A Treasury
of American
Folklore

A Treasury of American Folklore

Our Customs, Beliefs, and Traditions

EDITED BY TERRI HARDIN

BARNES
&NOBLE
BOOKS
NEW YORK

1994 Barnes & Noble Books

Book design by Charles Ziga, Ziga Design

ISBN 1-56619-370-2

Printed and bound in the United States of America

M 9 8 7 6 5 4 3 2

Contents

Part II   *Southern Folktales*

Part III   Midwestern and Prairie Folktales

Part IV   Western Folktales

Introduction

What we call "America" and what we think of as our nation is actually a composite of many peoples. For centuries, groups of individuals united by the common threads of race, ethnic (or national) background, and religion have come to the New World, bringing with them their customs, traditions, and beliefs.

Belief played an important role in the Old World's discovery of the New. Belief brought Columbus to America; in search of a new trade route to China, he found America, instead. However, unwilling to admit his mistake, he named the people living on this land "Indians"—a term that is still commonly used today in referring to America's indigenous peoples.

The wealth Columbus discovered spurred rumors that even more fantastic wealth was here to unearth. Conquistadors, intrigued by the myths of El Dorado and the Seven Cities of Cíbola, conquered and claimed the new land for Spain. Hungry for booty, other kingdoms of the Old World soon followed Spain's lead.

The belief that untold opportunities exist here for religious and political freedom—as well as for economic advancement—enticed many immigrants to this great land—and still does. The idea that every person, regardless of race, creed, or color, has an equal opportunity to share in this wealth holds the greatest attraction. However, even though our belief in equality, freedom, and the right to live as we choose brings us together as a nation, it is the customs, legends, and lore of all Americans—culled from our different pasts—that makes our country a land of such spiritual richness.

Commonly held beliefs strengthen group identity, and stories handed down from generation to generation provide a past that is both vivid and personal. In the New World (which was only fully conquered by the Old less than two centuries ago), the legends and folk wisdom of each group provided a psychological shelter against the harsh realities of both pioneer life and urban struggle.

These tales often became an integral part of the frontier societies that emerged. It is possible today to travel throughout our country and be amazed at the variety of cuisines, celebrations, and customs that distinguish America's different groups of settlers. Milwaukee, for example, is proud of its German past, as is Minnesota of its Swedish and Danish origins; California glories in its Spanish legacy, as does Louisiana in its Cajun and Creole roots; and African Americans all over the country are rediscovering the brilliance of their heritage.

America's first settlers were, of course, the Native Americans. Even though some of their legends remain, they have been defeated by war and disease, leaving behind only names in places where the race once prospered. The next to arrive on America's shores were the Europeans, who came in search of riches; the first settlers from Europe, by contrast, were looking for religious and economic freedom. The stories of the terrors, hardships, and struggles these men and women braved have been preserved in both lore and law.

Even as our young nation weathered many calamities (which included two wars with England and a divisive civil war), people from other lands were not deterred, and they continued to immigrate to this land seeking a better life. Some homesteaded the lonely prairies of the South and Midwest, while others found employment building the railroad system that would link the East with the West. This influx of immigrants provided ever more diversity.

Ironically, the "tired, poor, and huddled masses" that were wooed by the hope of liberty were met with ambivalence by those who had settled in this country before them. Some of this friction was relieved by the push west; even so, life was not easy for the new immigrants as they sought to establish themselves. Ultimately, subjugated and beleaguered by intolerance, they found spiritual sustenance in the common belief in the right to personal freedom.

However, the juxtaposition of so many nationalities excited interest in the groups' respective customs and folklore. When the nation had consisted of small, homogeneous communities, the customs peculiar to each community had gone unnoticed. But the less homogeneous these communities became, the more the status quo was challenged, and curiosity about each other's "peculiarities" developed. Toward the end of the nineteenth century, compilations of American legends began to be made, and the American Folk-Lore Society was founded to preserve authentic American experience.

The process of recording popular beliefs and customs scientifically— that is, without placing moral judgments on their value—is relatively recent. Therefore, one reads of Southern plantation owners who, though faithfully recording the folklore of neighbors and employees of African descent, insist on viewing blacks as children, and of missionaries who denounced Chinese immigrants as godless and immoral.

Chroniclers of folklore often praised or extolled a custom or piece of folklore in ways that reflected their own bias. Such tales are usually full of the chroniclers' preconceptions of immigrant life—and they were far from tolerant. In fact, one of the most troubling aspects about researching this subject is having to sift through documents of racial, ethnic, and religious intolerance and to admit that these arguments—some centuries old—are still very much alive today. It is easy, then, to realize how the borders of our country are jealously guarded against people who basically have the same hopes and dreams as ourselves, and who might have been ourselves, in another period.

Since many of these tales were collected at a time when American society was undergoing great changes—and were collected, for the most part, in an "objective" manner—it is disconcerting, but not surprising, to find that they reflect the sentiments of the times. While the tales are often raw with the sometimes-despicable views of their observers, they are also raw with firsthand information and detail, and as such they cannot be discounted.

America's past is also blessedly filled with kindness and generosity. For example, the Acadians, evicted from their homes in the North, found succor in Maryland and then in Louisiana; benevolent societies were developed to aid new immigrants; and charity workers brought education to the poor.

In time, the superstitions, beliefs, and customs of individual groups gave way to shared American experiences that produced genres such as the tall tale and concepts such as the Wild West. Both of these literary inventions celebrate the vastness of our country and the greatness of our spirit.

In this century, with large, centralized communication networks making America more homogeneous, we stand to lose the richness of our own story. An effort, however, is being made to understand the heritages of the different groups of Americans. More than ever, we need to respect and appreciate our nation's cultural diversity. The legends and lore that each of these groups brought to America, and the legends that grew around them as they struggled to make their place in the New World, should be gathered together so that we might all have the opportunity to remember, treasure, and reflect on them.

In this collection are stories and folklore from around the country as they were collected and recorded at the turn of the century. While hardly exhaustive, this selection of tales will provide a small introduction not only to the extraordinary diversity of our nation, but also to the ideas and beliefs that we share.

In this book, one will read, for example, how the Scotch and the Irish brought their fancies and healing practices with them, and of America's strong belief in witches, which is manifested in legends and superstitions of almost every culture. Many are the means of detecting witches; many too are the charms and remedies for keeping them at bay! In fact, some believe there are good reasons never to let one's guard down, for there are other supernatural agencies besides witches. Ghosts and demonic animals are to be found everywhere, and the Devil himself has left his mark on much of our land. A great deal of lore has been collected on movements of the sun and the moon, on how to recognize lucky and unlucky portents, and on how to guard against apparitions and the "evil eye." Also collected are records of the folk medicine of many peoples. Some of these cures are simply common sense, others are fantastic and have their roots in pre-Christian beliefs.

Since New World settlers were mainly avowed Christians, most of the tales collected in this treasury affirm this belief. Among various Christian sects, however, a wide spectrum of divergence exists. Recounted are the pagan and "Christian" dances of the Native Americans, the mysterious voodoo rituals of the inhabitants of the Louisiana delta, the strange practices of the New Mexican Penitentes, and the religious practices of the Chinese immigrants of New York.

Making analogies between animals and human behavior is another popular folklore motif, as in many Native-American legends and in the *ananci* and "rabbit" stories of the African Americans. The latter were popularized by Joel Chandler Harris, the compiler of the enormously popular Uncle Remus tales. These tales are rather controversial: Some feel that the preservation of the stories about Brer Fox, Brer Rabbit, and the Tar Baby is a reminder to African Americans of their humiliation at the hands of the white man; others point to their widespread popularity as evidence that the tales are generally subversive and part of a unique and vivid culture gone underground.

Material for this book is culled from a variety of sources, chief among which are the earliest publications of the American Folk-Lore Society. Also represented are tales from regional folklore societies, from the memoirs of pioneers, from journalists, and from anthologists of the time. Readers wishing to expand their knowledge of a particular subject can refer to the note at the end of each story citing its source. Many of the stories, for reasons of clarity and cohesiveness, have been adapted and edited.

The legends and folklore in this book are divided by region—Northern, Southern, Midwestern and Prairie, and Western. These divisions are some-what random, since southern Pennsylvania (placed in the North) has much in common with the South; and tales of Dodge City, which mostly evoke the Wild West, are set in the Midwest. Indeed, as frontiers were pushed west, the "West" came to mean several, different areas. Attempts have been made to keep the subject matter from being ghettoized by ethnic group. Within regions, chapters are separated by legend type in order to have the legends of different peoples set side by side for comparison.

Do not think that folklore and legends have ceased to be important aspects of our lives. Not only do they exist, but they continue to influence our lives even without our knowing it. The stories collected in this book, as well as the ones we will continue to hear on our lifelong journey, serve to remind us of the wealth of imagination and experience that surrounds us all.

I hope you will enjoy these tales and add them to your own personal trove.

—*Terri Hardin*
1994

Part I

Northern Folktales

Legends and Legendary Figures

· *Condemned to the Noose* ·

(English)

Ralph Sutherland, who, early in the last century, occupied a stone house a mile from Leeds, in the Catskills, was a man of morose and violent disposition, whose servant, a Scotch girl, was virtually a slave, inasmuch as she was bound to work for him without pay until she had refunded to him her passage money to this country. Becoming weary of bondage and of the tempers of her master, the girl ran away. The man set off in a raging chase, and she had not gone far before Sutherland overtook her, tied her by the wrists to his horse's tail, and began the homeward journey. Afterward, he swore that the girl stumbled against the horse's legs, so frightening the animal that it rushed off madly, pitching him out of the saddle and dashing the servant to death on rocks and trees; yet, knowing how ugly-tempered he could be, his neighbors were better inclined to believe that he had driven the horse into a gallop, intending to drag the girl for a short distance, as a punishment, and to rein up before he had done serious mischief. On this supposition he was arrested, tried, and sentenced to die on the scaffold.

The tricks of circumstantial evidence, together with pleas advanced by influential relatives of the prisoner, induced the court to delay sentence until the culprit should be ninety-nine years old, but it was ordered that, while released on his own recognizance, in the interim, he should keep a hangman's noose about his neck and show himself before the judges in Catskill once every year, to prove that he wore his badge of infamy and kept his crime in mind. This sentence he obeyed, and there were people living recently who claimed to remember him as he went about with a silken cord knotted at his throat. He was always alone, he seldom spoke; his rough, imperious manner had departed. Only when children asked him what the rope was for were his lips seen to quiver, and then he would hurry away. After dark his house was avoided, for gossips said that a shrieking woman passed it nightly, tied at the tail of a giant horse with fiery eyes and smoking nostrils; that a skeleton in a winding sheet had been found there; that a curious thing, somewhat like a woman, had been known to sit on his garden wall, with lights shining from her fingertips, uttering unearthly laughter; and that domestic animals reproached the man by groaning and howling beneath his windows.

These beliefs he knew, yet he neither grieved nor scorned nor answered when he was told of them. Years sped on. Every year deepened his reserve and loneliness, and some began to whisper that he would take his own way out of the world, though others answered that men who were born to be hanged would never be drowned; but a new republic was created; new laws were made; new judges sat to minister them; so, on Ralph Sutherland's ninety-ninth birthday anniversary, there were none who would accuse him or execute sentence. He lived yet another year, dying in 1801. But was it from habit, or was it in self-punishment and remorse, that he never took off the cord? For, when he drew his last breath, though it was in his own house, his throat was still encircled by the hangman's rope.

From: Charles M. Skinner, *Myths & Legends of Our Own Land*, vol. 1 (Philadelphia and London: J. B. Lippincott Co., 1896).

· *A Romantic Legend* ·

(English)

"For my part," said Aunt Lois, "I never had much opinion of Sir Harry Frankland, or Lady Frankland, either. I don't think such goings-on ever ought to be countenanced in society."

"They both repented bitterly—repentd in sackcloth and ashes," said Miss Mehitable. "And if God forgives such sins, why shouldn't we?"

"What was the story?" said Major Broad.

"Why," said Aunt Lois, "haven't you heard of Agnes Surridge, of Marblehead? She was housemaid in a tavern there, and Sir Harry fell in love with her, and took her and educated her. That was well enough; but when she'd done going to school he took her home to his house in Boston, and called her his daughter; although people became pretty sure that the connection was not what it should be, and they refused to have anything to do with her. So he bought this splendid place out in the woods, and built a great palace of a house, and took Miss Agnes out there. People who wanted to be splendidly entertained, and who were not particular as to morals, used to go out to visit them."

"I used to hear great stories of their wealth and pomp and luxury," said my grandmother, "but I mourned over it; that it should come to this in New England, that people could openly set such an example and be tolerated. It wouldn't have been borne a generation before, I can tell you. No, indeed—the magistrates would have put a stop to it. But these noblemen, when they came over to America, seemed to think themselves lords of God's heritage, and free to do just as they pleased."

"But," said Miss Mehitable, "they repented, as I said. He took her to England, and there his friends refused to receive her; and then he was appointed ambassador to Lisbon, and he took her there. On the day of the great earthquake Sir Harry was riding with a lady of the court when the shock came, and in a moment, without warning, they found themselves buried under the ruins of a building they were passing. He wore a scarlet cloak, as was the fashion; and they say that in her dying agonies the poor creature bit through this cloak and sleeve into the flesh of his arm, and made a mark that he carried to his dying day. Sir Harry was saved by Agnes Surridge. She came over the ruins, calling and looking for him, and he heard her voice and answered, and she got men to come and dig him out. When he was in that dreadful situation, he made a vow to God, if he would save his life, that he would be a different man. And he was a changed man from that day. He was married to Agnes Surridge as soon as they could get a priest to perform the ceremony; and when he took her back to England all his relations received her, and she was presented in court and moved in society with perfect acceptance."

"I don't think it ever ought to have been," said Aunt Lois. "Such women never ought to be received."

"What!—is there no place of repentance for a woman?" said Miss Mehitable. "Christ said, 'Neither do I condemn thee; go and sin no more.'"

I noticed again that sort of shiver of feeling in Miss Mehitable; and there was a peculiar thrill in her voice, as she said these words, that made me sensible that she was speaking from some inward depth of feeling.

"Don't you be so hard and sharp, Lois," said my grandmother. "Sinners must have patience with sinners."

"Especially with sinners of quality, Lois," said Uncle Bill. "By all accounts Sir Harry and Lady Frankland swept all before them when they came back to Boston."

From: Harriet Beecher Stowe, *Oldtown Folks* (Boston: Fields, Osgood & Co., 1869).

· *Saved By the Bible* ·

(German)

It was on the day after the battle of Germantown that Warner, who wore the blue, met his hated neighbor, the Tory Dabney, near that bloody field. By a common impulse the men fell upon each other with their knives, and Warner soon had his enemy in a position to give him the deathblow, but Dabney began to bellow for quarter. "My brother cried for quarter at Paoli," answered the other, "and you struck him to the heart."

"I have a wife and child. Spare me for their sakes."

"My brother had a wife and two children. Perhaps you would like to beg your life of them."

Though made in mockery, this proposition was caught at so earnestly that Warner at length consented to take his adversary, firmly bound, to the house where the bereaved family was living. The widow was reading the Bible to her children, but her grief was too fresh to gather comfort from it. When Dabney was flung into the room he groveled at her feet and begged piteously for mercy. Her face did not soften, but there was a kind of contempt in the settled sadness of her tone as she said, "It shall be as God directs. I will close this Bible, open it at chance, and when this boy shall put his finger at random on a line, by that you must live or die."

The book was opened, and the child put his finger on a line: "That man shall die."

Warner drew his knife and motioned his prisoner to the door. He was going to lead him into the wood to offer him as a sacrifice to his brother's spirit.

"No, no!" shrieked the wretch. "Give me one more chance; one more! Let the girl open the book."

The woman coldly consents, and when the book is opened for the second time, she reads, "Love your enemies." There are no other words. The knife is used, but it is to cut the prisoner's bonds, and he walks away with head hung down, never more to take arms against his countrymen. And glad are they all at this, when the husband is brought home—not dead, though left among the corpses at Paoli, but alive and certain of recovery, with such nursing as his wife will give him. After tears of joy have been shed she tells him the story of the Bible judgment, and all the members of the family fall on their knees in thanksgiving that the blood of Dabney is not upon their heads.

From: Charles M. Skinner, *Myths & Legends of Our Own Land*, vol. 1 (Philadelphia and London: J. B. Lippincott Co., 1896).

· *Mr. King at the Quaker Meeting* ·

(English)

I heard a story, formerly, from a friend of very high character as a man and lawyer, the late Honorable William Baylies, of West Bridgewater, Massachusetts. It seems that while Mr. King, then a young man, was in the practice of his profession in Boston, he was detained in attendance upon court at Plymouth, until late on Saturday evening. It was necessary for him to be at home seasonably on Monday morning, and accordingly he mounted his horse early on Sunday, the ordinary mode of travel in those days, and proceeded leisurely on his way. It was summertime; and in passing through the township of Hanover, in Plymouth County, he approached a plain wooden structure by the roadside, in which, as he could see by the assemblage within, the door and windows being open, that it was a time of religious service. Alighting, out of deference to the character of the day, he hitched his horse and quietly entered the building. It proved to be a Quaker meeting, and perfect silence prevailed. At length tiring of this state of things, Mr. King arose and began to address the assembly upon topics suitable to the day. He was an uncommonly handsome young man, and then and ever afterwards distinguished for extraordinary powers of eloquence. The Quakers listened with mute amazement and admiration to the discourse of some twenty minutes' duration, when the speaker slipped out, remounted, and proceeded on his journey. The incident was the occasion of great and mysterious interest, for a long time afterwards, in the quiet country neighborhood. No imagination could conceive who the wonderful speaker might be, and many insisted it must have been, indeed, "an angel from heaven." Some years afterwards, at the session of a constitutional convention in Massachusetts, Mr. King rose to make a motion. He had no sooner begun than a Quaker member started up from a back seat, and, carried away by the first glimpse at solution of the long-standing mystery, cried out, "That's the man that spoke in our meetin'!"

From: George Lunt, ed., *Old New England Traits* (New York: Hurd & Houghton, 1893).

• *The Consecration of George Washington* •

(German)

In 1773 some of the Pietist monks were still living in their rude monastery whose ruins are visible on the banks of the Wissahickon. Chief among these mystics was an old man who might have enjoyed the wealth and distinction warranted by a title had he chosen to remain in Germany, but he had forsworn vanities, and had come to the New World to pray, to rear his children, and to live a simple life. Some said he was an alchemist, and many believed him to be a prophet. The infrequent wanderer beside the romantic river had seen lights burning in the window of his cell and had heard the solemn sound of song and prayer. On a winter night, when snow lay untrodden about the building and a sharp air stirred in the trees with a sound like harps, the old man sat in a large room of the place, with his son and daughter, waiting. For a prophecy had run that on that night, at the third hour of morning, the "deliverer" would present himself.

In a dream was heard a voice, saying, "I will send a deliverer to the New World who shall save my people from bondage, as my Son saved them from spiritual death."

The night wore on in prayer and meditation, and the hours tolled heavily across the frozen wilderness, but, at the stroke of three, steps were heard in the snow and the door swung open. The man who entered was of great stature, with a calm, strong face, a powerful frame, and a manner of dignity and grace.

"Friends, I have lost my way," said he. "Can you direct me?"

The old man started up in a kind of rapture. "You have not lost your way," he cried, "but found it. You are called to a great mission. Kneel at this altar and receive it."

The stranger looked at the man in surprise and a doubt passed over his face. "Nay, I am not mad," urged the recluse, with a sight smile. "Listen. Tonight, disturbed for the future of your country, and unable to sleep, you mounted horse and rode into the night air to think on the question that cannot be kept out of your mind: Is it lawful for the subject to draw sword against his king? The horse wandered, you knew and cared not whither, until he brought you here."

"How do you know this?" asked the stranger, in amazement.

"Be not surprised, but kneel while I anoint thee deliverer of this land."

Moved and impressed, the man bowed his knee before one of his fellows for the first time in his life. The monk touched his finger with oil, and laying it on the brow of the stranger, said, "Do you promise, when the hour shall strike, to take the sword in defense of your country? Do you promise, when you shall see your soldiers suffer for bread and fire, and when the people you have led to victory shall bow before you, to remember that you are but the minister of God in the work of a nation's freedom?"

With a new light burning in his eyes, the stranger bent his head.

"Then, in His name, I consecrate thee deliverer of this oppressed people. When the time comes, go forth to victory, for, as you are faithful, be sure that God will grant it. Wear no crown, but the blessings and honor of a free people, save this." As he finished, his daughter, a girl of seventeen, came forward and put a wreath of laurel on the brow of the kneeling man. "Rise," continued the prophet, "and take my hand, which I have never before offered to any man, and accept my promise to be faithful to you and to this country, even if it cost my life."

As he arose, the son of the priest stepped to him and girt a sword upon his hip, and the old man held up his hands in solemn benediction. The stranger laid his hand on the book that stood open on the altar and kissed the hilt of his sword. "I will keep the faith," said he. At drawn he went his way again, and no one knew his name, but when the fires of battle lighted the western world, America looked to him for its deliverance from tyranny. Years later it was this spot that he revisited, alone, to pray, and here Sir William Howe offered to him, in the name of his king, the title of regent of America. He took the parchment and ground it into a rag in the earth at his feet. For this was George Washington.

From: Charles M. Skinner, *Myths & Legends of Our Own Land*, vol. 1 (Philadelphia and London: J. B. Lippincott Co., 1896).

CHAPTER 2

Pirates and Buried Treasure

· *The Party from Gibbet Island* ·

(English)

Ellis Island, in New York Harbor, once bore the name of Gibbet Island, because pirates and mutineers were hanged there in chains. During the times when it was devoted to this fell purpose, there stood in Communipaw the Wild Goose tavern, where Dutch burghers resorted to smoke, drink Hollands, and grow fat, wise, and sleepy in each others' company. The plague of this inn was Yan Yost Vanderscamp, a nephew of the landlord, who frequently alarmed the patrons of the house by putting powder into their pipes and attaching briers beneath their horses' tails, and who naturally turned pirate when he became older, taking with him to sea his boon companion, an ill-disposed, ill-favored blackamoor named Pluto, who had been employed about the tavern. When the landlord died, Vanderscamp possessed himself of this property, fitted it up with plunder, and at intervals he had his gang ashore—such a crew of singing, swearing, drinking, gaming devils as Communipaw had never seen the like of; yet the residents could not summon activity enough to stop the goings-on that made the Wild Goose a disgrace to their village. The British authorities, however, caught three of the swashbucklers and strung them up on Gibbet Island, and things that went on badly in Communipaw after that went on with quiet and secrecy.

The pirate and his henchmen were returning to the tavern one night, after a visit to a rakish-looking vessel in the offing, when a squall broke in such force as to give their skiff a leeway to the place of executions. As they rounded that lonely reef a creaking noise overhead caused Vanderscamp to look up, and he could not repress a shudder as he saw the bodies of his three messmates, their rags fluttering and their chains grinding in the wind.

"Don't you want to see your friends?" sneered Pluto. "You, who are never afraid of living men, what do you fear from the dead?"

"Nothing," answered the pirate. Then, lugging forth his bottle, he took a long pull at it, and holding it toward the dead felons, he shouted, "Here's fair weather to you, my lads in the wind, and if you should be walking the rounds tonight, come in to supper."

A clatter of bones and a creak of chains sounded like a laugh. It was midnight when the boat pulled in at Communipaw, and as the storm continued, Vanderscamp, drenched to the skin, made quick time to the Wild Goose. As he entered, a sound of revelry overhead smote his ear, and, being no less astonished than in need of cordials, he hastened upstairs and flung open the door. A table stood there, furnished with jugs and pipes and cans, and by light of candles that burned as blue as brimstone could be seen the three gallows birds from Gibbet Island, with halters on their necks, clinking their tankards together and trolling forth a drinking song.

Starting back with affright, as the corpses hailed him with lifted arms and turned their fishy eyes on him, Vanderscamp slipped at the door and fell headlong to the bottom of the stairs. Next morning he was found there by the neighbors, dead to a certainty and was put away in the Dutch churchyard at Bergen on the Sunday following. As the house was rifled and deserted by its occupants, it was hinted that the Negro had betrayed his master to his fellow buccaneers, and that he, Pluto, was no other than the devil in disguise. But he was not, for his skiff was seen floating bottom up in the bay soon after, and his drowned body lodged among the rocks at the foot of the pirates' gallows.

For a long time afterwards the island was regarded as a place that required purging with bell, book, and candle, for shadows were reported there and faint lights that shot into the air, and to this day, with the great immigrant station on it and crowds going and coming all the time, the Battery boatmen prefer not to row around it at night, for they are likely to see the shades of the soldier and his mistress who were drowned off the place one windy night, when the girl was aiding the fellow to escape confinement in the guardhouse, to say nothing of Vanderscamp and his felons.

From: Charles M. Skinner, *Myths & Legends of Our Own Land*, vol. 1 (Philadelphia and London: J. B. Lippincott Co., 1896).

· *Dungeon Rock* ·

(English)

Lynn's first historian, who dealt somewhat in tradition, among other things, says, in substance, "Early in 1658, on a pleasant evening, a little after sunset, a small vessel was seen to anchor near the mouth of the Saugus River. A boat was presently lowered from her side, into which four men descended and moved up the river a considerable distance, when they landed and proceeded directly into the woods. They had been noticed by only a few individuals; but in those early times, when the people were surrounded by danger and easily susceptible to alarm, such an incident was well calculated to awaken suspicion, and in the course of the evening the intelligence was conveyed to many houses. In the morning the vessel was gone, and no trace of her or her crew could be found."

He further states that on going into the foundry connected with the then-existing ironworks, a quantity of shackles, handcuffs, hatchets, and other articles of iron were ordered to be made and left at a certain place, for which a return in silver would be found. "This was done" (so says the historian), and the mysterious contractors fulfilled their part of the obligation, but were undiscovered. Some months afterward the four men returned and made their abode in what has, to this day, been called Pirates' Glen, where they built a hut and dug a well. It is supposed that they buried money in this vicinity, but our opinion is that most of the money then, as now, was kept aboveground. Their retreat being discovered, one of the king's cruisers appeared on the coast, and three of them were arrested and carried to England and probably executed.

The other, whose name was Thomas Veal, escaped to a rock in the woods, in which was a spacious cavern, where the pirates had previously deposited some of their plunder. There the fugitive practiced the trade of shoemaking. He continued his residence here till the great earthquake of 1658, when the top of the rock was unloosed and crashed down into the mouth of the cavern, enclosing the unfortunate man in what has been called to this day Pirates' Dungeon, or Dungeon Rock. We cannot vouch for the complete truthfulness of this historian's statements.

In 1852, one Hiram Marble purchased from the city of Lynn a lot of woodland in which Dungeon Rock is situated. He came, as was claimed, influenced by Spiritualistic revelations.

Directed by the spirit of the departed pirate Tom Veal, Mr. Marble commenced to excavate from this very hard porphyry rock in search of a subterranean vault, into which had been poured, as was supposed, the ill-gotten gain of all the pirates, from Captain Kidd down to the last outlaw of the ocean. Twenty-seven years the sound of the hammer and the drill and the thud of blasting powder echoed through the leafy forests, and then all was hushed.

Hiram Marble died in his lonely residence at Dungeon Rock, November 10, 1868, age sixty-five. He was widely known for his perseverance in the work in which he was engaged. Sixteen years he labored without a realization of his ardent hopes. He remained a Spiritualist to the last, and those of a like faith were invited to the funeral services, which took place on the day following his death.

His faith has not been without works, nor his courage barren of results, and centuries hence, if his name and identity should be lost, the strange labor may be referred to some recluse Cyclops who had strayed hither from mystic lands.

Edwin Marble, who succeeded his father in the strange search for treasure, died January 16, 1880, age forty-eight. He was buried near the foot of the rock on the southwestern slope, it having been his express desire to be interred near the scene of his hopeful, though fruitless, labors.

The broken rock, which they removed solely with their own hands, makes quite a mountain of itself.

From: Frank Harriman, "Dungeon Rock, Lynn," *The Bay State Monthly* (April 1884): 235–39.

· *Buried Treasure* ·

(German)

The myth of buried treasure, the tale of the local Nibelungen hoard, was one with which I was early familiar. At a remote corner of my father's farm was a stagnant pool and swamp, in summer studded with the graceful stalks of the cattail or sweet flag. Rising beyond the swamp was a barren hillside scantily covered with tufts of wire grass and stunted trees. The legend was that once, early in the century, "after the Revolution," and before the old people could remember, there was a lonely log cabin by the pond. In it lived a solitary and misanthropic man. No one knew his history, nor even his full name. At last he fell sick, and some neighbors charitably came to attend him. As death approached, he called them to his bedside, and told them that during the Revolution he had been a spy for the British; that for this traitorous service he had been paid much gold, but through avarice or remorse he had spent none of it. He had placed it in a crock and buried it in the hillside above his cabin. He desired that they should dig it up, and give it to some good object. But, alas! just as he was proceeding to state exactly the spot where to dig, the death rattle seized him, and his tongue refused its function.

So ran the story, and it was so well believed that many a pit in the hillside testified to the labors of the treasure seekers. It was believed that if one sleeps over a buried treasure he will dream of it, and I remember finding men sleeping in the grass on the hillside, hoping that the lucky inspiration would come to them.

I have now my doubts whether the whole story was not an echo of some one of the Old World myths of the concealed hoard.

It will be noted that the treasure is stated to have been blood money, the price of treachery, and that it brought no happiness to the owner. Like the hoard of the Nibelungs, it was lost through hiding, since the owner failed to give clear enough directions as to its whereabouts. These traits seem to brand it as a modern and localized form of that ancient and cosmopolite folktale which inspired the Nibelungenlied, Siegfried and the Dragon, and so on.

Thunderstorms are frequent and often severe in that locality. Prudent housewives were careful to put out the fire when they saw one approaching, as it was believed that the smoke attracted the lightning. All held firmly to the opinion that a tree which had been once struck would not be liable to the accident again. The stone arrowheads left by the aboriginal population were sometimes pointed out as "thunderbolts," formed or deposited where the lightning struck the ground. Stones in general were believed to "grow" in the ground, and the lightning aided their development; for that reason the upland fields were stonier than those in the valley.

From: D. G. Brinton, "Reminiscences of Pennsylvania Folk-Lore," *Journal of American Folk-Lore* 5 (1892): 177–85.

Chapter 3

Superstitions

· *Superstitions from Pennsylvania* ·

(German)

We are all aware of the frequency with which the divining rod is used in the search for water, ores, and hidden treasure; and we learn, occasionally, of certain individuals claiming to possess the power of curing sickness and healing wounds by the mere laying on of hands; of exorcising evil spirits, and combating the spells of rival witches; laying ghosts, and giving charms and amulets; and pretending, in fact, to be able to accomplish almost anything that may be desired.

Who has not heard of carrying a potato, or a horse chestnut, to ward off rheumatism; having secreted somewhere about the person, the left hind foot of a graveyard rabbit for luck; or, placing within the purse the dried heart of a bat for success in gambling?

We are all more or less uncomfortably impressed at hearing unaccountable noises; many persons dread going upon a journey or cutting out a garment on Friday. Thus we perceive that the mere reference to the trifles which are apt to control our actions bring to our minds such a startling array of superstitions, observed by us in others, or perhaps, even, entertained to a limited degree by ourselves, that it becomes impracticable to continue further entering so prolific a subject at this moment when time is so limited.

From: "Popular Superstitions," *The Pennsylvania-German Society Proceedings and Addresses*, vol. 5 (Reading, PA: 1895).

· *Superstitions from Boston* ·

(Armenian)

When the left eye twitches it is bad luck. When the right eye twitches it is good luck.

If one's left ear rings, he will hear bad news; if his right ear, good news.

If the palm of one's right hand itches, his debtor wants to pay him money. If the left palm itches, then he is going to pay out money.

If one's feet itch, he is going to travel. If his face burns, someone is speaking evil of him.

To sneeze is a sign that someone is talking about you.

When one has pimples on his face it is a sign that his mother stole an egg while she was pregnant with him.

When one hiccoughs, it is a sign that he has stolen the dough of a priest.

In some parts of Armenia people account for an eclipse of the sun or moon by saying, "There is war going on somewhere." In other parts they believe the devil to be between them and the eclipsed object. In the places where this latter view is held they will beat drums and tin pans, yell, and make all the noise possible, so as to drive the devil away. As the eclipse passes away they rejoice in their success. If the eclipse occurs in January, it is believed there will be little produce raised the following season. If in February, a contagious disease will sweep away many people; if in March, there will be much loss of stock, and so on.

Dead bodies are said to rise out of their graves in the nighttime and go about the country. They are not, however, flesh and blood as long as the darkness lasts, but are supposed to be so far spiritualized that they have power to assume any form they may choose. Once a dead person, who was strolling about in the night and had taken on the form of a puppy, was picked up by a man who, thinking to keep it, carried it home with him. Next morning the puppy was gone, and in its place was a dead body. Armenians avoid going by a graveyard after night, for fear the dead will follow them.

A shooting star is the sign of someone's death.

When a light is seen rising from a grave (the result of decaying matter), they think it is an indication of holiness.

In a certain part of Armenia there are seven hills in the same community. The Armenians account for them in the following manner: Once upon a time Nero and his army were marching against the city of Harpud with the intention of capturing it. On the spot marked by one of these hills he pitched his camp. During the night the earth opened and swallowed both him and his army. Six other kings hostile to the Armenians have in the course of time encamped in this same neighborhood. Each time the earth has engulfed them. Over the places of burial of the seven armies with their kings have come these seven hills.

The villages nestling around the bases of different hills here and there throughout the country oftentimes have names that indicate that they have been battlegrounds in the past. One is named "Sharp to Sharp," having reference to the clashing of swords. Another is called "Judgment," and so on.

At twelve o'clock on New Year's Eve all rivers and springs stop flowing for five minutes. If one should go to a spring when it starts again he would find gold dust pouring from it for a moment or two. There was once a woman who went for a pitcher of water just at this time. On coming to the light the water looked dirty, and without thinking what was the matter she threw it out. Next morning she found a little gold in the bottom of the pitcher.

If neighbor A is not friendly with neighbor B, and one desires that he should be, all he has to do is to secure a lock of B's hair and burn it so that A will get a scent of it. Henceforth he will be friendly with B.

Seeds sown in the new moon will do well; in the dark of the moon they will not.

From: G. D. Edwards, "Items of Armenian Folk-Lore Collected in Boston," *Journal of American Folk-Lore* 12 (1899): 97–107.

· *Superstitions from Boston* ·

(Irish)

If you meet a funeral, you must turn and go back a few steps before continuing your journey.

The oldest member of a family takes the children, from the oldest to the youngest, and makes them walk three times across the grave. It cures disease.

When a funeral goes by, you must say: "Lord have mercy on them."

Turn everything upside down in the room when the dead is laid out.

Stop the clock and cover the mirrors. This is still said to be always done among Irish in Boston.

When the first child dies, the mother must not attend the funeral; if she does, she will die also.

A newborn baby, when dressed, is to be shaken, holding it up by the feet. This will bring good luck.

In a strange house, put a garter at the head of your bed, and think on the one you are to marry, naming the bedposts.

Place your clothes in the four corners of the room, and you will dream of the one you are to marry.

If you have the hiccough, and think of the right person, it will go away.

If your hand itches, rub it on a wooden object, saying:

> Rub on wood,
> Something good.

If you rub your forefinger, and it itches, you will be disappointed.

For the first baby, a cradle must be bought.

If you have two, you will be married twice, or go twice to a wedding.

If a knife is dropped, the first visitor will be a lady; if a fork, a man.

If you spill salt, put some on the stove, or on your right shoulder, three times.

If you put your shoes in the shape mentioned, saying,

> Place your shoes in the form of a T,
> Hoping my true love for to see,

you will dream of the person.

From: Jane H. Newel, "Superstitions of Irish Origin in Boston," *Journal of American Folk-Lore* 5 (1892): 242–43.

· Superstitions from Boston ·

(Syrian)

If a person sees blackbirds in the morning, he will have bad luck.

If a man goes to look for a position, and when halfway there remembers something he has forgotten and left at home, he will not go and try for the position that day.

If one person is relating something to another and a child sneezes, it shows that he is speaking the truth.

When the new moon appears, a Syrian takes a piece of silver money, and, holding it up before the moon, says, "May it be a happy moon."

A Syrian will not plant when the moon is full, and never under any circumstances when it begins to wane. He always plants when the moon is new.

If a person meets a blackbird as he starts off on a journey, he will have bad luck.

When one member of a family has started on a journey, the others will not dust a room in the house until he has crossed a river.

If two persons are spending the evening together, and one of them speaks of bad luck to come, it is *very* bad luck indeed. The reason, it was explained, is because a Syrian abhors the darker side of life and tries to have his mind continually filled with glad and happy thoughts.

Twins always bring good luck, both to their parents and to themselves.

Never begin a journey on Tuesday or on Friday, for it will be a failure!

If a person breaks a piece of pottery on the departure of a visitor, it means he does not wish his return.

If a woman puts on a garment of her husband while he is away, she desires him to meet with bad luck. The reason being that, when a man dies, it is customary for his wife to put on one of his garments and sing funeral songs. The Syrians have very many of these funeral songs.

To carry a small piece of bone which comes from Rome from the skeleton of St. Peter or of St. Paul, or a lock of hair, or a piece of the garment of any saint, brings good luck.

If a person carries hằbĕ́k, he will have bad luck.

Hábék is a plant native to Syria. My informant thought that it did not grow in America, and knew it only by its Arabic name. The reason being that, when a man dies, a considerable amount of it is placed about the corpse.

A cross-eyed person loves *two* persons *equally*.

If a company of people, while dining, speak of someone who is far away, and a spoon, or some other article from the table, happens to fall on the floor as his name is being mentioned, it means that he is dying of hunger.

A Syrian will not go near a graveyard at night, for he fears the spirits of the dead, which are thought to rise from the ground in the evening and linger about the village. If the ghost appears in a black garment, the man is in trouble; but if the garment is white, the man is at rest.

Every Syrian fancies that he is under the thralldom of a certain witch, who appears to him in his dreams. She endeavors to separate him from his own mother. If the man finds, after waking, that his nose has been bleeding, or is still bleeding, it means that the bonds uniting him with his witch are broken, and that he is free. But if he finds the next morning that the tassels on the sash of his nightrobe are cross tied into a knot, it means that he will be a slave of that witch, and can only with great difficulty extricate himself from her power.

When a newly married bride enters for the first time the door of her husband's house, she breaks a loaf of unleavened bread and sticks it upon the door for good luck.

If a person's left hand itches, he is to receive some money; but if it is the right hand that itches, he is to pay some money.

If a person's left eye twitches, something unpleasant will happen to him; but if it is the right eye that twitches, it will be something pleasant.

If a little baby always keeps his hands tightly clenched, he will live long; but if he holds them loosely, his life will be short.

If a person cuts his fingernails in the evening, he will have bad luck.

If a person, as he stands on the threshold of a room, curses another, he will meet with the evil he has wished the other man.

From: Howard Barrett Wilson, "Notes of Syrian Folk-Lore Collected in Boston," *Journal of American Folk-Lore* 16 (1903): 133–47.

· Good- and Bad-Luck Superstitions ·

(Unidentified)

Amulets are worn for good luck. A scapula wards off disease. A heart worn as a charm will bring a sweetheart. Books of magic "speak true." Dreams are prophetic, they foretell sorrow, joy, and the arrival of letters. Fortunes may be determined by tea leaves. It is unsafe to go out by another door than the one by which you enter a room. If a dog howls bad luck "is sure to come before sundown." It is unlucky to comb your hair after dark. Never attempt anything new on Friday. Peacock feathers have an evil influence. Relics of the saints, of the cross, and mantles worn by them all have healing power. The grandmother of a child whose right side was paralyzed took her to the Church of John the Baptist, she laid her in the pew, the priest placed the relics of Saint Anne on her as she slept, then he prayed. When she awoke she was cured. She walked to the elevated station. Saint Anne had heard the prayer and the child prays to Anne daily.

From: Elsa G. Herzfeld, *Family Monographs: The History of Twenty-four Families Living in the Middle West Side of New York City* (New York: The James Kempster Printing Co., 1905).

· Of Death and Funerals ·

(Irish)

No cooking is done in the house of death. No one must touch a *crepe* on the door of a house in which death has occurred. It is "God's sin" to do so. One day I came upon a small boy on a doorstep, crying bitterly. His friend said that he was sure he was going to die. Through curiosity he had touched some of the wax flowers and *crepe* at the door of a dead neighbor. His playfellows had said, "God will damn you."

The Irish fear that wearing green will cause death. One girl bought green material for a dress. It was "made up." Soon after she and her brother were "seized with a fever." Her brother died and she was sick for a long time. It is unlucky to wear the clothes of a deceased person. The family must avoid moving to rooms in which death has occurred, otherwise there will be more deaths. There are certain houses where "people just die off" (this has nothing to do with unsanitary conditions). When a young child dies, it is best not to mourn, because it is better off in heaven, or because it is an angel. An unbaptized child is mourned because it is not buried in consecrated ground.

The warnings of approaching death are many. The belief in the banshee is widespread among the Irish residents. One family represented her as a woman in a trailing white dress who hovers about the precincts and wails loudly when death is approaching. She is a good woman, but she foretells death. The banshee never comes to America. She is afraid to cross the ocean, but there are plenty of ghosts and spirits in New York without her. In County Cavan, Ireland, "a nice girl" is not buried without "salie rods" (sticks of the salie tree are peeled, decorated with white ribbons, and stuck in the newly made grave as a symbol of purity). In one of the lakes of Cavan there is a "round castle with a round tower." This castle became drowned when its lord was defending it from the invading Danes. "The water came up" and "it sank into the lake." "At times you can see the tower." Blessed is he who is buried on a rainy day. When a certain child was about to die, his mother heard a noise as if "the devil himself were falling downstairs." The same woman is not afraid of ghosts. "There is only one ghost, the Holy Ghost, and he won't follow you if you behave yourself. The Devil is too busy somewhere else."

It is possible "for a dead person to wish someone away." Ghosts are quite likely to deceive persons by deceptive allurements. If the vision comes as a "Sister" it is the "Lord's will" that a thing is to happen.

If you do not attend your neighbor's wake you are likely to have no mourners at your own. If there are not plenty of coaches, a fine casket, and an elaborate display of flowers, your neighbors will say "you do not mean well by the dead." Mrs. Green says she "would rather any day go to a funeral than a wedding."

In many cases not only all the "insurance money" is used up, but large sums are borrowed in order to have a big funeral. Frequently the family pays for the coaches used by the neighbors.

From: Elsa G. Herzfeld, Family Monographs: The History of Twenty-four Families Living in the Middle West Side of New York City (New York: The James Kempster Printing Co., 1905).

· Foundation Sacrifice ·

(English)

In 1824, or thereabouts, when some repairs or changes were being made in my grandfather's, Thorndike Deland's, house at the corner of Essex and Newberry streets in Salem, a china image was placed, or replaced, in the brickwork.

As my mother, who was born in 1808, recalls this incident of her childhood, the image was eight or ten inches in height and was inserted; not in the foundations of the chimney, but on the first floor, at about the level of a person's head. Inquiries made of the antiquarians of Salem and Newburyport have failed to elicit information of any other case of the survival of foundation sacrifice in either of those towns.

From: N. D. C. Hodges, "Survival in New England of Foundation Sacrifice," *Journal of American Folk-Lore* 12 (1899): 290–91.

· Vampire Superstitions ·

(English)

In New England the vampire superstition is unknown by its proper name. It is there believed that consumption is not a physical but a spiritual disease, obsession, or visitation; that as long as the body of a dead consumptive relative has blood in its heart it is proof that an occult influence steals from it for death and is at work draining the blood of the living into the heart of the dead and causing his rapid decline.

It is a common belief in primitive races of low culture that disease is caused by the revengeful spirits of man or other animals—notably among some tribes of North American Indians as well as of African Negroes.

Gilbert Stuart, the distinguished American painter, when asked by a London friend where he was born, replied: "Six miles from Pottawoone, ten miles from Poppasquash, four miles from Conanicut, and not far from the spot where the famous battle with the warlike Pequots was fought." In plainer language, Stuart was born in the old snuff mill belonging to his father and Dr. Moffat, at the head of Petaquamscott Pond, six miles from Newport, across the bay, and about the same distance from Narragansett Pier, in the state of Rhode Island.

By some mysterious survival, occult transmission, or remarkable atavism, this region, including within its radius the towns of Exeter, Foster, Kingstown, East Greenwich, and others, with their scattered hamlets and more pretentious villages, is distinguished by the prevalence of this remarkable superstition—a survival of the days of Sardanapalus, of Nebuchadnezzar, and of New Testament history in the closing years of what we are pleased to call the enlightened nineteenth century. It is an extraordinary instance of a barbaric superstition outcropping in and coexisting with a high general culture, of which Max Müller and others have spoken, and which is not so uncommon, if rarely so extremely aggravated, crude, and painful.

The region referred to, where agriculture is in a depressed condition and abandoned farms are numerous, is the tramping ground of the book agent, the chromo peddler, and the patent medicine man, and the home of the erotic and neurotic modern novel. The social isolation away from the larger villages is as complete as a century and a half ago, when the boy Gilbert Stuart tramped the woods, fished the streams, and was developing and absorbing his artistic inspirations, while the agricultural and economic conditions are very much worse.

Farmhouses deserted and ruinous are frequent, and the once-productive lands, neglected and overgrown with scrubby oak, speak forcefully and mournfully of the migration of the youthful farmers from country to town. In short, the region furnishes an object lesson in the decline of wealth consequent upon the prevalence of a too-common heresy in the district that land will take care of itself, or that it can be robbed from generation to generation without injury, and suggests the almost criminal neglect of the conservators of public education to give instruction to our farming youth in a more scientific and more practical agriculture. It has been well said by a banker of well-known name in an agricultural district in the midlands of England that "the depression of agriculture is a depression of brains." Naturally, in such isolated conditions the superstitions of a much lower culture have maintained their place and are likely to keep it and perpetuate it, despite the church, the public school, and the weekly newspaper. Here Cotton Mather, Justice Sewall, and the host of medical, clerical, and lay believers in the uncanny superstitions of bygone centuries could still hold high carnival.

The first visit in this farming community of native-born New Englanders was made to ———, a small seashore village possessing a summer hotel and a few cottages of summer residents not far from Newport—that mecca of wealth, fashion, and nineteenth-century culture. The ——— family is among its well-to-do and most intelligent inhabitants. One member of this family had some years since lost children by consumption, and by common report claimed to have saved those surviving by exhumation and cremation of the dead.

In the same village resides Mr. ———, an intelligent man, by trade a mason, who is a living witness of the superstition and of the efficacy of the treatment of the dead which it prescribes. He informed me that he had lost two brothers by consumption. Upon the attack of the second brother his father was advised by Mr. ———, the head of the family before mentioned, to take up the first body and burn its heart, but the brother attacked objected to the sacrilege and in consequence subsequently died. When he was attacked by the disease in his turn, ———'s advice prevailed, and the body of the brother last dead was accordingly exhumed, and "living" blood being found in the heart and in circulation, it was cremated, and the sufferer began immediately to mend and stood before me a hale, hearty, and vigorous man of fifty years. When questioned as to his understanding of the miraculous influence, he could suggest nothing and did not recognize the superstition even by name. He remembered that the doctors did not believe in its efficacy, but he and many others did. His father saw the brother's body and the arterial blood. The attitude of several other persons in regard to the practice was agnostic, either from fear of public opinion or other reasons, and their replies to my inquiries were in the same temper of mind as that of the blind man in the Gospel of Saint John (9:25), who did not dare to express his belief, but "answered and said, 'Whether he be a sinner or no, I know not; one thing I know, that whereas I was blind, now I see.'"

At ———, a small isolated village of scattered houses in a farming population, distant fifteen or twenty miles from Newport and eight or ten from Stuart's birthplace, there have been made within fifty years a half dozen or more exhumations. The most recent was made within two years, in the family of ———. The mother and four children had already succumbed to consumption, and the child most recently deceased (within six months) was, in obedience to the superstition, exhumed and the heart burned. Dr. ———, who made the autopsy, stated that he found the body in the usual condition after an interment of that length of time. I learned that others of the family have since died, and one is now very low with the dreaded disease. The doctor remarked that he had consented to the autopsy only after the pressing solicitation of the surviving children, who were patients of his, the father at first objecting, but finally, under continued pressure, yielding. Dr. ——— declares the superstition to be prevalent in all the isolated districts of southern Rhode Island, and that many instances of its survival can be found in the large centers of population. In the village now being considered, known exhumations have been made in five families; in the village previously named, in three families; and in two adjoining villages, in two families. In 1875 an instance was reported in Chicago, and in a New York journal of recent date I read the following: "At Peukuhl, a small village in Prussia, a farmer died last March. Since then one of his sons has been sickly, and believing that the dead man would not rest until he had drawn to himself the nine surviving members of the family, the sickly son, armed with a spade, exhumed his father and cut off his head." It does not by any means absolutely follow that this barbarous superstition has a stronger hold in Rhode Island than in any other part of the country. Peculiar conditions have caused its manifestation and survival there, and similar ones are likely to produce it elsewhere. The singular feature is that it should appear and flourish in a native population which from its infancy has had the ordinary New England educational advantages; in a state having a larger population to the square mile than any in the Union, and in an environment of remarkable literacy and culture when compared with some other sections of the country. It is perhaps fortunate that the isolation of which this is probably the product, an isolation common in sparsely settled regions, where thought stagnates and insanity and superstition are prevalent, has produced nothing worse.

In neighboring Connecticut, within a few miles of its university town of New Haven, there are rural farming populations, fairly prosperous, of average intelligence, and furnished with churches and schools, which have made themselves notorious by murder, suicides, and numerous cases of melancholia and insanity.

Other abundant evidence is at hand pointing to the conclusion that the vampire superstition still retains its hold in its original habitat—an illustration of the remarkable tenacity and continuity of a superstition through centuries of intellectual progress from a lower to a higher culture, and of the impotency of the latter to entirely eradicate from itself the traditional beliefs, customs, habits, observances, and impressions of the former.

From: George R. Stetson, "The Animistic Vampire in New England," *The American Anthropologist* 9 (January 1896): 1–13.

CHAPTER 4

Portents, Charms, and Remedies

· *Portents on Death* ·

(German)

Signs and presages of death were sufficiently numerous, but I doubt if any of them were peculiar to the locality. To carry a hoe through the house, to rock an empty chair in an absentminded manner with the foot, to dream of the loss of a front tooth, were intimations of the decease of some friend or neighbor or member of the family. The "death tick" was often referred to, and I have heard its peculiar sound, like the ticking of a large, old-fashioned clock, reckoning time toward eternity.

The incident of death itself was held to be frequently associated with some physical, external manifestation. At the moment of the departure of the spirit, a weight would be heard to drop in some unoccupied room, or there would be a buzzing sound, like that of a swarm of bees, outside the window. What these might signify was not stated.

From: D. G. Brinton, "Reminiscences of Pennsylvania Folk-Lore," *Journal of American Folk-Lore* 5 (1892): 177–85.

· Portents on Luck ·

(German)

A sign of bad luck on a journey was for one to return to the house for something forgotten, after he had passed out the gate. I believe it could be neutralized by not closing the door or gate on returning. Persons would rather suffer some inconvenience than take the risk of incurring this evil presage. It was deeply impressed upon me by an incident of my boyhood. Some miles from us there lived a widow, one of whose sons was drowned while bathing. I heard with awe that, as he was leaving the house to go with his companions, he returned three times to get some trifle. His mother implored him not to join the party, fearing the omen of these returns, but he laughed at her fears as silly, and went forth to his death.

The folklore of food-taking offered nothing that I remember which was peculiar. We held that it was bad luck to upset the salt, but that the effect could be neutralized by throwing some over the left shoulder. If one inadvertently helped himself to a dish of which he already had some, it was a sign that a hungry visitor would soon come. To take the last piece of bread on the plate was a sign that you would go hungry.

From: D. G. Brinton, "Reminiscences of Pennsylvania Folk-Lore," *Journal of American Folk-Lore* 5 (1892): 177–85.

· Dream Interpretations ·

(Various)

Dreams
(Armenian)

If one dreams of digging potatoes he will have money come to him, or some other good fortune.

If one dreams of money being at some particular spot, and on waking goes in search of it, he will find it as he dreamed. However, he must tell no one of his dream. If he does so, he will find only coal.

If one dreams of the living as being dead, he may expect good luck.

If one dreams of the dead as living, it is because the dead person's angel has come to visit his spirit while he slept.

To dream of a river, or of a spring, is a good sign, provided it is running. But if it is dry, then someone is going to die.

If one dreams of a snake, it is the sign of some enemy undertaking to injure him. If the snake bites him, then the troubles that are coming will be too much for him; if he kills the snake, the trouble will arise, but he will overcome it.

To dream of horses is always a good sign, but when the horse is black the good fortune will come sooner than if it were white.

To dream of being at a wedding is always a sign of bad luck.

If one dreams of seeing a preacher it is a sign that he is going to see the devil.

If one dreams of a person dressing, it is a sign of coming trouble. The person putting on the clothes is the one who will be afflicted.

To dream about a baby is always a sign of misfortune. If the babe is still in the womb, it is not as bad luck as if it is born. From first to last, the larger the babe the worse the luck. The person who has the babe is the one who will suffer the misfortune.

From: G. D. Edwards, "Items of Armenian Folk-Lore Collected in Boston," *Journal of American Folk-Lore* 12 (1899): 97–107.

Dreams
(Syrian)

If a person dreams that a tooth is pulled without starting blood, it means that some member of his family is going to die. If it is a back tooth, the person will be an aged one; if a middle tooth, the person will be of medium age; if a front tooth, the person will be young.

If a person dreams that he is eating white grapes, it means that it will surely rain the next day.

To dream that a certain man, attired in his finest clothes, is in a company where the others are not so attired means that the man is going to die.

To dream of blood means that nothing will happen.

If a person dreams that he sees his deceased father or mother talking angrily to him, it means that he or she wishes him to pray or make some atonement for him, or her.

If a person dreams that a large sore breaks and the matter is discharged, it means that he will be able to settle up all his debts.

If a married man dreams that he is being married, and sees himself attired in his wedding garments, it means that he is going to die.

A man (A) has a certain number of troubles to pass through. If another man (B) dreams that he (A) is dead, he (A) has already passed the first trouble. If a second man (C) dreams that he (A) is dead, he (A) has passed the second trouble. This continues till all are passed.

To dream that the leaves fall to the ground yellow means that there will be an epidemic in the town.

If a person dreams that he sees a naked figure dancing in the air, it means that death will come and release a soul from its body.

If a person dreams that he sees a line of camels traveling single file, it means that angels from heaven are descending to inspire the little children.

If a person dreams of a river, it means that something stands between him and his wishes.

If a person dreams of a woman, it means that he will have happiness. If, however, her hair is disheveled, it means that some member of his family will die soon.

To dream of seeing a cloud in the shape of a camel means there will be no rain and consequently a poor harvest.

To dream of snakes brings bad luck.

To dream of a leafless tree means it will rain the next day.

If a person dreams of an old woman carrying a baby in her arms, it means that some man of the town will die.

The reason being, according to my informant, that the earth is looked upon as the mother of mankind, who carries her children in her bosom when they are dead.

If a person dreams that there are many priests in his house, he may be sure that on that same day a year hence some member of his household will die.

In Lebanon when a man dies it is the custom for thirty or more priests to attend the funeral ceremony. My informant tells me that the number of priests in each town in Syria is very large in proportion to the population. In B'shory, a town of about seven thousand inhabitants, there are some forty priests.

If a person dreams of eating human flesh, his life will be short, and his children will perish from the face of the earth.

From: Howard Barrett Wilson, "Notes of Syrian Folk-Lore Collected in Boston," *Journal of American Folk-Lore* 16 (1903): 133–47.

· *Various Cures for Sickness* ·

(Armenian)

When one is sick, his friends will go to a bush which happens to be growing near the grave of some saint, or near some spot where a saint is once known to have been, and they will tie a rag on the bush and pray to the saint that the sick may get well. The tree will have so many rags sometimes, and of such various colors, that it will look at a distance as if it were in bloom.

Another remedy for sickness is to bathe in a stream and hang a rag on a tree close by.

Still another is to place an egg in a stream of water, but back in a little nook from the current so that it will not be swept away. Anyone who picks up the egg will get the disease it was intended to cure.

When a baby is sick it is bathed over the grave of some martyr. In the wintertime, water is heated and carried to the grave for this purpose.

When one is possessed with devils, a bowl of water is set in his presence, and a fortune-teller or soothsayer then charms the demons and gets them into the water. They are then taken one at a time and put into a ram's horn, after which the horn is plugged and given to the afflicted one with instructions to bury it deep in his yard.

In case of fever and ague, the sick bathes in a brook which is called "fever and ague brook." Every community has such a brook.

Sometimes when one is sick he will have four priests come. All of them will read aloud and at the same time, but each one will be reading a different scriptural passage. This is expected to cure the sick.

When one is sick he will oftentimes hunt up a fortune-teller who is supposed to know how to charm away disease. The fortune-teller will write something on a piece of paper (no one knows what), and, folding it up, give it to the man with instructions to wear it over his heart, or on his right or left arm, or on his head, or to put it in the water at some place, or anything else which he is disposed to tell him. His instructions faithfully carried out are to work a cure.

A piece of paper which has been blessed by a priest is sometimes put in a silver box and carried about with one in the belief that it will ward off disease.

Some take a blue bead which has been blessed by a priest and carry it concealed on their persons for the purpose of warding off the influence of witches. If there is a bright, pretty child in the family, a blue bead is nearly always concealed in its hair at just about the point "*bregma*," or a little in front of that, for fear some jealous person will bewitch him.

When one is bewitched, if a piece of the witch's garment can be cut off and burned so that the bewitched person may sniff the smoke from it, he will recover.

If one person meets another individual regularly as he goes to or from his work, and he continually has either good or bad luck, he will attribute it to this individual; or if on the days he meets him his luck is the reverse of what it is on the days when he does not meet him, then the result is the same.

Trees are prevented from being bewitched by putting the skulls of horses or dogs on them. These protect the tree from evil influences and insure its fruitfulness.

From: G. D. Edwards, "Items of Armenian Folk-Lore Collected in Boston," *Journal of American Folk-Lore* 12 (1899): 97–107.

· *Wart Remedies* ·

(German)

The dispersion of those trifling but disfiguring excrescences, warts, was generally by magical means. The warts should be bathed in the water in which the blacksmith cooled his irons, when the latter was not looking;

or they should be rubbed with a piece of raw meat which had been stolen, and the meat should be buried under a stone. As it decayed, the warts would disappear. Or a string should be stolen, and as many knots tied in it as there were warts to remove; the string should then be buried. I remember trying the first mentioned of these plans myself, with very successful results.

Warts were firmly believed to be "catching," and it was well to avoid shaking hands with a person who had them. They could also be caught from the udders of cows; but the most certain method of producing them was to handle a toad. This doubtless arose from the similarity of the dermic corrugations on the animal to warts on the hands. The toad was also said to eject a saliva which would cause a wart to grow where it touched the skin.

From: D. G. Brinton, "Reminiscences of Pennsylvania Folk-Lore," *Journal of American Folk-Lore* 5 (1892): 177–85.

· Charms and Remedies ·

(German)

To Bring Cherries Ripe by Martinmas

Graft the scion on the stock of a mulberry tree and your desire is accomplished.

To Drive Away Frights and Fantasies—
Also to Catch Fish

If you have in your hand the plant called arsesmant, and also caraway, you are safe from frights and fantasies, with which people are often befooled. If they are mixed with the juice of housewort, and the hands are smeared with it, and the refuse put into water where there are fish, you can easily catch the fish with the hands or in nets. If you take the hands out of the water the fish leave.

Sonnen-Werbel—Sun-Whist—Sun-Turn
Is it Heliotrope or Sunflower?
To Prevent Evil Reports and Discourse the Infidelity of a Wife

The virtue of this plant is wonderful, if gathered in the sign of the lion, in the month of August, and folded up in a laurel leaf, or a wolf's tooth.

If one wears it on his person, no one can say contradictory things to him, but only pleasant words; and if anything has been taken from anyone, and he lays this under his head at night, he will see the form and all the characteristics of the one who has done it.

If it is laid in any place where many women are, in a church, if anyone among them has violated her honor, she cannot go from the place till it is removed out of the way. This is proved.

For Sore Mouth

Hast thou the scurvy gum or brown,
So breathe I thrice mine own breath in.

To Overcome and End Battles and Quarrels—To Divine Whether a Sick Person Will Recover or Die—Also for Dimness or Glare of the Eyes

This root grows at the time that swallows and eagles make their nests. If one wears it about him, together with the heart of a mole, he will overcome in battle and end all quarrels. If it is laid on the head of a sick person, then if he weeps, he is about to get well again; if he sings with cheerful voice, he is about to die.

When it is in blossom, bruise it and steep it in a vessel of water over the fire, and skim it well, when it is thoroughly done, strain it through a towel and preserve it. This is a good wash for weak or dazzling eyes.

To Heal Shot Blister on the Eyes

Take a dirty plate; if you have none make one so. Then he for whom you use it will lose his pain in one minute. Put the side of the plate that is eaten from towards the eyes and say:

Dirty plate, I press thee
Blister sore, repress thee.

To Make Chickens Lay Well

Take hare's dung, bruise it fine, mix it with bran wet, feed it to the hens continually, and they lay abundantly.

To Consecrate a Divining Rod

When one makes a divining rod, or luck rod, he breaks it as before said
and says while making it and before he uses it: Luck rod, retain thy
strength, retain thy virtue, whereto God hath ordained thee.

To Drive Away the Worm

Worm, I conjure thee by the living God that thou avoid this blood and
this flesh, as God, the Lord will avoid the judge who pronounces unjust
judgment, it being in his power to pronounce right judgment.

For Consumption

I command thee out of the bone into the flesh; out of the flesh into the
skin; out of the skin into the wide world.

For a Burn

There went three holy men over the land,
They blessed the heat and they helped the burn
They blessed it that it consumed him.

For a Snake Bite

God enacted everything, and everything was good,
But thou alone, viper, art accursed.
Accursed shalt thou be and thy poison.

tsing, tsing, tsing

For a Bad Dog

Hound, hold your mouth to the ground.
Me God made, thee he suffers, hound.

You must do this toward the place where the dog is. You must make the
three crosses at the dog, and before he sees you, but you must say the
words first of all.

For Hollow Horn, in the Cow

Bore a hole in the horn that is hollow. Milk some milk from the same
cow and squirt it into the horn. This is an *allbest* cure.

A Very Good Cure for the Botts

Stroke the horse three times and lead it around three times with the head towards the sun and say: The holy one says, Joseph went over a field where he found three little worms; one was black, another was brown, the third was red:

Thou shalt die; go dead.

To Take Away Pain and Heal Wounds with Three Rods

With this rod and Christ's blood
Take I the pain and suppuration.

You must cut a piece from a young branch of a tree, towards sunrise, into three small pieces; rub them around on the wound one after another, beginning with that which is in the right hand first. In all cases of forms of words in this book, repeat them three times, whether the . . . stand or not. Let a half hour intervene between the first and second time, and the third be overnight. Wrap the sticks in a piece of white paper and put in a warm place.

A Sovereign Remedy for Colic

Jerusalem, thou Jewish City,
Which Christ, the Lord, has borne;
Water and blood thou must become,
That is good for N. for colic and worms.

For Weakness of the Limbs

The buds of the birch tree, or the inner bark of the root taken when the trees are in bud, makes a good tea for weakness of the limbs. Drink it in fourteen days, and then wait a while before drinking again; and during the fourteen days, change a couple of days and drink water.

Another, for the Same

Take bedonia and johnswort, put it into good corn brandy, and drink of it in the morning before eating. It is very wholesome and good. A tea made of white acorns is also good for weakness of the limbs.

Against Mice

When you harvest your grain, say as you bring the first three sheaves into the barn:

> Rats and mice, the first three sheaves to you I give,
> That my grain all the rest to me you leave.

Name each kind of grain.

To Drive Away the Ringbone, or Excrescence on the Leg of a Horse

Take a bone where you find but must not be looking for it, rub the excrescence of the horse with it in the old of the moon, lay the bone where you found it and the sore will disappear.

To Make a Horse Eat Again—This is Applicable on a Journey

Hold up the mouth of the horse that will not eat and strike it three times on the inside or the roof of the mouth. It will certainly help it, that it will eat again and continue to travel.

A Good Eye Water

Take eleven cents' worth of white vitriol and one ounce of sugar of lead (acetate L.); dissolve them in oil of rosemary; put it into a tolerably large bottle, and fill it with rosewater.

To Hold a Thief Fixed, that He Cannot Move—It is the Best Charm for This Purpose in the Book

O Peter, O Peter! Take from God the power; may I find—what I would bind—with the band, of Jesus' hand—that robbers all, great and small—that none can go no step more, neither backwards nor before—till I then with my eyes perceive, till I then with my tongue relieve—till first they count me every stone, twixt heaven and earth, and drop of rain—each leaf of tree and blade of grass; this pray I to my foe for Mass.

Say the Creed and the Paternoster. To compel him to stand, say this thrice. If the thief is to be permitted to win, the sun must not shine on him before you loose him. This loosing is done in two forms. The first is: Bid him in the name of St. John to go forth. The second is this: With the words with which you (or *those*, if only *one*, or a woman) were stopped, you are loosed.

For the Pining or Dwindling Away of the Leg of a Horse
Take a pound of old bacon, cut it small, put it in a pan, roast it well, put in a handful of fish worms, a gill of oats, and three spoonfuls of salt; roast it all right black and strain it through a towel; then add a gill of Dutch soap, and half gill of corn brandy, a half gill of vinegar, and half gill of boys' urine, stir them together and rub the leg with it crosswise, on the third, sixth, and ninth day after the new moon, and warm it in with an oak board.

To Make Molasses
Take pumpkins, stew them, strain (press) out the liquid, and boil it down till it is thick as molasses. The author of this book has eaten such, and thought it was the real molasses, till the people told him.

How to Make Good Beer
Take a handful of hops, about three spoonfuls of ginger, and a half gallon of molasses—strain it into a tub. Then it is good beer.

For Falling Sickness
Take a turtledove, cut off the neck, and give the blood to the patient.

To Make Poor Paper Not Flow When You Write on It
Dip the paper in alum water. I, Hohman, will hereafter pour a little water on the alum and moisten the paper. Then I will see whether one can write on it.

For Stone in the Bladder
The author of this book, Johann Geog Hohman, am using this remedy and it is helping me. Another man sought help from the doctors a long time in vain; he then found this serviceable, viz. He ate every morning forty-seven peach stones, and it helped him. If the case is very bad, continue it. I, Hohman, have used it only a few weeks. I began to perceive its good effects immediately, though I had the disease so bad, that I was forced to cry aloud when I made water. To the loving God and my wife I owe a thousand thanks for this relief.

For Incontinence—Not Able to Hold One's Water
Take a hog's bladder, burn it to a powder, and take it.

To Take Away an Excrescence in the Increase of the Moon
Look directly over the excrescence and say: What increases, increases; what decreases, decreases. Say this thrice in one breath.

To Drive Away Mice or Moles
Put a piece of unslacked lime in the hole.

To Remove a Film from the Eyes
Dig the root of bissibet on St. Bartholomew's day before sunrise, eight or five roots; take off the ends of the roots over the trench from which they are dug; get a patch of cloth and thread which have not been in water; see that the thread has no knot in it; tie up the roots in the patch, hang them on the neck till the film is gone, with a band which also has not touched water.

For Bad Hearing—and Roaring in the Ears— Also for Toothache
Moisten some cotton with a few drops of tincture of camphor and lay it on the tooth affected. It eases the pain very much.

Put in the ear it strengthens the hearing and prevents the buzzing and roaring of the ears.

To Make Children's Teeth Grow Without Pain
Boil the brain of a hare, and rub the gums of the children with it, and the teeth will grow without pain.

For Puking and Purging
Take cloves and pound them fine; take bread and soak it in red wine and eat it, and you will soon be better. Or, put the cloves in the bread.

To Heal a Burn
Anoint the burnt part with the juice of the flag bruised and pressed; or better, saturate a rag in the juice and bind it on.

Another Good Cure for Weak Limbs—for Purifying the Blood, Strengthening the Head and Heart—for Dizziness, etc.

In the morning, before eating take two little drops of oil of cloves in a glass of white wine. It is good also against the constant vomiting of the mother—also for cold stomach. It strengthens and warms it and checks the vomiting. A couple of drops on a little cotton laid on an aching tooth stills the pain.

The oil of cloves is obtained as follows: Take a "good bit" of the clove spice, pulverize it, pour on a half ounce of water, let it stand in warm sand four days, then distill it into a tin or copper vessel and separate the oil with cotton or a separating glass.

For Dysentery and Diarrhea

Take moss of trees, boil it in red wine, and give it to the patient to drink.

For the Toothache

The author of this book, Hohman, has cured himself more than sixty times with this remedy of the severest toothache; and of the sixty times that he has used it, it has failed but once. Take, namely, vitriol: When the tooth begins to ache, put a little piece in the sore tooth; spit all the saliva out, but not too often. I know not whether it would help a tooth that is not hollow, but think it would, if laid on it.

Caution for Pregnant Women

Pregnant women must be careful to avoid camphor. It must not be given to them; they cannot endure the smell of it when they are sick.

For Bite of a Mad Dog—Hydrophobia

A certain Valentine Kettering of Dauphin County, has made known to the senate of Pennsylvania a remedy which will cure the bite of a rabid animal without fail. He says it has been used by his forefathers in Germany for 250 years, and by himself since he came to the U.S., now over sixty years, and has always been found infallible. He publishes it purely from notions of humanity, this remedy is the red chickweed or pimpernal (Bot. name *anogallis Phœnicea?*). It is a summer plant, known in Germany and Switzerland under the name of *Gauchkeil* and red meyer or red heehner-dorn. It must be gathered in June, when in full bloom, dried in the shade, and pulverized. The dose of this for an adult is a small egg-glass full, or a drachm and a scruple, at once, taken in beer or water. For a child the dose is the same, only it is to be given at three separate times.

When it is for beasts, it is to be used green, and may be cut and mixed in bran and other fodder. If for swine, use the dust, and put it in their swill. It can be eaten on buttered bread, or honey, or molasses, etc.

The Honorable Henry Muhlenberg says that in Germany they give thirty grains of the powder four times a day, and so continue for a week with decreasing doses, and at the same time wash the wound with a decoction of the plant and sprinkle the powder in it. Mr. Kettering says he has always found a single dose followed by the happiest results.

It is said this is the remedy used so successfully by the late Dr. Wm. Stoy.

To Guard Against Various Diseases in Sheep, and to Promote the Growth of the Wool

William Ellies, in his admirable treatise on the sheep culture in England relates the following: I know a farmer who has a flock of sheep which yields a remarkable crop of wool. He secures that result by this means: When he shears his sheep he washes them thoroughly in buttermilk. Buttermilk makes not only the sheep's wool, but also the hair of all animals to grow strong. Those who have not buttermilk at hand, can take other milk, mixing a little salt and water with it. I can assure also that, by the proper use of this means, the sheep tick will be exterminated from the lambs. It also cures the scab or itch, prevents colds from attacking them, and makes the wool grow rapidly and thick.

Plaster for a Burn

Take a gill of fat in which chickens have been cooked; six eggs roasted in live embers hard; take out the yolk, cook them in the fat till they are right black, add a handful of rue, steep it, and strain through a towel. When ready cool it with a gill of olive oil. It is best that the plaster for a man should be made by a woman, and for a woman by a man.

A Right Good Plaster

Take a wormwood rue, ———, yarrow, and beeswax, of each an equal part, but of the beeswax a little more, add tallow and a little spirits of turpentine, simmer together in an oven and strain them.

For Poll-Evil

Apply turpentine, rub it in with the hand, and baste with a hot iron; then take goose fat, baste it in three days in succession, and the last day in the last quarter (of the moon).

To Stop Blood

I go through a green wold,
Where bloom three flowers, fresh and cold;
The first is called might, the second, good, is height,
The third says, still the blood.

To Stop Blood and Cure Wounds in Man or Beast

On Jesus' grave there grew three roses: the first is goodly, the second all-pervading. Blood stands still, the wounds they heal.

To Gain a Law Suit

It is said that if one has a law suit, and will take of the largest sage, and will write the names of the twelve apostles on a leaf and put them in his shoe before he goes to the courthouse, he will gain his case.

For the Swelling of Cattle

To desh break no flesh, but to desh! While saying this run your hand along the back of the animal.

Note.—The hand must be put upon the bare skin in all cases of using sympathetic words.

To Catch Small Fish—Civet and Beavers

Castor liquid, nine grains each; eel fat, two ounces; unsalted fresh butter, four ounces; mix in a vessel of white glass, stop or cover the vessel close, set it in the sun or a tolerably warm place nine or ten days; stir the composition with a small spoon till they all come together.

From: John George Hohman, "The Long Hidden Friend," *Journal of American Folk-Lore* 17 (1904): 89–152.

CHAPTER 5

The Supernatural

· Witches and Witchcraft ·

(Various)

Witchcraft in Salem
(English Puritan)

The extraordinary delusion recorded as Salem witchcraft was but a reflection of a kindred insanity in the Old World that was not extirpated until its victims had been counted by thousands. That human beings should be accused of leaguing themselves with Satan to plague their fellows and overthrow the powers of righteousness is remarkable, but that they should admit their guilt is incomprehensible, albeit the history of every popular delusion shows that weak minds are so affected as to lose control of themselves and that a whimsy can be as epidemic as smallpox.

Such was the case in 1692 when the witchcraft madness, which might have been stayed by a seasonable spanking, broke out in Danvers, Massachusetts—the first victim being a wild Irishwoman, named Glover—and speedily involved the neighboring community of Salem. The mischiefs done by witches were usually trifling, and it never occurred to their prosecutors that there was an inconsistency between their pretended powers and their feeble deeds, or that it was strange that those who might live in regal luxury should be so wretchedly poor. Aches and pains, blight of crops, disease of cattle were charged to them; children complained of being pricked with thorns and pins (the pins are still preserved in Salem); and if hysterical girls spoke the name of any feeble old woman, while in flighty talk, they virtually sentenced her to die. The word of a child of eleven years sufficed to hang, burn, or drown a witch.

Giles Corey, a blameless man of eighty, was condemned to the medieval *peine forte et dure*, his body being crushed beneath a load of rocks and timbers. He refused to plead in court, and when the beams were laid upon him he only cried, "More weight!" The shade of the unhappy victim haunted the scene of his execution for years, and always came to warn the people of calamities. A child of five and a dog were also hanged after formal condemnation. Gallows Hill, near Salem, witnessed many sad tragedies, and the old elm that stood on Boston Common until 1876 was said to have served as a gallows for witches and Quakers. The accuser of one day was the prisoner of the next, and not even the clergy were safe.

A few escapes were made, like that of a blue-eyed maid of Wenham, whose lover aided her to break the wooden jail and carried her safely beyond the Merrimac, finding a home for her among the Quakers; and that of Miss Wheeler, of Salem, who had fallen under suspicion, and whose brothers hurried her into a boat, rowed around Cape Ann, and safely bestowed her in "the witch house" at Pigeon Cove. Many, however, fled to other towns rather than run the risk of accusation, which commonly meant death.

When the wife of Philip English was arrested he too asked to share her fate and both were, through friendly intercession, removed to Boston, where they were allowed to have their liberty by day on condition that they would go to jail every night. Just before they were to be taken back to Salem for trial they went to church and heard the Reverend Joshua Moody preach from the text, "If they persecute you in one city, flee unto another." The good clergyman not only preached goodness, but practiced it, and that night the door of their prison was opened. Furnished with an introduction from Governor Phipps to Governor Fletcher, of New York, they made their way to that settlement, and remained there in safe and courteous keeping until the people of Salem had regained their senses, when they returned. Mrs. English died, soon after, from the effects of cruelty and anxiety, and although Mr. Moody was generally commended for his substitution of sense and justice for law, there were bigots who persecuted him so constantly that he removed to Plymouth.

According to the belief of the time a witch or wizard compacted with Satan for the gift of supernatural power, and in return was to give up his soul to the evil one after his life was over. The deed was signed in blood of the witch and horrible ceremonies confirmed the compact. Satan then gave his ally a familiar in the form of a dog, ape, cat, or other animal, usually small and black, and sometimes an undisguised imp. To suckle these "familiars" with the blood of a witch was forbidden in English law, which ranked it as a felony; but they were thus nourished in secret, and by their aid the witch might raise storms, blight crops, abort births, lame cattle, topple over houses, and cause pains, convulsions, and illness.

If she desired to hurt a person she made a clay or waxen image in his likeness, and the harms and indignities wreaked on the puppet would be suffered by the one bewitched, a knife or needle thrust in the waxen body being felt acutely by the living one, no matter how far distant he might be. By placing this image in running water, hot sunshine, or near a fire, the living flesh would waste as this melted or dissolved, and the person thus wrought upon would die. This belief is still current among Negroes affected by the voodoo superstitions of the South.

The witch too had the power of riding winds, usually with a broomstick for a conveyance, after she had smeared the broom or herself with magic ointment, and the flocking of the unhallowed to their Sabbaths in snaky bogs or on lonely mountaintops has been described minutely by those who claim to have seen the sight. Sometimes they cackled and gibbered through the night before the houses of the clergy, and it was only at Christmas that their power failed them. The meetings were devoted to wild and obscene orgies, and the intercourse of fiends and witches begot a progeny of toads and snakes.

Naturally the Indians were accused, for they recognized the existence of both good and evil spirits, their medicine men cured by incantations in the belief that devils were thus driven out of their patients, and in the early history of the country the red man was credited by white settlers with powers hardly inferior to those of the oriental and European magicians of the middle ages.

Cotton Mather detected a relation between Satan and the Indians, and he declares that certain of the Algonquins were trained from boyhood as powahs, powwows, or wizards, acquiring powers of second sight and communion with gods and spirits through abstinence from food and sleep and the observance of rites. Their severe discipline made them victims of nervous excitement and the responsibilities of conjuration had on their minds an effect similar to that produced by gases from the rift in Delphos on the Apollonian oracles, their manifestations of insanity or frenzy passing for deific or infernal possession.

When John Gibb, a Scotchman, who had gone mad through religious excitement, was shipped to this country by his tired fellow countrymen, the Indians hailed him as a more powerful wizard than any of their number, and he died in 1720, admired and feared by them because of the familiarity with spirits out of Hobbomocko (hell) that his ravings and antics were supposed to indicate.

Two Indian servants of the Reverend Mr. Purvis, of Salem, having tried by a spell to discover a witch, were executed as witches themselves. The savages, who took Salem witchcraft at its worth, were astonished at its deadly effect, and the English may have lost some influence over the natives in consequence of this madness. "The Great Spirit sends no witches to the French," they said.

Barrow Hill, near Amesbury, was said to be the meeting place for Indian powwows and witches, and at late hours of the night the light of fires gleamed from its top, while shadowy forms glanced athwart it. Old men say that the lights are still there in winter, though modern doubters declare that they were the aurora borealis.

But the belief in witches did not die even when the Salem people came to their senses. In the Merrimac Valley the devil found converts for many years after: Goody Mose, of Rocks Village, who tumbled downstairs when a big beetle was killed at an evening party, some miles away, after it had been bumping into the faces of the company; Goody Whitcher, of Amesbury, whose loom kept banging day and night after she was dead; Goody Sloper, of West Newbury, who went home lame directly after a man had struck his ax into the beam of a house that she had bewitched, but who recovered her strength and established an improved reputation when, in 1794, she swam out to a capsized boat and rescued two of the people who were in peril; Goodman Nichols, of Rocks Village, who "spelled" a neighbor's son, compelling him to run up one end of the house, along the ridge, and down the other end, "troubling the family extremely by his strange proceedings"; Susie Martin, also of Rocks, who was hanged in spite of her devotions in jail, though the rope danced so that it could not be tied, but a crow overhead called for a withe and the law was executed with that; and Goody Morse, of Market and High streets, Newburyport, whose baskets and pots danced through her house continually and who was seen "flying about the sun as if she had been cut in twain, or as if the devil did hide the lower part of her."

The hill below Easton, Pennsylvania, called *Hexenkopf* (Witch's head), was described by German settlers as a place of nightly gathering for weird women, who whirled about its top in "linked dances" and sang in deep tones mingled with awful laughter. After one of these women, in Williams Township, had been punished for enchanting a twenty-dollar horse, their Sabbaths were held more quietly.

Mom Rinkle, whose "rock" is pointed out beside the Wissahickon, in Philadelphia, "drank dew from acorn cups and had the evil eye." Juan Perea, of San Mateo, New Mexico, would fly with his chums to meetings in the mountains in the shape of a fireball. During these sallies he left his own eyes at home and wore those of some brute animal. It was because his dog ate his eyes when he had carelessly put them on a table that he had always afterward to wear those of a cat. Within the present century an old woman who lived in a hut on the Palisades of the Hudson was held to be responsible for local storms and accidents. As late as 1889 two Zuñi Indians were hanged on the wall of an old Spanish church near their pueblo in Arizona on a charge of having blown away the rainclouds in a time of drought. It was held that there was something uncanny in the event that gave the name of Gallows Hill to an eminence near Falls Village, Connecticut, for a strange black man was found hanging, dead, to a tree near its top one morning.

Moll Pitcher, a successful sorcerer and fortune-teller of old Lynn, has figured in obsolete poems, plays, and romances. She lived in a cottage at the foot of High Rock, where she was consulted, not merely by people of respectability, but by those who had knavish schemes to prosecute and who wanted to learn in advance the outcome of their designs. Many a ship was deserted at the hour of sailing because she boded evil of the voyage. She was of medium height, big-headed, tangle-haired, long-nosed, and had a searching black eye. The sticks that she carried were cut from a hazel that hung athwart a brook where an unwedded mother had drowned her child. A girl who went to her for news of her lover lost her reason when the witch, moved by a malignant impulse, described his death in a fiercely dramatic manner. One day the missing ship came bowling into port, and the shock of joy that the girl experienced when the sailor clasped her in his arms restored her erring senses. When Moll Pitcher died she was attended by the little daughter of the woman she had so afflicted.

John, or Edward, Dimond, grandfather of Moll Pitcher, was a benevolent wizard. When vessels were trying to enter the port of Marblehead in a heavy gale or at night, their crews were startled to hear a trumpet voice pealing from the skies, plainly audible above the howling and hissing of any tempest, telling them how to lay their course so as to reach smooth water. This was the voice of Dimond, speaking from his station, miles away in the village cemetery. He always repaired to this place in troubling weather and shouted orders to the ships that were made visible to him by mystic power as he strode to and fro among the graves. When thieves came to him for advice he charmed them and made them take back their plunder or caused them to tramp helplessly about the streets bearing heavy burdens.

> Old Mammy Redd, of Marblehead,
> Sweet milk could turn to mould in churn.

Being a witch, and a notorious one, she could likewise curdle the milk as it came from the cow, and afterward transform it into blue wool. She had the evil eye, and, if she willed, her glance or touch could blight like palsy. It only needed that she should wish a bloody cleaver to be found in a cradle to cause the little occupant to die, while the whole town ascribed to her the annoyances of daily housework and business.

Her unpleasant celebrity led to her death at the hands of her fellow citizens who had been "worrited" by no end of queer happenings: Ships had appeared just before they were wrecked and had vanished while people looked at them; men were seen walking on the water after they had been comfortably buried; the wind was heard to name the sailors doomed never to return; footsteps and voices were heard in the streets before the great were to die; one man was chased by a corpse in its coffin; another was pursued by the devil in a carriage drawn by four white horses; a young woman who had just received a present of some fine fish from her lover was amazed to see him melt into the air, and was heartbroken when she learned next morning that he had died at sea. So far away as Amesbury the devil's power was shown by the appearance of a man who walked the roads carrying his head under his arm, and by the freak of a windmill that the miller always used to shut up at sundown but that started by itself at midnight. Evidently it was high time to be rid of Mammy Redd.

Margaret Wesson, "old Meg," lived in Gloucester until she came to her death by a shot fired at the siege of Louisburg, five hundred miles away, in 1745. Two soldiers of Gloucester, while before the walls of the French town, were annoyed by a crow, that flew over and around them, cawing harshly and disregarding stones and shot, until it occurred to them that the bird could be no other than old Meg in another form, and, as silver bullets are an esteemed antidote for the evils of witchcraft, they cut two silver buttons from their uniforms and fired them at the crow. At the first shot its leg was broken; at the second, it fell dead. On returning to Gloucester they learned that old Meg had fallen and broken her leg at the moment when the crow was fired on, and that she died quickly after. An examination of her body was made, and the identical buttons were extracted from her flesh that had been shot into the crow at Louisburg.

As a citizen of New Haven was riding home—this was at the time of the goings-on at Salem—he saw shapes of women near his horse's head, whispering earnestly together and keeping time with the trot of his animal without effort of their own. "In the name of God, tell me who you are," cried the traveler, and at the name of God they vanished. Next day the man's orchard was shaken by viewless hands and the fruit thrown down. Hogs ran about the neighborhood on their hind legs; children cried that somebody was sticking pins into them; one man would roll across the floor as if pushed, and he had to be watched lest he should go into the fire; when housewives made their bread they found it as full of hair as food in a city boardinghouse; when they made soft soap it ran from the kettle and over the floor like lava; stones fell down chimneys and smashed crockery. One of the farmers cut off an ear from a pig that was walking on its hind legs, and an eccentric old body of the neighborhood appeared presently with one of her ears in a muffle, thus satisfying that community that she had caused the troubles. When a woman was making potash it began to leap about, and a rifle was fired into the pot, causing a sudden calm. In the morning the witch was found dead on her floor. Yet killing only made her worse, for she moved to a deserted house near her own, and there kept a mad revel every night; fiddles were heard, lights flashed, stones were thrown, and yells gave people at a distance a series of cold shivers; but the populace tried the effect of tearing down the house, and quiet was brought to the town.

In the early days of this century a skinny old woman known as Aunt Woodward lived by herself in a log cabin at Minot Corner, Maine, enjoying the awe of the people in that secluded burg. They moved around but little at night, on her account, and one poor girl was in mortal fear lest by mysterious arts she should be changed, between two days, into a white horse. One citizen kept her away from his house by nailing a horseshoe to his door, while another took the force out of her spells by keeping a branch of "round wood" at his threshold. At night she haunted a big, square house where the ghost of a murdered infant was often heard to cry, and by day she laid charms on her neighbors' provisions and utensils, and turned their cream to butter-milk. "Uncle" Blaisdell hurried into the settlement to tell the farmers that Aunt Woodward had climbed into his sled in the middle of the road, and that his four yoke of oxen could not stir it an inch, but that after she had leaped down one yoke of cattle drew the load of wood without an effort. Yet she died in her bed.

From: Charles M. Skinner, *Myths & Legends of Our Own Land,* vol. 1 (Philadelphia and London: J. B. Lippincott Co., 1896).

Mrs. Ann Hibbins
(English)

Mrs. Ann Hibbins was the wife of William Hibbins, a wealthy and influential merchant of Boston. Hutchinson says that he was one of the principal merchants in all the colony. At this early day in its history he had served the colony with credit, first as its agent in England, and again as one of the assistants, or chief magistrates. These important trusts denote the high esteem in which he was held, and they confirm his admitted capacity for public affairs. A series of unlucky events, how-ever, brought such heavy losses upon him in his old age as seriously to impair his estate; but what was perhaps worse to bear, the sudden change from affluence to a more straitened way of living is alleged not only to have soured his wife's naturally unstable temper, but to have so far unset-tled her mind that she became in turn so morose and so quarrelsome as to render her odious to all her neighbors. Instead of being softened by misfortune, she was hardened and embittered by it. And it is thought that some of these neighbors were led to denounce her as a witch, as presently they did, through motives of spite, or in revenge for her malice toward, or her abusive treatment of, them.

It was a credulous age, when the spirit of persecution was easily aroused. The eye of the whole town was presently turned upon Mrs. Hibbins. There is little room to doubt that she was the unfortunate possessor of a sharp tongue and of a crabbed temper, neither of which was under proper restraint. Most unfortunately for her, as it fell out, a superior intelligence and penetration enabled her to make shrewd guesses about her neighbors and their affairs, which the old wives and gossips believed and declared no one else but the Devil or his imps could have known or told her of. From dislike they advanced to hatred, then to fear, and then it no doubt began to be freely whispered about that she was a witch. Such a reputation would naturally cast a fatal blight over her life. No wife or mother believed herself or her infant for one moment safe from the witch's detestable arts, since she might take any form she pleased to afflict them. Presently, the idle gossip of a neighborhood grew into a formal accusation. How much could be made in those days of a little, or how dangerous it then was to exercise any gift like that of clairvoyance or mind reading, the following fragment will make clear to the reader's mind. Upon this point Mr. Beach a minister in Jamaica, writes to Dr. Increase Mather as follows:

> You may remember what I have sometimes told you your famous Mr. Norton once said at his own table, before Mr. Wilson the pastor, Elder Penn, and myself and wife, etc., who had the honour to be his guests—that one of your magistrates' wives, as I remember, was hanged for a witch, only for having more wit than her neighbours. It was his very expression, she having, as he explained it, unhappily guessed that two of her persecutors, whom she saw talking in the street, were talking of her; which, proving true, cost her her life, notwithstanding all he could do to the contrary, as he himself told us.

One can hardly read this fragment without shuddering.

The increasing feeling of detestation and fear having now broken out into a popular clamor for justice upon the witch, Mrs. Hibbins was first publicly expelled from the communion of her church, and then publicly accused and thrown into prison. When the prison door closed behind her, her doom was sealed.

Fortunately, perhaps, for him, for he died a year before this bitter disgrace sullied his good name, the husband was not alive to meet the terrible accusation or to stem the tide setting so strongly and so pitilessly against the wife whom he had sworn at the altar to love, cherish, and protect. If her brother, Richard Bellingham, then holding the second place in the colony, made any effort to save her, that fact nowhere appears. Her three sons, whom she seems to have loved with the affectionate tenderness of a fond mother, were all absent from the colony. Alone, friendless, an object of hatred to her own neighbors, her heart may well have sunk within her.

Under such distressing circumstances was poor old Dame Hibbins, who once held her head so high, dragged from her dungeon before the court which was to try her as the worst of criminals known to the law. The jury, however, failed to convict her of any overt act of witchcraft. But she could not escape thus. The people, it is said, demanded her blood, and nothing short of this would satisfy them. So the magistrates, having the power to set aside the verdict, obeying the popular voice, brought her before the bar of the general court, where, in presence of the assembled wisdom of the colony, she was again required to plead guilty or not guilty to being a witch. She answered with firmness and spirit that she was not guilty, and said she was willing to be tried by God and the court. The evidence already taken against her was then read, witnesses were heard, and her answers considered; and the whole case being then submitted for its decision, the court by its vote this time found her guilty of witchcraft according to the tenor of the bill of indictment. Governor Endicott, rising in his place, then pronounced in open court the awful sentence of death upon the doomed woman for a crime which had no existence save in the imagination of her accusers. The warrant for her execution was made out in due form, the fatal day was fixed, and the marshal-general was therein directed to take with him "a sufficient guard." Then the poor, infirm, superannuated old woman, as innocent as the babe unborn, was led back to prison a condemned felon. Then the members of the great and general court, satisfied that they had done God's work in hanging a witch, dispersed in peace to their homes, made more secure, as they believed, by this act of justice.

As the sentence was not carried into effect for a whole year, it is

probable that the intercession of friends may have procured for the condemned woman this reprieve. But it could not avert her final doom,
however it might delay it. That was sealed. On the day that she was to
suffer she made and executed in prison a codicil to her will, clearly disposing of all her property. She was then taken to the usual place of execution,
and there, hanged.

The "usual place of execution" being the Common, it is a tradition
that Mrs. Hibbins, as well as others who suffered at the hands of the
public executioner, was launched into eternity from the branch of the
great elm tree that stood, until within a few years, a commanding and
venerated relic of the past, near the center of this beautiful park. Her
remains were shamefully violated. A search was immediately made upon
the dead body of the poor woman for the distinguishing marks that all
witches were supposed to have on their persons. Her chests and boxes
were also ransacked for the puppets or images by which their victims were
afflicted, but none were found. The remains were then probably thrust
into some obscure hole, for the sufferer, being excommunicated and a
condemned witch, would not be entitled to Christian burial, although she
earnestly begged this poor boon in her will. Hubbard, who writes nearest
to the event, says that they who were most forward to condemn Mrs.
Hibbins were afterward observed to be special marks for the judgments of
divine Providence.

And all this really happened in the good town of Boston in the year
1656!

From: Samuel Adams Drake, A *Book of New England Legends and Folk Lore* (Boston: Roberts
Brothers, 1888).

The Baker's Dozen
(Dutch)

B aas (Boss) Volckert Jan Pietersen Van Amsterdam kept a bake shop
in Albany, and lives in history as the man who invented New Year's
cakes and made gingerbread babies in the likeness of his own fat offspring.
Good churchman though he was, the bane of his life was a fear of being
bewitched, and perhaps it was to keep out evil spirits, who might make
one last effort to gain the mastery over him, ere he turned the customary

leaf with the incoming year, that he had primed himself with an extra glass of spirits on the last night of 1654. His sales had been brisk, and as he sat in his little shop, meditating comfortably on the gains he would make when his harmless rivals—the knikkerbakkers (bakers of marbles)—sent for their usual supply of olie-koeks and mince pies on the morrow, he was startled by a sharp rap, and an ugly old woman entered. "Give me a dozen New Year's cookies!" she cried, in a shrill voice.

"Vell, den, you needn' sbeak so loud. I aind teaf, den."

"A dozen!" she screamed. "Give me a dozen. Here are only twelve."

"Vell, den, dwalf is a dozen."

"One more! I want a dozen."

"Vell, den, if you vant anodder, go to de duyvil and ged it."

Did the hag take him at his word? She left the shop, and from that time it seemed as if poor Volckert was bewitched, indeed, for his cakes were stolen; his bread was so light that it went up the chimney, when it was not so heavy that it fell through the oven; invisible hands plucked bricks from that same oven and pelted him until he was blue; his wife became deaf, his children went unkempt, and his trade went elsewhere.

Thrice the old woman reappeared, and each time was sent anew to the devil; but at last, in despair, the baker called on Saint Nicholas to come and advise him. His call was answered with startling quickness, for, almost while he was making it, the venerable patron of Dutch feasts stood before him. The good soul advised the trembling man to be more generous in his dealings with his fellows, and after a lecture on charity he vanished, when, lo! the old woman was there in his place.

She repeated her demand for one more cake, and Volckert Jan Pietersen, etc., gave it, whereupon she exclaimed, "The spell is broken, and from this time a dozen is thirteen!" Taking from the counter a gingerbread effigy of Saint Nicholas, she made the astonished Dutchman lay his hand upon it and swear to give more liberal measure in the future. So, until thirteen new states arose from the ruins of the Colonies—when the shrewd Yankees restored the original measure—thirteen made a baker's dozen.

From: Charles M. Skinner, *Myths & Legends of Our Own Land*, vol. 1 (Philadelphia and London: J. B. Lippincott Co., 1896).

· Specters ·

(Various)

Ghosts
(German)

Ghosts, it is needless to say, were familiar to us as children. One of them used to haunt a certain hillock at no great distance from the paternal mansion. From time to time it would be seen there in the gray night light. The tradition was that on that spot a Hessian soldier had been killed and buried during the Revolution, and that his spirit was restless in his foreign grave.

There were other legends which, like this one, were connected with the battle of the Brandywine, the scene of which was but a few miles distant. On the floor of the old Quaker meetinghouse, into which the wounded were carried, could still be seen certain dark spots which we were told were the stains of human blood, and that no washing could erase them. I remembered looking at these discolorations with even more awe than I have since regarded those on the marble basin in the Hall of the Abencerrages, to your right as you enter the Alhambra, where the members of that unfortunate family were beheaded to the last man. Perhaps sober science would tell us that the latter stains are but the ferruginous veins in the marble, and the former but progressive dry rot in the old boards; but we do not wish to be dragging science into everything, or what should we have thrilling and romantic left?

To return to ghosts. There was another spot which they frequented. It bore the uncanny name "Gallows Hill," because in some early days a gallows had been erected there, and one or more men hanged thereon. In a community which had been peopled by Quakers, who disapprove of capital punishment, such an occurrence was felt as a deep shock to the moral sense, and the spot was shunned, and fell into the worse repute as the belief grew that the restless spirits of the criminals still hovered around the windy hilltop where they met their fate.

Though I cannot speak from personal observation of these particular ghosts, I can of others, as I was somewhat of a ghost seer myself in those days; a faculty which I regret I lost as I advanced in years. I remember on two occasions seeing distinctly such supernal visitors. Both times it was in broad daylight and I was in sound health.

Once it was out of doors in a garden, the next time at the entrance of the roomy garret of my father's house. Of course, with such evidence of my own, I was quite prepared to accept without question the statements of others on such points.

From: D. G. Brinton, "Reminiscences of Pennsylvania Folk-Lore," *Journal of American Folk-Lore* 5 (1892): 177–85.

Storm Ship of the Hudson
(Dutch)

It was noised about New Amsterdam, two hundred years ago, that a round and bulky ship flying Dutch colors from her lofty quarter was careering up the harbor in the teeth of a north wind, through the swift waters of an ebbing tide, and making for the Hudson. A signal from the Battery to heave to and account for herself being disregarded, a cannon was trained upon her, and a ball went whistling through her cloudy and imponderable mass, for timbers she had none.

Some of the sailor folk talked of mirages that rose into the air of northern coasts and seas, but the wise ones put their fingers beside their noses and called to memory the Flying Dutchman, that wanderer of the seas whose captain, having sworn that he would round Cape Horn in spite of heaven and hell, has been beating to and fro along the bleak Fuegian coast and elsewhere for centuries, being allowed to land but once in seven years, when he can break the curse if he finds a girl who will love him.

Perhaps Captain Vanderdecken found this maiden of his hopes in some Dutch settlement on the Hudson, or perhaps he expiated his rashness by prayer and penitence; howbeit, he never came down again, unless he slipped away to sea in snow or fog so dense that watchers and boatmen saw nothing of his passing. A few old settlers declared the vessel to be the *Half Moon*, and there were some who testified to seeing that identical ship with Hudson and his specter crew on board making for the Catskills to hold carouse.

This fleeting vision has been confounded with the storm ship that lurks about the foot of the Palisades and Point-no-Point, cruising through Tappan Zee at night when a gale is coming up. The Hudson is four miles wide at Tappan, and squalls have space enough to gather force; hence, when old skippers saw the misty form of a ship steal out from the shadows of the western hills, then fly like a gull from shore to shore, catching the moonlight on her topsails, but showing no lanterns, they made to wind-ward and dropped anchor, unless their craft were staunch and their pilot's brains unvexed with liquor. On summer nights, when falls that curious silence which is ominous of tempest, the storm ship is not only seen spinning across the mirror surface of the river, but the voices of the crew are heard as they chant at the braces and halyards in words devoid of meaning to the listeners.

From: Charles M. Skinner, *Myths & Legends of Our Own Land*, vol. 1 (Philadelphia and London: J. B. Lippincott, 1896).

The Galloping Hessian
(Unidentified)

In the flower-gemmed cemetery of Tarrytown, where gentle Irving sleeps, a Hessian soldier was interred after sustaining misfortune in the loss of his head in one of the Revolutionary battles. For a long time after he was buried it was the habit of this gentleman to crawl from his grave at unseemly hours and gallop about the country, sending shivers through the frames of many worthy people, who shrank under their blankets when they heard the rush of hoofs along the unlighted roads.
they heard the rush of hoofs along the unlighted roads.

In later times there lived in Tarrytown—so named because of the tarrying habits of Dutch gossips on market days, though some hard-minded people insist that "Tarwe town" means "Wheat town"—a gaunt schoolmaster, one Ichabod Crane, who cherished sweet sentiments for Katrina Van Tassell, the buxom daughter of a farmer, also a famous maker of pies and doughnuts. Ichabod had been calling late one eve-ning, and, his way home being long, Katrina's father lent him a horse to make the journey; but even with this advantage the youth set out with misgivings, for he had to pass the graveyard. As it was near the hour when the Hessian was to ride, he whistled feebly to keep his courage up, but when he came to the dreaded spot the whistle died in a gasp, for he heard the tread of a horse.

On looking around, his hair bristled and his heart came up like a plug in his throat to hinder his breathing, for he saw a headless horseman coming over the ridge behind him, blackly defined against the starry sky. Setting spurs to his nag with a hope of being first to reach Sleepy Hollow bridge, which the specter never passed, the unhappy man made the best possible time in that direction, for his follower was surely overtaking him. Another minute and the bridge would be reached; but, to Ichabod's horror, the Hessian dashed alongside and, rising in his stirrups, flung his head full at the fugitive's back. With a squeal of fright the schoolmaster rolled into a mass of weeds by the wayside, and for some minutes he remained there, knowing and remembering nothing.

Next morning farmer Van Tassell's horse was found grazing in a field near Sleepy Hollow, and a man who lived some miles southward reported that he had seen Mr. Crane striding as rapidly along the road to New York as his lean legs could take him, and wearing a pale and serious face as he kept his march. There were yellow stains on the back of his coat, and the man who restored the horse found a smashed pumpkin in the broken bushes beside the road. Ichabod never returned to Tarrytown, and when Brom Bones, a stout young plowman and tap-haunter, married Katrina, people made bold to say that he knew more about the galloping Hessian than anyone else, though they believed that he never had reason to be jealous of Ichabod Crane.

From: Charles M. Skinner, *Myths & Legends of Our Own Land*, vol. 1 (Philadelphia and London: J. B. Lippincott, 1896).

· *The Ramapo Salamander* ·

(German)

A curious tale of the Rosicrucians runs to the effect that more than two centuries ago a band of German colonists entered the Ramapo Valley and put up houses of stone, like those they had left in the Hartz Mountains, and when the Indians saw how they made knives and other wonderful things out of metal, which they extracted from the rocks by fire, they believed them to be manitous and went away, not wishing to resist their possession of the land. There was treasure here, for High Tor, or Torn Mountain, had been the home of Amasis, youngest of the magi who had followed the star of Bethlehem. He had found his way, through Asia and Alaska, to this country, had taken to wife a native woman, by whom he had a child, and here on the summit he had built a temple. Having refused the sun worship, when the Indians demanded that he should take their faith, he was set upon, and would have been killed had not an earth-quake torn the ground at his feet, opening a new channel for the Hudson and precipitating into it every one but the magus and his daughter. To him had been revealed in magic vision the secrets of wealth in the rocks.

The leader in the German colony, one Hugo, was a man of noble origin, who had a wife and two children: a boy named after himself; a girl, Mary. Though it had been the custom in the other country to let out the forge fires once in seven years, Hugo opposed that practice in the forge he had built as needless. But his men murmured and talked of the salamander that once in seven years attains its growth in unquenched flame and goes forth doing mischief. On the day when that period was ended the master entered his works and saw the men gazing into the furnace at a pale form that seemed made from flame, that was nodding and turning in the fire, occasionally darting its tongue at them or allowing its tail to fall out and lie along the stone floor. As he came to the door, he was transfixed, and the fire seemed burning his vitals, until he felt water sprinkled on his face, and saw that his wife, whom he had left at home too ill to move, stood behind him and was casting holy water into the furnace, speaking an incantation as she did so. At that moment a storm arose, and a rain fell that put out the fire; but as the last glow faded the lady fell dead.

When her children were to be consecrated, seven years later, those who stood outside of the church during the ceremony saw a vivid flash, and the nurse turned from the boy in her fright. She took her hands from her eyes. The child was gone. Twice seven years had passed and the daughter remained unspotted by the world, for, on the night when her father had led her to the top of High Torn Mountain and shown her what Amasis had seen—the earth spirits in their caves heaping jewels and offering to give them if Hugo would speak the word that binds the free to the earth forces and bars his future for a thousand years—it was her prayer that brought him to his senses and made the scene below grow dim, though the baleful light of the salamander clinging to the rocks at the bottom of the cave sent a glow into the sky.

Many nights after the glow was seen on the height and Hugo was missing from his home, but, for lack of a pure soul to stand as interpreter, he failed to read the words that burned in the triangle on the salamander's back, and returned in rage and jealousy. A knightly man had of late appeared in the settlement, and between him and Mary a tender feeling had arisen, that, however, was unexpressed until, after saving her from the attack of a panther, he had allowed her to fall into his arms.

She would willingly then have declared her love for him, but he placed her gently and regretfully from him and said, "When you slept I came to you and put a crown of gems on your head: that was because I was in the power of the earth spirit. Then I had power only over the element of fire, which either consumes or hardens to stone; but now water and life are mine. Behold! Wear these, for thou art worthy." And touching the tears that had fallen from her eyes, they turned into lilies in his hands, and he put them on her brow.

"Shall we meet again?" asked the girl.

"I do not know," said he. "I tread the darkness of the universe alone, and I peril my redemption by yielding to this love of earth. Thou art redeemed already, but I must make my way back to God through obedience tested in trial. Know that I am one of those that left heaven for love of man. We were of that subtle element which is flame—burning and glowing with love—and when thy mother came to me with the power of purity to cast me out of the furnace, I lost my shape of fire and took that of a human being—a child. I have been with thee often, and was rushing to annihilation, because I could not withstand the ordeal of the senses. Had I yielded, or found thee other than thou art, I should have become again an earth spirit. I have been led away by wish for power, such as I have in my grasp, and forgot the mission to the suffering. I became a wanderer over the earth until I reached this land, the land that you call new. Here was to be my last trial and here I am to pass the gate of fire."

As he spoke voices arose from the settlement. "They are coming," said he. The stout form of Hugo was in advance. With a fierce oath he sprang on the young man. "He has ruined my household," he cried. "Fling him into the furnace!" The young man stood waiting, but his brow was serene. He was seized, and in a few moments had disappeared through the mouth of the burning pit. But Mary, looking up, saw a shape in robes of silvery light, and it drifted upward until it vanished in the darkness. The look of horror on her face died away, and a peace came to it that endured until the end.

From: Charles M. Skinner, *Myths & Legends of Our Own Land*, vol. 1 (Philadelphia and London: J. B. Lippincott, 1896).

· *Goblins* ·

(Various)

Dunderberg
(Dutch)

D underberg, "Thunder Mountain," at the southern gate of the Hudson Highlands, is a wooded eminence, chiefly populated by a crew of imps of stout circumference, whose leader, the Heer, is a bulbous goblin, clad in the dress worn by Dutch colonists two centuries ago, who carries a speaking-trumpet, through which he bawls his orders for the blowing of winds and the touching off of lightnings. These orders are given in Low Dutch, and are put into execution by the imps aforesaid, who troop into the air and tumble about in the mist, sometimes smiting the flag or topsail of a ship to ribbons, or laying the vessel over before the wind until she is in peril of going on beam ends.

At one time a sloop passing the Dunderberg had nearly foundered, when the crew discovered the sugarloaf hat of the Heer at the masthead. None dared to climb for it, and it was not until she had driven past Pollopel's Island—the limit of the Heer's jurisdiction—that she righted. As she did so the little hat spun into the air like a top, creating a vortex that drew up the storm clouds, and the sloop kept her way prosperously for the rest of the voyage. The captain had nailed a horseshoe to the mast.

The "Hat Rogue" of the Devil's Bridge in Switzerland must be a relative of this gamesome sprite, for his mischief is usually of a harmless sort; but, to be on the safe side, the Dutchmen who plied along the river lowered their peaks in homage to the keeper of the mountain, and for years this was a common practice.

Mariners who paid this courtesy to the Heer of the Dunderberg were never molested by his imps, though skipper Ouselsticker, of Fishkill—for all he had a parson on board—was once beset by a heavy squall, and the goblin came out of the mist and sat astraddle of his bowsprit, seeming to guide his schooner straight toward the rocks. The dominie chanted the song of Saint Nicholas, and the goblin, unable to endure either its spiritual potency or the worthy parson's singing, shot upward like a ball and rode off on the gale, carrying with him the nightcap of the parson's wife, which he hung on the weathercock of Esopus steeple, forty miles away.

From: Charles M. Skinner, *Myths & Legends of Our Own Land*, vol. 1 (Philadelphia and London: J. B. Lippincott, 1896).

The Culprit Fay
(Unidentified)

The wood tick's drum convokes the elves at the noon of night on Cro' Nest top, and, clambering out of their flower-cup beds and hammocks of cobweb, they fly to the meeting, not to freak about the grass or banquet at the mushroom table, but to hear sentence passed on the fay who, forgetting his vestal vow, has loved an earthly maid.

From his throne under a canopy of tulip petals, borne on pillars of shell, the king commands silence, and with severe eye but softened voice he tells the culprit that while he has scorned the royal decree he has saved himself from the extreme penalty, of imprisonment in walnut shells and cobweb dungeons, by loving a maid who is gentle and pure.

So it shall be enough if he will go down to the Hudson and seize a drop from the bow of mist that a sturgeon leaves when he makes his leap; and after, to kindle his darkened flame-wood lamp at a meteor spark. The fairy bows, and without a word slowly descends the rocky steep, for his wing is soiled and has lost its power; but once at the river, he tugs mightily at a mussel shell till he has it afloat; then, leaping in, he paddles out with a strong grass blade till he comes to the spot where the sturgeon swims, though the water sprites plague him and toss his boat, and the fish and the leeches bunt and drag; but, suddenly, the sturgeon shoots from the water, and before the arch of mist that he tracks through the air has vanished, the sprite has caught a drop of the spray in a tiny blossom, and in this he washes clean his wings.

The water goblins torment him no longer. They push his boat to the shore, where, alighting, he kisses his hand, then, even as a bubble, he flies back to the mountaintop, dons his acorn helmet, his corselet of beehide, his shield of ladybug shell, and grasping his lance, tipped with wasp sting, he bestrides his firefly steed, and off he goes like a flash. The world spreads out and then grows small, but he flies straight on. The ice ghosts leer from the topmost clouds, and the mists surge round, but he shakes his lance and pipes his call, and at last he comes to the Milky Way, where the sky sylphs lead him to their queen, who lies couched in a palace ceiled with stars, its dome held up by northern lights and the curtains made of the morning's flush. Her mantle is twilight purple, tied with threads of gold from the eastern dawn, and her face is as fair as the silver moon.

She begs the fay to stay with her and taste forever the joys of heaven, but the knightly elf keeps down the beating of his heart, for he remembers a face on earth that is fairer than hers, and he begs to go. With a sigh she fits him a car of cloud, with the firefly steed chained on behind, and he hurries away to the northern sky whence the meteor comes, with roar and whirl, and as it passes it bursts to flame. He lights his lamp at a glowing spark, then wheels away to the fairyland. His king and his brothers hail him stoutly, with song and shout, and feast and dance, and the revel is kept till the eastern sky has a ruddy streak. Then the cock crows shrill and the fays are gone.

From: Charles M. Skinner, *Myths & Legends of Our Own Land*, vol. 1 (Philadelphia and London: J. B. Lippincott, 1896).

Catskill Gnomes
(Native American)

Behind the New Grand Hotel, in the Catskills, is an amphitheater of mountain that is held to be the place of which the Mohicans spoke when they told of people there who worked in metals, and had bushy beards and eyes like pigs. From the smoke of their forges, in autumn, came the haze of Indian summer; and when the moon was full, it was their custom to assemble on the edge of a precipice above the hollow and dance and caper until the night was nigh worn away. They brewed a liquor that had the effect of shortening the bodies and swelling the heads of all who drank it, and when Hudson and his crew visited the mountains, the pygmies held a carouse in his honor and invited him to drink their liquor. The crew went away, shrunken and distorted by the magic distillation, and thus it was that Rip Van Winkle found them on the eve of his famous sleep.

From: Charles M. Skinner, *Myths & Legends of Our Own Land*, vol. 1 (Philadelphia and London: J. B. Lippincott, 1896).

Rip Van Winkle
(Dutch)

The story of Rip Van Winkle, told by Irving, dramatized by Boucicault, acted by Jefferson, pictured by Darley, set to music by Bristow, is the best known of American legends. Rip was a real personage, and the Van Winkles are a considerable family to this day. An idle, good-natured, happy-go-lucky fellow, he lived, presumably, in the village of Catskill, and began his long sleep in 1769. His wife was a shrew, and to escape her abuse Rip often took his dog and gun and roamed away to the Catskills, nine miles westward, where he lounged or hunted, as the humor seized him.

It was on a September evening, during a jaunt on South Mountain, that he met a stubby, silent man of goodly girth, his round head topped with a steeple hat, the skirts of his belted coat and flaps of his petticoat trousers meeting at the tops of heavy boots, and the face—ugh!—green and ghastly, with unmoving eyes that glimmered in the twilight like phosphorus. The dwarf carried a keg, and on receiving an intimation, in a sign, that he would like Rip to relieve him of it, that cheerful vagabond shouldered it and marched on up the mountain.

At nightfall they emerged on a little plateau where a score of men in the garb of long ago, with faces like that of Rip's guide, and equally still and speechless, were playing at bowling with great solemnity, the balls sometimes rolling over the plateau's edge and rumbling down the rocks with a boom like thunder. A cloaked and snowy-bearded figure, watching aloof, turned like the others, and gazed uncomfortably at the visitor who now came blundering in among them. Rip was at first for making off, but the sinister glare in the circle of eyes took the run out of his legs, and he was not displeased when they signed to him to tap the keg and join in a draught of the ripest schnapps that ever he had tasted—and he knew the flavor of every brand in Catskill. While these strange men grew no more genial with passing of the flagons, Rip was pervaded by a satisfying glow; then, overcome by sleepiness and resting his head on a stone, he stretched his tired legs out and fell to dreaming.

Morning. Sunlight and leaf shadow were dappled over the earth when he awoke, and rising stiffly from his bed, with compunctions in his bones, he reached for his gun. The already venerable implement was so far gone with rot and rust that it fell to pieces in his hand, and looking down at the fragments of it, he saw that his clothes were dropping from his body in rags and mold, while a white beard flowed over his breast. Puzzled and alarmed, shaking his head ruefully as he recalled the carouse of the silent, he hobbled down the mountain as fast as he might for the grip of the rheumatism on his knees and elbows, and entered his native village.

What! Was this Catskill? Was this the place that he left yesterday? Had all these houses sprung up overnight, and these streets been pushed across the meadows in a day? The people, too: Where were his friends? The children who had romped with him, the rotund topers whom he had left cooling their hot noses in pewter pots at the tavern door, the dogs that used to bark a welcome, recognizing in him a kindred spirit of vagrancy: Where were they?

And his wife, whose athletic arm and agile tongue had half disposed him to linger in the mountains: How happened it that she was not awaiting him at the gate? But gate there was none in the familiar place: An unfenced yard of weeds and ruined foundation wall were there. Rip's home was gone. The idlers jeered at his bent, lean form, his snarl of beard and hair, his disreputable dress, his look of grieved astonishment. He stopped, instinctively, at the tavern, for he knew that place in spite of its new sign: an officer in blue regimentals and a cocked hat replacing the crimson George III of his recollection, and labeled "General Washington." There was a quick gathering of ne'er-do-wells, of tavern haunters and gaping apprentices, about him, and though their faces were strange and their manners rude, he made bold to ask if they knew such and such of his friends.

"Nick Vedder? He's dead and gone these eighteen years." "Brom Dutcher? He joined the army and was killed at Stony Point." "Van Brummel? He too went to the war, and is in Congress now."

"And Rip Van Winkle?"

"Yes, he's here. That's him yonder."

And to Rip's utter confusion he saw before him a counterpart of himself, as young, lazy, ragged, and easy-natured as he remembered himself to be, yesterday—or, was it yesterday?

"That's young Rip," continued his informer. "His father was Rip Van Winkle too, but he went to the mountains twenty years ago and never came back. He probably fell over a cliff, or was carried off by Indians, or eaten by bears."

Twenty years ago! Truly, it was so. Rip had slept for twenty years without waking. He had left a peaceful colonial village; he returned to a bustling republican town. How he eventually found, among the oldest inhabitants, some who admitted that they knew him; how he found a comfortable home with his married daughter and the son who took after him so kindly; how he recovered from the effect of the tidings that his wife had died of apoplexy, in a quarrel; how he resumed his seat at the tavern tap and smoked long pipes and told long yarns for the rest of his days, were matters of record up to the beginning of this century.

And a strange story Rip had to tell, for he had served as cupbearer to the dead crew of the *Half Moon*. He had quaffed a cup of Hollands with no other than Henry Hudson himself. Some say that Hudson's spirit has made its home amid these hills, that it may look into the lovely valley that he discovered; but others hold that every twenty years he and his men assemble for a revel in the mountains that so charmed them when first seen swelling against the western heavens, and the liquor they drink on this night has the bane of throwing any mortal who lips it into a slumber whence nothing can arouse him until the day dawns when the crew shall meet again. As you climb the east front of the mountains by the old carriage road, you pass, halfway up the height, the stone that Rip Van Winkle slept on, and may see that it is slightly hollowed by his form. The ghostly revelers are due in the Catskills in 1909, and let all tourists who are among the mountains in September of that year beware of accepting liquor from strangers.

From: Charles M. Skinner, *Myths & Legends of Our Own Land*, vol. 1 (Philadelphia and London: J. B. Lippincott, 1896).

· The Devil ·

(Various)

The Devil's Dance Chamber
(Unidentified)

Most-storied of our New World rivers is the Hudson. Historic scenes have been enacted on its shores, and Indian, Dutchman, Briton, and American have invested it with romance. It had its source, in the red man's fancy, in a spring of eternal youth; giants and spirits dwelt in its woods and hills, and before the river—Shatemuc, king of streams, the red men called it—had broken through the highlands, those mountains were a pent for spirits who had rebelled against the manitou. After the waters had forced a passage to the sea these evil ones sought shelter in the glens and valleys that open to right and left along its course, but in time of tempest, when they hear manitou riding down the ravine on wings of storm, dashing thunderbolts against the cliffs, it is the fear that he will recapture them and force them into lightless caverns to expiate their revolt, that sends them huddling among the rocks and makes the hills resound with roars and howls.

At the Devil's Dance Chamber, a slight plateau on the west bank, between Newburg and Crom Elbow, the red men performed semireligious rites as a preface to their hunting and fishing trips or ventures on the warpath. They built a fire, painted themselves, and in that frenzy into which savages are so readily lashed, and that is so like to the action of mobs in trousers, they tumbled, leaped, danced, yelled, sang, grimaced, and gesticulated until the manitou disclosed himself, either as a harmless animal or a beast of prey. If he came in the former shape the augury was favorable, but if he showed himself as a bear or panther, it was a warning of evil that they seldom dared to disregard.

The crew of Hudson's ship, the *Half Moon*, having chanced on one of these orgies, were so impressed by the fantastic spectacle that they gave the name Duyvels Dans-Kamer to the spot. Years afterwards, when Stuyvesant ascended the river, his doughty retainers were horrified, on landing below the Dans-Kamer, to discover hundreds of painted figures frisking there in the firelight. A few surmised that they were but a new generation of savages holding a powwow, but most of the sailors fancied that the assemblage was demoniac, and that the figures were spirits of bad Indians repeating a scalp dance and reveling in the mysterious firewater that they had brought down from the river source in jars and skins. The spot was at last once profaned with blood, for a young Dutchman and his wife, of Albany, were captured here by an angry Indian, and although the young man succeeded in stabbing his captor to death, he was burned alive on the rock by the friends of the Indian whose wrath he had provoked. The wife, after being kept in captivity for a time, was ransomed.

From: Charles M. Skinner, *Myths & Legends of Our Own Land*, vol. 1 (Philadelphia and London: J. B. Lippincott, 1896).

The Devil's Stepping-Stones
(Unidentified)

When the devil set a claim to the fair lands at the north of Long Island Sound, his claim was disputed by the Indians, who prepared to fight for their homes should he attempt to serve his writ of ejectment. Parley resulted in nothing, so the bad one tried force, but he was routed in open fight and found it desirable to get away from the scene of action as soon as possible. He retreated across the sound near the head of East River. The tide was out, so he stepped from island to island, without trouble, and those reefs and islands are to this day the Devil's Stepping-Stones.

On reaching Throgg's Neck he sat down in a despairing attitude and brooded on his defeat, until, roused to a frenzy at the thought of it, he resolved to renew the war on terms advantageous entirely to himself.

In that day Connecticut was free from rocks, but Long Island was covered with them; so he gathered all he could lay his hands on and tossed them at the Indians that he could see across the sound near Cold Spring until the supply had given out. The red men who last inhabited Connecticut used to show white men where the missiles landed and where the devil struck his heel into the ground as he sprang from the shore in his haste to reach Long Island. At Cold Spring other footprints and one of his toes are shown.

Establishing himself at Coram, he troubled the people of the country for many years, so that between the devil on the west and the Montauks on the east they were plagued indeed; for though their guard at Watch

Hill, Rhode Island, and other places often apprised them of the coming of the Montauks, they never knew which way to look for the devil.

From: Charles M. Skinner, *Myths & Legends of Our Own Land*, vol. 1 (Philadelphia and London: J. B. Lippincott, 1896).

The Stone-Throwing Devil
(English)

Under the title of "Lithobolia," the story of the stone-throwing devil was printed in London in the year 1698. It purports to be the narrative of an eyewitness, and is signed with the initials "R. C." This tract, consisting of a few leaves only, is now extremely rare; but a synopsis of its contents may be found in the "Wonderful Providences" of Increase Mather.

George Walton was an inhabitant of Portsmouth in the year 1682. He had incurred the bitter enmity of an old woman of the neighborhood by taking from her a strip of land to which she laid claim; and it is the opinion of the writers whom we have quoted that she, being a witch, was at the bottom of all the mischief that subsequently drove Walton's family to the brink of despair. This bedlam had in fact told Walton that he should never peacefully enjoy the land he had wrested from her.

One still Sabbath night in June all at once a shower of stones rattled against the sides of the roof of Walton's house. It came as fiercely and as unexpectedly as a summer hailstorm. As soon as it had ceased, the startled inmates, who were in bed, hurried on their clothes and sallied out to see if they could discover the perpetrators of this outrage upon the peace and quiet of the family. It was ten o'clock, and a bright moonlit night. They found the gate taken off the hinges and carried to a distance from the house, but could neither see nor hear anything of the stone throwers.

While thus engaged, a second volley of stones whistled about their heads, which drove them, much terrified by its suddenness and fury, back to the shelter of the house. They first went into the porch; but, the stones reaching them here, they were quickly pelted out of this into an inner chamber, where, having bolted and barred all the doors, they awaited in no calm frame of mind the next demonstration of their assailants. Some had been struck and hurt, and all were in consternation. But to the dismay of these poor people, this proved no secure refuge; for the stone battery opened again presently, filling the room itself with flying missiles, which crashed through the casements, scattering the glass in every direction, came down the chimney, bounding and rebounding along the floor like spent cannonballs, while the inmates looked on in helpless amazement at what threatened to demolish the house over their heads. This bombardment continued, with occasional intermission, for four hours.

While it was going on, Walton was walking the floor of his chamber in great disorder of mind, when a sledgehammer cast with vindictive force thumped heavily along the floor overhead, and, narrowly missing him, fell at his feet, making a great dent in the oak floor; at the same time the candles were swept off the table, leaving him in total darkness.

All this, it is true, might have been the work of evil-minded persons; but certain things hardly consistent with this theory convinced the family beyond any reasonable doubt that the stones which bruised and terrified them were hurled by demon hands. In the first place, some of the stones which were picked up were found to be hot, as if they had just been taken out of the fire. In the second, notwithstanding several of them were marked, counted, and laid upon a table, these same stones would afterward be found flying around the room again as soon as the person's back was turned who had put them there. In the third, upon examination, the leaden crossbars of the casements were found to be bent outwardly, and not inwardly, showing conclusively that the stones came from within, and not from without. Finally, to settle the matter, some of the maidens belonging to the household were frightened out of their wits upon seeing a hand thrust out of a window, or the apparition of a hand—there being, to their certain knowledge, no one in the room where it came from.

This was not all. After Walton had gone to bed, though not to sleep, a heavy stone came crashing through his chamber door. He got up, secured the unwelcome intruder, and locked it in his own chamber; but it was taken out by invisible hands, and carried with a great noise into the next room. This was followed by a brickbat. The spit flew up the chimney, and came down again, without any visible agency. This carnival continued from day to day with an occasional respite. Wherever the master of the house showed himself—in the barn, the field, or elsewhere, by day or by night—he was sure to receive a volley. No one who witnessed them doubted for a moment that all these acts proceeded from the malevolence of the aforesaid witch; and an attempt was accordingly made to brew a powerful witch broth in the house, to exorcise her. But for some reason or other its charm failed to work; and so the spell remained hanging over the afflicted family.

Some of the pranks of the demon quite outdo the feats of Harlequin in the Christmas pantomimes. Walton had a guest staying with him, who became the faithful recorder of what happened while the storm of stones rained down upon the doomed dwelling. In order to soothe and tranquilize his mind, he took up a musical instrument and began to play; when "a good big stone" rolled in to join the dance, while the player looked on in amazement. Among other tricks performed by the mischievous demon who had taken up its unwelcome residence among the family was that of taking a cheese from the press and crumbling it over the floor; then the iron used in the press was found driven into the wall, and a kettle hung upon it. Several cocks of hay that had been mowed near the house were adroitly hung upon trees nearby; while the mischievous goblin, twisting bunches of hay into wisps, stuck them up all about the house kitchen— "*cum multis aliis.*"

The relater of all these unaccountable doings indeed admits that certain skeptical persons persisted in believing that any or all of them might have been the work of human beings; but as everyone credits what he wishes to credit, so this ancient writer appears to mention the fact only with the view of exposing its absurdity. Our own purpose is not to decide between two opinions, but to declare that people in general considered George Walton to be a victim of supernatural visitation, or, in other words, bewitched; and to show that the temper of his day was such that any occurrence out of the common was sure to be considered according to its character, either as emanating from heaven or from the bottomless pit. There were no such things as accidents; everything had some design.

From: Samuel Adams Drake, *A Book of New England Legends and Folk Lore* (Boston: Roberts Brothers, 1888).

The Spuyten Duyvil
(Dutch)

The tidewater creek that forms the upper boundary of Manhattan Island is known to dwellers in tenements round about as "Spittin' Divvle." The proper name of it is Spuyten Duyvil, and this, in turn, is the compression of a celebrated boast by Anthony Van Corlaer. This redoubtable gentleman, famous for fat, long wind, and long whiskers, was trumpeter for the garrison at New Amsterdam, which his countrymen had just bought for twenty-four dollars, and he sounded the brass so sturdily that in the fight between the Dutch and Indians at the Dey Street peach orchard his blasts struck more terror into the red men's hearts than did the matchlocks of his comrades. William the Testy vowed that Anthony and his trumpet were garrison enough for all Manhattan Island, for he argued that no regiment of Yankees would approach near enough to be struck with lasting deafness, as must have happened if they came when Anthony was awake.

Peter Stuyvesant—Peter the Headstrong—showed his appreciation of Anthony's worth by making him his esquire, and when he got news of an English expedition on its way to seize his unoffending colony, he at once ordered Anthony to rouse the villages along the Hudson with a trumpet call to war. The esquire took a hurried leave of six or eight ladies, each of whom delighted to believe that his affections were lavished on her alone, and bravely started northward, his trumpet hanging on one side, a stone bottle, much heavier, depending from the other. It was a stormy evening when he arrived at the upper end of the island, and there was no ferryman in sight, so, after fuming up and down the shore, he swallowed a mighty draught of Dutch courage—for he was as accomplished a performer on the horn as on the trumpet—and swore with ornate and voluminous oaths that he would swim the stream "in spite of the devil" (en spuyt den Duyvil).

He plunged in, and had gone halfway across when the Evil One, not to be spited, appeared as a huge moss bunker, vomiting boiling water and lashing a fiery tail. This dreadful fish seized Anthony by the leg; but the trumpeter was game, for, raising his instrument to his lips, he exhaled his last breath through it in a defiant blast that rang through the woods for miles and made the devil himself let go for a moment. Then he was dragged below, his nose shining through the water more and more faintly, until, at last, all sight of him was lost. The failure of his mission resulted in the downfall of the Dutch in America, for, soon after, the English won a bloodless victory, and St. George's cross flaunted from the ramparts where Anthony had so often saluted the setting sun. But it was years, even then, before he was hushed, for in stormy weather it was claimed that the shrill of his trumpet could be heard near the creek that he had named, sounding above the deeper roar of the blast.

From: Charles M. Skinner, *Myths & Legends of Our Own Land*, vol. 1 (Philadelphia and London: J. B. Lippincott, 1896).

The Devil's Footprint
(English)

The eastern end of Long Island, New York, is divided into two long points which partially enclose a bay. The northern point is named Orient, and the southern, which is longer, is named Montauk. Between these points lies Gardiner's Island, and within the bay thus sheltered from the ocean is Shelter Island.

One of the natural curiosities of Shelter Island is what appears to be a footprint in a rock. This footprint is that of a right foot. The impression of the heel and instep is deep and well formed, but the toeprints are lost where the rock slopes suddenly away. The tradition about this is that when the Evil Spirit left the island he took three long strides, the first on Shelter Island, the second on Orient Point, and the third on Montauk, whence he plunged into the sea. The rock on which there was a corresponding footprint at Orient Point has been removed to the rooms of the Long Island Historical Society in Brooklyn.

It is said on Shelter Island that if anyone makes a wish when he places his foot into this footprint for the first time, he will certainly get it. This unfortunately is not true; but another saying, that the footprint will fit the right foot of anyone from a little child to the largest man, is a striking fact; for as the bottom is narrow and the top wide, and there is no limit in length, it supports comfortably any foot that is placed in it. Finally it is said that no horse will pass this stone without being seized with terror on drawing near it, snorting, rearing, and trembling in every limb.

From: Cornelia Horford, "A Tradition of Shelter Island," *Journal of American Folk-Lore* 12 (1899): 43–44.

The Fiddler and the Devil
(Dutch)

Before Brooklyn had spread itself beyond Greenwood Cemetery a stone could be seen in Martense's Lane, south of that burial ground, that bore a hoof mark.

A Negro named Joost, in the service of the Van Der Something-or-others, was plodding home on Saturday night, his fiddle under his arm. He had been playing for a wedding in Flatbush and had been drinking schnapps until he saw stars on the ground and fences in the sky; in fact, the universe seemed so out of order that he seated himself rather heavily on this rock to think about it. The behavior of the stars in swimming and rolling struck him as especially curious, and he conceived the notion that they wanted to dance.

Putting his fiddle to his chin, he began a wild jig, and though he made it up as he went along, he was conscious of doing finely, when the boom of a bell sent a shiver down his spine.

It was twelve o'clock, and here he was playing a dance tune on Sunday. However, the sin of playing for one second on the Sabbath was as great as that of playing all day; so, as long as he was in for it, he resolved to carry the tune to the end, and he fiddled away with a reckless vehemence.

Presently he became aware that the music was both wilder and sweeter than before, and that there was more of it. Not until then did he observe that a tall, thin stranger stood beside him, and that he was fiddling too— composing a second to Joost's air, as if he could read his thought before he put it into execution on the strings. Joost paused, and the stranger did likewise.

"Where de debble did you come frum?" asked the first. The other smiled. "And how did you come to know dat music?" Joost pursued.

"Oh, I've known that tune for years," was the reply. "It's called 'The Devil's Joy at Sabbath Breaking.'"

"You're a liar!" cried the Negro. The stranger bowed and burst into a roar of laughter. "A liar!" repeated Joost, "for I made up dat music dis very minute."

"Yet you notice that I could follow when you played."

"Humph! Yes, you can follow."

"And I can lead, too. Do you know the tune 'Go to the Devil and Shake Yourself'?"

"Yes; but I play second to nobody."

"Very well, I'll beat you at any air you try."

"Done!" said Joost. And then began a contest that lasted until daybreak. The stranger was an expert, but Joost seemed to be inspired, and just as the sun appeared he sounded, in broad and solemn harmonies, the hymn of Von Catts:

> Now behold, at dawn of day,
> Pious Dutchmen sing and pray.

At that the stranger exclaimed, "Well, that beats the devil!" and striking his foot angrily on the rock, disappeared in a flash of fire like a burst bomb. Joost was hurled twenty feet by the explosion, and lay on the ground insensible until a herdsman found him some hours later.

As he suffered no harm from the contest and became a better fiddler than ever, it is supposed that the recording angel did not inscribe his feat of Sabbath breaking against him in large letters. There were a few who doubted his story, but they had nothing more to say when he showed them the hoofprint on the rock. Moreover, there are fewer fiddlers among the Negroes than there used to be, because they say that the violin is the devil's instrument.

From: Charles M. Skinner, *Myths & Legends of Our Own Land*, vol. 1 (Philadelphia and London: J. B. Lippincott, 1896).

Chapter 6

Nature

· *Various Animal Lore* ·

(German)

Various animals could predict the weather. The apparition of the groundhog on a certain day in February was watched for. If he looked around and went promptly back, the spring would be late; if he remained out most of the day, it would be early.

The croak of the tree frog foretold rain, and the color of the breastbone of a fall goose indicated the severity of the winter; the darker the bone, the harder would be the cold.

From: D. G. Brinton, "Reminiscences of Pennsylvania Folk-Lore," *Journal of American Folk-Lore* 5 (1892): 177–85.

· *Cats* ·

(German)

Cats, though as favorite household pets as elsewhere, were looked upon as uncanny creatures. It was surely bad luck to kill one. It was unsafe to leave one in the room with a babe, as pussy would suck its breath and thus take away its life. Nor should a cat be permitted in the room with a corpse. At an unguarded moment it would fly at the dead face and tear it with its sharp claws.

From: D. G. Brinton, "Reminiscences of Pennsylvania Folk-Lore," *Journal of American Folk-Lore* 5 (1892): 177–85.

· *Snakes* ·

(Various)

Snake Beliefs
(German)

A very common belief is to the effect that if one kills the first snake met with in the spring, no others will be observed during the remainder of that year. In Swabia, tales are still told of home snakes which appear to bring good luck, but which must under no circumstances be killed. These snakes come to the children and sip milk with them out of their bowls. Tales of this class were common a score of years ago, and I remember hearing of a child eating bread and milk from a saucer, while a huge black snake drank freely from the same dish, but at short intervals the child would playfully tap its spoon upon the snake's head, saying, *du musht men mokka fressa,* to cause it to drink less milk and eat more of the bread.

Occasionally, we hear of black snakes found in pastures where they suckle cows, so that these animals daily resort to certain localities to secure relief from a painful abundance of milk.

As an illustration of the belief in the transformation of human beings into serpents, I will relate a circumstance said to have occurred during the first half of the present century. Near Trexlertown, Lehigh County, dwelt a farmer named Weiler. His wife and three daughters had, by some means or other, incurred the enmity of a witch, who lived but a short distance away, when the latter, it is supposed, took her revenge in the following manner. Whenever visitors came to the Weiler residence, the girls, without any premonition whatever, would suddenly be changed into snakes, and after crawling back and forth along the top ridge of the wainscoting for several minutes, they were restored to their natural form. This curious transformation occurred quite frequently, and the circumstance soon attained widespread notoriety. About the end of the third month the spell was broken and everything went on as before.

The rattlesnake, because of its venomous bite, is universally dreaded, and numerous curious beliefs are current respecting this reptile, also the use to which various parts may be put, and the treatment of its bite.

Another curious superstition held by young men, is that if one places a snake's tongue upon the palm of his hand—beneath the glove—it will cause any girl, regardless of her previous indifference, to ardently return his passion if he be enabled but once to take her hand within his own.

There are numerous popular methods of treating snake bites, from the internal use of alcoholic liquors, to the external application of warm, raw flesh, obtained by cutting a live chicken in two.

I ascertained a short time since the secret of alleged success claimed by various mountain powwows both in this state and in Maryland. The remedy is termed the *meister wurzel*, or "master root," commonly known as the *sanicle* or *Sanicula marylandica*. The roots of the plant are crushed, one part being made into a poultice and applied to the wound, while the remainder is boiled in milk which is freely administered internally.

The following procedure was formerly practiced in northern Lehigh County, but is still performed even at this day in Cumberland County. The operator recites the following words:

> *Gott hot alles arshaffa, und alles war gut;*
> *Als du allen Schlang, bisht ferflucht,*
> *Ferflucht solsht du sain and dain gift.*

> God created everything, and it was good;
> Except thou alone snake art cursed,
> Cursed art thou and thy poison.

The speaker then, with the extended index finger, makes the sign of the cross three times over the wound, each time pronouncing the word *tsing*.

In connection with the extraction of serpent venom may be mentioned the use of the snakestone, or madstone, the latter, without doubt, having originally been employed in snake bites.

It would appear that the Old World custom of employing calculi or stones for the extraction of serpent venom, gradually led to the practice in modern times of applying similar substances to the wounds made by the bite of rabid dogs. These calculi are of a cretaceous or chalky nature, and anything of a cretaceous character, may, if dry, possess absorbant properties, and it is probable that to this property may be attributed the first employment of the oriental bezoar stones as capable of extracting or expelling poisons.

From: "Popular Superstitions," *The Pennsylvania-German Society Proceedings and Addresses*, vol. 5 (Reading, PA: 1895).

Snakes and Snake Bites
(Syrian)

For snake bites a very rare and mysterious stone is used. The priests keep these stones and are said to have always had them. The stone itself is thought to be artificial, and to have been made by the Greeks. In shape it is circular, about two inches in diameter, and half an inch or so thick. The color is bright yellow on one side, and black on the other. The stone is applied directly to the wound, the black side down if the snake were black, and vice versa. Milk is put on the stone, and it bubbles as if the stone were hot. After a short time the stone has drawn out all the poison. My informant says he cannot explain this phenomenon, but that he himself has seen it operate, and that it is the only thing he knows of that is efficacious in bringing about a cure for snake bites.

From: Howard Barrett Wilson, "Notes of Syrian Folk-Lore Collected in Boston," *Journal of American Folk-Lore* 16 (1903): 133–47.

· Eggs ·

(Various)

Egg Beliefs
(German)

One of the most conspicuous characteristics of the Teutonic race is a devout attachment to ancestral customs and beliefs, a trait which among the less intelligent and truly illiterate becomes proportionately intensified. It is more than probable that to this trait may be attributed the preservation of fragments of myths and folklore, as well as a remarkable adherence to Old World formulæ relating to witchcraft and folk medicine, relics of customs and superstitions which are probably contemporary with the birth of the human race itself.

We are all familiar with the custom of having eggs served at Easter breakfast, and also that of children receiving presents of dyed eggs; sometimes toy rabbits or hares—made of soft, fluffy goods, and stuffed with cotton or sawdust—were also given as presents. Children were told that the hare laid the eggs, and nests were prepared for the hare to lay them in. The custom obtains as well in south Germany. The figure of a hare is placed among the Easter eggs when given as a present.

The association of the hare with Easter observances was much more common in former times, and in England it was customary for the hare to be eaten at such times. Hare hunting, as an Easter custom, began to fall into disuse about the middle of the last century.

Germans to this day term April *Ostermonat*, or Easter month, an old form of the word *Ostarmanoth*, occurring as early as the time of Charlemagne. The old High German name was *ostara*, the plural form being retained as two days were usually kept at Easter. The association of the hare with eggs is curious, and the explanation is found in the belief that originally the hare seems to have been a bird which the ancient Teutonic goddess Ostara turned into a quadruped. For this reason the hare, in grateful recognition of its former quality as a bird and swift messenger of the spring goddess, is able to lay eggs on her festival at Easter time.

From: "Popular Superstitions," *The Pennsylvania-German Society Proceedings and Addresses,* vol. 5 (Reading, PA: 1895).

Egg Beliefs
(Armenian)

For three days before Easter the Armenians will gather at a churchyard for the purpose of breaking eggs. Two persons will each take an egg, and one of them will hold his egg stationary while the other strikes it with the point of his egg. If A is holding the stationary egg and B is doing the striking, then, in case A's egg cracks, he turns the other end and lets B strike again. If the other end is cracked, B gets the egg and A must produce another egg to be treated as before and with like possible results. If B's egg cracks, then he turns the other end of the egg and strikes again. If it suffers in like manner, he loses his egg and must supply another, whereupon A does the striking until he forfeits his right by losing an egg. Thus they go on breaking eggs, until oftentimes one couple has broken as many as a hundred. The man with the strongest egg will of course win the most eggs from his opponent. These cracked eggs which he has won he sells at a reduced price. Sometimes a man will pay a dollar for a strong egg before he enters into a contest, if there is evidence to prove that he is really getting a strong one.

Formerly, Easter eggs were always colored red in order to represent the blood of Christ. They are usually colored red now, but are beginning to vary somewhat.

From: G. D. Edwards, "Items of American Folk-Lore Collected in Boston," *Journal of American Folk-Lore* 12 (1899): 97–107.

Egg Beliefs
(Syrian)

During Lent, and especially on Easter Sunday, the Syrians have a custom of playing with eggs. The game is as follows: Two persons take a number of eggs apiece, testing them upon their teeth to get as strong-shelled ones as possible. The sharper end is called the head, and the other the heel. Then A says, "With my head I will break your head," or, if he thinks he has a very hard-shelled egg, he may say, "With my head I will break your head and your heel, too." B may then make the threat to take A's egg and with its heel break both ends of his own egg.

But suppose he does not, and the game goes on with A's threat to B. B then wraps his hand tightly about the egg and, leaving only the very tip exposed, says, "Well, break it!" A says, "You are not showing very much of it." B then moves his hand down a trifle, and A, if he thinks he can break it, strikes. But if he thinks that he cannot break it, he says, "I will show you more than that," and takes B's egg and gives B his egg. B then does the striking, and if he succeeds in breaking A's egg he wins it. If, on the contrary, B's egg is broken by the blow, A wins it. The one who loses then produces a new egg, and the game continues until the supply of either one or the other is exhausted.

From: Howard Barrett Wilson, "Notes of Syrian Folk-lore Collected in Boston," *Journal of American Folk-Lore* 16 (1903): 133–47.

· *The Moon* ·

(German)

Another belief which I remember was accepted without question was that which gave us our word *lunatic*; to wit, that insanity, especially periodical recurrent insanity, is caused by exposure to the rays of the moon. I believe it is acknowledged by alienists that the increased light at the time of full moon excites certain classes of patients; but in my early days I recall several "moonstruck" persons who regularly became unmanageable for the three days of full moon, and were quite sane at other dates. They were all colored people, and I doubt if it was anything more than a hallucination.

Many of the superstitions which Grimm narrates as occurring among the Scotch and North Germans were familiar beliefs in the neighborhood where I passed my boyhood. I was often told that one should have his hair cut in the waxing moon if a strong growth was wished for; while, if it was desired to extirpate weeds and briars so that they should not sprout again, they must be cut down in the wane of the moon. For some allied notion, it was the custom to cut trees for use as firewood in the wane of the moon, as the timber cured more soundly, and was less apt to become soggy and sputtery.

One of the "signs" to which considerable attention was paid was the first sight of the new moon. If this was to the left, especially if it was over the left shoulder, the presage was unfavorable, and some bad luck would occur during that moon; but if on the right hand, then the lunar month would be a prosperous one. So permanent are the impressions of childhood that I think I now never see the new moon without this ancient superstition recurring to my mind. Of course, its roots run far back into those archaic associations which led the left hand to be considered that tending toward evil fortune, and which imparted to the adjective *sinister* its peculiar and ill-boding significance.

By some it was held that the sign varied with the nature of the crop to be planted. Root crops, such as turnips, potatoes, carrots, and the like, which ripen their edible portions beneath the soil, should be planted in the wane of the moon, or, as the local expression was, in the "sinking" sign, in contradistinction to the "rising" signs, which were those of the increasing orb.

Even such a matter as fence-building should be carried on with due respect to these potent influences. A fence should be constructed in the "rising" signs, for if the posts be planted, and the cornerstones which support the rails in a worm fence be located in the "sinking" signs, the former will rot more readily, and the latter will sink into the ground and allow the bottom rails to decay.

There was, I remember, some discrepancy in the opinions of the times when the moon indicated the weather about to prevail. Some said it would be at the quarters; others, the third day after the quarters; and others again, the fifth and sixth days after the new moon.

From: D. G. Brinton, "Reminiscences of Pennsylvania Folk-Lore," *Journal of American Folk-Lore* (1892): 177–85.

· The Eliot Oak ·

(English)

When John Eliot had become a power among the Indians, with far-reaching sagacity he judged it best to separate his converts from the whites, and accordingly, after much inquiry and toilsome search, gathered them into a community at Natick—an old Indian name formerly interpreted as "a place of hills," but now generally admitted to mean simply "my land." Anticipating the policy which many believe must eventually be adopted with regard to the entire Indian question, Eliot made his settlers landowners, conferred upon them the right to vote and hold office, impressed upon them the duties and responsibilities of citizenship, and taught them the rudiments of agriculture and the mechanic arts.

In the summer of 1651, the Indians built a framed edifice, which answered, as is the case today in many small country towns, the double purpose of a schoolroom on weekdays, and a sanctuary on the Sabbath. Professor C. E. Stowe, once called that building the first known theological seminary of New England, and said that for real usefulness it was on a level with, if not above, any other in the known world.

It is assumed that two oaks, one of the red, and the other of the white, species, of which the present Eliot Oak is the survivor, were standing near this first Indian church. The early records of Eliot's labors make no mention of these trees.

Adams, in his *Life of Eliot*, says: "It would be interesting if we could identify some of the favorite places of the Indians in this vicinity," but fails to find sufficient data. Bigelow (or Biglow, according to ancient spelling), in his *History of Natick*, 1830, states: "There are two oaks near the South Meeting-house, which have undoubtedly stood there since the days of Eliot." It is greatly to be regretted that the writer did not state the evidence upon which his conclusion was based.

Bacon, in his *History of Natick*, 1856, remarks: "The oak standing a few rods to the east of the South Meeting-house bears every evidence of an age greater than that of the town, and was probably a witness of Eliot's first visit to the 'place of hills.'" It would be quite possible to subscribe to this conclusion, while dissenting entirely from the premises. It will be noticed that Bacon relies upon the appearance of the trees as a proof of its age. His own

measurement, fourteen and a half feet circumference at two feet from the
ground, is not necessarily indicative of more than a century's growth.

The writer upon Natick, in Drake's *Historic Middlesex*, avoids expressing
an opinion. "Tradition links these trees with the Indian Missionary." For
very long flights of time, tradition—as far as the age of trees is concerned—cannot at all be relied upon; within the narrow limits involved
in the present case, it may be received with caution.

The Red Oak which stood nearly in front of the old Newell Tavern,
was the original Eliot Oak. Mr. Austin Bacon, who is familiar with the
early history and legends of Natick, states that "Mr. Samuel Perry, a man
who could look back to 1749, often said that Mr. Peabody, the successor
to Eliot, used to hitch his horse by that tree every Sabbath, because Eliot
used to hitch his there."

This oak was originally very tall; the top was probably broken off in
the tremendous September gale of 1815; as it was reported to be in a
mutilated condition in 1820. Time, however, partially concealed the disaster by means of a vigorous growth of the remaining branches. In 1830, it
measured seventeen feet in circumference two feet from the ground. It
had now become a tree of note, and would probably have monopolized
the honors to the exclusion of the present Eliot Oak, had it not met with
an untimely end. The keeper of the tavern in front of which it stood had
the tree cut down in May 1842. This act occasioned great indignation,
and gave rise to a lawsuit at Framingham, "which was settled by the
offenders against public opinion paying the costs and planting trees in the
public green." A cartload of the wood was carried to the trial, and much
of it was taken home by the spectators to make into canes and other relics.

The King is dead, long live the King!

Upon the demise of the old monarch, the title naturally passed to the
White Oak, its neighbor, another of the race of Titans, standing conve-
niently near, of whose early history very little is positively known beyond
the fact that it is an old tree; and with the title passed the traditions and
reverence that gather about crowned heads.

Mrs. Stowe has given it a new claim to notice, for beneath it, according
to Drake's *Historic Middlesex*, "Sam Lawson, the good-natured, lazy storyteller, in Oldtown Folks, put his blacksmith's shop. It was removed when
the church was built."

The present Eliot Oak stands east of the Unitarian meetinghouse, which church is on or near the spot where Eliot's first church stood. It measured, January 1884, seventeen feet in circumference at the ground; fourteen feet two inches at four feet above. It is a fine old tree, and it is not improbable—though it is unproven—that it dates back to the first settlement of Natick.

From: L. L. Darney, "Historic Trees," *The Bay State Monthly* 1 (February 1884): 87.

· *The Weather* ·

(English)

As is the weather the last Friday of every month, so will be the majority of days during the next month.

Add the day of the month and the age of the moon, at the time of the fall of the first snow, and the sum will tell the number of snows which will fall during the winter.

If the equinoctial or line storm, which occurs about September 20, clears off cold, every storm for six months will clear off cold.

A warm November is a sign of a cold winter. "Winter never rots in the sky."

When the sun sets clear on Friday night, it will storm before Sunday.

> Wind from the east
> Is bad for man and beast;
> Wind from the west
> Is softest and best.

When the cat runs about the house and plays, it is a sign of high winds. If the rooster crows:

> When the rooster crows on the ground,
> The rain will fall down;
> When he crows on the fence,
> The rain will depart hence.

After a storm from the east, if the wind goes round by the north to the northwest, it will be warm; but if it goes round by the south, it will clear off cold.

Wild geese passing over is a sign of a storm.

A white frost is a sign of rain.

Three successive cloudy mornings, and it will rain on the third.

Smoke falling from the chimney is a sign of rain.

Wasps coming out thick, in the fall, is a sign that winter is about to set in.

If on a cloudy morning blue sky is seen sufficient to make a pair of pants, the sun will come out.

From: Emma Backus, "Weather-signs from Connecticut," *Journal of American Folk-Lore* 8 (1895): 26.

Chapter 7

Customs and Beliefs

· Customs from Boston ·

(Armenian)

The nails of babies are never cut, because they would then become robbers. The first time the nails are cut, they are buried in the graveyard. Even the older Armenians never allow the parings of their nails to be cast about at random. They gather them together and bury them, or wrap them in paper or rags and hide them in a crack of the wall, fence, or some other place which will afford storage for them. Armenians never give fire from their hearths when it has but lately been lighted, since it would be bad luck to do so. However, when it has been started for several hours, the privilege may be granted without danger.

It is the custom of Armenians always to face the east when worshipping.

In making the sign of the cross, they always use the thumb and two fingers, in order to represent the Trinity. The motions are made from the forehead to the breast, then to the left, back to the right, and finally to the center of the breast.

On holidays they take food and incense and go to the cemetery. They burn the incense at the graves and offer prayer. The Spirit comes down from heaven, and rests on the grave while they are offering their devotions. They cry, kiss the ground or stone which marks the burial place, and burn candles about it.

From: G. D. Edwards, "Items of Armenian Folk-Lore Collected in Boston," *Journal of American Folk-Lore* 12 (1899): 97–107.

· Customs from Boston ·

(Syrian)

When a person falls ill, if the trouble is slight he may cure himself by carrying around a small, round, white stone tied to the end of a ribbon.

For many ailments branding is resorted to, a hot iron, or brick, or even a thick piece of cloth being used for the purpose. For rheumatism a person would be branded on the hand or arm; for trouble with the eyes, on the head, etc.

Tattooing is very common, but it is practiced for ornamentation only, no religious significance being attached to it. The designs represent nearly everything from fishes to patron saints, and are usually on the hand or arm. A Catholic generally has a cross on one hand or the other to mark the fact. A young man of exceptional physique often has a round design about the size of a five-cent piece, on the right side of his head near the eye, to denote strength and prowess.

Among the Arabs when two tribes have had a fight and the members of a third tribe wish to make peace again between them, they ask either tribe to send a few men halfway. When they meet, the members of the third tribe kill a black sheep, thus symbolizing that hatred is killed, and that the earth has drunk its blood, so that only love remains.

From: Howard Barrett Wilson, "Notes of Syrian Folk-Lore Collected in Boston," *Journal of American Folk-Lore* 16 (1903): 133–47.

· Customs from New England ·

(English)

Fifty years ago, and even at a later date, the good New Englanders kept Saturday night, taking the evening meal before sundown, and so having the work "done up." Just as the sun set behind the western hills, the household disposed itself to reading and quiet, but when Sunday evening came, and the sun had gone down, if there were young women in the family, their beaux came, a circumstance always causing the evening to be looked for with pleasant anticipation.

Last summer I visited a church where during my childhood a very tall man and a very small woman occupied the front pew, he leading the singing with unction, while she quietly chewed the fennel, now and then passing a sprig to a neighbor less fortunate than herself; perhaps in order to help them keep awake during the long prayer, which often consumed an hour, or the longer sermon, which frequently required two hours in delivery, more especially if the minister was expatiating on some doctrine. Most of the congregation had come long distances, and therefore waited through a short recess for the afternoon meeting, which gave the good dames an opportunity to sift the gossip of the neighborhood.

Church choirs were an interesting feature, consisting of a great bass viol, with from fifteen to thirty singers. When such a choir sang "Before Jehovah's Awful Throne," there was awe and reverence among the worshippers, even although among the singers there might be a quarrel as to who should take the first seat.

During the winter, a very prominent object was the footstove, on which the women rested their feet in order to keep them warm. It was no unusual thing to see a woman sit during service with her footstove in hand, and pass it to another at a distance of three or four seats. As stoves were not in use in churches, many amusing incidents happened at their introduction. In the history of the town of Litchfield, Connecticut, I find this record:

> Opposition had been made to the introduction of a stove in the old meeting-house, and an attempt made in vain to induce the society to purchase one. Seven young men purchased a stove and requested permission to put it up in the meeting-house on trial. Consent was obtained. It was ready for use on the first Sunday in November. It being a warm, pleasant day, it was thought best not to light the fire.
>
> These young men were at the church early, as the historian records, "to see the fun." The stove stood in the middle aisle. People came in and stared. Deacon Trowbridge had been persuaded to give up his opposition. He shook his head, however, as he felt the warm air from the stove, and gathered up the skirts of his great-coat as he passed up the broad aisle to the deacon's seat. Another old farmer scowled and muttered at the effect of

the heat. One woman took her seat, and, after fanning herself, fainted entirely away. One good brother stood, and holding out his hands to warm them, rubbed them together to show how he enjoyed the heat. There was not, nor had there been, a fire in the stove; and when on Monday morning it was rumored that such was the fact, the opposers succumbed, and this was the means of reconciling the congregation to the use of a stove in church.

In Connecticut, and in New York, the bringing home of the bride was called a "Second-day Wedding"; in New Jersey, an "Infair."

From: M. F. Hoagland, "Notes on New England Customs," *Journal of American Folk-Lore* 6 (1893): 301–303.

· Childbirth Beliefs and Practices ·

(Unidentified)

Although "it is God's will and not man's that the child comes to us," frequently the women prolong the lactation period to avoid conception. All the mothers complain that they have to bear too many children. One mother believed that the parent who "wished hardest" could control the sex of the unborn child. "Some women have no luck with boys."

A pregnant woman must avoid all fright or the child will die. If the mother is frightened by injuries received by her husband, the child will be born with the same flaw. It is unlucky to be born with a birthmark. A pregnant woman must never catch her breath nor cross her hands over her heart or the child will be born with heart trouble. A woman in "the family way" must never go to a funeral or the child is sure to die. Great importance is placed in the desire a pregnant woman may have to eat a certain thing. The child will never want to eat that article of food. A pregnant woman is supposed to abstain from certain foods before delivery. After the child is born she may not eat meat lest the child should suffer. One woman stole meat from the supper table and ate it. She says it made the "baby sick." "A child born in May is always lucky." "The Sunday child (*Sonntagskind*) is born with gold in its pocket" When a child comes "right after a dead one, the child may be stillborn." Only the female sex may be present at birth. The women prefer having a midwife to a physician because they are "ashamed."

The period of nursing varies with the nationality, but a child must not be nursed for a period of more than three years, otherwise it will "grow up to be stupid." A child that is weaned on Good Friday "forgets quickest." A child once weaned must never be nursed again or "bad luck" will follow it. If a child is born with teeth it will surely turn out to be a murderer. It is unlucky to rub babies' gums. If you do it, the child will have a sharp temper. A mother's milk is used to transmit health and strength. One child had sore eyes, they were washed with the mother's milk. "The eyes were well again in a few days." An infant's fingernails must be torn or bitten off, otherwise the child will be a thief. If you pass a baby through a window, "it will become a thief." The person who discovers a child's first tooth must make it a gift. If a baby looks in the glass while teething it makes the teeth harder to cut. If there are two boys and two girls in a family both boys will not grow up.

From: Elsa G. Herzfeld, *Family Monographs: The History of Twenty-four Families Living in the Middle West Side of New York City* (New York: The James Kempster Printing Co., 1905).

• Christening Beliefs and Practices •

(Unidentified)

The mother and child are unclean until they are churched. It is only after the holy water has been applied that the uncleanliness is removed. In Catholic families the child is christened before the end of the first week, until then "it is not safe from harm." An unbaptized child will die much more easily. In the case of the approaching death of an unbaptized child, anyone present may rescue it from the evil one. It is unlucky to give the child a name before christening. Frequently the son is named for the father, but the mother does not "like" to give her name to the female child. The child is not to be named after a dead relative, otherwise it is sure to die. If an additional name is given it is to "give the child good luck."

The invitation to "stand for a child" is regarded as an honor which it is unlucky to refuse. The mother thinks her child will grow to be like its godparents. It is unlucky for the child if its godparents die. The godmother must wear clean clothes to church or the child will be "dirty." Frequently the child must have a new dress, but the christening robe may be worn by all the children in the family and become an heirloom. It is unlucky to borrow a christening robe.

Before going to church the child ought to be carried through the house to protect it from disease. A child must be taken to church "on a straight line" or it will lose its way in later life. A child on the way to church must not meet a funeral. It will die if it does. If it does not cry during the performance of the sacrament it will never grow up. The name given the child is a symbol of its new life. The godmother and friends congratulate the parents because the child is a "Christian."

From: Elsa G. Herzfeld, *Family Monographs: The History of Twenty-four Families Living in the Middle West Side of New York City* (New York: The James Kempster Printing Co., 1905).

· *Baptism* ·

(English)

It has of course been noticed that a large proportion of the entries I have quoted relate to discipline administered in cases of fornication, in many of which confession is made by husband and wife, and is of acts committed before marriage. The experience of Braintree in this respect was in no way peculiar among the Massachusetts towns of the last century. While examining the Braintree records I incidentally came across a singular and conclusive bit of unpublished documentary evidence on this point in the records of the church of Groton; for, casually mentioning one day in the rooms of the Society the Braintree records to our librarian, Dr. S. A. Green, he informed me that the similar records of the Groton church were in his possession, and he kindly put them at my disposal. Though covering a later period (1765–1803) than the portion of the Braintree church records from which the extracts contained in this paper have been made, the Groton records supplement and explain the Braintree records to a very remarkable degree. In the latter there is no vote or other entry showing the church rule or usage which led to these postnuptial confessions of premarital relations: but in the Groton records I find the following among the preliminary votes passed at the time of signing the church covenant, regulating the admission of members to full communion:

> June 1, 1765. The church then voted with regard to Baptizing children of persons newly married, That those parents that have not a child till seven yearly months after Marriage are subjects of our Christian Charity, and (if in a judgment of Charity otherwise qualified) shall have the privilege of Baptism for their Infants without being questioned as to their Honesty.

This rule prevailed in the Groton church for nearly forty years, until in January 1803, it was brought up again for consideration by an article in the warrant calling a church meeting "to see if the church will reconsider and annul the rule established by former vote and usage of the church requiring an acknowledgment before the congregation of those persons who have had a child within less time than seven yearly months after marriage as a term of their having baptism for their children."

The compelling cause to the confessions referred to was therefore the parents' desire to secure baptism for their offspring during a period when baptism was believed to be essential to salvation, with the Calvinistic hell as an alternative. The constant and not infrequently cruel use made by the church and the clergy of the parental fear of infant damnation—the belief "that Millions of Infants are tortured in Hell to all Eternity for a Sin that was committed thousands of Years before they were born"—is matter of common knowledge. Not only did it compel young married men and women to shameful public confessions of the kind which has been described, but it was at times arbitrarily used by some ministers in a way which is at once ludicrous and, now, hard to understand. Certain of them, for instance, refused to baptize infants born on the Sabbath, there being an ancient superstition to the effect that a child born on the Sabbath was also conceived on the Sabbath; a superstition presumably the basis on which was founded the provision of the apocryphal Blue Laws of Connecticut:

> Whose rule the nuptial kiss restrains
> On Sabbath day, in legal chains

and there is one well-authenticated case of a Massachusetts clergyman whose practice it was thus to refuse to baptize Sabbath-born babies, who in passage of time had twins born to him on a Lord's Day. He publicly confessed his error, and in due time administered the rite to his children.

From: Charles F. Adams, *Some Phases of Sexual Morality and Church Discipline in Colonial New England* (Cambridge: John Wilson & Son University Press, 1891).

· *Wedding and Marriage Customs* ·

(Various)

Wedding Beliefs and Practices
(Unidentified)

Fortunate is the bride whom the sun shines upon. A girl must not "stand for" a bride more than three times or she will never be married. If the rice is thrown on any but the bride, ill luck is sure to come. Misfortune is sure to come if you sell or pawn a wedding gift. Above all, never "hock" your wedding ring. Be sure to keep it on the finger a long time if you want to be happy. If you work on the day of your wedding you will have to work always.

From: Elsa G. Herzfeld, *Family Monographs: The History of Twenty-four Families Living in the Middle West Side of New York City* (New York: The James Kempster Printing Co., 1905).

Wedding Customs
(English)

Marriage celebrations and marriage customs followed in the New World many of the customs of the Old World. Sack-posset, the drink of Shakespeare's time, a rich, thick concoction of boiled ale, eggs, and spices, was drunk at New England weddings, as we learn from the pages of Judge Sewall's diary; but it did not furnish a very gay wassail, for the Puritan posset-drinking was preceded and followed by the singing of a psalm—and such a psalm! a long, tedious, drawling performance from the Bay Psalm Book.

The bride and groom and bridal party walked in a little procession to the meetinghouse on the Sabbath following the marriage. We read in the Sewall diary of a Sewall bride thus "coming out," or "walking-out bride," as it was called in Newburyport. Cotton Mather thought it expedient to thus make public with due dignity the marriage. In some communities the attention of the interested public was further drawn to the newly married couple in what seems to us a very comic fashion. On the Sabbath following the wedding, the gayly dressed bride and groom occupied a prominent seat in the gallery of the meetinghouse, and in the middle of the sermon they rose and slowly turned around to display complacently on every side their wedding finery.

In Larned's *History of Windham County, Conn.*, we read a description of such a scene in Brooklyn, Connecticut. Further attention was paid to the bride by allowing her to choose the text for the sermon preached on the first Sunday of the coming-out of the newly married couple. Much ingenuity was exercised in finding appropriate and unusual Bible texts for these wedding sermons. The instances are well known of the marriage of Parson Smith's two daughters, one of whom selected the text, "Mary hath chosen that good part"; while the daughter Abby, who married John Adams, decided upon the text, "John came neither eating bread nor drinking wine, and ye say he hath a devil." This latter ingenious and curious choice has given rise to an incorrect notion that the marriage of Abigail Smith with John Adams was distasteful to her father and her family. Mr. Charles Francis Adams tells me that this supposition is entirely unfounded, and that old President Adams would fairly rise in his grave to denounce any such slander, should it become current.

In some communities still rougher horseplay than unexpected volleys of musketry was shown to the bridal party or to wedding guests. Great trees were felled across bridle paths, or grapevines were stretched across to obstruct the way, and thus delay the bridal festivities.

A custom prevailed in many New England towns that was doubtless an ameliorated and semicivilized survival of the customs of savage peoples, when young girls were carried off and made wives by force. A group of those young men who had not been invited to the wedding would invade the house when the marriage ceremony had been performed, and drag away the bride to an inn or some other house, when the groom and his party would follow and rescue her by paying a forfeit of a dinner to the bride stealers. In western Massachusetts this custom lingered until Revolutionary times; on page 245 of Judd's *History of Hadley* the names of stolen brides are given. Mrs. Job Marsh, married in 1783, is said to have been the last bride thus stolen. A very rough variation of this custom is reported to be still in vogue in some localities. In the town of Charlestown, Rhode Island, last summer, a very respectable young married woman, a native of the town and wife of a farmer, was asked whether she had ever ridden on the cars. She answered that she had once done so, when she went to Stonington to be married. When asked why she had not been married at home, she said that she knew better than to do that, that the young men of the neighborhood went at dead of night to the house sheltering the newly married couple, pulled them out of bed, and carried the bride downstairs. If the rough invaders found the door locked, they beat it down with an ax.

Madam Sarah Kemble Knights, in her journal of a horseback ride from Boston to New York in 1704, tells of a curious variation of this marriage custom in Connecticut. She writes thus:

> They generally marry very young; the males oftener, as I am told, under twenty than above: they generally make public Weddings, and have a way something Singular (as they say) in some of them, viz., just before joining hands the Bridegroom quits the place, who is soon followed by the Bridesmen, and, as it were, dragged back to duty—being the reverse to the former practice among us to steal Mistress Bride.

I think this is the most despicable, ungallant bridal custom that I ever heard of, and Connecticut maids must have been poor-spirited, downtrodden jades to endure meekly any such sneaking desertion, an it were merely an empty following of a local fashion.

The most eccentric marriage custom that I have noted in America is what has been termed a "smock marriage," or "marriage in a shift." It was believed in this country, and in Old England (and I have heard that the notion still prevails in parts of England to this day), that if a widow should wear no garment but a shift at the celebration of her second marriage, her new husband would escape liability for any debt previously contracted by her or by her former husband. Mr. William C. Prime, in his delightful book, *Along New England Roads*, page 25 et seq., gives an account of such a marriage in Newfane, Vermont. In February 1789, Major Moses Joy married widow Hannah Ward; the bride stood with no clothing on within a closet, and held out her hand to the major through a diamond-shaped hole in the door, and the ceremony was thus performed. She then appeared resplendent in brave wedding attire, which the gallant major had previously deposited in the closet for her assumption. Mr. Prime tells also of a marriage in which the bride, entirely unclad, left her room by a window by night, and, standing on the top round of a high ladder, donned her wedding garments, and thus put off the obligations of the old life. In some cases the marriage was performed on the public highway. In Hall's *History of Eastern Vermont*, page 587, we read of a marriage in Westminster, Vermont, in which the widow Lovejoy, while nude and hidden in a chimney recess behind a curtain, wedded Asa Averill. "Smock marriages" are recorded in York, Maine, in 1774, as shown on page 419 et seq. of *History of Wells and Kennebunkport*. It is said that in one case the pitying minister threw his coat over the shivering bride, one widow Mary Bradley, who in February, clad only in a shift, met the bridegroom on the highway, halfway from her home to his.

The traveler Kalm, writing in 1748, says that one Pennsylvania bridegroom saved appearances by meeting the scantily clad widow-bride halfway from her house to his, and announcing formally, in the presence of witnesses, that the wedding clothes which he then put on her were only lent to her for the occasion. This is curiously suggestive of the marriage investiture of eastern Hindustan.

In Westerly, Rhode Island, other smock marriages are recorded, showing that the belief in this vulgar error was universal. The most curious variation of this custom is given on page 224, vol. 2, of the *Life of Gustavus Vassa*, wherein that traveler records that he saw a shift marriage take place on a gallows in New York in 1784. A malefactor, condemned to death and about to undergo his execution, was reprieved and liberated through his marriage to a woman thus scantily clad. This traveler's yarn deserves not, of course, the credence accorded to the previously stated authentic records.

In the early days of the Colonies a marriage "contraction" or betrothal sometimes took place—so states Cotton Mather; this custom was abandoned after a few years of life in the New World. It could never have been of any use or much significance, nor, indeed, productive of high moral results.

A more formal method of courtship is suggested by what is termed a "courting stick"; one is preserved in Longmeadow, Massachusetts. It is a hollow tube eight feet in length, through which lovers, in the presence of an assembled family, could whisper tender nothings to each other.

Judging from the pages of the Sewall diary of the length of time elapsing between a proposal or agreement of marriage and its consummation, it is evident that short engagements were the mode, and that wedding arrangements were begun as soon as the engagement was announced. I find no indication of the use of betrothal rings, though Judith Sewall's lover sent her, after her acceptance of his offer, a "stone ring with a noble letter." Neither were wedding rings in common use.

Wedding gloves were sent by the bridal couple as gifts to friends, as were mourning gloves at funerals. Judge Sewall records many gifts of gloves from newly married friends. I have seen old wedding gloves, gold-laced and fringed, with rich gauntlets, far from an inexpensive gift. I do not learn that it was customary to give presents to the bride, though Judge Sewall tells of his presentation of a psalm book at a wedding. A bride cake was made in early days, and was served with cheese at the wedding. A rich wedding feast was frequently given, and the bride was kissed by all present, though I must state that in some parts of New England bride-kissing was discountenanced. So, also, was dancing at weddings, especially at taverns, as "abuses and disorders" arose. This was specially in early days, when marriage was held to be merely a civil contract and was performed by magistrates, not by ministers.

In a community that opened every function—a training, bridge planning, christening, house raising, or journeying—with prayer and psalm-singing, it was plain that the benediction of religion would not long be withheld at weddings, and by the close of the seventeenth century the Puritan ministers solemnized marriages.

Curiously enough, the Quakers, professedly simple in living, made a vast deal of celebration of weddings, though the wedding ceremony itself was simply "passing the meeting." Much feasting took place, and the bride seems to have had to pass through a most trying ordeal of promiscuous and unlimited kissing from every male Quaker for miles around. Visiting the bride was a favorite fashion. We read of one Boston bride, Mrs. Jervis, who received her guests, in 1774, "dressed in a white sattan night gound."

Other old-time English wedding customs are reported to have been in vogue in New England, such as throwing the stocking of the bride, to be scrambled for as a luck-bearing trophy. Along the coast from Marblehead to Castine, the bridesmaids and unmarried girls strove to steal the bride's garter by dexterity or craft. At a Pennsylvania Dutch wedding the bride's shoe was sought for, and the groomsmen protected the bride from the theft, and if ineffectual in their protection were obliged to redeem the shoe with a bottle of wine. I find no record of our modern fashions of throwing slippers and rice after the departing bride.

It is said that along the New Hampshire and upper Massachusetts coast the groom was led to the bridal chamber clad in a brocaded nightgown. This may have occasionally taken place among the gentry, but I fancy brocaded satin nightgowns were not common wear among New England settlers. I have also seen it stated that the bridal chamber was invaded, and healths there were drunks and prayers offered. The only proof of this custom which I have is the negative one which elderly Judge Sewall gives when he states of his own wedding that "none came to us" after he and his bride had retired. There is no reason to suppose, when the wedding of an English nobleman of that period was attended by most indecorous observances, that provincial and colonial weddings were entirely free from similar rude practices, but the greater simplicity of life in the New World naturally crowded out many roystering customs.

From: Alice Morse Earle, "Old-time Marriage Customs in New England," *Journal of American Folk-Lore* 6 (1893): 97–107.

Wedding Customs from New England
(English)

The superstition which made Friday an ill-omened day for any enterprise of course applied with peculiar force to weddings. Wednesday, recommended in the rhyme, has always been a favorite day, its position midway in the week being a convenient one, though few persons were aware of any other reason.

A New England matron, more learned in wedding cake than etymology, once remarked: "Oh, yes! Wednesday's the day for weddin's—of course, Wed'ns-day—Weden's-day," slowly pronouncing each syllable and strongly sounding the *d*, evidently supposing some association of matrimony in the derivation, and all unwitting the fact that it was the day named for Woden, the god of battles.

Sunday, not named in the rhyme, was a common evening for a quiet wedding, and its selection was a sufficient reason for the number of guests being small.

The preparations made by a bride, though so different, were perhaps as elaborate as those of the present day. She might have been for years collecting the articles suited to the furnishing or adorning of her future dwelling. Instances are known where friends commenced such preparations even in the childhood of the prospective bride, while still other cases are on record where only superstition prevented, lest the work done so very long beforehand might never be needed.

Where spinning and weaving were done at home, where the flax field and the fleecy sheep gave employment to wheel and loom, all the needful supply for household and personal wear was homemade. There was a blending of pleasant memories and neighborly good offices when it was customary to "change works," and some deft spinner or weaver was ready to give a few days' work in exchange for some other kindness; then the quilting, when friends came to do those elaborate patterns that even now adorn many a bed in quaint, old-fashioned chambers—the "Job's troubles," the "wild goose," the "rising sun," and many more—when she who set the last stitch would be the first of the company to be married, and she who dropped scissors, spool, or thimble must be careful about picking it up, for whosoever rashly looked at the underside of the unfinished quilt would never be married at all.

Newspapers were few, and engagements were not announced in them, but the secret, communicated to a few intimate friends, was allowed to "ooze out" gradually to an expectant public, which, in its thirst for news and its interest in courtship, differed little from the public of today. "Flirtations" were not "a thing unknown," but by a persistent course of Sunday-evening visiting, a young gentleman was supposed to "mean something" —and usually he did.

In some places the parties were "cried" in meeting; more generally the "intentions of marriage" were posted by the town clerk in the meeting-house entry three successive "Sundays or public days." Runaway matches might be supposed to be prevented by the law concerning "publishments," but this was not always the case; however, such a notice might cause guardians, in case of disapproval, to redouble their vigilance. Vigilance might in time be lulled asleep; and though usually the publishment directly preceded the marriage, yet it "held good" through the year.

It was somewhat embarrassing to walk into church facing one's own name posted up in the town clerk's best "large hand," and usually surrounded by a group of one's friends, who always seemed to consider such occasions extremely entertaining. Sometimes any awkwardness was avoided by having the notice posted on some other church than that in which either of the parties worshipped, but in the early days, when there was but one congregation in a village, there was no choice.

The duty of going to make the necessary announcement to the town clerk devolved on the individual supposed to be best able to endure hardships. In a certain town of Plymouth County, Massachusetts, one diffident swain, having gone on this errand to the official residence on Saturday evening, finding his courage completely fail him, stayed and made a social call. He was not on especially intimate terms with the family, and they were rather surprised at the attention. His engagement was not generally known, the object of his vows lived in a distant place, and all were at a loss to account for his singular conduct. At last, having wearied out the patience of the family, and stayed until an hour of the clock utterly unprecedented in a Saturday evening's call, he took his leave, to the relief of all concerned, and, rousing his courage, modestly confided his wishes to his host, who was thankfully lighting him to the door. Great was the mirth of his entertainers when the matter was explained.

The strictness of the law concerning publishments was often preventive of imposition and deception. It saved many a heartache.

The wedding was usually at the home of the bride, and on the next day the bridal pair, with a large party of friends, was entertained at the house of the parents or some near relative of the groom. This was called in Maine "the second-day wedding."

Sometimes, but rarely, a marriage took place at the new home of the young couple. It is an old superstition that a wedding should not be the first festivity held in a new house. We have recently seen persons high in culture and position strive to avert the omen by giving a large party shortly before the first marriage in their new dwelling.

A marriage in church was rare indeed. This might have been a "sur-

vival" from the old Puritan times, when marriage, being considered merely
a civil contract, was celebrated, not by a clergyman, but by a magistrate,
prayers and religious rites not belonging to it at all. But later (at the time
referred to in this sketch) the ceremony was performed by a minister, if
possible, and a magistrate, if called to officiate, gave a religious form to
the occasion by "making a prayer," as the phrase went.

"Priscilla," cried a friendly matron to a young bride as she stood beside
the groom, just ready to enter the parlor, where a goodly host of friends
and kindred were assembled to see the two made one—"Priscilla, is everything you've got on your own?"

"Certainly," was the prompt reply.

"Nothing borrowed! Dear me! it will never answer—'tis the worst of
luck!" and detaining the group she glanced up and down the bride's figure
to see if perchance she might detect some want; no, all in order.

"Here, here," she exclaimed, "you shall wear these"; and the bride,
despite her protestations, was compelled to assume a necklace, the string
of gold beads which was her sister-in-law's most precious ornament.

Whether the spell was efficacious, who can tell? But tradition avers the
union blessed that evening to have been "an uncommonly happy one,"
and loving hearts still cherish the memory of the bride and bridegroom,
who have long ere this met in the land where partings are no more.

This was on an evening of March—March, the "reign of blast and
storm"—more than seventy years ago.

Summer weddings were less fashionable then than now. Wedding journeys were less frequent, and cold weather was the season of festivities,
generally, in New England country villages. How many charming stories
we have heard from old persons brought up in some faraway country home
of the winter visitings, when a merry party would "pack into" two or
three sleighs, and go off in full force for a three or four days' visit to the
house of some uncle or cousin, fifteen or twenty miles distant—a home
of abundance, where the visitors, biped and quadruped, received the best
of cheer, seasoned with the genuine New England welcome which is
every bit as hearty as the traditional "Highland welcome" famous in song
and story!

Thanksgiving evening was (indeed, it is still) a favorite time for weddings, especially suitable as the time of family gatherings, the general
mustering of kinsfolk "from near and from far."

The old English calendars gave the "seasons for marriages," the times allowed by the church. Beside these were various lucky and unlucky days. The New England girl, though she paid no heed to these, yet remembered the old "wedding rhymes":

> Monday for health,
> Tuesday for wealth,
> Wednesday the best day of all;
> Thursday for losses,
> Friday for crosses,
> And Saturday no luck at all.

Quakers were allowed to be "a law unto themselves." They published and married themselves in their public meetings with a simple formula, which the law acknowledged, if duly recorded by "the clerk of the meeting," and forwarded to the legal authorities.

The attendants, "bridesmaids and groomsmen," were, naturally, relatives or intimate friends, but some delicacy was required in making the selection. One would surely not choose, to walk together in the bridal procession, two persons who found each other's companionship unpleasant; yet, on the other hand, there was a risk in selecting those who betrayed an incipient tenderness for one another—the "auroral dawn of love"—for superstition said those who stood up together as bridesmaid and groomsman would never stand together in a nearer relation. Then, again, it was certain that "every wedding makes a wedding," and Love might cheat Fate after all.

During the progress of her toilette the bride should, of course, consult her mirror as often as she pleased; but when once the toilette was complete, not another look! What would be the result, apparently no one knew, but at least it was "dreadful unlucky"—good and sufficient reason for avoiding it.

The superstition concerning "telling the bees" of a death, as recorded in Whittier's poem, is well known. There was a similar fancy, though less general, concerning weddings. The little workers were to be informed of the event, and receive a bit of wedding cake. As members of the family they were entitled to such attentions, and were supposed to resent the neglect of them.

Many of these customs and traditions are of British origin; a few are still more general.

From: Pamela MacArthur Cole, "New England Weddings," *Journal of American Folk-Lore* 6 (1893): 103–107.

Wedding Customs
(Syrian)

Customs relating to marriage, from what I can learn, would seem to vary considerably in different parts of Syria, and in different classes of society. The following account is of a wedding I attended in Boston. On hearing that there was to be a wedding in "Little Syria," I hastened to call on the bishop (who, incidentally, is the head of all the Maronite churches in the United States) and to find out from him when it was to occur, and, also, some of their customs concerning marriage. He told me that in Syria a girl was marriageable as soon as she reached puberty (twelve to fourteen years of age); a boy after he was fourteen. The young people themselves have very little voice in the affair, their parents making the match with or without consulting the preferences of their children.

However, if two young people fall in love, and their parents will not sanction the affair, they may take matters into their own hands and elope. Then all of the bride's family turn out and search far and near, and, if they are able to find her, bring her back home. One man told me that his sister eloped, and they brought her back three times. The fourth time, however, they were unable to find any trace of her. After a few months she returned with her husband, and her father gave him a job in his business.

A girl is never allowed to go to the house of her betrothed, and must never see him, unless it be a chance meeting on the street. He, also, is not supposed to go to her house, but if, for any reason, he finds it necessary to do so, he must not see her. In Syria the wedding ceremony is held in the bride's house.

The details of the wedding I attended are as follows: The ceremony took place in the Maronite chapel on Tyler Street. It was early New Year's morning, and high mass was just about over when I reached the church, which was packed to overflowing with devout worshippers. After the mass many left the church, but a few remained to see the ceremony. While the bishop was removing the robe he had worn during the mass, and putting on a special robe for the ceremony, candles were distributed to everyone present, and lighted.

Lighted candles play a large role in the life of the Syrians, but their exact significance I have been unable to determine. In some localities of Syria, to quote Mr. Huxley (*Journal of the American Oriental Society*, vol. 23, 1902, p. 193), "before leaving her father's house, the bride, holding a candle in each hand, and supported by old women, walks slowly back and forth three times through the length of the room." Also at funerals, I am told, everyone holds a lighted candle, the number of candles used varying with the position of the man in the community. When a priest dies lighted candles are carried from his house to the church, where the ceremony occurs, and from the church to the grave. Nor is their use limited to affairs of a religious nature. One evening I was invited to dine at the home of one of the better-to-do Syrians, and the light in both the front room and in the dining room was furnished by candles. The bishop, who was present, explained to me that "mine host" had used candles instead of lamps to do me honor. I noticed that when dinner was over and we had repaired to the front room the candlestick from the table was brought in, and that a lamp was lighted in the dining room.

After repeating a number of prayers the bishop took two rings and blessed them. These rings do not necessarily belong to the bride and groom, but are often borrowed for the occasion, as they were in this instance. After having been blessed, they were put on the little finger of the left hand of the bride and groom respectively. Then both were crowned with rosaries. A widow or widower is crowned on the hand, as a person must not be crowned on the head but once. A divorced person cannot be remarried. The customary questions were asked and the usual answers given. The two were uncrowned, the rings removed from their fingers, the candles blown out, and the ceremony was over. As the bride leaves the church, generally, flowers and small pieces of candy are thrown at her. They are also thrown at her when she leaves her father's house and starts for the church.

The bride and groom were driven back to the house of her father and, when the rest of us, who walked, arrived, were seated at the head of the long table, which was to hold the wedding breakfast. Everyone went up and offered congratulations. The male relations kissed the groom four times alternately, first on the right cheek, then on the left.

When breakfast was ready all sat down, the bride and groom remaining at the head of the table. Dishes piled with food of every description were placed side by side along the edge of the table, which had been pieced with boards and boxes to reach the length of the two rooms. The center of the table was filled with loaves, or discs, of bread. Each person then, without ceremony, helped himself from any dish within reach that happened to strike his fancy. Of course no knives or forks were used, but every one ate with his fingers, wiping them on the bread in true Syrian fashion. The women who were gathered at the rear of the room to replenish the dishes as soon as emptied, at short intervals set up a deafening yell, pronouncing lo! lo! lo! etc., in the shrillest tones they could command. This was a sign of welcome to all present. After the breakfast was over everything was cleared away, and dancing began, and was continued during the rest of the day and most of the night. Sometimes the dancing is kept up every night for a month. Very often special dancers are hired and come long distances to perform.

From: Howard Barrett Wilson, "Notes of Syrian Folk-Lore Collected in Boston," *Journal of American Folk-Lore* 16 (1903): 133–47.

Wedding Customs
(Scots-Irish)

Perhaps the most curious wedding customs obtained among the Scotch-Irish settlers; for instance, the Presbyterian planters of Londonderry, New Hampshire, as told in Parker's history of that town. The ancient wedding sport known in various parts of the British Isles as "riding for the kail," or "for the broose"—a pot of spiced broth—and also called "riding for the ribbon," took the form in America of riding a daredevil race over breakneck, half-cleared roads to the house of the bride to secure a beribboned bottle of whiskey. The privileged Protestants had been in Ireland the only subjects permitted to carry or discharge firearms, and they ostentatiously paraded, at every celebration or festivity, their franchised condition by frequent volleys of blank cartridges. Their descendants kept up the same noisy custom in the new land, and the firing of guns formed a large part of a wedding celebration.

A Scotch-Irish marriage in Londonderry was prefaced by widespread formal invitations at least three days previous to the wedding day. An invitation of a single day's warning was almost an insult. The wedding festivities began by a gathering of the groom's friends at his home as an escort; the groom and his party proceeded with frequent discharges of musketry at every house they passed, until they met about halfway a party of the male friends of the bride. Each group of wedding guests then appointed a champion, who "ran for the bottle" to the bride's home, and the victorious one returned with it to the advancing party. Upon reaching the scene of the wedding, the bride-groom and his party of friends entered a room, and sat there till the best man brought the bride into the room, and stationed her before the parson by the side of the groom. The best man and the bridesmaid stationed themselves behind the bridal couple, and at a certain point in the ceremony bride and groom each thrust the right hand behind the back and the attendant couple withdrew the gloves, taking care to have the two gloves removed at precisely the same moment. At the end of the ceremony all kissed the bride, and the beribboned bottle of whiskey was not the only one that regaled the company. The bride and groom started on their journey with many parting volleys of musketry. In some neighborhoods, as a further pleasing attention, hidden groups of men discharged blank cartridges from ambush at the bridal pair as they rode through the woods.

Occasionally the wedding bells did not ring smoothly. One Scotch-Irish lassie seized the convenient opportunity, when the rollicking company of her male friends had set out to meet the bridegroom, to mount a pillion behind a young New Hampshire Lochinvar and ride boldly off to a neighboring parson and marry the man of her choice. Such an unpublished marriage was known in New Hampshire as a "Flagg marriage," from one Parson Flagg, of widespread notoriety, of Chester, Vermont, whose house was a sort of Yankee Gretna Green. The government of New Hampshire, previous to the Revolution, as a means of increasing its income, issued marriage licenses at the price of two guineas each. Sometimes easygoing parsons kept a stock of these licenses on hand, ready for issue, at a slightly advanced price, to eloping couples. Such a marriage, without proper public publishing in meeting, was not, however, deemed very reputable.

From: Alice Morse Earle, "Old-time Marriage Customs in New England," *Journal of American Folk-Lore* 16 (1893): 97–107.

Wedding Customs
(Acadian)

In Acadia, as we prized temperance, sobriety, and simplicity of manners more than riches, early marriages were highly favored. Early marriages foster the virtues which give to man the only true happiness, and from which he derives health and longevity.

No obstacle was thrown in the way of a loving couple who desired to marry. The lover accepted by the maiden obtained the ready consent of the parents, and no one dreamed of inquiring whether the lover was a man of means, or whether the destined bride brought a handsome dowry, as we are wont to do nowadays. Their mutual choice proved satisfactory to all; and, indeed, who better than they could mate their hearts, when they alone were staking their happiness on the venture? and, besides, it is not often that marriages founded on mutual love turn out badly.

The bans were published in the village church, and the old curate, after admonishing them of the sacredness of the tie that bound them forever, blessed their union, while the holy sacrifice of mass was being said. It is useless for me to describe the marriage ceremony and the rejoicings attending the nuptials, as you have witnessed the like here, but I will speak to you of an old Acadian custom which prevails no more among us, one which we no longer observe.

As soon as the marriage of a young couple was determined, the men of the village, after having built a cozy little home for them, cleared and planted the land parceled out to them; and while they so generously extended their aid and assistance, the women were not laggards in their kindness to the bride. To her they made presents of what they deemed most necessary for the comfort and utility of her household, and all this was done and given with honest and willing hearts.

Everything was orderly and neat in the home of the happy couple, and after the marriage ceremony in the church and the wedding feast at the home of the bride's father, the happy couple were escorted to their new home by the young men and the young maidens of the village. How genial was the joy that warmed our hearts and brightened our souls on these occasions; how noisy and light the gaiety of the young people; how unalloyed their merriments and happiness!

From: Felix Voorhies, *Acadian Reminiscences* (Opelousas, LA: The Jacob News Depot Co., 1907).

· Funerals ·

(Various)

Funeral Customs
(Native American)

Indians have considerable light on the immortality of the soul. They conduct their burials and funerals in this way:

First they bathe the dead body, dressing it in the best clothes they have, keeping it some hours in its own house where there is in the meantime much moaning. They provide a great quantity of pinole, corn, and all they have to eat. If it is man, they add his bow, arrows, knife, and other things that he may need—and if a woman, all the womanly implements, mill for grinding, earthen vessels, and so on, because they will need them where they go.

On asking them where the souls of those who die go, they say that when they go from the body they journey on to the side of the setting sun, and from there they continue on through the air to where the Grand Captain is—Caddi Ayo; and from there they go to stop at a house situated to the south called the house of death (and what is death but eternal life?), and there they imagine, and the old men persuade them, that they are very happy—and that they all remain in the state that death found them; that is, if a woman dies nursing a baby, she always walks burdened, and many other erroneous beliefs. But they do not say that husband and wife live in an eternal married life.

I asked if everybody went to this place without pain, and they said: "Yes, unless they are wicked." They have for the wicked, the house of Tescino, that is, the Devil, and there he punishes them severely. They do not believe that adulterers, concubines, thieves, etc., merit this inferno, because they can conceive only of perceptible evil.

The funerals of those who die in war or absent from home are conducted in this form: They invite all the people for a certain day, and prepare all the food they have at the time. Distant a stone's throw from the house they make a pyre of prepared wood. Men and women seated together on the bed are all mourning, and a captain entering speaks a few words with them and then begins a moaning—we should more properly say a howling—which the mourning women answer. Then seven men go out of the house and, turning their faces to the east, pray, having before them a small vessel with ground and moistened corn; and the petition of the principal old man being finished, they take from the little vessel part of the moistened corn and scatter it to the four winds, and three of them who serve as sponsors of the funeral eat the remainder of the corn, and all return together to the house and renew the clamor. All the captains seat themselves in their order, and the sponsors seat themselves together and offer to an old Santones tobacco and flour, and taking it, he returns to the fire, makes a prayer, and casts some of it into the fire, and returns the remainder to the sponsors. This done, two or three Indians go out and deliver a bow and arrow to the mother or wife of the deceased.

Then the captains, one by one, go offering to the director (or master of ceremonies) some six, some eight arrows, according to the rank or state of each. The women follow giving their condolences, and contributing knives and clothes. Adding to this all the precious things or jewels that belong to the deceased, they roll it all together and cover it with a mat. Meanwhile, an old man and a youth are singing in a high key a funeral hymn, and one of the sponsors puts the roll on his shoulders; another carries fire; another a bundle of grass; and going to the funeral pyre they scatter the fire to all parts, and casting on it the mat with the arrows and clothes, reduce them to ashes. Some of the company are now mourning and grieving, while others are laughing and chatting. To crown the function they have a dinner that is free to all the company, and the company is dismissed. They say they do this so that when the soul goes to the house of rest, and the body and soul come together, they may find all that is needed.

From: Adina DeZavala, "Religious Beliefs of the Teajas or Hasanias Indians," *Publications of the Folk-Lore Society of Texas* 1 (1916): 19–43

Funeral Customs
(English)

In New England villages, where all the inhabitants were acquainted with each other, the news of a death circulated rapidly, and "everybody went" to the funeral, which was usually held at the house, involving much care at a time when the friends were least able to bear it.

The relatives and most intimate friends were generally seated in an upper room, and the officiating minister stood on the stairs, where he could be heard above and below. The service over, "the person having charge of the funeral," known on festive occasions as the master of ceremonies, standing on the stairs, called in a loud tone the names of the mourners in the order in which they were to come down, and family after family passed out to take their proper place in the procession. This list was carefully prepared, and it had need to be: To give the names of the immediate family was easy enough, but when it came to settling the precise place of the far-off branches, the task was a hard one, and there was often much bitter feeling when by some inadvertence the shade and degree of kindred had been forgotten or misunderstood. Brothers and their families must come before sisters, nephews took precedence over nieces. "The Woman's Hour," of which we hear so much now, had not struck in the New England of 1800.

To us looking back upon those days, how grim and forbidding many of the customs seem! The idea of dressing the dead in the garments they had worn in life was almost unknown, and the unnatural dress added one more to the painful associations. As late as fifty years ago, young girls were dressed for the grave with plaited-bordered caps, concealing sometimes the loveliest and most luxuriant hair. The floral decorations, now so abundant, were a thing unknown. The custom of strewing the bier or the grave with flowers is old, older than Christianity—though to that, as to so many ancient customs, the gospel gave a new and beautiful significance—but New England has long retained traces of the harsh and unlovely characteristics of her early days, not only derived from a gloomy ancestry, but also strengthened by the struggle with life and labor—a struggle which, giving so little opportunity for the amenities of life, sometimes destroyed all inclination for them.

I have been told by a friend that in 1855 she was assisting in some preparations for the funeral of a young girl who had died, after a short illness, away from home. As she stood beside the coffin, she felt that she could not endure its cold, bare look, void of all beauty, and she said: "I cannot bear the thought of laying her away without a flower; can't we get some flowers?" It was in the very earliest days of spring, and having no flowers accessible, she asked if some one would go to the woods nearby, and bring a handful of the tender young sprays of leaves just budding— something to suggest a thought of the freshness of hope and of life—but her proposition was received with such a stare of surprise and an air of disapproval that she said no more.

It was understood that every person must have an opportunity to look at the dead, and indeed there are many persons living today who would consider themselves defrauded if such an opportunity were refused. I have heard a ghastly story of a woman who some eighty years ago was burned to death. Contrary to all modern ideas of propriety, her poor remains were, according to the custom of the time, exposed to view at the funeral. Two elderly women persuaded several young girls who were averse to the painful sight to go and look, adding the remark which then, as now, supplemented any especially unpleasant requirement: "It is your duty to do it." The result of the duty was, in the case of two sensitive young creatures, such a shock to the nerves that for weeks they were unable to sleep in quiet, and their parents watched a part of every night at their bedside.

There is still a belief among the superstitious that the dead will reappear in the dreams of one who has looked at them unless he has taken the precaution of touching them.

Refreshments were offered at the house when the company had assembled, and when friends gathered, as they often did, from great distances, it was a proper and natural custom; but it was too often merely an excuse for drinking, in the days when liquor flowed on any and every occasion. We are told in the *History of Norton* that it was the custom to offer liquor not only at weddings and funerals and informal social calls, but even at town meetings, and notably at the time of "venduing the poor."

Formerly, the friends remained by the grave until it was filled; in later time the coffin was placed beside the open grave, and the person in charge said, "I will see that the corpse is decently interred." The chief mourner, or nearest male relative, then turning to the persons present thanked them for their attention and kindness. This speech of thanks has sometimes been made by the master of ceremonies "in behalf of the friends of the deceased."

A century ago the custom of wearing mourning was universal. It would have shown a sad want of respect to the departed had their nearest friends failed to make this change of dress. And I have heard old persons speak of their recollection of the labor and expense involved when a large family was "called into mourning," as the phrase went. Although there have always been a few vigorous protestants against this custom, yet until recently they have been but few, and little heed has been paid to their words. It is but a few years since a zealous but illiterate preacher in Maine, called to officiate at a funeral, commenced his service with the following impressive words: "It is sad to see so many persons clad in the *habliments* of woe."

Whittier's beautiful poem has made many persons familiar with the custom of telling the bees of a death in the family. The news should be told at each hive, and at the same time a bit of crepe tied on the hive. This is with most of us a matter of tradition only; I know a few persons who remember seeing it done in 1842.

There were many superstitions connected with death: It is an old fancy that mirrors should be covered when there is a death in the house; it seems to have been feared that if they were left exposed, the face of the dead might be seen in them. The breaking of a mirror, which in so many nations and ages was supposed to foretell misfortune, in New England was thought to have been a warning of death; so too was the falling of a picture from the wall, especially if it were the portrait of some individual. Mysterious sounds, ghostly tappings at the windows, the howling of some restless, uneasy dog, the creaking of stairs—the manifold sounds which the stillness of night allows a wakeful ear to catch—all these were among the signs and omens remembered after the coming of calamity, and treasured for future warnings. If a body lay unburied over Sunday, it was "a sure sign" that there would be another death in town before the end of the week. Suicides too never came singly; one was sure to be soon followed by another. These old beliefs cling to the memory of those who deny having any faith in them, yet who will go a long way round to avoid meeting a hearse, which, whether filled or empty, is equally of ill omen.

It was once common for families to have private burial places near the house, and in a long ride through a scattered country village one may pass many of these little home cemeteries, where two or three white stones gleam among the trees. In some instances, when farms change owners, these graves are leveled and their contents removed to the nearest burying ground, or farms have been sold with the agreement that the graves shall be cared for and not disturbed. But in the course of time, and probably not a long time, they will all disappear.

It was the custom (in many places still prevalent) for the relatives to go back to the house to tea. We refuse to believe the cynical remark, attributed to Dean Swift, that "the merriest faces are seen in mourning coaches," but it is certain that these assemblies of mourning relatives were not a very sorrowful company. In a large family circle, there were many whose connection with the departed was distant, and their knowledge of him slight; and sorrow had been so diluted as to become little more than a mild gravity.

These tea drinkings were a survival of the funeral feasts known in some form in all lands and ages, recalling to readers of Shakespeare those "funeral-baked meats" so thriftily used for the marriage which "followed hard upon."

Formerly the bell was tolled while the procession was on its way to the grave, and at intervals during the burial. In some towns the bell is tolled to announce a death—usually at sunrise after the death occurs. After tolling some minutes there is a pause, and then commences a series of more rapid strokes in number equaling the years of the deceased. This custom too is rapidly passing away. Holmes refers to it in his story of Elsie Venner.

Hearses in New England villages are a modern innovation. Formerly the dead were carried to the grave on a bier, and where the distance was short this was not inconvenient. But in some cases it involved much hardship and discomfort. In the extremes of heat and cold, the task was sometimes almost unendurable; and we must remember the extremes of age, too, for the bearers were generally, as far as practicable, near the age of the deceased. There were usually eight persons chosen to perform the office: The first four, the more prominent by reason of position or of intimacy, were called the bearers; the others, who were expected to relieve them from time to time, were called "underbearers." When the family turned to leave the grave, the eight, bearers and underbearers, generally preceded them, and stood uncovered at the entrance of the cemetery, four on each side, till the procession had passed out.

New measures, even if improvements, are seldom welcome, and in many towns the proposal to purchase a hearse met with fierce opposition. It was thought to be treating the dead with disrespect if any but human strength were employed to carry them to their last resting place—it was inhuman to deny them the last service that neighbor or friend could render them. For some time the hearse was driven only to the gate of the cemetery, the bier then carried to the grave. A bier was seen in the cemetery of South Middleboro' in May 1893.

The mourning rings—many are still in existence—were sometimes presented at the funeral to the bearers, sometimes purchased with money left by will for that purpose. They were of different styles, some set with hair, others inscribed with name and date, or the popular "skull and cross-bones." I have seen one in the form of a wreath in black and gold, encircled with the inscription MADM. L. DUDLEY, OB. 24 OCTO. 1756. Æ 72. It was presented, I am told, to Judge Cushing, of Massachusetts.

Funeral cards, sent to friends, sometimes gave the date and place both of death and interment, sometimes adding a verse of Scripture or of elegiac poetry. The custom has never been so general here as abroad. In British newspapers the words *no cards* sometimes follow the notice of a death.

In walking through old cemeteries, one must be impressed with the lack of variety among epitaphs and decorations. Of the latter it is a question which are in worse taste—the unpleasant little cherubs suggestive of the place whither the departed is supposed to have gone, or the ghastly skull and crossbones belonging to the earthly tabernacle which he has left behind. Of the former, one is almost tempted to say, as the dying French critic remarked of the "style" of his confessor who tried to describe the bliss of heaven, they are "enough to put one out of conceit with the subject." Scripture furnishes consolatory passages enough to express the sorrow and hope of every afflicted soul beneath the skies; but, reading many of these trite old-fashioned phrases, I am reminded of the words of the old stonecutter in Hawthorne's sketch: "these inscriptions seem to stretch to suit a great grief, and shrink to fit a small one."

I cannot tell when the custom arose, but I know that it was customary in New England some sixty or seventy years ago, to announce a suicide in the list of deaths by a euphemism—as, "In this city, first instant, A. B. suddenly . . ." It was so common that, on seeing such a notice, anyone would understand at once that the deceased had taken his own life. Those were the days when newspapers understood and respected a certain degree of reserve in regard to personal feeling, whether of joy or sorrow. Individuals had some privacy.

Another euphemism in regard to death is the phrase "if anything should happen." Persons speak of making their will, or making any definite arrangement concerning their possessions, "in case anything should happen to them." The phrase is almost invariably used where death is hourly expected, certain things are to be done, or certain persons called, "if anything should happen"—meaning that one thing which is sure to happen.

Another old fashion which I observed in Great Britain is not yet extinct in New England. It is applying the word *poor* to departed friends, whatever may have been their condition or circumstances. There are still old-fashioned persons who always speak of relatives, perhaps half a century dead, as "my poor mother," "my poor sister." It sounds strange to unaccustomed ears, but it is a tender old fashion, after all.

Mourning pieces, as they are called, are still occasionally to be seen; a monument surmounted by a funeral urn bears the name of some dead relative, and weeping friends stand beside the grave. These were prepared to suit all sorts of bereavements, and the group is selected accordingly. In one, the ornament of a parlor that I have often seen, a father and two little daughters, all clad in mourning, are gazing at the tomb of the wife and mother. Some, of an early date, are specimens of fine embroidery. They are far more pleasing than the ghastly decoration which many persons even now preserve—a funeral wreath surrounding a coffin plate.

To those of us who are fond of the study of language, and remember that words are history, it is interesting to observe that we retain in common speech many phrases that belong to customs now obsolete. We speak of the ashes of the dead in our cemeteries, although we may be bitter opponents of cremation; the bier is a figurative term in common use; the "bearers" are still chosen, though their office is merely nominal; and the very word *funeral*, applied to a ceremony almost always performed by day, is derived from the torches or tapers (from the Latin *funiculi*, small cords covered with wax) burned at the last rites, which usually took place at night.

We have heard of persons who "enjoyed a funeral," and there is more truth than poetry in the statement. Sir Walter Scott speaks of his father as having enjoyed a funeral; he adds that his presence adorned one, and among his qualifications was the fact of his being a thorough and enthusiastic genealogist. To one who has ever heard the comments by some aged person on hearing of the death of a contemporary, the remark is interesting and intelligible. How the history of the family is recalled, marriages, births, and deaths detailed, with anecdotes of the defunct and all his kin! All this information came in play when the list of mourning relatives was prepared, when the due order of precedence must be observed with as much care as was ever needed by seneschal renowned in song and romance.

The gathering of friends and neighbors—the opportunity of a social chat with those from a distance—for persons whose life was barren of incident, to whom there came no daily news, whose journeys were few and far between, let us have charity if sometimes, where the heart was untouched, they did not find a funeral an occasion of unrelieved sadness. Then too to one with a keen sense of humor, even now, perhaps, it is a milder way of stating a fact to say that the sources of smiles and tears lie very near together.

That is a touching story told of the funeral of Sir Walter Scott: The road by which the procession took its way wound over a hill whence can be seen one of the most beautiful of landscapes. It was his habit to pause there to gaze upon the scene, and when taking a friend out to drive, he never failed to stop there and call the attention of his companion to the most beautiful points of the view. Few could refrain from tears when, carrying their master on his last journey, the horses stopped at the old familiar spot, as it were for him to give a last look at the scene he had loved so well.

Extremes meet. I told this anecdote of Scott's funeral to a friend, who in turn told me a story: A little less than a century ago, there lived in a certain New England village a graceless fellow who spent most of his time at the grog shop, to the neglect of all honest calling. When the summons had at last come for him

> To join
> The innumerable caravan that moves
> To the pale realms of shade,

as his funeral procession, on its way to the place of burial, passed his favorite haunt, the bearers inadvertently turned a little aside, at the same time slackening their pace. The wag of the neighborhood spoke hastily: "Go on! go on!" said he; "don't stop here, for mercy's sake! He'll be sure to go in!"

From: Pamela McArthur Cole, "New England Funerals," *Journal of American Folk-Lore* 7 (1894): 217–23.

Funeral Customs
(German)

In Pennsylvania it was formerly the custom, when a death occurred, for men to be sent out in various directions, within a circle of from fifteen or twenty miles radius, in order to "warn the people" to attend the funeral. Hundreds would often assemble, and the day was made one of feasting, many of the neighbors assisting the bereaved family to bake the meats, fry the sausages, and make the rusk and cake.

From: M. F. Hoagland, "Notes on New England Customs," *Journal of American Folk-Lore* 6 (1893): 301–303.

Funeral Customs
(Chinese)

The humblest Chinaman cannot be induced to leave his native land until assured that, should he die while abroad, his remains will be returned for final interment in the sacred soil of the Celestial Empire. Their anxiety in this respect has much to do with the company craze which possesses them. The famous Six Companies, which now figure so prominently in all that relates to the Chinese residing in this country, were originally formed chiefly to attend to the return of the remains of dead Chinamen to China. When other matters began to engross the attention of those companies to such an extent that they grew careless in the discharge of their original duty, the immigrants began to form other societies composed of those coming from any particular district, with no other purpose than the rescue and return home of the bones of their members. Then, as trade organizations began to multiply among them, their leaders charged themselves, as a part of their vocation, with the pious duty of guarding the remains of their members who might die, and seeing that they were returned to the sacred soil.

The insistence of the Chinese on having their remains returned to China for final burial is based wholly upon the superstition that otherwise their spirits will be troubled and without rest or peace in their future state of existence. They will also be exposed to the assaults and persecutions of every form of malevolent devils; will be beaten, tortured, and driven about, and will, in fact, be compelled to exist in a veritable hell until their bones find shelter beneath the sacred soil of the Celestial Land, when their troubles will end and their spirits will be at rest.

Chinamen have been coming to this city for fully half a century, but not in any great numbers until within the last fifteen or twenty years. The earlier immigrants were notably of a higher grade, intellectually and physically, at least, than those who have more recently poured in upon us. But these earlier comers, being stragglers, had nobody to look after their remains if they died while here. And so it happens that occasional burials of these people have been made in these years. Many of the early comers were undoubtedly buried in the paupers' burying ground, and their graves are now indistinguishable. But since there has been a regular colony of them here more care has been taken in the disposal of the remains of their dead, with a view to their subsequent recovery and shipment to their native land. With this end in view ground was purchased in the New York Bay Cemetery, in the Greenville section of Jersey City, where they were interred. For ceremony's sake bodies were buried as many as possible in a single grave, the coffins resting one on top of the other, until so near the surface that no more would be permitted by the cemetery authorities. This arrangement sadly mixed the bodies, so that now it is found difficult to separate and identify them. At least fifty have been buried in those grounds; others found burial in Greenwood, while still others lie scattered in various cemeteries throughout all this region.

Later a plot was secured in the Cemetery of the Evergreens, Brooklyn, which is commonly known as Celestial Hill, and here the Chinamen who have died of late years have been interred. Hundreds of burials have taken place there, and they are still being added to continually. It is now the only recognized Chinese burial ground in this vicinity.

The exhumation of the remains of the neglected ones was made a philanthropic duty by Ching Wah and Kung Saw a few years ago, acting under the auspices of the Chinese legation. They employed two Chinese laborers to assist them, though the graves were opened by the regular grave diggers of the cemetery. These, however, are only permitted to uncover the coffins, the actual remains being considered too sacred to be even touched by other hands than those of their countrymen. When recovered the remains are taken to a tent near at hand where a charcoal furnace is provided, over which the portions of the body, after being carefully segregated, are dried and the remaining flesh burned off. The bones are then scraped and thoroughly cleaned, after which they are wrapped in excelsior and packed in boxes, each box containing only the bones of one individual, and marked with the name and date of death of the person in Chinese characters, for identification in China. The boxes are then ready for shipment.

There is a legend afloat in Chinatown that the spirit of a deceased Chinaman who was buried in Greenwood Cemetery appeared to the mayor of Chinatown and complained that he, and others buried with him, could get no rest because of the "white devils" among whom they were lying. This apparition, so the story goes, was followed by others, until the matter was referred to a committee of the Chong Wah Gong Shaw, who decided to purchase the plot in the Cemetery of Evergreens, where all the Chinamen who have since died have been buried.

In this connection a queer and superstitious custom of these people regarding their dead may properly be briefly noticed. Ts'ing Ming is the period in the Chinese calendar corresponding with the early part of our month of April. At this time is performed the rite of worship at the ancestral tombs. This is regarded as a most sacred duty by all Chinamen, and he who would willfully fail in performing it would be looked upon as an outcast. Hence its observance by the Chinamen of New York.

As but few of these have ancestors buried in this country, while those who are buried here have only occasionally relatives in this country to pay their remains this reverence, it has become the custom for "cousins" and friends to perform the ceremony. On the morning of the day in question the male members of the family in China, or the friends and relatives of the deceased in this country, repair to the place of burial, where, having weeded and swept the grave, they light incense and arrange beside or upon it sacrificial offerings of roast pigs and fowls, fish, cakes, tea, wine, cigarettes, and whatever else may minister to the comfort of the departed one. The family representative (or here the nearest relative) then performed the Ko-t'ow in honor of the deceased, and each in turn follows his example. Papers representing money are then burned, on the ashes of which are poured libations of wine. A second Ko-t'ow ends the ceremony.

This ceremony can be observed in Evergreen Cemetery at Celestial Hill, on the first Sunday of April in every year and on the Monday following. It calls Chinamen by the hundreds to the burying ground. The prosperous merchant and his friends come in carriages, their offerings being brought in express wagons; the laundrymen ride to the cemetery gates in the surface or elevated street cars, and then proceed on foot, carrying their offerings in baskets and huge bundles.

They chatter and laugh and smoke on the way as if never troubled with sorrow, and perform the ceremony at the grave in the same hilarious, unconcerned manner. When through they wait for the spirit of the departed to make a hurried meal of the essential and immaterial elements of the viands offered, and then, gathering up the substantial food, return to town and enjoy the feast it affords. Whole roasted pigs by the score appear among these offerings; chickens and ducks by the hundreds; besides boiled rice and various kinds of cakes and sweetmeats.

From: Louis J. Beck, *New York's Chinatown* (New York: Bohemia Publishing Co., 1898).

A New York City Funeral Custom
(Unidentified)

There are a few small and poorly equipped flower shops in the district. These are patronized chiefly for wreathes, which are most frequently made of straw, wax, or other artificial flowers. I found one stationery store which fills orders for "memory cards" elaborately edged in gilt with pictures of angels above. The card expresses the sorrow of the family and gives the dates of birth and death of the deceased (dates of confirmation and communion are sometimes added). Below these is a quotation from the Bible. They are sent to friends by the family of the deceased.

I also found in the homes several instances of wax wreathes, ornamented with silver and framed in glass and wood. In one case the photograph of the dead father with the date of birth, death, and marriage, names of wife, children, etc., were inscribed in gold lettering, a variation probably of the "memory card." One woman had a photograph of the tombstone she had erected in Ireland in memory of her father. She showed it with great pride.

From: Elsa G. Herzfeld, *Family Monographs: The History of Twenty-four Families Living in the Middle West Side of New York City* (New York: The James Kempster Printing Co., 1905).

· *Medicine* ·

(Unidentified)

The Irish frequently speak of the physician as a "charmer." On one occasion a man with a severe cold went to the "charmer" to be cured. The latter "pulled out his hair as much as a cap could cover; roasted two eggs and put them on the bald spot, then he muttered to himself, when he got through the man could swaller and holler as loud as any one." "In the owld country," when a person has a sore throat ("they call it dipthery here"), "the charmer takes a frog, ties a string to him and lets him go up and down till he takes out the lump." In some cases the physicians of New York City are regarded as quacks "who don't come up to the Irish charmer."

The Irish Catholic mother believes that praying over a sick child will cure it, and placing "holy bones" on the body of a crippled child will make it whole. In Ireland there is a church where even the blind are "cured." One woman has seen cripples walk out of the church "just like other people." The men of the family do not, as a rule, care to call in the doctor unless it is absolutely necessary. They prefer "to let things go on." Often a man will go without telling his family that he is sick. "The women folks do not understand men anyway." As a usual thing the man also avoids hospitals and clinics. Sometimes he goes and doesn't tell his wife about it.

Usually a "pay" doctor is preferred as a matter of pride, and because he "gives more attention to the patient." One woman has an alopath for herself and a homeopath for the children, "because he used home cures." For general illnesses "she saved" and used patent medicines. The usual charges of a "pay" doctor are from a dollar to a dollar fifty. One woman refused to go to a "pay doctor" in " 'Arlem" because "he charged two dollars a visit and that's special rates and without medicine at that." The charges for services at confinement are regularly ten dollars.

I have known of cases in which the woman refused to go to a man physician to explain her "female troubles." One woman felt sick before the birth of her child, but she was "ashamed" to consult a man doctor so she went to a "lady doctor." Most of the women say that they have been "opirated" for "female troubles." Sometimes a girl is taken to a "lady doctor who advertises" a "sure cure" within a specified time "or your money back."

Numerous patent medicines are in use to cure illnesses, as "Rickey's Drug Bargains" or "Doctor Humphrey's Patent Medicines." The father of the family will secretly go off to a doctor who cures consumption in a week "or your money back."

Occasionally there is a "family doctor." His choice is purely fortuitous. In one case of confinement a doctor was called in because he lived around the corner. The doctor had come from a dinner. He was intoxicated and did not give the right kind of help. As a result, the patient states that she has suffered from "piles" ever since. (Of course she has used every "pile cure" in existence.) Nevertheless she continued to employ the same doctor for a number of years.

In another case the doctor's instruments, according to the mother, distorted the shape of the child's head. "The baby died from this," but the mother continued to call on the same doctor. In this same family, in the case of a later confinement, the "Fifth Avenue doctor" had been engaged beforehand. The physician took no interest because "we was poor"; he was careless and the "head bones" were driven together. "The eyes had an extra skin over them." "It was the doctor's fault that Annie's sight is queer."

In one case a woman was with difficulty persuaded to change her physician. She preferred the inefficient one because he "told her things."

The physician is not engaged many weeks before confinement. One mother never engages the midwife until the day before. The mother usually says "what's the sense, he'll come round soon enough."

From: Elsa G. Herzfeld, *Family Monographs: The History of Twenty-four Families Living in the Middle West Side of New York City* (New York: The James Kempster Printing Co., 1905).

· *Drinking* ·

(English)

It is certain that, at the time of which we are speaking, some of the old laws affecting the drinking habits of society were openly disregarded. Drinking healths, for instance, though under the ban of the law, was still practiced in Cotton Mather's day by those who met at the social board. We find him defending it as a common form of politeness, and not the invocation of heaven it had once been in the days of chivalry. Drinking at funerals, weddings, church raisings, and even at ordinations, was a thing everywhere sanctioned by custom. The person who could have refused to furnish liquor on such an occasion would have been the subject of remarks not at all complimentary to his motives.

It seems curious enough to find that the use of tobacco was looked upon by the fathers of the colony as far more sinful, hurtful, and degrading than indulgence in intoxicating liquors. Indeed, in most of the New England settlements, not only the use but the planting of tobacco was strictly forbidden. Those who had a mind to solace themselves with the interdicted weed could do so only in the most private manner. The language of the law is "Nor shall any take tobacco in any wine or common victual house, except in a private room there, so as the master of said house nor any guest there shall take offence thereat; which, if any do, then such person shall forbear upon pain of two shillings sixpence for every such offence."

It is found on record that two innocent Dutchmen, who went on a visit to Harvard College—when that venerable institution was much younger than it is today—were so nearly choked with the fumes of tobacco smoke, on first going in, that one said to the other, "This is certainly a tavern."

It is also curious to note that, in spite of the steady growth of the smoking habit among all classes of people, public opinion continued to uphold the laws directed to its suppression, though, from our standpoint of today, these do seem uncommonly severe. And this state of things existed down to so late a day that men are now living who have been asked to plead "guilty or not guilty," at the bar of a police court, for smoking in the streets of Boston. A dawning sense of the ridiculous, it is presumed, led at last to the discontinuance of arrests for this cause; but for some time longer officers were in the habit of inviting detected smokers to show respect for the memory of a defunct statute of the Commonwealth, by throwing their cigars into the gutter.

As further fixing the topographical character of taverns, it may be stated that in the old almanacs distances are always computed between the inns, instead of from town to town, as the practice now is.

Of course such topographical distinctions as we have pointed out began at a time when there were few public buildings; but the idea almost amounts to an instinct, because even now it is a common habit with everyone to first direct the inquiring stranger to some prominent landmark. As such, tavern signs were soon known and noted by all travelers.

Then again, tavern titles are, in most cases, traced back to the old country. Love for the old home and its associations made the colonist like to take his mug of ale under the same sign that he had patronized when in England. It was a never-failing reminiscence to him. And inn-keepers knew how to appeal to this feeling.

One board had painted on it a bird, a tree, a ship, and a foaming can with the legend:

> This is the bird that never flew,
> This is the tree which never grew,
> This is the ship which never sails,
> This is the can which never fails.

THE DOG AND POT; TURK'S HEAD; and TUN AND BACCHUS were also old and favorite signs. Some of the houses which swung these signs were very quaint specimens of our early achitecture. So, also, the signs themselves were not unfrequently the work of good artists. Smibert or Copley may have painted some of them. West once offered five hundred dollars for a red lion he had painted for a tavern sign.

Not a few boards displayed a good deal of ingenuity and mother wit, which was not without its effect, especially upon thirsty Jack, who could hardly be expected to resist such an appeal as this one of the SHIP IN DISTRESS:

> With sorrows I am compass'd round;
> Pray lend a hand, my ship's aground.

We hear of another signboard hanging out at the extreme south end of the town, on which was depicted a globe with a man breaking through the crust, like a chicken from its shell. The man's nakedness was supposed to betoken extreme poverty.

So much for the sign itself. The story goes that early one morning a continental regiment was halted in front of the tavern, after having just made a forced march from Providence. The men were broken down with fatigue, bespattered with mud, famishing from hunger. One of these veterans doubtless echoed the sentiments of all the rest when he shouted out to the man on the sign, " 'List, darn ye! 'List, and you'll get through this world fast enough!"

From: Samuel Adams Drake, *Old Boston Taverns and Tavern Clubs* (Boston: W. A. Butterfield, 1917).

· *Bundling* ·

(Unidentified)

For my present purpose it is only necessary for me to say that the practice of "bundling" has long been one of the standing taunts or commonplace indictments against New England, and has been supposed to indicate almost the lowest conceivable state of sexual immorality; but, on the other hand, it may safely be asserted that "bundling" was, as a custom, neither so vicious or so immoral as is usually supposed; nor did it originate in, nor was it peculiar to, New England. It was a practice growing out of the social and industrial conditions of a primitive people, of simple, coarse manners and small means.

Two young persons proposed to marry. They and their families were poor; they lived far apart from each other; they were at work early and late all the week. Under these circumstances Saturday evening and Sunday were the recognized time for meeting. The young man came to the house of the girl after Saturday's sundown, and they could see each other until Sunday afternoon, when he had to go back to his own home and work. The houses were small, and every nook in them occupied; and in order that the man might not be turned out of doors, or the two be compelled to sit up all night at a great waste of lights and fuel, and that they might at the same time be in each other's company, they were "bundled" up together on a bed, in which they lay side by side and partially clothed. It goes without saying that, however it originated, such a custom, if recognized and continued, must degenerate into something coarse and immoral. The inevitable would follow. The only good and redeeming feature about it was the utter absence of concealment and secrecy. All was open and recognized. The very "bundling" was done by the hands of mother and sisters.

The most singular, and to me unaccountable, fact connected with the custom of "bundling" is that, though it unquestionably prevailed—and prevailed long, generally and from an early period—in New England, no trace has been reported of it in any localities of England itself, the mother country. There are well-authenticated records of its prevalence in parts at least of Ireland, Wales, Scotland, and Holland; but it could hardly have found its way as a custom from any of those countries to New England. I well remember hearing the late Dr. John G. Palfrey remark—and the remark will, I think, very probably be found in some note to the text of his *History of New England*—that down to the beginning of the present century, or about the year 1825, there was a purer strain of English blood to be found in the inhabitants of Cape Cod than could be found in any county of England. The original settlers of that region were exclusively English, and for the first two centuries after the settlement there was absolutely no foreign admixture. Yet nowhere in New England does the custom of "bundling" seem to have prevailed more generally than on Cape Cod; and . . . it was on Cape Cod that the practice held out longest against the advance of more refined manners.

From: Charles F. Adams, *Some Phases of Sexual Morality and Church Discipline in Colonial New England* (Cambridge: John Wilson & Son University Press, 1891).

· *Abolition* ·

(English)

Major Broad and my grandfather drew their chairs together and began a warm discussion of the Constitution of the United States, which had been recently presented for acceptance in a convention of the state of Massachusetts.

"I haven't seen you, Major Broad," said my grandfather, "since you came back from the convention. I'm very anxious to have our state of Massachusetts accept that Constitution. We're in an unsettled condition now; we don't know fairly where we are. If we accept this Constitution, we shall be a nation—we shall have something to go to work on."

"Well, Deacon Badger, to say the truth, I could not vote for this Constitution in convention. They have adopted it by a small majority; but I shall be bound to record my dissent from it."

"Pray, Major, what are your objections?" said Miss Mehitable.

"I have two. One is it gives too much power to the president. There's an appointing power and a power of patronage that will play the mischief some day in the hands of an ambitious man. That's one objection. The other is the recognizing and encouraging of slavery in the Constitution. That is such a dreadful wrong—such a shameful inconsistency—when we have just come through a battle for the doctrine that all men are free and equal, to turn round and found our national government on a recognition of African slavery. It cannot and will not come to good."

"O, well," said my grandfather, "slavery will gradually die out. You see how it is going in the New England states."

"I cannot think so," said the Major. "I have a sort of feeling about this that I cannot resist. If we join those states that still mean to import and use slaves, our nation will meet some dreadful punishment. I am certain of it."

"Well, really," said my grandfather, "I'm concerned to hear you speak so. I have felt such anxiety to have something settled. You see, without a union we are all afloat—we are separate logs, but no raft."

"Yes," said Miss Mehitable, "but nothing can be settled that isn't founded on right. We ought to dig deep, and lay our foundations on a rock, when we build for posterity."

"Were there many of your way of thinking at the convention, Major?" said my grandfather.

"Well, we had a pretty warm discussion, and we came very near to carrying it. Now, in Middlesex County, for instance, where we are, there were only seventeen in favor of the Constitution, and twenty-five against; and in Worcester County there were only seven in favor and forty-three against. Well, they carried it at last by a majority of nineteen; but the minority recorded their protest. Judge Widgery of Portland, General Thompson of Topsham, and Dr. Taylor of Worcester rather headed the opposition. Then the town of Andover instructed its representative, Mr. Symmes, to vote against it, but he didn't, he voted on the other side, and I understand they are dreadfully indignant about it. I saw a man from Andover last week who said that he actually thought Symmes would be obliged to leave the town, he was so dreadfully unpopular."

"Well, Major Broad, I agree with you," said my grandmother, heartily, "and I honor you for the stand you took. Slavery is a sin and a shame; and I say, with Jacob, 'O my soul, come not thou into their secret—unto their assembly, mine honor, be not thou united.' I wish we may keep clear on 't. I don't want anything that we can't ask God's blessing on heartily, and we certainly can't on this. Why, anybody that sees that great scar on Caesar's forehead sees what slavery comes to."

My grandmother always pointed her antislavery arguments with an appeal to this mark of ill usage which old Caesar had received at the hands of a brutal master years before, and the appeal never failed to convince the domestic circle.

"Well," said my grandfather, after some moments of silence, in which he sat gazing fixedly at the great red coals of a hickory log, "you see, Major, it's done, and can't be helped."

"It's done," said the Major, "but in my opinion mischief will come of it as sure as there is a God in heaven."

"Let's hope not," said my grandfather, placidly.

From: Harriet Beecher Stowe, *Oldtown Folks* (Boston: Fields, Osgood & Co., 1869).

· *Fire Worship* ·

(Native American)

The tribes of the Hasanias have a particular form of worship with fire. There is a certain house in which there is a perpetual fire. And there is a certain old man who has charge of it and keeps it alive, and he is the "*Chenesi*"—or their grand high priest. They believe that if the fire should go out they would all die. This house which they renovated in December 1716, is between the Naiches and the Hainai, and is common to both towns and is said to be the house of the "Great Captain." It is large, round, and made of straw, and has a canopy made of mats, and on the bed are three coverings, two of them very small. At each side of the door there are other mats in a roll. Before the bed is a bench with four legs, and upon the bench they are accustomed to place tobacco and pipes, with feathers and earthen vessels which they use in their idolatrous rites for incense. The fire is always made of four very large and heavy tree trunks and are always placed to point to the four principal winds. The wood is brought and placed in piles outside.

Here the old men come together for their consultations and war dances, and when they need water for their crops here they meet and make supplication. The ashes from this fire they pile up outside, and when they move the bones of the enemy they have killed, they bury them in these ashes.

Near this large house are two smaller ones within rifle shot, and they call these two houses "*Coninicis.*" These, they say, are two boys, or children who their Grand Captain sent from the sky that they might be consulted on any doubts. They think these little gods have been in their houses two years. (It was at the time that the two religions of the Holy Cross were negotiating for entrance to Texas that they made their appearance.) And, according to the Indian interpreter, when their enemies, the Tojienes, burned these houses, they say they saw them go up in the smoke and they have never come down. In these little houses are four little posts with coverings of painted red grass raised above an altar of wood. Within I found they had four or five plates or dishes of black wood, round and curiously carved, with four feet. Some were made with head and tail of an owl; others with head, tail, and feet of an alligator or lizard. Besides this there were many feathers of all sizes and color—plumes of peacocks, white feathers, loosened from the breast; some banners of feathers; crowns of skins; with many bones of cranes that served for flutes and fifes, and some of reed grass; and other instruments that they used to make music for their dances. These little houses were well swept and cared for.

The house of fire is for the Hanaii and the other tribes of Naiches, Nacogdoches, and Nazonis, as the parish church or cathedral (would be to us). From this, fire is carried to their houses. It is customary for the Naiches and Hanaii to come together in one mosque or house of fire, and for the Nacogdoches and Nazonis to gather in the mosque that is in Nacogdoches. On the principal feasts of the year all the houses or most of them take fire (serve themselves with fire) from that principal house (not that they need it)—but because when it was built they carried it from there and preserved it; and if at any time it should go out, they hold that it is an omen that all that family will die, and (therefore they continue to replenish or) bring it anew from the house of the mosque with great ceremony.

They fear that the fire will become angry and they bring it the first tobacco and the first fruits of the corn and all their crops, and of the meat they kill. They believe the fire created them, although some of them say that man came out from the sea and was scattered throughout all the earth by those creatures called Niacaddi—water and fire, but they always go to the fire in all their ceremonies. They say that they were the descendants of bears, others of dogs, others of coyotes and other animals. Asking them how it was, they answered that their forefathers seeing the evils that the demons wrought transformed themselves into these animals, though at the same time they were rational men, women, and children.

From: Adina DeZavala, "Religious Beliefs of the Teajas or Hasanias Indians," *Publications of the Folk-Lore Society of Texas* 1 (1916): 39–43.

· *The Dress at Ceremonies* ·

(English)

Even at a later date in the rather hungry little Pilgrim colony at Plymouth much ceremony was observed, though the people were extreme Puritans without rank. At beat of drum on Sunday morning the men came to Captain Standish's door with their cloaks on, each bearing a musket or matchlock. They proceeded to church three abreast, led by a sergeant. In the rear walked the governor, in a long robe. On his right was Elder Brewster, wearing a cloak. On the governor's left was Captain Miles Standish, who also wore a cloak and side arms, and carried a small cane as a sort of baton of authority perhaps. Thus "they march in good order, and each sets his arms down near him."

It was only in an age such as this that resistance to the celebration of rites and the observance of forms could be made a capital article of faith by the Puritan, and later by the Quaker. The wearing of a surplice, the propriety of doffing the hat on certain occasions, was a matter for scruple and violent debate, for the grave consideration of the lawgiver and magistrate, and for severe penalties.

From: Edward Eggleston, *The Beginners of a Nation* (New York: D. Appleton and Co., 1896).

· St. Patrick's Day ·

(Irish)

The Ordinance

1. Be it ordained by the Mayor, Aldermen, and Commonality of the city of New York in Common Council convened, That if any person shall, on the Seventeenth day of March, commonly called St. Patrick's Day, or any other day, carry or drag through or along the street, alley or highway, within this city, or shall exhibit to public view in any street, alley or highway, or from any window, roof of any house, or other building, or shall exhibit to public view in any place, or in any manner within this city, an effigy of St. Patrick, or any other titular saint, or of any person or persons whomsoever, or any shew of a similar kind, whether the same is intended as an effigy of St. Patrick or any other titular saint, or any person or persons, or whether the same is disguised to ridicule such titular saint, or any person or persons whomsoever, he or she shall forfeit and pay for each offence the penalty of Ten Dollars, to be recovered with costs of suit.

2. And be it further ordained, That every person who shall be aiding, assisting, or countenancing any such transaction as aforesaid, shall be deemed to have acted contrary to this ordinance, and shall, for each offence, forfeit and pay the like penalty, to be recovered as aforesaid.

3. And it is further ordered, That if any person who shall contravene this ordinance shall be a minor, an apprentice, a bound servant, or a slave, his or her parent or guardian, master or owner, as the case may be, shall be deemed liable to pay the penalty so incurred, and shall and may be prosecuted for the same as aforesaid.

A true copy of its original

T. Wortman, City Clerk.

St. Patrick's Reply

My dear Crature.

By just inserting the following little bit of petition, you will confer a lasting obligation on

An Afflicted Saint.

To the honorable the mayor, aldermen, and commonality of
the city of New York, in common council convened.

The petition of Saint Patrick, of the kingdom of Ireland, most respectfully sheweth:

That, whereas it has been a custom prevailing since time immemorial,
among the young, ragged, and sunburnt order of citizens in this city, to
testify their respect and veneration of your petitioner, by forming, on the
17th day of March, solemn and splendid processions, and (with shouts
and other vehement expressions of joy, highly pleasing and grateful to
the citizens) "carrying or dragging through or along the streets, alleys, and
highways within this city," various pretty effigies of rags and straw, decorated with potatoes and codfish, whereby your petitioner was most *honorably* represented.

And whereas, it has pleased your honorable body, in the plenitude of
your care and tenderness for the public welfare and tranquility, among
other decrees of equal wisdom and importance, to publish an ordinance,
prohibiting under penalty of ten dollars, all such magnificent testimonies
of public respect (as they were calculated to instill into the minds of the
young and vulgar a taste for show and parade, highly dangerous to the
prosperity of a republic.)

And whereas your said most gracious and laudable decree, in the magni-
tude of its beneficial influence, doth not extend to the abolishing of a
custom also established, since time immemorial, by the aforesaid young,
ragged, and sunburnt gentry, of "carrying and dragging through or along
the streets, alleys and highways within the city," on the 18th day of
March, the effigy of your petitioner's beloved wife Shelah; your prohibition
being against the carrying or dragging the effigy of St. Patrick, or any other
titular saint, person or persons whomsoever—and Shelah (dear jewel) not
having the good fortune to be either saint or person at all, at all.

And whereas your humble petitioner hath not enough of the modern
husband in his composition to be satisfied with having his wife gallanted
about the streets by any other person but himself—especially without his
being present:

Now therefore, your petitioner most humbly, respectfully, and earnestly
entreats and prays your honorable body, that amidst the many important
considerations with which your honorable body is continually engaged,
that it would please your honorable body to listen to the private distresses

of your distressed petitioner; and insert a little bit of a clause in your aforesaid highly important and valuable ordinance; where is shall be decreed, that your petitioner's beloved wife Shelah, aforesaid, shall not be allowed to appear in public on the day aforesaid, but shall stay at home and console her confined husband; otherwise your petitioner much fears that she will exhibit herself about the city, to the annoyance of your most honorable body's most humble petitioner.

And your petitioner further prays, that it may be explained by your honorable body, that any person who carries a potato or codfish on the end of a stick, pole, or any other thing, or in any other manner, on the day aforesaid, shall come within the sense of your most gracious decree aforesaid.

And also, that if any bull shall be found running "through or along the streets, alleys, or highways within this city," on the day aforesaid, he shall be slain for the benefit of the poor of this city.

And so bad luck to the man that eats bull beef on that day.

And your petitioner, as in duty bound, will forever pray.

Saint Patrick.

St. Patrick's Day Toasts

The Saint of Shillelah—We regret that the social festivity of his day is abused by the orgies of tories, and that any sons of St. Patrick disgrace his memory and insult the American people by the insolent display of a British Crown

The memory of St. Patrick—May his virtues—his patriotism—his benevolence—his worth—ever be held in sacred estimation.

Ireland—The best blood of this land has been shed by the most iniquitous government that ever insulted heaven and oppressed mankind, but may she like the "shivering tenants of the frigid zone," enjoy a day proportioned to the dreary darkness of her long and gloomy night.

That little island in the western Ocean, called Erin, or Patrick's Potato Garden—Patrick expelled the four-legged venomous reptiles which infected it at that day. May his sons soon extinguish the swarm of two-legged ones, which are preying on its vitals, from a neighboring island.

Shelah.

The Irish Harp—Mournful are its sounds among the hills. It groans under the weight of a foreign crown. Soon may it be relieved from its oppressive burden; soon may Ireland "take her place among the nations of the earth."

The three-leaved shamrock of Ireland—May it ever remind republicans of the three theological virtues, Faith, Hope, and Charity, imperative of their duty to relieve a republican in distress, and ameliorate his situation.

The harp of Erin, decorated with the shamrock, and the cap of liberty substituted for the crown.

The starving human property of George the 3d on the Island of Britain— May hunger (if nothing else can) make them partake of the spirit of their ancestors of the seventeenth century, and prompt them to avenge the injuries of mankind, by breaking their chains on the guilty heads of their blood-stained tyrants.

The memory of the martyrs for Irish freedom—Heroes fired with the soul of Erin—Alas! closed are their eyes in the narrow house, careless of the beams of the morning, their deeds are untold, for silent are the bards, and the high-sounding harp of their fathers is mute. Sons of the bards awake—raise the echoing song, strike ten thousand strings, if there is aught of music in the harp pour it on the memory of the brave.

Irish heroes and patriots—Montgomery, Lord Edward Fitzgerald, Russel, Emmet, and the thousand others whom "memory cannot count nor choice elect," may every son of Erin emulate their shining virtues and devotion to liberty.

The Catholics of Ireland—Their cause is a good one: May their spirited exertions and manly perseverance be crowned with the rich reward of "emancipation."

Irish slavery—may the chains of coercion, the cords of enslavement, which are already stretched to their utmost extent, be by the energetic efforts of our countrymen rent asunder like cobwebs—and may they enjoy their portion of liberty and happiness after such a long, long absence.

Disguise thyself as thou wilt, still slavery, still thou art a bitter draught. May the spirit of freedom move over the whole globe, that all mankind may partake of its sweets. Its liberty, sweet liberty.

May Negro slavery, that degrading remnant of colonial dependence, be speedily abolished.

May Irishmen flourish in every climate, and always substantiate the character they profess:—"a lion in battle, a saint in love, and a brother in charity."

The Republican Irish who have sought an asylum in this country from persecution—We hail them as brothers—No alien law.

The emigrants from Europe—Every republican will hail them as friends—every philanthropist will welcome them as strangers—"Hail to the Chief."

Adopted citizens—With native hearts, attached to the principles upon which our political institutions are founded, and those natives with foreign predilections who are opposed to them—may both be where they ought to be—"A man's a man for a' that."

The land we inhabit; incense to the memory of Columbus who discovered it; honors to the heroes who bled for it; dignities to the patriots who preserve it; the bulwark of Liberty; the school for self-government; the envy of regal power, the asylum of persecuted worth.

The American people—Firm amidst the injustice of foreign aggression, the infamous designs of domestic traitors, the croakings of unprincipled speculators, and the howlings of intriguing tories.

Washington—he fought for independence; Jefferson—writer of the Declaration of Independence; Madison—the man of the people's choice—he will support independence. Then let every man whose heart ever formed an independent wish drink Washington, Jefferson, and Madison compared with whom the kings and emperors of the earth are no more than glowworms to the sunbeams. "Go where glory waits thee."

From: John D. Crimmins, *St. Patrick's Day: Its Celebration in New York and Other American Places, 1737-1845* (New York: 1902).

· Haik's Day ·

(Armenian)

On the festival called Haik's Day, it is the custom for persons to deluge each other with water at every opportunity. It is related that Haik, first king of Armenia, worshipped an image, and that sprinkling was connected with his worship. When Christianity was accepted, the worship of the former image became obsolete. It was deprived of its sacredness, and hence the day upon which such worship was rendered became a gala day. For the sprinkling, which was the custom upon that day, was substituted what has already been referred to—the lying in wait to drench each other with water.

The story of the Cross Day is told as follows: The cross on which Christ was crucified was left on Mount Calvary, where in time it became covered up with dirt and rubbish. A queen who desired to rescue it from eternal entombment came to Calvary in search of it. She threw money on the ground, and the people scrambled to pick it up. This action she performed over and over again, looking each time that the people arose from their scrambling to see if the cross was in sight. After a while, together with the money, there had been picked away so much dirt, that the cross came to view. The day upon which it was found was called "Cross Day." Henceforth, the anniversary of that day has been observed. Religious services are held in the church, and ceremonies are performed. The crosses which are in the church are removed from their places and put in water, where they remain for three days. After this they are taken out and restored to their former positions.

On Easter morning the sun dances, and there is no other morning in the year when such is the case. Since they cannot look directly at the sun; they have mirrors into which they look in order to see it dance. It is said too that very seldom is there an Easter morning which is not clear. Prior to Easter there is a seven weeks of self-denial, and, in a measure, fasting. Before the fasting begins there is a week given up to feasting, dancing, and frivolity. The period of fasting has become personified, until they imagine that a spirit oversees its observance. The name of the spirit is "Great Fast." The seven weeks' fast begins at midnight, and on the evening previous they talk of Great Fast being over behind the mountain.

At twilight they say: "Now he is on top of the mountain." A little later, when it is dark, they will say: "Now he is in the valley." Still later: "He is leaving the valley." Thus they go on speaking of him as drawing nearer and nearer, until they will finally say: "He is now on the housetop waiting to come down." At midnight he comes down the chimney, and sits in the fireplace. He goes to everything in the room and smells of it, to the cooking vessels, etc.; and even smells of the mouths of those who are asleep, to see if they have been eating butter, grease, or any other forbidden article of food. In preparation for this scrutinizing investigation, on this night after supper it is customary to scour all the dishes with ashes. Everything must be clean. Some people will even wash their mouths with ashes. After his examination, Great Fast goes back and takes his seat in the chimney, where he sits for forty days in order to watch the people, and to be sure that they do not do any of the things forbidden for that period. However, though he sees everything, he cannot be seen himself. He is invisible.

From: G. D. Edwards, "Items of Armenian Folk-Lore Collected in Boston," *Journal of American Folk-Lore* 12 (1899): 97–107.

· *The Corpus Christi Festival* ·

(German)

The traveler by the Philadelphia and Erie railroad, when in the heart of the Appalachian chain, comes suddenly upon a German village set in the midst of a green oasis of meadows and grain fields reclaimed from the surrounding forests. This village bears the pretty name of St. Mary's, and is one of the loftiest towns in Pennsylvania, being situated on the great divide between the waters of the Susquehanna and the Ohio. Certain Redemptorist fathers and devout Catholic laymen of Philadelphia and Baltimore founded it as a Catholic community some fifty-three years ago, and settled it with adherents of their faith from Alsace, Bavaria, and Belgium. These people, owing in part no doubt to their isolation, have clung to the language, customs, dress, and religion of the fatherland with great tenacity, and form an interesting study for the student of sociology, who finds here a bit of medieval Germany transplanted to American soil and flourishing therein. As one walks the streets of St. Mary's he hears the guttural tongue of the fatherland on every hand, and sees women in peasant dress busy at household tasks, the weaver at his hand loom, the butcher, baker, and shoemaker plying their craft in Old World style. There is a German church, German schools, German societies.

The Redemptorist fathers moved farther west after a time, and were succeeded by monks of the Benedictine order, who are now the spiritual fathers of the village. Christmas and Easter are duly observed, but the great day of the year is the Festival of Corpus Christi, in honor of Christ's triumphant entry into Jerusalem, and the institution of the Sacrament of the Lord's Supper which followed. The festival was observed this year on Sunday, June 20, with great pomp and ceremony, and we were so fortunate to see it. Preparations for it began in St. Mary's and the outlying farms a week before. The large and beautiful German Catholic Church, where the procession was to form, was decorated with evergreens and flowers more profusely than at Christmas or Easter. On the Saturday before, the farmers brought green saplings and boughs from the woods and stuck them in the earth along the route of the procession. Baskets of cut flowers, green leaves, fresh ferns, and grasses were provided for strewing in the road before the Host, and in all German homes great preparations were made for the feast which was to follow at the close of the ceremonies, the day having as great significance in this respect as Thanksgiving in New England. The route of the procession was to be from the German church to the pretty hilltop cemetery a half mile distant, and return by another road. At intervals along the way, wayside altars were erected— bowers of greenery bedecked with flowers and bearing a Christ on the cross, pictures of the Virgin and saints, and other emblems of the Catholic faith. Lighted candles burned before these shrines during the ceremonies.

The day began with the celebration of low mass at eight o'clock. Long before this, the streets were filled with happy groups winding their way towards the church, all attired in gala dress—girls in white, with long white veils floating behind, and bearing bouquets of flowers in their hands; boys each with a boutonnière in his coat lapel; mothers with babes in arms, and fathers escorting them. Great farm wagons, drawn by horses or mules, came lumbering in from the farms, their seats filled with farmer folk having the rugged German features, clad in the garb of the German peasant, and addressing one another in the language of the fatherland.

When the celebration of high mass began, at nine o'clock, the church was crowded to suffocation, the worshippers filled the portico and esplanade without. At ten, on the conclusion of the service, the procession was formed, the father prior acting as master of ceremonies. First came three acolytes in altar vestments, bearing emblems of the Catholic faith; then a standard-bearer with the banner of the Holy Childhood Society of the parish. The members of the society followed—the boys first, and then the girls, the latter, some five hundred in number, clad in white dresses and veils, and bearing baskets of flowers, which they strewed along the road; after them the St. Mary's Silver Cornet Band, then one each of the men's and women's societies of the parish, bearing banners; after them, under a rich canopy borne by four men, came three Benedictine fathers in full canonicals, the central one, a monk of imposing presence, bearing the Sacred Host. Next came more parish societies of both sexes bearing banners; then the St. Mary's Citizen Band; then devotees in general, the whole procession numbering fully two thousand persons, and stretching from the church to the cemetery.

As the head of the procession approached the first of the wayside altars, the boys uncovered their heads, and all chanted hymns in praise of the Christ and of the Sacrament. As the priests with the Sacred Host arrived before the altar, the procession halted, and the priests, kneeling before it, performed the appropriate service for Corpus Christi, and bestowed the benedictus, the whole body of people kneeling during the ceremony. The procession then continued on to the German cemetery, with its quaint Old World tombs and crosses, past the little chapel in its midst, where prayers and masses for the dead are said, and out by another entrance. As the priests arrived at the door of the chapel the people again halted, the celebrants entered and performed the same service as at the altar. This concluded, the march was again resumed, and the procession returned to the church by another road, passing a second wayside altar, before which the solemn service was again performed. Arrived at the church, the procession was disbanded, the members returning to their homes to enjoy the feast which had been prepared for the occasion, perhaps to meet long-sundered members of the family around the board.

From: Charles Burr Todd, "The Corpus Christi Festival at St. Mary's, Pennsylvania," *Journal of American Folk-Lore* 11 (1899): 126–32.

· *The Sabbath* ·

(English Puritan)

The Law

The legislature of 1884 has placed an act upon our statute book which rounds out and completes an act looking in the same direction passed by the legislature of 1877. Chapter 37 of the Acts of 1884 provides that "The provisions of chapter ninety-eight of the Public Statutes relating to the observance of the Lord's Day shall not constitute a defense to an action for a tort or injury suffered by a person on that day."

Chapter 232 of the Acts of 1877 provided that common carriers of passengers should no longer escape liability for their negligence in case of accidents to passengers, by reason of the injury being received on Sunday. This act marked a long step forward in the policy of this Commonwealth, and made it no longer possible for a corporation openly violating the law to escape the consequences of its illegal acts by saying to the injured passenger, "You were breaking the law yourself, and therefore you have no redress against us." This was a condition of things which worked a confusion of relations, and lent "doubtful aid to morality"; resting on "no principle of justice" or law, and creating a "species of judicial outlawry which ignored alike the principles of humanity and the analogies of the law."

The provisions more particularly referred to in these acts are those relating to traveling on the Lord's Day, found in the statutes as follows:

> Whoever travels on the Lord's day, except from necessity or charity, shall be punished by fine not exceeding ten dollars for each offence. Pub. Stat., Chap. 98, Sect. 2.

It is an interesting and curious study to follow the changes made in the Sunday law, so called, with the accompanying judicial decisions, as one by one the hindrances to the attainment of simple justice by travelers injured on the Lord's Day have been swept away.

The Pilgrims brought many strange ideas with them to their new home, as we all well know, and we find these reflected in their statute books in the form of many "blue laws," some of which may yet be found in changed garb in the form of constantly disregarded "dead letter" laws in our own public statutes. Interesting as a general discussion of this subject is, as showing the character and purposes of the founders of the Republic, we can follow but one division of the Sunday law in its various forms since it was first framed by our "Puritan ancestors who intended that the day should be not merely a day of rest from labor, but also a day devoted to public and private worship and to religious meditation and repose, undisturbed by secular cares or amusements," and among whom were found some who thought death the only fit punishment for those who, as they considered it, "prophaned," the Lord's Day.

As early as 1636 it was enacted by the court of the Plymouth colony that, "Whereas, complaint is made of great abuses in sundry places of this Government of prophaning the Lord's day by travellers, both horse and foot, by bearing of burdens, carrying of packs, etc., upon the Lord's day to the great offence of the Godly welafected among us. It is, therefore, enacted by the Court and the authoritie thereof that if any person or persons shall be found transgressing in any of the precincts of any township within this Government, he or they shall be forthwith apprehended by the Constable of such a town and fined twenty shillings, to the Collonie's use, or else shall sit in the stocks four hours, except they can give a sufficient reason for theire soe doeing; but they that 'soe transgresse' must be apprehended on the Lord's day and 'paye theire fine or sitt in the stockes as aforesaide' on the second day thereafter." It seems, however, that in spite of the pious sentiments of the framers of the law it was not, or could not be enforced, for in 1662 it was further enacted that "This Court doth desire that the transgression of the foregoing order may be carefully looked into and p'r'vented if by any due course it may be."

But even now it seems that the energies of the lawmakers were of no avail in preventing prophanation of the holy day by "foraignors and others," so that twenty years later, in 1682, we find that "To prevent prophanation of the Lord's day by foraignors or any others unessesary travelling through our Townes on that day. It is enacted by the Court that a fitt man in each Towne be chosen, unto whom whosoever hath necessity of travell on the Lord's day in case of danger of death, or such necessitous occations shall repaire, and makeing out such occations satisfyingly to him shall receive a Tickett from him to pas on about such like occations"; but, "if he attende not to this," or "if it shall appear that his plea was fake," the hand of the law was likely to fall upon him while he contributed twenty shillings "to the use of the Collonie."

In the Massachusetts Bay province it was early enacted that "no travel- ler . . . shall travel on the Lord's day . . . except by some adversity they are belated and forced to lodge in the woods, wilderness, or highways the night before, and then only to the next inn," under a penalty of twenty shillings.

In 1727 it was found that notwithstanding the many good and whole- some laws made to prevent the "prophanation of the Lord's day," this same "prophanation" was on the increase, and so it was enacted that the penalty for the first offense should be thirty shillings, and for the second, three pounds, while the offender, presumably a "foraignor," was to be put under a bond to observe the Sabbath day and keep it holy according to the ideas of the straitlaced Puritans.

From: Chester F. Sanger, "Sunday Travel and the Law," *The Bay State Monthly* 1 (1885): 231–33.

The Observance

The so-called "False Blue Laws" of Connecticut, which were foisted upon the public by the Reverend Samuel Peters, have caused much indignation among all thoughtful descendants and all lovers of New England Puritans. Three of his most bitterly resented false laws which refer to the observance of the Sabbath read thus:

> No one shall travel, cook victuals, make beds, sweep house, cut hair, or shave on the Sabbath Day.
> No woman shall kiss her child on the Sabbath or fasting day.
> No one shall ride on the Sabbath Day, or walk in his garden or elsewhere except reverently to and from meeting.

Though these laws were worded by Dr. Peters, and though we are disgusted to hear them so often quoted as historical facts, still we must acknowledge that, though in detail not correct, they are in spirit true records of the old Puritan laws which were enacted to enforce the strict and decorous observance of the Sabbath, and which were valid not only in Connecticut and Massachusetts, but in other New England states. Even a cursory glance at the historical record of any old town or church will give plenty of details to prove this.

Thus in New London we find in the latter part of the seventeenth century a wicked fisherman presented before the court and fined for catching eels on Sunday; another "fined twenty shillings for sailing a boat on the Lord's Day"; while in 1670 two lovers, John Lewis and Sarah Chapman, were accused of and tried for "sitting together on the Lord's Day under an apple tree in Goodman Chapman's Orchard"—so harmless and so natural an act. In Plymouth a man was "sharply whipped" for shooting fowl on Sunday; another was fined for carrying a grist of corn home on the Lord's Day, and the miller who allowed him to take it was also fined. Elizabeth Eddy of the same town was fined, in 1652, "ten shillings for wringing and hanging out clothes." A Plymouth man, for attending to his tar pits on the Sabbath, was set in the stocks. James Watt, in 1658, was publicly reproved "for writing a note about common business on the Lord's Day, *at least in the evening somewhat too soon.*" A Plymouth man who drove a yoke of oxen was "presented" before the court, as was also another offender, who drove some cows a short distance "without need" on the Sabbath.

In Newbury, in 1646, Aquila Chase and his wife were presented and fined for gathering peas from their garden on the Sabbath, but upon investigation the fines were remitted, and the offenders were only admonished. In Wareham, in 1772, William Estes acknowledged himself "Gilty of Racking Hay on the Lord's Day" and was fined ten shillings; and in 1774 another Wareham citizen, "for a breach of the Sabbath in pulling apples," was fined five shillings. A Dunstable soldier, for "wetting a piece of an old hat to put in his shoe" to protect his foot—for doing this piece of heavy work on the Lord's Day—was fined, and paid forty shillings.

Captain Kemble of Boston was in 1656 set for two hours in the public stocks for his "lewd and unseemly behavior," which consisted in his kissing his wife "publicquely" on the Sabbath day, upon the doorstep of his house, when he had just returned from a voyage and absence of three years. The lewd offender was a man of wealth and influence, the father of Madam Sarah Knights, the "fearfull female travailler" whose diary of a journey from Boston to New York and return, written in 1704, rivals in quality if not in quantity Judge Sewall's much-quoted diary. A traveler named Burnaby tells of a similar offense of an English sea captain who was soundly whipped for kissing his wife on the street of a New England town on Sunday, and of his retaliation in kind, by a clever trick upon his chastisers; but Burnaby's narrative always seemed to me of dubious credibility.

Abundant proof can be given that the act of the legislature in 1649 was not a dead letter which ordered that "whosoever shall prophane the Lords daye by doeing any seruill worke or such like abusses shall forfeite for euery such default ten shillings or be whipt."

The Vermont "Blue Book" contained equally sharp "Sunday laws." Whoever was guilty of any rude, profane, or unlawful conduct on the Lord's Day, in words or action, by clamorous discourses, shouting, hallooing, screaming, running, riding, dancing, jumping, was to be fined forty shillings and whipped upon the naked back not to exceed ten stripes. The New Haven code of laws, more severe still, ordered that "Profanation of the Lord's Day shall be punished by fine, imprisonment, or corporeal punishment; and if proudly, and with a high hand against the authority of God—*with death.*"

Lists of arrests and fines for walking and traveling unnecessarily on the Sabbath might be given in great numbers, and it was specially ordered that none should "ride violently to and from meeting." Many a pious New Englander, in olden days, was fined for his ungodly pride, and his desire to "show off" his "new colt" as he "rode violently" up to the meetinghouse green on Sabbath morn. One offender explained in excuse of his unnecessary driving on the Sabbath that he had been to visit a sick relative, but his excuse was not accepted. A Maine man who was rebuked and fined for "unseemingly walking" on the Lord's Day protested that he ran to save a man from drowning. The court made him pay his fine, but ordered that the money should be returned to him when he could prove by witnesses that he had been on that errand of mercy and duty. As late as the year 1831, in Lebanon, Connecticut, a lady journeying to her father's home was arrested within sight of her father's house for unnecessary traveling on the Sabbath; and a long and fiercely contested lawsuit was the result, and damages were finally given for false imprisonment. In 1720 Samuel Sabin complained of himself before a justice in Norwich that he visited on Sabbath night some relatives at a neighbor's house. His morbidly tender conscience smote him and made him "fear he had transgressed the law," though he felt sure no harm had been done thereby. In 1659 Sam Clarke, for "Hankering about on men's gates on

Sabbath evening to draw company out to him," was reproved and warned not to "harden his neck" and be "wholly destroyed." Poor stiff-necked, lonely, "hankering" Sam! to be so harshly reproved for his harmlessly sociable intents. Perhaps he "hankered" after the Puritan maids, and if so, deserved his reproof and the threat of annihilation.

Sabbath breaking by visiting abounded in staid Worcester town to a most base extent, but was severely punished, as local records show. In Belfast, Maine, in 1776, a meeting was held to get the "Town's Mind" with regard to a plan to restrain visiting on the Sabbath. The time had passed when such offenses could be punished either by fine or imprisonment, so it was voted "that if any person makes unnecessary Vizits on the Sabeth, They shall be Look't on with Contempt." This was the universal expression throughout the Puritan colonies; and looked on with contempt are Sabbath breakers and Sabbath slighters in New England to the present day.

Even if they committed no active offense, the colonists could not passively neglect the church and its duties. Of course, the Quakers contributed liberally to the support of the court, and were fined in great numbers for refusing to attend the church which they hated, and which also warmly abhorred them; and they were zealously set in the stocks, and whipped and caged and pilloried as well—whipped if they came and expressed any dissatisfaction, and whipped if they stayed away.

Severe and explicit were the orders with regard to the use of the "Creature called Tobacko" on the Sabbath. In the very earliest days of the colony means had been taken to prevent the planting of the pernicious weed except in very small quantities "for meere necessitie, for phisick, for preseruaceon of health, and that the same be taken privatly by auncient men." In Connecticut a man could by permission of the law smoke once if he went on a journey of ten miles (as some slight solace for the arduous trip), but never more than once a day, and never in another man's house. Let us hope that on their lonely journeys they conscientiously obeyed the law, though we can but suspect that the one unsocial smoke may have been a long one. In some communities the colonists could not plant tobacco, nor buy it, nor sell it, but since they loved the fascinating weed then as men love it now, they somehow invoked or spirited it into their pipes, though they never could smoke it in public unfined and unpunished. The shrewd and thrifty New Haven people permitted the raising of it for purposes of trade, though not for use, this supplying the "devil's weed" to others, chiefly the godless Dutch, but piously spurning it themselves—

in public. Its use was absolutely forbidden under any circumstances on the Sabbath within two miles of the meetinghouse, which (since at that date all the homes were clustered around the church green) was equivalent to not smoking it at all on the Lord's Day, if the law were obeyed. But wicked backsliders existed, poor slaves of habit, who were in Duxbury fined ten shillings for each offense, and in Portsmouth, not only were fined, but to their shame be it told, set as jailbirds in the Portsmouth cage. In Sandwich and in Boston the fine for "drinking tobacco in the meetinghouse" was five shillings for each drink, which I take to mean chewing tobacco rather than smoking it; many men were fined for thus drinking, and solacing the weary hours, though doubtless they were as sly and kept themselves as unobserved as possible. Four Yarmouth men—old sea dogs, perhaps, who loved their pipe—were, in 1687, fined four shillings each for smoking tobacco around the end of the meetinghouse. Silly, ostrich-brained Yarmouth men! to fancy to escape detection by hiding around the corner of the church; and to think that the tithingman had no nose when he was so Argus-eyed.

Not content with strict observance of the Sabbath day alone, the Puritans included Saturday evening in their holy day, and in the first colonial years these instructions were given to Governor Endicott by the New England Plantation Company: "And to the end that the Sabeth may be celebrated in a religious man ner wee appoint that all may surcease their labor every Satterday throughout the yeare at three of the clock in the afternoone, and that they spend the rest of the day in chatechizing and preparaceon for the Sabeth as the minister shall direct." Cotton Mather wrote thus of his grandfather, old John Cotton: "The Sabbath he begun the evening before, for which keeping from evening to evening he wrote arguments before his coming to New England, and I suppose 'twas from his reason and practice that the Christians of New England have generally done so too." He then tells of the protracted religious services held in the Cotton household every Saturday night—services so long that the Sabbath-day exercises must have seemed in comparison like a light interlude.

John Norton described these Cotton Sabbaths more briefly thus: "He (John Cotton) began the Sabbath at evening; therefore then performed family-duty after supper, being longer than ordinary in Exposition. After which he catechized his children and servants and then returned unto his study. The morning following, family-worship being ended, he retired into his study until the bell called him away. Upon his return from meeting he returned again into his study (the place of his labor and prayer) unto his private devotion; where, having a small repast carried him up for his dinner, he continued until the tolling of the bell. The public service being over, he withdrew for a space to his pre-mentioned oratory for his sacred addresses to God, as in the forenoon, then came down, *repeated the sermon in the family*, prayed, after supper sang a Psalm, and towards bedtime betaking himself again to his study he closed the day with prayer. Thus he spent the Sabbath continually." Just fancy the Cotton children and servants listening to his long afternoon sermon a second time!

All the New England clergymen were rigid in the prolonged observance of Sunday. From sunset on Saturday until Sunday night they would not shave, have rooms swept nor beds made, have food prepared, nor cooking utensils and tableware washed. As soon as their Sabbath began they gathered their families and servants around them, as did Cotton, and read the Bible and exhorted and prayed and recited the catechism until nine o'clock, usually by the light of one small "dip candle" only; on long winter Saturdays it must have been gloomy and tedious indeed. Small wonder that one minister wrote back to England that he found it difficult in the new colony to get a servant who *"enjoyed catechizing and family duties."* Many clergymen deplored sadly the custom which grew in later years of driving, and even transacting business, on Saturday night. Mr. Bushnell used to call it "stealing the time of the Sabbath," and refused to countenance it in any way.

It was very generally believed in the early days of New England that special judgments befell those who worked on the eve of the Sabbath. Winthrop gives the case of a man who, having hired help to repair a milldam, worked an hour on Saturday after sunset to finish what he had intended for the day's labor. The next day his little child, being left alone for some hours, was drowned in an uncovered well in the cellar of his house. "The father freely, in open congregation, did acknowledge it the righteous hand of God for his profaning his holy day."

Visitors and travelers from other countries were forced to obey the rigid laws with regard to Saturday-night observance. Archibald Henderson, the master of a vessel which entered the port of Boston, complained to the Council for Foreign Plantations in London that while he was in sober Boston town, being ignorant of the laws of the land, and having walked half an hour after sunset on Saturday night, as punishment for this unintentional and trivial offense, a constable entered his lodgings, seized him by the hair of his head, and dragged him to prison.

The Puritans found in Scripture support for this observance of Saturday night, in these words, "The evening and the morning were the first day," and they had many followers in their belief. In New England country towns to this day, descendants of the Puritans regard Saturday night, though in a modified way, as almost Sunday, and that evening is never chosen for any kind of gay gathering or visiting. As late as 1855 the shops in Hartford were never open for customers upon Saturday night.

Sunday night, being shut out of the Sabbath hours, became in the eighteenth century a time of general cheerfulness and often merrymaking. This sudden transition from the religious calm and quiet of the afternoon to the noisy gaiety of the evening was very trying to many of the clergymen, especially to Jonathan Edwards, who preached often and sadly against "Sabbath evening dissipations and mirth-making." In some communities singing schools were held on Sunday nights, which afforded a comparatively decorous and orderly manner of spending the close of the day.

Sweet to the Pilgrims and to their descendants was the hush of their calm Saturday night, and their still, tranquil Sabbath—sign and token to them, not only of the weekly rest ordained in the creation, but of the eternal rest to come. The universal quiet and peace of the community showed the primitive instinct of a pure, simple devotion, the sincere religion which knew no compromise in spiritual things, no halfway obedience to God's Word, but rested absolutely on the Lord's Day—as was commanded. No work, no play, no idle strolling was known; no sign of human life or motion was seen except the necessary care of the patient cattle and other dumb beasts, the orderly and quiet going to and from the meeting, and at the nooning, a visit to the churchyard to stand by the side of the silent dead. This absolute obedience to the letter as well as to the spirit of God's Word was one of the most typical traits of the character of the Puritans, and appeared to them to be one of the most vital points of their religion.

From: Alice Morse Earle, *The Sabbath in Puritan New England* (New York: Charles Scribner's Sons, 1891).

· Religions ·
(Various)

Theology from New York's Chinatown
(Chinese)

Confucianism

There is a disciple of Confucius among them who assembles as many of the faithful as he can gather on Sunday afternoons in the halls of the Chong Wah Gong Shaw and discourses to them on the teachings of their master; exhorting them to perseverance in the faith. This man's name is Chi Kai Pik, one of the secretaries of the Chinese consulate. His topics sound very queer to outsiders. Thus he has given a series of three discourses, the topics of which were:

1. "*Kut Pot ching, pot shak*" (Not cut squarely, I shall not eat).
2. "*Pot she, pot shak, pot*" (Not in season, I shall not eat).
3. "*Tuck ke tsou, pot shak*" (Without sauce, I shall not eat).

The word used to mean "squarely" implies honesty. *Season* implies time and circumstances, a clear conscience. *"Tsou"* means, literally, "sauce"; but as used here implies grace. Thus it can be readily seen that under these hyperbolic titles a vast deal of substantial truth and sound moral principle can be conveyed. And that is far more profitable and elevating than prostrating oneself before a wooden image or a hideous daub and appealing to it for help in gambling or guidance in the purchase of human flesh for beastly uses. The two are radically antagonistic. The one possesses a smattering of religion—moral improvement; the other is debasing, demoralizing, and utterly devoid of any religious flavor. The expenses of this weekly Confucian service are defrayed by the Chinese government through its minister at Washington.

Buddhism

According to Buddhist belief, when a man dies he is immediately born again, or appears in a new shape, and the same shape may, according to his merit or demerit, be any of the innumerable order of beings composing the Buddhist universe, from a clog to a divinity. If his demerit would be sufficiently punished by a degraded earthly existence—in the form, for instance, of a woman or a slave; of a persecuted or disgusting animal; of a plant, or even a piece of inorganic matter—he will be born in some one of the 136 Buddhist hells situated in the interior of the earth. These places of punishment have a regular gradation in the intensity of the suffering and in the length of time the sufferer lives, the least term of life being ten million years; the longer terms being almost beyond the power of notation to express.

A meritorious life, on the other hand, secures the next birth either in an exalted and happy position on earth, or as a blessed spirit or even divinity in one of the many heavens in which the least duration of life is about ten billion years. But however long the life, whether of misery or bliss, it has an end, and at its close the individual must be born again, and may again be either happy or miserable, either a god or, it may be, the vilest animate object.

This system, it will be observed, recognizes a superior power, and also a future state of reward and punishment for deeds done in the body. More strictly, it is said to be a belief binding the spiritual nature of man to a supernatural being on whom he is conscious that he is dependent; also the practice that springs out of the recognition of such relations, including the personal life and experience, the doctrine, the duties, and rites founded on it. More generally and more comprehensively, while it means any system of faith and worship, it implies essentially a belief in a superior power or powers governing the world, and the worship of such power or powers, and the practice in life of what, by those authorities, are pronounced virtues.

Joss

Thus it is that the American people look upon the so-called Joss House of every Chinatown as a house of worship under one or the other of those forms of belief. It is no such thing. It is an innovation—rather, a fraud. And, by the way, it is as well to note here as elsewhere, that the name or title, "Joss," is not Chinese, but a pigeon-English word invented to signify the image worshipped, or possibly it is a corruption of the Portuguese "*deos*"—God.

The Chinese, having forgotten the high moral principle inculcated by

Confucius, and not comprehending the transcendentalism of either Buddha or Lao-Tzu, their accepted and avowed religious teachers, have set up a religion of their own, differing from either, having only ignorance and superstition for its base, and immorality for its sheet anchor. This monstrosity or travesty on religion recognizes "gods many and lords many." The image is in itself the god, not a mere representation of him. Though a divinity he is not a supreme being. It is perfectly competent and usual for any colony or company of Chinamen to set up any divinity they please, only it must be some departed being endowed with some particular claim to merit and virtue from the Chinese standpoint. Thus "Chinese Gordon," the soldier of fortune, originally of the British Army, then a leader of the government forces in China in the suppression of the Taiping Rebellion, and later a victim of Mahdist violence in Egypt, is now a "Joss" in Chinatown.

Other josses represent departed Chinamen of alleged standing, or mythological persons of antiquity endowed with some particular virtue, or vice, for the code of these strange people recognizes but little distinction between the two elements. Monsters conspicuous in legend only for their depravity or the general viciousness of their lives, are deified as unquestionably as the purest characters in Chinese history. When a god is required to serve the purposes of any particular trade, profession, or vocation, one is readily found in the musty annals of the Mongolian race, is hewed out of a block of wood, or fabricated from other materials by clever workmen, and is set up in a convenient place to receive the worship of those in need of his services.

Another point illustrating the absence of any religious element among these people is that, though they claim these images to be gods and make their prayers to and incense before them, they do not pray for forgiveness of sins, for help to lead better lives, or for a happy future existence, but solely for material prosperity in the present life and for aid in immediately impending enterprises. The gambler prays for luck, the merchant for success in business, the highbinder for assistance in crimes; the young man for aid in securing a wife; the farmer for a good crop; the prostitute for abundant patronage; and so on through the whole range of human wants, whether good or bad. If a Chinaman wants to secure a fortune by a lottery drawing he appeals to Joss to help him. Another is encumbered with female offspring, and he calls upon joss to aid in disposing of them. One has committed a serious crime, and asks for deliverance from its consequences. This one has a quarrel on his hands, and prays for aid in killing his enemy. And all these are equally devout and alike representatives of the "religion" of China.

That religion has no Sunday or holy day. With its adherents one day is as good as another, and Joss is ever ready to receive the prayers and offerings of his worshippers. There is no sacredness about his dwelling place; he sits as comfortably in one place as in another, and smiles as benignantly amid clouds of opium smoke, the rivalries of a commercial rendezvous, and the orgies of a vile resort where human passions have full sway, or under the gaze of a company of mere idle and curious sightseers. Nor is he at all proud and consequential. He requires no priestly intercessor between his motley worshippers and himself, nor does he call for the services of ministers or preachers to exalt his virtues and bring men to his feet. He is ever ready—for a suitable consideration—to give immediate audience to whoever wishes to approach his awful presence and proffer petitions, whether they are highborn or lowly, educated or ignorant, saints or sinners. The red-handed murderer catches his ear as readily as does the innocent victim of violence and wrong.

Joss usually sits enthroned upon a platform or dais surrounded with more or less gaudy hangings and drapings, according to the ability of those under whose patronage he may be to provide them. Essentials of his outfit are a basin filled with sand for holding the burning sticks of incense and a prayer box. The latter is a cylindrical vessel of wood, perhaps twelve inches in height and six inches in diameter. It is filled with wooden strips slightly longer than the box itself, having an oval-shaped end. These strips are about an eighth of an inch thick, and from a half to three-quarters of an inch in width. They are all inscribed with Chinese characters which form ready-made prayers or the use of the worshippers. There is a human attendant, though having no priestly character or office. His business is to keep the place in order and to supply the customers with the essentials for their worship. These consist of a half dozen sticks of highly perfumed punk to serve as incense, two red candles, and sundry strips of papers. The whole outfit, at wholesale prices, could not cost more than four cents, but is sold to the worshipper for fifty cents. It must be purchased on the spot and at the established price, or that particular joss will decline to be interviewed.

The mode of worship is interesting, but can be best comprehended by watching the movements of the worshipper. Here, for instance, comes a laundryman who has faith in lotteries and is looking for a fortune from that source. He approaches with his half dollar, which he understandingly gives to the janitor or attendant, and receives in return the requisite outfit. He then lights his red candles and sticks of incense and places them in the bowl or basin of sand in front of Joss. Then he kneels and offers his prayer, which in English would be about this:

> Oh, thou great Joss, thou art greater than all other gods in the universe. Your clear head and your bright genius is able to indicate the winning numbers in this slip (showing lottery ticket) which I am going to play tonight in Wing Chong Chin Company at 11 Mott Street. If you bless me with eight spots of winning on my slip I, Sing Lee, will repay your blessing with a large roasted pig, a chicken, cakes of every variety, all the fruits of the season, firecrackers by the thousands, and paper money by the millions.

He then takes up the prayer box, which in this case contains one hundred sticks, each stick containing one character or number, and shakes it thoroughly until one stick falls out. Whatever number happens to be on this stick he accepts as Joss's indications of the winning number he is to play, and hurries away to the lottery shop to invest his money on that number—and lose it.

Now you observe the devotions of Mr. Lee Wah Sing, an earnest young man who is anxious to purchase a certain young girl for a concubine. He approaches Joss in the same manner as did Sing Lee, having obtained from the attendant a similar outfit. In addition he must have in writing the name of the girl who is for sale, her age, birthday, the town of her nativity, and the necessary data for her identification. He then lights incense sticks, kneels, and makes his prayer, beginning with a like fulsome laudation of Joss's powers, asking his aid in securing the girl he wants, and promises similar generous returns as did Sing Lee. He then takes the prayer box, the numbers in which in this case correspond to certain numbers and verses in a prayer book, which the attendant hands him free of charge after having paid fifty cents for his incense. If he finds that the indicated verse in the prayer book is favorable to his amorous wish he takes his girl and pays for her. But if the answer is unfavorable he drops her and goes in pursuit of another.

Here comes a man who wants to consult Joss in regard to the purchase of a certain laundry. He goes through the same preliminaries as the others, but does not make use of the prayer box. Instead he is supplied with two kidney-shaped pieces of wood. One side of each of these pieces is designated head and the other tail. After he has called upon Joss in the general terms of his predecessors, he tosses the two pieces of wood up. If they fall with two heads it means pretty good; if one head and one tail, very good; if two tails, the meaning is very bad. His negotiations for the laundry will be governed by these indications of the estimate Joss puts upon the business.

All Chinatown was greatly excited during the early part of the present year because of the prevalence of sickness among its denizens. Immediately after the Chinese New Year, January 27, there were more than twenty deaths. Nearly every day Chinamen of more or less distinction died.

At the beginning of the new year the mayor of Chinatown, according to custom, makes an official devotion to the joss enthroned at headquarters. He did so this year, and on taking the praying machine shook out stick number ten, which indicated this prophecy in the book of prophecies, meaning, according to Chinese lore, that sickness and death would prevail throughout the year in Chinatown. The translated prophecy reads:

> At time of sickness life lingers around;
> Why break the roof or chain the turtle?
> Strict obedience is sure to reign,
> But trust in Joss and Buddha is the only remedy.

This is much more like a religious act than the illustrations that precede it. But all alike show the basis of superstition and ignorance upon which the structure stands. Its absolute distinction from Buddhism or Taoism is manifest. It has nothing in common with either, though is doubtless an outgrowth of both systems, tinctured somewhat with Confucianism, the foundation of which is filial respect and duty, which might well lead to ancestral worship. But as practiced, the so-called religion calls for no worship, and none such is performed. What passes for worship is a mere superstitious invocation of assistance in impending need or distress. Nothing beyond the immediate temporal or sensual requirements of the devotee is even thought of. There is no adoration of the pretended divinity; no manifestation of repentance for sins or a desire for a holier life; no recogni-

tion of a future state of rewards or punishments. The same god is recognized and appealed to by the vilest or the most virtuous person.

From: Louis J. Beck, *New York's Chinatown* (New York: Bohemia Publishing Co., 1898).

The Minister's Wood-Spell
(English)

It was in the winter of this next year that the minister's "wood-spell"
was announced.

"What is a wood-spell?" you say. Well, the pastor was settled on the
understanding of receiving two hundred dollars a year and his wood; and
there was a certain day set apart in the winter, generally in the time of
the best sleighing, when every parishioner brought the minister a sledload
of wood; and thus, in the course of time, built him up a mighty woodpile.

It was one of the great seasons of preparation in the minister's family,
and Tina, Harry, and I had been busy for two or three days beforehand,
in helping Esther create the wood-spell cake, which was to be made in
quantities large enough to give ample slices to every parishioner. Two
days beforehand, the fire was besieged with a row of earthen pots, in
which the spicy compound was rising to the necessary lightness, and Harry
and I split incredible amounts of oven wood, and in the evening we sat
together stoning raisins round the great kitchen fire, with Mr. Avery in
the midst of us, telling us stories and arguing with us, and entering into
the hilarity of the thing like a boy. He was so happy in Esther, and
delighted to draw the shy color into her cheeks, by some sly joke or
allusion, when Harry's head of golden curls came into close proximity
with her smooth black satin tresses.

The cake came out victorious, and we all claimed the merit of it; and
a mighty cheese was bought, and every shelf of the closet, and all the
dressers of the kitchen, were crowded with the abundance.

We had a jewel of a morning—one of those sharp, clear, sunny winter
days, when the sleds squeak over the flinty snow, and the little icicles
tingle along on the glittering crust as they fall from the trees, and the
breath of the slow-pacing oxen steams up like a rosy cloud in the morning
sun, and then falls back condensed in little icicles on every hair.

We were all astir early, full of life and vigor. There was a holiday in the academy. Mr. Rossiter had been invited over to the minister's to chat and tell stories with the farmers, and give them high entertainment. Miss Nervy Randall, more withered and wild in her attire than usual, but eminently serviceable, stood prepared to cut cake and cheese without end, and dispense it with wholesome nods and messages of comfort. The minister himself heated two little old andirons red-hot in the fire, and therewith from time to time stirred up a mighty bowl of flip, which was to flow in abundance to every comer. Not then had the temperance reformation dawned on America, though ten years later Mr. Avery would as soon have been caught in a gambling saloon as stirring and dispensing a bowl of flip to his parishioners.

Mr. Avery had recently preached a highly popular sermon on agriculture, in which he set forth the dignity of the farmer's life, from the text, "For the king himself is served of the field"; and there had been a rustle of professional enthusiasm in all the mountain farms around, and it was resolved, by a sort of general consent, that the minister's woodpile this year should be of the best: none of your old makeshifts—loads made out with crooked sticks and snapping chestnut logs, most noisy, and destructive to good wives' aprons. Good straight shagbark hickory was voted none too good for the minister. Also the ax was lifted up on many a proud oak and beech and maple. What destruction of glory and beauty there was in those mountain regions! How ruthlessly man destroys in a few hours that which centuries cannot bring again!

What an idea of riches in those glorious woodland regions! We read legends of millionnaires who fed their fires with cinnamon and rolled up thousand-dollar bills into lamplighters, in the very wantonness of profusion. But what was that compared to the prodigality which fed our great roaring winter fires on the thousand-leafed oaks, whose conception had been ages ago—who were children of the light and of the day—every fragment and fiber of them made of most-celestial influences, of sunshine and raindrops, and nightdews and clouds, slowly working for centuries until they had wrought the wondrous shape into a gigantic miracle of beauty? And then snuffling old Heber Atwood, with his two hard-fisted boys, cut one down in a forenoon and made logs of it for the minister's woodpile. If this isn't making light of serious things, we don't know what is. But think of your wealth, O ye farmers!—think what beauty and glory every year perish to serve your cooking stoves and chimney corners.

To tell the truth, very little of such sentiment was in Mr. Avery's mind

or in any of ours. We lived in a woodland region, and we were *blasé* with
the glory of trees. We did admire the splendid elms that hung their
cathedral arches over the one central street of Cloudland Village, and on
this particular morning they were all aflame like Aladdin's palace, hanging
with emeralds and rubies and crystals, flashing and glittering and dancing
in the sunlight. And when the first sled came squeaking up the village
street, we did not look upon it as the funereal hearse bearing the honored
corpse of a hundred summers, but we boys clapped our hands and shouted,
"Hurrah for old Heber!" as his load of magnificent oak, well-bearded with
gray moss, came scrunching into the yard. Mr. Avery hastened to draw
the hot flip-iron from the fire and stir the foaming bowl. Esther began
cutting the first loaf of cake, and Mr. Rossiter walked out and cracked a
joke on Heber's shoulder, whereat all the cast-iron lineaments of his hard
features relaxed. Heber had not the remotest idea at this moment that
he was to be branded as a tree murderer. On the contrary, if there was
anything for which he valued himself, and with which his heart was at
this moment swelling with victorious pride, it was his power of cutting
down trees. Man he regarded in a physical point of view as principally
made to cut down trees, and trees as the natural enemies of man. When
he stood under a magnificent oak, and heard the airy rustle of its thousand
leaves, to his ear it was always a rustle of defiance, as if the old oak had
challenged him to single combat; and Heber would feel of his ax and say,
"Next winter, old boy, we'll see—we'll see!" And at this moment he and
his two tall, slab-sided, big-handed boys came into the kitchen with an
uplifted air, in which triumph was but just repressed by suitable modesty.
They came prepared to be complimented, and they were complimented
accordingly.

"Well, Mr. Atwood," said the minister, "you must have had pretty hard
work on that load; that's no ordinary oak; it took strong hands to roll
those logs, and yet I don't see but two of your boys. Where are they
all now?"

"Scattered, scattered!" said Heber, as he sat with a great block of cake
in one hand, and sipped his mug of flip, looking, with his grizzly beard
and shaggy hair and his iron features, like a cross between a polar bear
and a man—a very shrewd, thoughtful, reflective polar bear, however,
quite up to any sort of argument with a man.

"Yes, they're scattered," he said. "We're putty lonesome now 't our house. Nobody there but Pars, Dass, Dill, Noah, and 'Liakim. I ses to Noah and 'Liakim this mornin', 'Ef we had all our boys to hum, we sh'd haf to take up two loads to the minister, sartin, to make it fair on the wood-spell cake.' "

"Where are your boys now?" said Mr. Avery. "I haven't seen them at meeting now for a good while."

"Wal, Sol and Tim's gone up to Umbagog, lumberin'; and Tite, he's sailed to Archangel; and Jeduth, he's gone to th' West Injies for molasses; and Pete, he's gone to the West. Folks begins to talk now 'bout that 'ere Western kentry, and so Pete, he must go to Buffalo, and see the great West. He's writ back about Niagry Falls. His letters is most amazin'. The old woman, she can't feel easy 'bout him no way. She insists 'pon it them Injuns'll scalp him. The old woman is just as choice of her boys as ef she hadn't got just es many es she has."

"How many sons have you?" said Harry, with a countenance of innocent wonder.

"Wal," said Heber, "I've seen the time when I had fourteen good, straight boys—all on 'em a turnin' over a log together."

"Dear me!" said Tina. "Hadn't you any daughters?"

"Gals?" said Heber, reflectively. "Bless you, yis. There's been a gal or two 'long, in between, here an' there—don't jest remember where they come; but anyway, there's plenty of womenfolks 't our house."

"Why?" said Tina, with a toss of her pretty head, "you don't seem to think much of women."

"Good in their way," said Heber, shaking his head; "but Adam was fust formed, and then Eve, you know." Looking more attentively at Tina as she stood bridling and dimpling before him, like a bird just ready to fly, Heber conceived an indistinct idea that he must say something gallant, so he added, "Give all honor to the women, as weaker vessels, ye know; that's sound doctrine, I s'pose."

Heber having now warmed and refreshed himself, and endowed his minister with what he conceived to be a tip-top, irreproachable load of wood, proceeded, also, to give him the benefit of a little good advice, prefaced by gracious words of encouragement. "I wus tellin' my old woman this mornin' that I didn't grudge a cent of my subscription, 'cause your preachin' lasts well and pays well. Ses I, 'Mr. Avery ain't the kind of man that strikes twelve the fust time. He's a man that'll wear.' That's what I said fust, and I've followed y' up putty close in yer preachin'; but then I've jest got one word to say to ye. Ain't free agency a gettin' a leetle too top-heavy in yer preachin'? Ain't it kind o' overgrowin' sovereignty? Now, ye see, divine sovereignty hes got to be took care of as well as free agency. That's all, that's all. I thought I'd jest drop the thought, ye know, and leave you to think on 't. This 'ere last revival you run along considerable on 'Whosoever will may come,' an' all that. Now, p'r'aps, ef you'd jest tighten up the ropes a leetle t'other side, and give 'em sovereignty, the hull load would sled easier."

"Well," said Mr. Avery, "I'm much obliged to you for your suggestions."

"Now there's my wife's brother, Josh Baldwin," said Heber; "he was delegate to the last consociation, and he heerd your openin' sermon, and ses he to me, ses he, 'Your minister sartin doos slant a leetle toward th' Arminians; he don't quite walk the crack,' Josh says, ses he. Ses I, 'Josh, we ain't none on us perfect; but,' ses I, 'Mr. Avery ain't no Arminian, I can tell you. Yeh can't judge Mr. Avery by one sermon,' ses I. 'You hear him preach the year round, and ye'll find that all the doctrines gits their place.' Ye see I stood up for ye, Mr. Avery, but I thought 't wouldn't do no harm to kind o' let ye know what folks is sayin'."

Here the theological discussion was abruptly cut short by Deacon Zachary Chipman's load, which entered the yard amid the huzzahs of the boys. Heber and his boys were at the door in a minute. "Wal, railly, ef the deacon hain't come down with his shagbark! Wal, Wal, the revival has operated on him some, I guess. Last year the deacon sent a load that I'd ha' been ashamed to had in my backyard, an' I took the liberty o' tellin' on him so. Good, straight-grained shagbark. Wal, wal! I'll go out an' help him onload it. Ef that 'ere holds out to the bottom, the deacon's done putty wal, an' I shall think grace *has* made some progress."

The deacon, a mournful, dry, shivery-looking man, with a little round bald head, looking wistfully out of a great red comforter, all furry and white with the sharp frosts of the morning, and with his small red eyes weeping tears through the sharpness of the air, looked as if he had come as chief mourner at the hearse of his beloved hickory trees. He had cut down the very darlings of his soul, and come up with his precious load, impelled by a divine impulse like that which made the lowing kine, in the Old Testament story, come slowly bearing the ark of God, while their brute hearts were turning toward the calves that they had left at home. Certainly, if virtue is in proportion to sacrifice, Deacon Chipman's load of hickory had more of self-sacrifice in it than a dozen loads from old Heber; for Heber was a forest prince in his way of doing things, and, with all his shrewd calculations of money's worth, had an openhanded generosity of nature that made him take a pride in liberal giving.

The little man shrank mournfully into a corner, and sipped his tumbler of flip and ate his cake and cheese as if he had been at a funeral.

"How are you all at home, deacon?" said Mr. Avery, heartily.

"Just crawlin', thank you—just crawlin'. My old woman don't git out much; her rheumatiz gits a dreadful strong hold on her; and, Mr. Avery, she hopes you'll be round to visit her 'fore long. Since the revival she's kind o' fell into darkness, and don't see no cheerin' views. She ses sometimes the universe ain't nothin' but blackness and darkness to her."

"Has she a good appetite?" said Mr. Avery.

"Wal, no. She don't enjoy her vittles much. Some say she's got the jaunders. I try to cosset her up, and git her to take relishin' things. I tell her ef she'd eat a good sassage for breakfast of a cold mornin', with a good hearty bit o' mince pie, and a cup o' strong coffee, 't would kind o' set her up for the day; but, somehow, she don't git no nourishment from her food."

"There, Rossiter," we heard Mr. Avery whisper aside, "you see what a country minister has to do—give cheering views to a dyspeptic that breakfasts on sausage and mince pies."

And now the loads began coming thick and fast. Sometimes two and three, and sometimes four and five, came stringing along, one after another, in unbroken procession. For every one Mr. Avery had an appreciative word. Its especial points were noticed and commended, and the farmers themselves, shrewdest observers, looked at every load and gave it their verdict. By and by the kitchen was full of a merry, chatting circle, and Mr. Rossiter and Mr. Avery were telling their best stories, and roars of laughter came from the house.

Tina glanced in and out among the old farmers, like a bright tropical bird, carrying the cake and cheese to each one, laughing and telling stories, dispensing smiles to the younger ones—treacherous smiles, which meant nothing, but made the hearts beat faster under their shaggy coats; and if she saw a red-fisted fellow in a corner, who seemed to be having a bad time, she would go and sit down by him, and be so gracious and warming and winning that his tongue would be loosened, and he would tell her all about his steers and his calves and his last crop of corn, and his load of wood, and then wonder all the way home whether he should ever have, in a house of his own, a pretty little woman like that.

By afternoon the minister's woodpile was enormous. It stretched beyond anything before seen in Cloudland; it exceeded all the legends of neighboring woodpiles and wood-spells related by deacons and lay delegates in the late consociation. And truly, among things picturesque and graceful, among childish remembrances, dear and cheerful, there is nothing that more speaks to my memory than the dear, good old mossy woodpile. Harry, Tina, Esther, and I ran up and down and in and about the piles of wood that evening with a joyous satisfaction. How fresh and spicy and woodsy it smelt! I can smell now the fragrance of the hickory, whose clear, oily bark in burning cast forth perfume quite equal to cinnamon. Then there was the fragrant black birch, sought and prized by us all for the high-flavored bark on the smaller limbs, which was a favorite species of confectionary to us. There were also the logs of white birch, gleaming up in their purity, from which we made sheets of woodland parchment.

It is recorded of one man who stands in a high position at Washington, that all his earlier writing lessons were performed upon leaves of the white birch bark, the only paper used in the family.

Then there were massive trunks of oak, veritable worlds of mossy vegetation in themselves, with tufts of green velvet nestled away in their bark, and sheets of greenness carpeting their sides, and little white, hoary trees of moss, with little white, hoary apples upon them, like miniature orchards.

One of our most interesting amusements was forming landscapes in the snow, in which we had mountains and hills and valleys, and represented streams of water by means of glass, and clothed the sides of our hills with orchards of apple trees made of this gray moss. It was an incipient practice at landscape gardening, for which we found rich material in the woodpile. Esther and Tina had been filling their aprons with these mossy treasures, for which we had all been searching together, and now we all sat chatting in the evening light. The sun was going down. The sleds had ceased to come, the riches of our woodland treasures were all in, the whole air was full of the trembling, rose-colored light that turned all the snow-covered landscape to brightness. All around us not a fence to be seen—nothing but waving hollows of spotless snow, glowing with the rosy radiance, and fading away in purple and lilac shadows; and the evening stars began to twinkle, one after another, keen and clear through the frosty air, as we all sat together in triumph on the highest perch of the woodpile. And Harry said to Esther, "One of these days they'll be bringing in our wood," and Esther's cheeks reflected the pink of the sky.

"Yes, indeed!" said Tina. "And then I am coming to live with you. I'm going to be an old maid, you know, and I shall help Esther as I do now. I never shall want to be married."

Just at this moment the ring of sleigh bells was heard coming up the street. Who and what now? A little one-horse sleigh drove swiftly up the door, the driver sprang out with a lively alacrity, hitched his horse, and came toward the house. In the same moment Tina and I recognized Ellery Davenport!

From: Harriet Beecher Stowe, *Oldtown Folks* (Boston: Osgood & Co., 1869).

PART II

Southern
Folktales

CHAPTER 8

Legends and Legendary Figures

· *The Little Finger* ·

(African)

Before we came here, poor devils, we were all free, we were not obliged to work for any master. It is the whites who came into our country, Africa, to get us. They stole some of us; they bought some of us from our fathers for a red handkerchief, a bottle of tafia, or an old gun. When we went to war those who were caught were sold to the whites who came to trade on the seacoast. We were led away, tied together, tied two by two; and when we reached the seacoast like a herd of cattle, men, women, and children, we were exchanged, not for money, but for any kind of merchandise, and the whites put us into ships and brought us here. This is how we became slaves in America.

When Manga, my grandmother, arrived at the seacoast, she saw a pretty little town with small houses. There were many ships, and they seemed to be dancing on the sea; some were going up, others down. It was the wind, you know, that was blowing and shaking up the sea. My poor grandmother, who was young then, was afraid when she saw they were putting all the Negroes on board the ships. She thought they were going to drown them in the sea. A white man came to her and bought her from her master. He took her to his house and told her in her own language: "I bought you to take care of my little boy." He had a pretty house with a store in it, and a pretty garden. Behind the house was an orange grove, and the trees were so large that there was a fine shade underneath. To show you how my grandmother's country was a good one, I will tell you that the orange trees were in bloom the whole year; there were flowers and little oranges and ripe oranges all the time. The house was near the sea, and every morning Manga took little Florimond to take a bath. The little boy was so pretty, and his father and mother were so good, that Manga would not have left them for anything in the world. She loved little Florimond so much; his hair was curly, his eyes were blue, his skin was white and rosy. Everybody adored the poor little boy, he was so pretty and smart. He could sing so well and imitate all birds so admirably that often they thought it was the nita that was singing in the trees. Nita is a little bird in Africa which sings at night when the moon is shining. It perches on the top of the tallest tree; and if there is a light breeze it sings better, for the swinging of the branch helps the little bird to sing, as the rocking of the hammock helps a man's lullaby. Florimond imitated the nita so well that everybody was mistaken, and it amused the boy very much.

Florimond's father used to trade with the Negroes that lived far in the woods, so one day he started to get gold dust and elephants' teeth. On leaving he said to Manga: "Take good care of my wife and my little boy. You know I gave you already a pair of shoes; I will give you, on my return, a fine dress and a necklace." The first time Manga put on her shoes they hurt her so much that she could hardly walk. She took them off on arriving at the house, and sat on the steps looking at her toes: "Wiggle, wiggle, poor things," she said, "you were in prison just now: You are free now, you are glad, is it not? Oh! I shall never shut you up again. I don't understand how white folks can put their toes in such things!" From that time Manga never put shoes on.

Well, the master went into the big woods, and three days afterwards the lady said to Manga to take Florimond to the sea and give him a bath. While the little boy was playing with the shells and the white sand, they saw a skiff with several persons come ashore. A white man disembarked, and passed by Manga, and she felt a peculiar sensation, as if some misfortune was to happen. The eyes of the man shone like those of a cat in the dark. As he passed, he said: "Good morning, Florimond," but the little boy did not reply anything. When they arrived home the lady sent them to play in the yard, and every time the master was away the strange man would come to the house. Florimond did not want to see him, and he said one day he would tell his father about the stranger. The latter said to Manga: "You little black imp, if ever you open your mouth about what you see here, I will cut your tongue with my big knife; then I will carry you to my ship, sew you up in a sack, and throw you into the sea for the fish to eat you." Manga was so frightened that she would not have said a word even if they had whipped her for a whole day. In the evening Florimond cried so much that it was with great difficulty that Manga succeeded in putting him to sleep. Her cot was near the bed of the little boy, and during the night she saw the pirate enter the room with a big stick. He struck the little boy on the head and said: "He is dead. I will put him in the hole which I dug in the yard. Now I must attend to the black girl."

Manga, however, had already run away into the yard; but the man, thinking that she was in the road, ran out to catch her. Florimond's mother came into the room, took the little boy's body in her arms, and buried him in a hole near the place where Manga was. She was not quite through with her ugly work, when she heard a noise and ran away. She met the man, who said: "I believe the girl has gone to the woods; we need not trouble about her anymore; the lions and tigers will soon eat her up. Now I must go on board my ship, and when I come back I will take you with me."

The lady went into the house, and Manga came out of her hiding place. She felt so weak that she could hardly stand, but before she left she kissed the ground where her dear little master was buried. She said: "Farewell, little angel," and ran into the woods. She preferred to stay with the wild animals than with the cruel mother.

After walking for some time as fast as she could, she stopped by a bayou in the wood, drank some water, and sat down to rest. She fell asleep, but soon she was awakened by loud talking. She saw some men standing around her, and among them was her master, who seemed to be very angry: "What are you doing here so far from my house? I left you to take care of my little boy. I suppose you did something wrong and ran away." Manga did not reply anything, because she remembered the threats of the pirate. The master ordered his men to bring her back to his house, and he hastened to go home. He found his wife, who was weeping bitterly, and she said to him: "Oh! what a dreadful misfortune! Manga let Florimond fall on his head, and our poor little boy is dead. I wanted to kill the Negress, but she ran away, and I don't know where she is. If ever I catch her I will strangle her with my own hands."

When the poor man heard that his dear boy was dead, he fell in a swoon. They put him in bed, and he remained fifteen days delirious. During that time the lady said to Manga that she would kill her if she opened her mouth. She shut the girl in a cabin, and gave her nothing but bread and water.

At last Florimond's father got out of bed, but he would not be consoled, and he wept all day for his little boy. As Manga was still in her prison, her master did not see her, and did not think of her. One day as he was walking about in the yard, he looked from time to time at his dear boy's grave, and tears flowed from his eyes. In the meantime the nita was singing on a tree nearby, and its song was so sad that the poor man felt more sad than ever. It seemed to him it was his Florimond who was singing, and he came to the grave and looked at it a long time. All at once the poor father thought he was dreaming. He saw something that was so strange that many people will not believe it; but so many people told me the same story, that I believe it is as sure as the sun is shining. When the lady had buried the little boy, she had not had time to cover the body completely, and one little hand was out of the grave, and it was the pretty little finger which was moving as if it was making a sign to call someone. The little finger moved on one side and then on the other, and never stopped beckoning, so to say. The poor father dug up the earth with his hand and uncovered the body. He found it as fresh as if it had just been buried, and he took it in his arms and carried it to the house. He put the boy on a bed and rubbed him so long that the child came back to consciousness. The father sent for a surgeon, who began to attend to the boy, and said that he would revive. There was no danger for his life, as the skull was not broken; the child was only in a state of lethargy, and would soon be well again. Indeed, in a few days Florimond was running about as if nothing had happened, but he never said anything about his mother and the stranger, and the lady at last allowed Manga to leave her prison. Remorse had taken hold of Florimond's mother; she grew thinner every day, and one evening, in spite of the most tender care, she died. Her last words were, "Oh! my God, forgive me!" She was buried in the grave where her little boy had been; and as to the pirate, he never came back. They say that he was hanged.

After his wife's death Florimond's father left Africa, and sold poor Manga. She was put upon a ship, and this is how she became a slave in Louisiana, and related to me the story of the little finger.

From: Alcee Fortier, *Louisiana Folk-Tales* (Boston and New York: Houghton Mifflin Co., 1895).

· *The True Story of Evangeline* ·

(Acadian)

Emmeline Labiche was an orphan whose parents had died when she was quite a child. I had taken her to my home, and had raised her as my own daughter. How sweet-tempered, how loving she was! She had grown to womanhood with all the attractions of her sex, and, although not a beauty in the sense usually given to that word, she was looked upon as the handsomest girl of St. Gabriel. Her soft, transparent hazel eyes mirrored her pure thoughts; her dark-brown hair waved in graceful undulations on her intelligent forehead, and fell in ringlets on her shoulders; her bewitching smile, her slender, symmetrical shape, all contributed to make her a most attractive picture of maiden loveliness.

Emmeline, who had just completed her sixteenth year, was on the eve of marrying a most deserving, laborious, and well-to-do young man of St. Gabriel, Louis Arceneaux. Their mutual love dated from their earliest years, and all agreed that Providence willed their union as man and wife, she the fairest young maiden, he the most deserving youth of St. Gabriel.

Their bans had been published in the village church, the nuptial day was fixed, and their long love dream was about to be realized, when the barbarous scattering of our colony took place.

Our oppressors had driven us to the seashore, where their ships rode at anchor, when Louis, resisting, was brutally wounded by them. Emmeline had witnessed the whole scene. Her lover was carried on board one of the ships, the anchor was weighed, and a stiff breeze soon drove the vessel out of sight. Emmeline, tearless and speechless, stood fixed to the spot, motionless as a statue, and when the white sail vanished in the distance, she uttered a wild, piercing shriek, and fell fainting to the ground.

When she came to, she clasped me in her arms, and in agony of grief, she sobbed piteously. "Mother, mother, she said, in broken words, "he is gone; they have killed him; what will become of me?"

I soothed her grief with endearing words until she wept freely. Gradually its violence subsided, but the sadness of her countenance betokened the sorrow that preyed on her heart, never to be contaminated by her love for another one.

Thus she lived in our midst, always sweet-tempered, but with such sadness depicted in her countenance, and with smiles so sorrowful, that we had come to look upon her as not of this earth, but rather as our guardian angel, and this is why we called her no longer Emmeline, but Evangeline, or God's little angel.

The sequel of her story is not gay, and my poor old heart breaks whenever I recall the misery of her fate.

Emmeline had been exiled to Maryland with me. She was, as I have told you, my adopted child. She dwelt with me, and she followed me in my long pilgrimage from Maryland to Louisiana. I shall not relate to you now the many dangers that beset us on our journey, and the many obstacles we had to overcome to reach Louisiana; this would be anticipating what remains for me to tell you. When we reached the Teche country, at the Poste des Attakapas, we found there the whole population congregated to welcome us. As we went ashore, Emmeline walked by my side, but seemed not to admire the beautiful landscape that unfolded itself to our gaze. Alas! it was of no moment to her whether she strolled on the poetical banks of the Teche, or rambled in the picturesque sites of Maryland. She lived in the past, and her soul was absorbed in the mournful regret of the past. For her, the universe had lost the prestige of its beauties, of its freshness, of its splendors. The radiance of her dreams was dimmed, and she breathed in an atmosphere of darkness and of desolation.

She walked beside me with a measured step. All at once, she grasped my hand, and, as if fascinated by some vision, she stood rooted to the spot. Her very heart's blood suffused her cheeks, and with the silvery tones of a voice vibrating with joy: "Mother! Mother!" she cried out, "it is he! It is Louis!" pointing to the tall figure of a man reclining under a large oak tree.

That man was Louis Arceneaux.

With the rapidity of lightning, she flew to his side, and in an ecstacy of joy: "Louis, Louis," said she, "I am your Emmeline, your long lost Emmeline! Have you forgotten me?"

Louis turned ashy pale and hung down his head, without uttering a word.

"Louis," said she, painfully impressed by her lover's silence and coldness, "why do you turn away from me? I am still your Emmeline, your betrothed, and I have kept pure and unsullied my plighted faith to you. Not a word of welcome, Louis?" she said, as the tears started to her eyes. "Tell me, do tell me that you love me still, and that the joy of meeting me has overcome you, and stifled your utterance."

Louis Arceneaux, with quivering lips and tremulous voice, answered: "Emmeline, speak not so kindly to me, for I am unworthy of you. I can love you no longer; I have pledged my faith to another. Tear from your heart the remembrance of the past, and forgive me," and with quick step, he walked away, and was soon lost to view in the forest.

Poor Emmeline stood trembling like an aspen leaf. I took her hand; it was icy cold. A deathly pallor had overspread her countenance, and her eye had a vacant stare.

"Emmeline, my dear girl, come," said I, and she followed me like a child. I clasped her in my arms. "Emmeline, my dear child, be comforted; there may yet be happiness in store for you.

"Emmeline, Emmeline," she muttered in an undertone, as if to recall that name, "who is Emmeline?" Then looking in my face with fearful shining eyes that made me shudder, she said in a strange, unnatural voice: "Who are you?" and turned away from me. Her mind was unhinged; this last shock had been too much for her broken heart; she was hopelessly insane.

How strange it is that beings, pure and celestial like Emmeline, should be the sport of fate, and be thus exposed to the shafts of adversity. Is it true, then, that the beloved of God are always visited by sore trials? Was it that Emmeline was too ethereal a being for this world, and that God would have her in his sweet paradise? It does not belong to us to solve this mystery and to scrutinize the decrees of Providence; we have only to bow submissive to his will.

Emmeline never recovered her reason, and a deep melancholy settled upon her. Her beautiful countenance was fitfully lightened by a sad smile which made her all the fairer. She never recognized anyone but me, and nestling in my arms like a spoiled child, she would give me the most endearing names. As sweet and as amiable as ever, everyone pitied and loved her.

When poor, crazed Emmeline strolled upon the banks of the Teche, plucking the wildflowers that strewed her pathway, and singing in soft tones some Acadian song, those that met her wondered why so fair and gentle a being should have been visited with God's wrath.

She spoke of Acadia and of Louis in such loving words, that no one could listen to her without shedding tears. She fancied herself still the girl of sixteen years, on the eve of marrying the chosen one of her heart, whom she loved with such constancy and devotion, and imagining that her marriage bells tolled from the village church tower, her countenance would brighten, and her frame trembled with ecstatic joy. And then, in a sudden transition from joy to despair, her countenance would change and, trembling convulsively, gasping, struggling for utterance, and pointing her finger at some invisible object, in shrill and piercing accents, she would cry out: "Mother, mother, he is gone; they have killed him; what will become of me?" And uttering a wild, unnatural shriek, she would fall senseless in my arms.

Sinking at last under the ravages of her mental disease, she expired in my arms without a struggle, and with an angelic smile on her lips.

She now sleeps in her quite grave, shadowed by the tall oak tree near the little church at the Poste des Attakapas, and her grave has been kept green and flower-strewn as long as I have been able to visit it. Ah! how sad was the fate of poor Emmeline, Evangeline, God's little angel.

From: Felix Voorhies, *Acadian Reminiscences* (Opelousas, LA: The Jacob News Depot Co., 1907).

· *Daniel Boone* ·

(English)

The larger part of the mountains and plateaus in western North Carolina was held by the Cherokee Indians, the fiercest of the Southern tribes, and that country was late in being settled. But some venturesome pioneers began to settle in the northernmost parts. Here, in what is now Watauga County, there came to live, in 1750, a family of Quakers by the name of Boone. There is still standing, near the county seat, the blackened stone chimney of the cabin of one of the sons, Daniel Boone, best known and most worthy representative of the hunters, explorers, and frontiersmen of that day. He well deserves the fame that has come down with his name. Though one of the most enterprising and tireless of frontiersmen, Daniel Boone, true to his Quaker training, was a peace-loving man. Daring oftentimes, but never reckless, modest and peaceable, but restless and enterprising, he kept ever in the van of the western settlers, until he died, at the age of eighty-six, on the other side of the Mississippi, still on the western border of civilization.

At the age of eighteen, Daniel Boone married his seventeen-year-old bride, and for seven years, pressed with the cares of a growing family, he played the perfect part of a quiet Quaker farmer, a life varied only by an occasional trip to the coastal towns as a wagoner and by the annual hunt that replenished the winter larder. But in 1759 the Cherokee Indians, who had watched with jealous eyes the steady encroachments of the whites upon their mountain lands, broke in upon the border settlements with tomahawk and torch, and times of blood, of unrest, and of adventure began.

Two years of war, in which Daniel Boone bore his part, bought peace from the conquered Cherokees. Boone had during this time become somewhat acquainted with the upper part of the Tennessee River country, and had made several hunting trips thither from his North Carolina home. It was on one of these trips, while gazing from a mountaintop upon a herd of buffalo beneath, that he is said to have exclaimed, "I am richer than the man mentioned in Scripture, who owned the cattle on a thousand hills: I own the wild beasts of more than a thousand valleys!" It is safe to say that, despite his Quaker training, he was unacquainted with the identity of the "man mentioned in Scripture," or he would scarcely have made such a boast; but the exclamation reveals his delight in the wild and wide freedom which the wilderness gave him.

In May 1769, Boone, with five neighbors and a trapper guide, John Finley, undertook the journey to Kentucky through Cumberland Gap, famed as the great gateway for Indian war and hunting parties, and for settlers' caravans and armies yet to come.

Then begins the most romantic portion of Boone's life. Sometimes alone, sometimes with but one companion, sometimes with more, hunting, watching, dodging Indian war parties, once captured and hardly escaping with life, after two years he returned home to bring his family from the Yadkin to the bluegrass country. In 1773 a company started with him, including his own and several other families, among them the first women to dare the dangers of the journey to the plains of Kentucky. But the party was stopped by an Indian attack in the upper valley of the Tennessee, a circumstance which decided his more timid companions to remain for a while where they were, in the midst of the mountain settlements. It was nearly two years before Boone saw his family, with some others, settled in the bluegrass of Kentucky. With this event he passes for the most part out of the life of the mountains.

From: Arthur W. Spaulding, *The Men of the Mountains* (Nashville: Southern Publishing, 1915).

· Davy Crockett ·

(English)

While on the subject of election matters, I will just relate a little anecdote about myself, which will show the people to the east how we manage these things on the frontiers. It was when I first run for Congress; I was then in favor of the Hero, for he had chalked out his course so sleek in his letter to the Tennessee legislature that, like Sam Patch, says I, "There can be no mistake in him," and so I went ahead. No one dreamt about the monster and the deposits at that time, and so, as I afterward found, many like myself were taken in by these fair promises, which were worth about as much as a flash in the pan when you have a fair shot at a fat bear.

But I am losing sight of my story. Well, I started off to the Cross Roads dressed in my hunting shirt, and my rifle on my shoulder. Many of our constituents had assembled there to get a taste of the quality of the candidates at orating. Job Snelling, a gander-shanked Yankee, who had been caught somewhere about Plymouth Bay, and been shipped to the West with a cargo of codfish and rum, erected a large shanty, and set up shop for the occasion. A large posse of the voters had assembled before I arrived, and my opponent had already made considerable headway with his speechifying and his treating, when they spied me about a rifle shot from the camp, sauntering along as if I was not a party in business. "There comes Crockett," cried one. "Let us hear the colonel," cried another; and so I mounted the stump that had been cut down for the occasion, and began to bushwhack in the most approved style.

I had not been up long before there was such an uproar in the crowd that I could not hear my own voice, and some of my constituents let me know that they could not listen to me on such a dry subject as the welfare of the nation until they had something to drink, and that I must treat them. Accordingly I jumped down from the rostrum, and led the way to the shanty, followed by my constituents, shouting, "Huzza for Crockett," and "Crockett forever!"

When we entered the shanty Job was busy dealing out his rum in a style that showed he was making a good day's work of it, and I called for a quart of the best; but the crooked critter returned no other answer than by pointing to a board over the bar, on which he had chalked in large letters, PAY TODAY AND TRUST TOMORROW. Now that idea brought me up all standing; it was a sort of cornering in which there was no back out, for ready money in the West, in those times, was the shyest thing in all nature and it was most particularly shy with me on that occasion.

The voters, seeing my predicament, fell off to the other side, and I was left deserted and alone, as the government will be, when he no longer has any offices to bestow. I saw as plain as day that the tide of popular opinion was against me, and that unless I got some rum speedily I should lose my election as sure as there are snakes in Virginny; and it must be done soon, or even burnt brandy wouldn't save me. So I walked away from the shanty, but in another guess sort from the way I entered it, for on this occasion I had no train after me, and not a voice shouted, "Huzza for Crockett." Popularity sometimes depends on a very small matter indeed; in this particular it was worth a quart of New England rum, and no more.

Well, knowing that a crisis was at hand, I struck into the woods, with my rifle on my shoulder, my best friend in time of need; and, as good fortune would have it, I had not been out more than a quarter of an hour before I treed a fat coon, and in the pulling of a trigger he lay dead at the root of the tree. I soon whipped his hairy jacket off his back, and again bent my steps toward the shanty, and walked up to the bar, but not alone, for this time I had half a dozen of my constituents at my heels. I threw down the coon skin upon the counter, and called for a quart, and Job, though busy in dealing out rum, forgot to point at his chalked rules and regulations; for he knew that a coon was as good a legal tender for a quart in the West as a New York shilling any day in the year.

My constituents now flocked about me, and cried, "Huzza for Crockett," "Crockett forever," and finding the tide had taken a turn, I told them several yarns to get them in a good humor; and having soon dispatched the value of the coon, I went out and mounted the stump without opposition, and a clear majority of the voters followed me to hear what I had to offer for the good of the nation. Before I was half through one of my constituents moved that they would hear the balance of my speech after they had washed down the first part with some more of Job Snelling's extract of cornstalk and molasses, and the question being put, it was carried unanimously. It wasn't considered necessary to tell the yeas and nays, so we adjourned to the shanty, and on the way I began to reckon that the fate of the nation pretty much depended upon my shooting another coon.

While standing at the bar, feeling sort of bashful while Job's rules and regulations stared me in the face, I cast down my eyes, and discovered one end of the coon skin sticking between the logs that supported the bar. Job had slung it there in the hurry of business. I gave it a sort of quick jerk, and it followed my hand as natural as if I had been the rightful owner. I slapped it on the counter, and Job, little dreaming that he was barking up the wrong tree, shoved along another bottle, which my constituents quickly disposed of with great good humor, for some of them saw the trick; and then we withdrew to the rostrum to discuss the affairs of the nation.

I don't know how it was, but the voters soon became dry again, and nothing would do but we must adjourn to the shanty; and as luck would have it, the coon skin was still sticking between the logs, as if Job had flung it there on purpose to tempt me. I was not slow in raising it the counter, the rum followed, of course, and I wish I may be shot if I didn't, before the day was over, get ten quarts for the same identical skin, and from a fellow, too, who in those parts was considered as sharp as a steel trap and as bright as a pewter button.

This joke secured me my election, for it soon circulated like smoke among my constituents, and they allowed, with one accord, that the man who could get the whip hand of Job Snelling in fair trade, could outwit Old Nick himself, and was the real grit for them in Congress. Job was by no means popular; he boasted of always being wide awake, and that any one who could take him in was free to do so, for he came from a stock that, sleeping or waking, had always one eye open, and the other not more than half closed. The whole family were geniuses. His father was the inventor of wooden nutmegs, by which Job said he might have made a fortune, if he had only taken out a patent and kept the business in his own hands; his mother, Patience, manufactured the first white oak pumpkin seeds of the mammoth kind, and turned a pretty penny the first season; and his aunt Prudence was the first to discover that corn husks, steeped into tobacco water, would make as handsome Spanish wrappers as ever came from Havana, and that oak leaves would answer all the purpose of filling, for no one could discover the difference except the man who smoked them, and then it would be too late to make a stir about it. Job himself bragged of having made some useful discoveries, the most profitable of which was the art of converting mahogany sawdust into cayenne pepper, which he said was a profitable and safe business; for the people have been so long accustomed to having dust thrown in their eyes that there wasn't much danger of being found out.

The way I got to the blind side of the Yankee merchant was pretty generally known before election day, and the result was that my opponent might as well have whistled jigs to a milestone as attempt to beat up for votes in that district. I beat him out and out, quite back into the old year, and there was scarce enough left of him, after the canvass was over, to make a small grease spot. He disappeared without even leaving a mark behind; and such will be the fate of Adam Huntsman, if there is a fair fight and no gouging.

After the election was over, I sent Snelling the price of the rum, but took good care to keep the fact from the knowledge of my constituents. Job refused the money, and sent me word that it did him good to be taken in occasionally, as it served to brighten his ideas; but I afterwards learnt when he found out the trick that had been played upon him, he put all the rum I had ordered in his bill against my opponent, who, being elated with the speeches he had made on the affairs of the nation, could not descend to examine into the particulars of a bill of a vender of rum in the small way.

From: Henry Watterson, ed., *Oddities in Southern Life and Character* (New York: Houghton Mifflin Co., 1892).

· Martha Berry ·

(English)

Down in the hills of northern Georgia, just where the Blue Ridge and the Cumberlands halt their invasion of the plains, lies the thriving little city of Rome. Two miles north, on a green-swarded, shady hill, is the proud old ancestral home of the Berrys. The big oak grove that surrounds it serves scarcely to hide, down in one corner, a little, low, mud-daubed log cabin, with a stick chimney wide enough to swallow any Saint Nicholas. And many a time it did swallow one of the little Berrys who had forgotten the key to the door of their playhouse, where candy pulls and corn poppings and chestnut roastings marked many a holiday.

The children of the Berry household grew up in time; but for one of them the little cabin held all too hallowed memories to permit its being neglected or forgotten. Martha Berry chose it for her "den," and with coon skins and bear skins and plunder of field and wood she made it a lodge to match the legend over the fireplace, "Kyndle Friendship." The rafters above were hidden behind festoons of peppers and popcorn ears, and outside, by the door, hung the cedar water pail alongside the gourd dipper. Over in one corner was a little old rosewood melodeon, infirm in its legs, and with its keys yellow from age. Here Martha Berry spent many and many a quiet hour with her books and the wild things of the woods that visited her.

One balmy Sunday afternoon in April three other little wild things crept up to the cabin, and through some unchinked cracks stood peering in at this wondrous palace of beauty and the lady that lived therein. Miss Berry, suddenly conscious of the scrutiny, looked up from her book to encounter the three pairs of gray-blue eyes so wonderingly intent upon her paradise.

"Come in," she called to them. But the three little barefoot, ragged children shrank away in fear. Going to the door, Miss Berry tried to talk with them, but it was only when she held out the temptation of bright-cheeked apples that she could persuade them to cross the threshold. Then, remembering it was Sunday, she began to tell them Bible stories. These were all new to them, as she discovered when she asked them questions.

"Don't know," they said, "don't know. Hain't never been to no Sunday school. We-uns' Hardshells."

Did they have any brothers and sisters? she asked. Yes, indeed. "I got about eight," said one; and another, "I got about ten."

They were the children of tenant farmers nearby, men from the mountains or of kin to them. If Miss Berry, like Joseph, was seeking to prove these spies as to their families, the proof was forthcoming. She asked them to return next Sunday and bring their brothers and sisters. Then promptly with their departure, her other interests took back her mind, until she had nearly forgotten her promise. The next Sunday she was sitting with some visitors from the city upon the gallery of the "big house," when through the woods she saw a procession that recalled her appointment. Not only children were coming, but men, women, babies, and dogs. Excusing herself from her friends, she hurried down to meet the Sunday-school delegation at the little log cabin.

Forming an impromptu program in her mind, she said, "First we'll sing something." The wheezy little melodeon, upheld on all sides by eager children, did its best, a wondrous best, as they sang to Miss Berry's "lining out," "I'm so glad that Jesus loves me." And then she told them Bible stories, stories so new and fresh to these neglected "Hardshells" that not the children only, but the fathers and mothers, sat with rapt faces, while the babies kept silence, and not even a dog moved his tongue. For this Sunday school, mark you, was the laying of the cornerstone of a great temple of service.

Every succeeding Sunday brought more and more and more visitors, some with gifts of shuck mats for seats for the growing audience, which promptly filled the cabin and overflowed into the grove. Miss Berry had become, before she knew it, the head and front of a weekly camp meeting, an affair that promised an undefined extension. How many a lady, with such a distinction thrust upon her, would not gracefully have withdrawn on about the seventh Sunday? How many would not have found the hot summer good reason to terminate an enterprise that threatened leisure and forbade society? But not so Martha Berry. A Voice had called, "Whom shall I send? and who will go for us?" And out of her leisurely, sheltered life she came to respond, "Here am I; send me." And then a new glory came upon life, the glory of a revealed Christ.

The Sunday school grew. People would come, rain or shine; and soon, impelled by necessity, Miss Berry invested one hundred dollars in lumber, and the men and boys of the Sunday school put up a small schoolhouse, which soon added to itself a little room on the front, then a big room on the back.

Then the Sunday school grew into a circuit. Some of the members moved up to Possum Trot Creek, and they sent word for Miss Berry to come there and open a Sunday school. So she drove the eight miles to Possum Trot, and held Sunday school with them in an old, dilapidated house that had survived the war. One Sunday it rained, and though the superintendent fled from corner to corner, she was soaked before the Sunday school and the shower were over. So she asked the people to put on a new roof before the next Sunday. But that seemed to them a most unreasonable request.

"It might not rain for a whole month," said one man.

"Yes," replied Miss Berry, "but it mought rain next Sunday."

She pointed to an oak tree nearby which would make good "boards," and told the men that if they would cut it up and shingle the roof she would bring the nails, and treat the workers to lemonade. They came, and she came, and, most indispensable of all, the lemonade came, a most unaccustomed beverage, but one highly appreciated by all, even by the old man who remarked with an amused chuckle that he "never heard of a woman a-bossin' of a house-roofin' before."

From Possum Trot "the Sunday Lady," as the countryside began affectionately to call her, was soon extending her chain of Sunday schools in several directions. Her sister and others were enlisted as helpers. And soon mightily grew the Word of God.

From: Arthur W. Spaulding, *The Men of the Mountains* (Nashville: Southern Publishing, 1915).

· *Rene Leblanc* ·

(Acadian)

We met there a party of Canadian hunters and trappers who gave us a friendly welcome, and replenished our store of provisions with game and venison. They informed us that the easiest and least wearisome way to reach Louisiana was to float down the Tennessee and Meschacebe rivers. The plan suggested by them was adopted, and the men of our party, aided by our Canadian friends, felled trees to build a suitable boat.

There, a great misfortune befell us. We experienced a great loss in the death of Rene Leblanc, who had been our leader and adviser in the hours of our sore trials. Old age had shattered his constitution, and unequal to the fatigues of our long pilgrimage, he pined away, and sank into his grave without a word of complaint. He died the death of a hero and of a Christian, consoling us as we wept beside him, and cheering us in our troubles. His death afflicted us sorely, and the night during which he lay exposed, preparatory to his burial, the silence was unbroken, in our camp, save by our whispered words, as if we feared to disturb the slumbers of the great and good man that slept the eternal sleep. We buried him at the foot of the hill, in a grove of walnut trees. We carved his name with a cross over it on the bark of the tree sheltering his grave, and after having said the prayers for the dead, we closed his grave, wet with the tears of those he had loved so well.

From: Felix Voorhies, *Acadian Reminiscences* (Opelousas, LA: The Jacob News Depot, Co., 1907).

CHAPTER 9

Pirates and Buried Treasure

· *The Dismal Swamp Ship* ·

(English)

A mong the buccaneers from the West Indies who afflicted our coast, "Spade-beard" was one of the worst. He looked every bit the devil that he was. His eyes were like fire, his hair and beard were glossy and coal black, he was alternately treacherous and imperious. He had fallen in with an English merchant ship that had been separated from her convoy in a gale, and had turned her adrift after killing all of her crew and stealing all her treasure, for she was freighted with bullion. Before the frigate which was her convoy could attack, he had run in behind the Virginia sand keys and escaped. But heaven's vengeance he could not thwart. An immense tidal wave swept against the shore. The pirate vessel was lifted upon it and carried inland, mile after mile, through the cypresses, and left among the trees when the tide flowed back.

There, in the Dismal Swamp, among bayous barely wide enough to give her passage, this shattered hulk is doomed to cruise forever. Her rigging and sails are gone, but swamp moss has grown to her masts and spars in their place, and the crew, wasted to skeletons and gray with mold, still work the ship, reef in gales with dangling snakes, and yell oaths and blasphemies. Spade-beard, with one arm off at the shoulder and a piece broken out of his head, copes with phantom enemies and fires silent broadsides of green light from rusty cannon into the melancholy woods. Pale gleams flit over the deck and shine through seams in the hull. This dreadful ship is usually seen in thunderstorms, at night, and is often struck by lightning, though never disabled. Guides and hunters in the swamp dread it beyond all other things of this world, for whoever meets it is doomed to death within a year.

From: Charles M. Skinner, *American Myths & Legends*, vol. 2 (Philadelphia and London: J. B. Lippincott Co., 1903).

CHAPTER 10

Superstitions

· *Superstitions from Louisiana* ·

(Unidentified)

There are a great many superstitions among the people in Louisiana, but they may be common to all countries. They are, however, interesting:

1. A person must come out of a room by the same door through which he came in; otherwise there will be a misfortune.
2. Put nails in shape of a cross in the nest of a goose, that thunder should not spoil the eggs and prevent them from hatching.
3. When a woman whistles, it makes the Virgin Mary weep.
4. When little children in their sleep put their arms on their heads, we must put them down, for they are calling misfortune on their heads.
5. When the palate falls, we must tie very tight a lock of hair in the middle of the head, and the palate will resume its natural position.
6. A dog that howls at night announces the death of someone.
7. A horse that neighs where there is a dead body announces the death of someone.
8. When a hearse stops before your door it is a sign of misfortune.
9. To kneel on the threshold is an omen of misfortune.
10. When one eats a sweet potato one must eat first a piece of the peel in order that the potato should not be too heavy on the stomach.

11. If in walking your right ankle turns, you will have a pleasant surprise; if it is the left ankle, a disappointment.

12. If your right ear is hot, someone is speaking well of you; if it is the left ear, someone is speaking badly of you.

13. To pass a child through a window makes a thief of him.

14. To pass over a child lying down will prevent him from growing.

15. You must always burn and not throw away your hair, because the birds will pick it up to make their nest, and that will make you crazy.

16. If you make a child who stammers eat in the same dish as a little dog, that will cure the child.

17. If your nose itches an old bachelor is going to kiss you, and a young man is crazy to do so.

18. If you strike your "crazy bone," you will be disappointed.

19. If a child teething looks at himself in a mirror, his teething will be painful.

20. To pass in front of a carriage at a funeral is a bad omen.

21. When a fly bothers you, it is a sign that you are going to receive a letter.

22. When a snake is cut to pieces, its friends come to get it to put the pieces together.

23. When in taking leave four persons cross hands it is a sign of marriage.

24. To dream of death is a sign of marriage; to dream of a marriage is a sign of death.

25. It is a sign of misfortune to pass the loaf of bread turned down.

26. When you cut a banana you cut the cross of Christ.

27. If you have a sore on the tip of the tongue, it is a sign that you have lied.

28. If you forget what you were going to say, it is a sign that you were going to lie.

29. If you sweep the feet of a child with a broom, it will make him walk early.

30. To turn a chair on one leg is a bad omen.

31. If scissors fall down with one point in the floor you will receive a visit, and it will come in the direction in which the other point lies.

32. If you plant lettuce on Good Friday it will not grow.

33. If you plough on Good Friday the ground will bleed.

34. If you carry an Irish potato in your pocket it will cure your rheumatism.

35. To cure a wart take a green pea, cut it, rub it on the wart, then take the pea and wrap it in a piece of paper and throw it away. The person who will pick it up will get the wart.
36. To open an umbrella in the house chases away the lovers.
37. To put an umbrella on the bed causes disputes.
38. To throw black pepper on a table is a sign of marriage.
39. It chases chicken lice from a chicken house to put it in the head of a crocodile.
40. It cures rheumatism to tie an eel's skin on the leg or the arm.
41. You must watch for a full moon if you want to make soap.
42. It makes the hair healthier to cut the ends of it at the time of the new moon.
43. If you cut your nails on Monday you will secure a present during the week.
44. If you wear green garters you will often receive presents.
45. If you walk on the tail of a cat you will not marry during the year.
46. It is a sign of misfortune to stumble in a graveyard.
47. It is a sign of misfortune to light a candle in a room when there is already another light.
48. It is a sign of good luck to meet a person who squints.
49. It is a sign that you will hear good news if you see a white butterfly.
50. If a girl wears on her left leg a yellow garter which has been worn by a bride she will marry during the year.

From: Alcee Fortier, *Louisiana Studies* (New Orleans: F. F. Hansell & Brothers, 1894).

· Superstitions from Georgia ·

(Unidentified)

In spring, cow lice turn to gnats; hog lice turn to fleas.
A toadstool is called the Devil's snuffbox, and the Devil's imps come at midnight to get the snuff. In the morning you can tell when the imps have been for the snuff, as you will find the toadstool broken off and scattered about. The snuff is used as one of the ingredients of a "cunjer-bag."

If a terrapin bites you, it will never let go till it thunders.

A pregnant woman cannot assist in killing hogs, or in handling fresh meat. The meat will spoil.

If you want a hen to hatch all pullets, put the eggs under her out of the bonnet of a young girl.

To make a girl love you, take a piece of candy or anything she is likely to eat, and put it under either armpit, so that it will get your scent.

To milk a cow on the ground, she will go dry unless you throw some of the milk on her back.

To make a cow take a strange calf, rub the nose of the cow and the body of the calf with tea made of walnut leaves, so that the scent will be the same with both.

To make a stray dog follow and stay with you, put a piece of bacon in the shoe of the left foot, wear it till you see the dog and throw it to him; if he eats it, he will follow you and stay with you. If he don't, get some hair off the dog's left ear and put it in the left pocket, or rub his left hind foot with a piece of cornbread.

To keep a strange dog with you, cut some hair off the end of his tail and bury under your doorstep.

If you wish a strange cat to stay with you, grease it with any kind of grease, stick the cat to the chimney back, and throw it under your bed.

If you want a cat to stay with you and not return to the former owner, grease the four feet of the cat in the house before taking it away.

Never throw keys; always hand them or lay them down, and let those who want them pick them up.

Negroes will not throw a knife or a key to one another, for they will certainly lose them if thrown.

In handing a knife to another, let the blade be shut up, and let it be handed back shut up. If the blade of a knife is soft, put the blade into a piece of hot corn bread, and put bread and knife into water.

To find water before seeking a spot to dig a well, Negroes take a switch of willow or peach, hold it in both hands near the middle, and walk over the ground where the well is desired; when they come to the spot where the water is, the switch twists and turns in the hands, sometimes rubbing off the bark, the ends turning down to the ground.

To get fleas out of a house, take a pine pole and skin it. The fleas in hopping about will hop on the pole and stick to the resin that issues. Sheep about a yard will also carry them off.

When the dogwood tree blossoms, fish begin to bite. (Negroes always fish with a big cork, and put the lead close to the hook in order to keep terrapins from cutting the line.)

When fishing, spit on your bait for luck.

If anyone steps across the pole of another while fishing, the person whose pole has been so treated will catch no fish unless the pole is again stepped over backwards.

You can't swear and catch fish.

From: Roland Steiner, "Superstitions and Beliefs from Central Georgia," *Journal of American Folk-Lore* 12 (1899): 261–71.

· *Superstitions from North Carolina* ·

(German)

They Says About Babies

Must not cut baby's nails with scissors before 't is a year old: 't will make it steal.

Must not hand a baby out of a window, or it will be hanged.

The first time a baby is taken out of its room or its natal room, it must be taken up, or it will not go to heaven. If the door of the room steps down, as so many of these patched-up houses do, then the person carrying the baby must step up on a chair or book with baby in her arms.

A Sower's Charm

Many old people are looked upon as so successful as sowers that they are believed to be possessed of some charm. One kind of incantation, sung as each handful of seed is thrown, I have found; it is used by an old man who has been champion turnip-seed sower for fifty years or more:

> Some for de bug,
> Some for de fly,
> Some for de devil,
> And in comes I.

I cannot find any others, though there are more.

Doggerel

Whenever one of the red and black spotted bugs is seen, you must say:

> Ladybug, ladybug, fly away home,
> Your house is on fire and your children will burn.

Ask me no questions, I'll tell you no lies.

Pithy Sayings

Not every horn that blows, blows for dinner.

The hands are called in from the field for the noon meal by a horn, on the plantations and farms.

"I'd call my hounds off that track," is another old saying.

Sense enough to come in out of the rain.

Bred in the bone.

It's a bad bird that fouls its own nest.

Joy go with you; you'll leave peace behind you.

> Tit for tat,
> You kill my dog, I'll kill your cat.

"You'll find the latchstring on the outside" and "We'll put on the big pot and the little one" are forms of welcome or friendly invitation.

"Pot luck" is used here, and "Pot calling kettle black" is an old saying.

The sight of you is good for sore eyes.

Scarce as hen's teeth.

From: N. C. Hoke, "Folk-Custom and Folk-Belief in North Carolina," *Journal of American Folk-Lore* 5 (1892): 113–20.

· A Superstition from Arkansas ·

(African)

A curious sign is the turning-back sign; it is very unlucky to turn back after you have once started. If you must turn back, however, you can avert misfortune by making the sign of a the cross in the dust with your heel, and spitting in the cross. This is sure. Why the formula is completed in such a surprising manner I cannot say.

From: Octave Thanet, "Folk-Lore in Arkansas," *Journal of American Folk-Lore* 5 (1892): 121–25.

· Superstitions from Baltimore ·

(African)

Never comb your hair at night: It will make you forgetful.
If you try to burn the combings of your hair and they do not flame quickly, it a sure sign of death.

Do not sweep your house Friday night: bad luck.

You must not put your shoes higher than your head: It is also bad luck to put your bed crossways of the room.

If you are robbed of anything, take a rooster, put him under a pot, and let everybody touch the pot: When the thief touches the pot the rooster will crow.

The first dove you hear in the spring, take off your right shoe and you will find a strand of the man's hair you are to marry.

To stop the screech owl from screeching, put an iron poker in the fire, or tie a knot in your underskirt.

If your shoe comes untied somebody is thinking about you.

When a jack-o'-lantern leads you, turn your pocket wrongside out.

It is bad luck to carry fire to fire: If you carry fire from one room to another, spit on it.

If rats cut your clothes, do not allow your kin to mend them.

When you move out of a house, do not sweep it if you wish luck.

If your right hand itches, spit on it and you will shake hands with your best friend: If your left hand itches, spit on it and you will get money.

When a rooster comes in your house, somebody is coming from a journey.

When you are going anywhere and have to go back for something forgotten, make a crossmark and spit on it.

When a cat licks her face it is going to rain.

If you are going uphill when you hear the first dove in the spring, you will get something: If you are going downhill you will lose something.

If you drop a dishcloth while washing the dishes, a hungry person is coming.

Never plant in the dark of the moon: Do not kill in the dark of the moon, the meat will spoil.

To learn to pick a banjo, go to the forks of the road at midnight: You will see a man; that is *Satan*, and *he* will teach you to play.

To keep the witches from riding you at night, sleep with an open penknife on your breast, or a sifter over your face: To catch the witches if they try to get through the holes, place a three-prong fork under the sieve.

When the witches are coming through the keyhole they sing, "Skin, don't you know me? Skin, don't you know me? Jump out and jump in"; and if you are able to throw pepper and salt on the skin while they are out of it, they cannot get it on again.

If you scatter mustard seed all around your bed, they have to stop to pick them all up before they can ride you.

Witches plait horses' manes for their stirrups, and ride the horses very hard, sometimes to death.

If anyone brings a hoe into the house, it is bad luck: To do away with it, you must walk out backward with the hoe.

Jaybirds go down to hell every Friday with a grain of sand.

If a dog wallows on his back, he is measuring for somebody's grave.

To break a looking glass is seven years of trouble.

Tie salt in your skirt, and if anybody talks about you it will make their teeth ache.

If you sneeze with food in your mouth it is a sure sign of death among your friends.

To make a young cow gentle, pour milk on her back: Do not let a drop fall on the ground, for that will make her milk dry up.

If your right ear burns, somebody is "talking good" about you; if the left ear burns, someone is "talking bad" about you: To make the talker bite her tongue, spit on your finger and make a crossmark in the ear that burns.

If your nose itches, somebody is coming; if your left eye itches, you will cry; if your right eye itches, you will see something pleasant.

To spill salt is bad luck: To do away with it, throw some over your left shoulder.

If you want good luck, always carry about with you a rabbit's left hind foot.

To cure any pain, catch a mole and let it die in your hand.

To carry off a wen, place a dead man's hand on it.

When nuts are plenty and coons are fat the winter will be cold.

The skin of a rabbit's stomach tied around a baby's neck helps it cut its teeth: If it teethes very hard tie a "sawyer bug" around its neck, and when the bug dies the tooth will come through.

If you count one hundred red horses and begin with a red mule, the first person you shake hands with you will marry.

If you see the new moon through the trees, bad luck; if clear, good luck.

Never use water in a basin that anyone else has washed in, without making a crossmark and spitting over it.

Do not let the birds build their nests with the combings of your hair: It will drive you crazy.

Never leave a loaf of bread turned upside down, for ships will sink.

Always mash the eggshells after you have taken out the egg: The witches will make boats out of the shells and sink ships.

A wild bird flying in at the window is a sign of death.

Never cross a funeral or count the followers.

Never ride behind white horses, if you come just after the hearse, or you will be the next.

If a cat crosses your path, bad luck; if one follows you, good luck.

From: Lee Collins, "Some Negro Lore from Baltimore," *Journal of American Folk-Lore* 5 (1892): 110–12.

· Superstitions from Allegheny ·

(Scots-Irish)

Cabbage seed sowed March 17—St. Patrick's Day—is sure to prosper.
Shrove cakes on Shrove Tuesday, pancakes on Ash Wednesday, cross
buns at Easter, bring good luck. The first should be round and have a
hole in the center. If the grease used in frying them be preserved and
applied to the axles of wagons in which the harvest is hauled home, mice
will not eat the grain. One cross bun must be kept during the year if the
good influence is to be continued.

From: J. Hampden Porter, "Folk-Lore of the Mountain Whites of the Alleghanie," *Journal
of American Folk-Lore* 7 (1894): 105–17.

· Various Superstitions ·

(Unidentified)

To kill a ghost, it must be shot with a bullet made of a silver quarter
dollar. Silver nails or screws in a coffin will prevent the dead haunting
the scenes of its existence in the flesh.

An infant, measured, will die before its growing time is over. My mother
once started to measure her sleeping baby boy, when the nurse, an old
Negress, sprang forward crying: "Dat chile ain't dead yet, ter be measured."
Explanations ensued, and the measuring was deferred.

No person who touches a dead body will be haunted by its spirit.

To thank a person for combing your hair will bring bad luck.

Dog howls—the sign of death.

To cut a baby's fingernails deform it; if the baby is a month old such
action will cause the child to have fits.

To allow a child to look into a mirror before it is a month old will
cause it trouble in teething.

Tickling a baby causes stuttering.

Cut a dog's "dew-claws," and it will not die from poisonous snake bite.

A child will have a nature and disposition similar to that of the person
who first takes it out of doors.

To see the new moon through clouds or treetops means trouble; if the disk is clear, good luck; if seen over the right shoulder, joy; if over the left, anger and disappointment.

To dream of a live snake signifies enemies at large; if a dead snake, enemies dead or powerless.

To dream of unbroken eggs signifies trouble to come; if the eggs are broken, your trouble is past.

To throw out of a window hair combings is bad luck.

To hear a screech owl is a sign of bad luck. To prevent their cry, turn the pockets, and set the shoes soles upward.

Plant all seeds, make soap, and kill meat, on the increase of the moon. If done on the decrease, the seeds will not grow, the soap will not lather, and the meat will shrink.

Never begin a task or journey on Friday.

If one lets fall the dishcloth, someone is coming.

Spill the salt is a sign of anger; "itching palms," of money.

Stir jellies, butter, sauce, etc., to the right; also soap. Otherwise it will not "make."

If you kill frogs, your cows will "go dry."

To cut off a pup's tail, causes him to grow "smart."

If you kill "grandaddies" the cows will die.

If a person comes into your presence while you are talking about him, and puts his hands upon you anyhow or anywhere, you will die.

These and many others form a long list that still holds good among the superstitiously inclined.

From: Ruby Andrews Moore, "Superstitions from Georgia," *Journal of American Folk-Lore* 7 (1894): 305–306.

CHAPTER 11

Portents, Charms, and Remedies

· *Various Portents from Georgia* ·

(Unidentified)

For a cook to drop a dishrag is a sign that someone will come hungry. When you drop your knife and it sticks up, it is a sign of good luck.

To see a measuring worm crawling on anyone is a sign that the person will have a new suit of clothes.

If a butterfly lights on you, it is a sign that you will die soon.

To see a butterfly, catch it and bite off the head, you will have a new dress the color of the butterfly.

In sitting in front of the fire, if the fire pops on you, you are sure to get new clothes.

If the fire pops with a blowing noise, it is a sign that there is going to be a fuss in the family.

To sit by a fire and have a "chunk" roll out is a sign of company.

It is bad luck for a stick of wood to roll out of the fire on the floor.

A rooster crowing before a door is a sign of a visitor.

To hear a rooster crow when he first goes to roost is a sign of hasty news.

When a hen crows, some evil will befall the family to which the hen belongs.

A dog's howling is a sign of the house catching fire.

For a dog to go hunting at night in winter is a sign of snow.

To see the new moon through the trees is a sign of bad luck.

Wear a string round the neck with a piece of money on it for good luck.

From: Roland Steiner, "Superstitions and Beliefs from Central Georgia," *Journal of American Folk-Lore* 12 (1899): 261–71.

· *Portents from North Carolina* ·

(German)

Every seed has a certain sign in which it must be planted. Besides the signs, of course the moon is an all-powerful potentate. She seems to rule everything.

All vegetables which grow under the ground—turnips, radishes, etc.—must be planted in the "dark of the moon," and all on top in the "light of it." That is general, and universally observed.

Good Friday is a chosen day for planting everything, but especially beans.

All Fridays are good days for planting things that hang down, like beans or grapes, *i.e.*, stringy things, because Friday is "hangman's day."

Plant corn always when the "little moon" (new moon) points down; the ears grow low on the stalks, and make heavy ears. Also put the roof on a building when the little moon hangs down, so the shingles won't turn up.

Sow wheat before the full moon in October.

If hickory leaves turn a pretty yellow in the autumn, the next harvest will be a good, rich, golden one.

Of course signs can be multiplied innumerably, so I have confined myself to a few about the few oldest things—death, birth, marriage, moving. I find moving to be full of horrors apparently, and more encrusted in signs than anything else except death.

Move in the increase of the moon, and always carry something into the house first that the wind won't blow away.

It is lucky to move salt first.

Never move a broom or a cat.
Never marry when the sign is in the crawfish; you'll go backwards.
Never marry in May.

> Happy the bride the sun shines on,

and

> Something old and something new,
> Something borrowed, something blue,
> are two rhymes about marriage.

If two spoons are in the same cup of coffee or tea as it is handed, it is a sign of marriage.

There is a belief that fortunes can be told by coffee grounds, or rather a husband's coming can be foretold.

If, on rising from a chair, it falls over, the person causing the accident will not marry for twelve months.

The breastbone or wishbone of a chicken, if pulled apart by two people, will result in marriage coming first to the one having the shortest piece. If put over the door, the person who first comes under will be the bride or bridegroom elect.

From: N. C. Hoke, "Folk-Custom and Folk-Belief in North Carolina," *Journal of American Folk-Lore* 5 (1892): 113–20.

· *Portents on Death* ·

(German)

In burying or laying out the dead, the feet must always be to the east, the head to the west. Meg Merrilies herself could not enforce this more rigidly.

There is a custom prevailing among some of putting a piece of muslin over the face of the dead; and when the coffin is carried to the church, and opened for friends to see (in the country, where people live miles apart, and travel must be over terrible roads, this is the only way for friends to take a farewell of those gone before), the muslin is removed and laid over the hands: It is bad luck if anyone should put the muslin back over the face. In fact, *that would not be permitted under any circumstances*. I have not been able to form any conjecture as to why this should be so guardedly, almost fiercely, observed.

In other places, sheets and white spreads are put over everything in the room, even over the pictures, so that the entire room where the dead lies shall be white. It is sometimes beautiful.

To put up an umbrella in the house is a sign of death, sometimes of just bad luck, but it is a deep-seated belief that it is disastrous.

A bird coming in the house is a sure sign of death; even flying through it is the same.

In making garments for the dead, never bite the thread; it will make the teeth rot.

A screech owl screeching near the house is a sure sign of death's approach.

If two people look in a mirror at once, the younger will die within a year.

Three lights in a room, or thirteen at table, is death to someone of the party present.

If two people work with another's head at the same time, the person will die soon.

A dog's howl means the approach of death.

One death brings on another. There are always two together.

Rain falling on a new-made grave is a good sign.

Bad luck is to hear a hen crow; kill it immediately.

When you hear the first whippoorwill in the spring, turn a summersault three times and you'll never have backache.

The cows are bewitched when butter won't come: Pour the cream behind the backlog and it will run off the witches. (A common practice.)

Wean a calf when the sign is in the feet; the calf will not take it so to heart and bawl.

A chunk on fire, falling down on the hearth, is a sure sign that a guest is coming.

So, also, if the scissors fall and stick up in the floor.

Never thank anybody who gives you seed; if you do, they will never do any good.

Get out of bed and turn your shoes over if you cannot sleep; it will drive off the witches who are keeping you awake.

A rabbit running across the road in front of you is dreadful luck.

From: N. C. Hoke, "Folk-Custom and Folk-Belief in North Carolina," *Journal of American Folk-Lore* 5 (1892): 113–20.

· *Portents on Luck* ·

(Various)

Portents from Georgia
(Unidentified)

Negroes will not carry a hoe or ax through a house, or put one on the shoulder; to do so is very bad luck.

To step over a broom going forwards is bad luck; you must step over it backwards.

It is bad luck to sweep the dirt out of a house at night; sweep it up into a corner and sweep out in the daytime. If obliged to sweep it out at night, take a coal of fire and throw it first in front of you.

One Negro will not step over another while lying down. If he does, he must step over again backwards.

Never let the moon shine on fresh meat; it brings bad luck.

To pin bad luck, drive a rusty nail in the front doorstep.

If a Negro sees a pin, and picks it up with the point to him, it is blunt luck; he will walk about in order to take it point toward him, and then it is sharp luck.

If a Negro moves into another house, even if the house has been swept and scoured, he will scour and sweep it again for fear of "cunjer."

If a looking glass falls from a wall and breaks, it is a sign of death; if anyone lets it fall from his hands, of seven years' bad luck.

Never lend salt or red pepper; if you lend it, it will give bad luck.

From: Roland Steiner, "Superstitions and Beliefs from Central Georgia," *Journal of American Folk-Lore* 12 (1899): 261–71.

Portents from North Carolina
(Scots-English)

There are many signs and omens which portend good or bad luck; generally, without any special significance as to what it will be. One of the most generally believed is that it is bad luck for a hare to cross the road in front of a traveler. I find, however, that in some sections the direction of the crossing governs the luck; from right to left, bad; from left to right, good. A dog's howling is also a sign of bad luck.

These bad-luck signs are many and I shall give only a few. It brings bad luck to turn a spinning wheel backwards; to turn a chair around on one leg; to step over a broom or a person lying down—the spell may be broken, however, by immediately stepping backwards over the broom or person; for a bird to fly into the house; to carry a hoe on the shoulder into the house; to spill salt; the spell may be broken by throwing some of the salt over the left shoulder; for a hen to crow—we all know the old couplet:

A whistling woman and a crowing hen
Will never come to any good end.

It also brings bad luck to kill a cat; for a screech owl or hoot owl to make its peculiar noise near the house; to walk backward with one shoe off and one on; for the fruit trees to bloom the second time in one season; to step on or over a grave; to see the new moon first through the branches of a tree; to say "thank you" or show any gratitude when given seeds or shrubs; to have rain on the wedding day; for a marriage party to meet a funeral procession; to turn round and go back after starting on a journey—the evil spell may be broken, however, by making a crossmark on the ground and spitting on it. Making the crossmark may be a corruption of the custom of crossing one's self to ward off evil, but why spit in the crossmark? Can this be a vague reference to sprinkling with holy water?

While the good-luck signs are not so numerous, there are plenty of them to give hope and prove that life is not entirely a dodging of evil. It brings very good luck to see the new moon for the first time unobstructed over the left shoulder; to find a horseshoe in the road, some say it must have nails in it, and some that the points must be toward the finder; good luck for the right eye to itch so that you rub it; bad for the left, however. Very good luck to have snow on your wedding day; to find a spider on one's clothes; to kill the first snake you see in the spring; to have a strange cat take up with you; to keep a horseshoe tacked over the door, the points must turn up, however, or the luck will spill; to find a pin or needle with point toward you, but you must pick it up

> Find a pin and pick it up,
> All that day you'll have good luck.

From: Haywood Parker, "Folk-Lore of the North Carolina Mountaineers," *Journal of American Folk-Lore* 20 (1907): 241–50.

· *Portents on Disease* ·

(Unidentified)

We frequently have one in our midst whose language we do not understand—a baby. And, poor baby! how many times we play at cross-purposes with you! Much of our time is spent in ingenious translation of sounds, making words out of grunts, and sentences for senseless babble. Our answers to your wants are often random shots, and when we prescribe for real or fancied ills we do no more than guess.

It is one of these guesses to which the Virginia mountain mother has given the name of Go-backs. The baby coming into one of these homes makes no acquaintance with the scales nor measuring tape, but it at once assumes in the parents' eyes a ponderous weight, proportionate to its importance. This weight must daily increase, and height or length must receive its share of gain. Sometimes there appears to be a cessation in this steady growth; the wise dames and anxious mother agree that something is the matter. The scales are not yet asked to give a casting vote, but the gap between the growth which mother wants and that which baby yields seems to widen, and the reason becomes more and more mysterious until some wiser dame whispers the dreaded words, "It has the Go-backs," and others echo, "It has the Go-backs."

When this ailment is suggested, the diagnosis will speedily follow, for time is an important element in the cure.

The mother then must go alone with the babe to some old lady duly instructed in the art or science of curing this blighting disease. She, taking the infant, divests it of its clothing, and places it on its back. Then with a yarn string she measures its length or height from the crown of the head to the sole of the heel, cutting off a piece which exactly represents this length. This she applies to the foot, measuring off length by length to see if the piece of yarn contains the length of the foot an exact number of times. This operation is watched by the mother with the greatest anxiety, for on this coincidence of measure depends the child's weal or woe. If the length of the string is an exact multiple of the length of the foot, nothing is wrong, but if there is a remainder, however small, the baby has the Go-backs, and the extent of the malady is proportional to this remainder. Of course in this measuring the elasticity of the yarn is not regarded, nor repetitions tried as a test of accuracy.

The diagnosis has in it an element of the exact science of measuring, but without its exactness; this latter feature does not detract in the minds of the believers from the confidence which the former suggests. To them it is a question of fact: Is the height an exact number of times the length of the foot? If not, treatment must follow. This is very simple, entailing no suffering on the part of the patient, and no further expense to the parent. The string with which the determination was made must be hung on the hinge of a gate on the premises of the infant's parents, and as the string by gradual decay passes away, so passes away the Go-backs. But if the string should be lost, the ailment will linger until a new test is made, and the string once more hung out to decay. Sometimes the cure is hastened by fixing the string so that wear will come upon it.

And thus the Go-backs is cured; at least there are many people in Virginia who think so.

From: J. Howard Gore, "The Go-Backs," *Journal of American Folk-Lore* 5 (1892): 107–109.

· A Cure for Flesh Decay ·

(Unidentified)

To cure this disease, a baby is measured by a seventh son or a seventh daughter three days in succession, before sunrise or after sunset, being passed through the measuring string each day; while, during the process, an unintelligible charm is repeated over the child. After the third measuring, the string is doubled and tied to the hinge of a door or window, and if it rots out in a certain time, the baby will recover; but if the child is "foot-and-a-half gone," there is no possible cure.

To cure the same disease in Pennsylvania, the baby, wrapped in blankets, is put in the oven after bread has been taken out and the oven has cooled down. Then, with the oven door open, the baby is "baked" for one hour.

From: Ann Weston Whitney, "Items of Maryland Belief and Custom," *Journal of American Folk-Lore* 12 (1899): 273–74.

· Portents on Spirits and Witches ·

(Unidentified)

Children born with a caul see spirits.

Negroes say that all animals can see spirits at night.

Negroes contend that hogs can see the wind; some maintain that all animals can do so.

If one is riding at night and feels a warm current of air on his face, Negroes say that a spirit is passing by.

If you are walking or riding along, and see a mist rising from the ground, it is a sign of the presence of spirits.

Dogs frequently "run" spirits at night, but spirits will whip a dog, unless the dog has dewclaws. When the dog sees a spirit, he will come back whining and get behind you. The dog does not wish to fight a spirit if he can help it. I have hunted coons and possums at night with Negroes, and, when the dogs kept running and did not see anything, the Negroes "quit" and went home, saying the dogs were running spirits.

The left hind foot of a graveyard rabbit is a talisman against spirits, also productive of good luck generally. I asked a Negro if spirits ever bothered him. He replied, "No, sir; I totes the left hind foot of a graveyard rabbit."

Negroes deem an *ignis fatuus*, or "Jack o' the Lantern," a spirit doomed to wander in swamps, seeking something it will never find.

To pass a haunted place, turn your pockets inside out; the haunt will not trouble you.

Some Negroes wear the coat turned inside out, to keep off evil spirits, or to keep witches from riding them.

To prevent a witch from riding a person, put a case knife, pair of scissors, or some mustard seed under the bed or pillow.

If a horse's mane is tangled in the morning, it is a sign that a witch has been riding him; the little knots seen in the mane are "witches' stirrups."

To prevent a witch from riding horses, nail a horseshoe over the door of the stable.

Horseshoes, when nailed on doors or posts for good luck, are placed with the round part uppermost. No witch or evil spirit can enter when they are so nailed.

From: Roland Steiner, "Superstitions and Beliefs from Central Georgia," *Journal of American Folk-Lore* 12 (1899): 261–71.

· Conjuring in Georgia ·

(African)

To conjure a well, throw graveyard dirt into the well, or an old pipe of a conjure doctor, or some devil's snuff.

Devil's snuff, a large species of mushroom, when broken, is full of a powder of a slatish color, and is used in conjure, singly or in combination with graveyard dirt and other things.

If a person is conjured by a Negro with a blue and a black eye, he will surely die.

If conjured by a blue-gummed Negro, death is certain.

To produce blindness by conjure, take a toadfrog and dry it, then powder it up, and mix with salt, and sprinkle in the hat of the person to be conjured, or on the head if possible; when the head sweats, and the sweat runs down the face, blindness takes place.

Wherever anyone gets killed, the spot is haunted.

All old houses, that stand off by themselves, and are unoccupied, generally get the reputation of being haunted. A conjure doctor can lay haunts.

Graveyard dirt must be got off the coffin of the dead person, on the waste of the moon at midnight.

If you go through a place that is haunted, to keep from seeing the haunts and from their harming you, take your hat off and throw it behind you, then turn around to the right and take up your hat and walk fast by the place, so as not to aggravate the haunts to follow.

Spirits come in any shape—as men, cows, cats, dogs—but are always black. Some whine like a cat.

To see spirits, take a rain-crow's egg, break it in water, and wash your face in it.

To put a root with a conjure spell on it on the ground and let a person walk over it will hurt him.

If a man dies and leaves money buried, so that nobody knows where it is, his spirit will come back, and the color of the spirit is red.

A conjure bag contains either devil's snuff, worms, a piece of snakeskin, some leaves or sticks tied with horsehair, black owl's feather, wing of a leather-wing bat, tail of a rat, or foot of a mole; any or all of these things may be used as needed.

To carry about the person a bone from the skeleton of a human being is proof against conjure, but the bone must be gotten out of a grave by the person.

In excavating an Indian mound on the Savannah River, Georgia, the Negroes working took each a metacarpal bone to protect them against conjure.

If a Negro finds a coat or article of dress lying nicely folded, with a stick lying on it, he will not touch it for fear of conjure. On one occasion, where some cotton was left in the field, and thought to be conjured, I could not get a Negro to touch it. When I picked it up and put it in a basket, the spell left it, as the spell leaves after being touched by a human hand, the conjure going to the person touching it. Conjure can only be effectual against those of the same race. A Negro cannot conjure a white man.

To prevent a hunting dog from "running spirits," take a glass button and tie around his neck.

To stop a dog from hunting, rub an onion over his nose, and he will not trail anything; a piece of wild onion is sometimes found in a conjure bag.

To keep witches from riding, you make an x on a Bible, and put it under your pillow.

Fish bone is good for conjure when swelling has occurred.

Pecune root is good for conjure to rub with.

Any trouble that befalls a Negro that he can't explain is laid at the door of "cunjer."

Many Negroes say that they travel round with spirits, but they are generally considered conjurers.

To keep from being conjured, wear a piece of money in either shoe, or both. If you eat where anyone is who you fear may conjure you, keep a piece of silver money in your mouth while eating and drinking.

Red pepper in your shoe will prevent conjure.

To conjure by means of a hat, take a toadfrog dry and powder, and put the powder in the hat, or the dried toad may be put up over the door, or under steps. Toads, frogs, lizards, etc., must all be gotten at night on the waste of the moon, as that will insure a wasting away of the body.

From: Roland Steiner, "Observations on the Practice of Conjuring in Georgia," *Journal of American Folk-Lore* 14 (1901): 173–80.

· A Voodoo Charm ·

(African)

Take a dried one-eyed toad, a dried lizard, the little finger of a person who committed suicide, the wings of a bat, the eyes of a cat, the liver of an owl, and reduce all to a powder. Then cut up into fine pieces a lock of hair from the head of a dead (natural) child, and mix it with the powder. Make a bag of a piece of sheet that has been used as a shroud, put all of the material into it and put it into the pillow of the intended victim, when nobody is aware of your action. He will pine away and die. A few feathers run through the bag will expedite matters.

From: Henry M. Wiltse, "In the Southern Field of Folk-Lore," *Journal of American Folk-Lore* 13 (1900): 209–12.

· *Body Parts* ·

(Unidentified)

When the left ear burns, it is a sign that someone is talking about you; when the right ear burns, that he is talking evil. You must pull the ear and say:

> Bad betiger, good betiger;
> Hope the Devil may ride yer.

Betiger is a corruption of "Betide you." If good is said of you, the burning or itching will continue; if bad, it will stop.

If the lower part of your ear burns, someone is talking about you.

When your left nostril itches, it is a sign that some man whom you have never seen is coming to your house. When your right nostril itches, some woman whom you have never seen is coming.

When your nose itches while coming to your own house, you will see a stranger.

When your eye quivers, it is a sign you are going to cry about something.

When your left eye jumps, it is a sign that you are going to see some trouble.

If the palm of your hand itches, don't tell anyone about it, but put your hand under your arm and you will have some money.

If the right palm itches, you are going to get some money. If the left palm itches, it is a sign that you are going to shake hands with a stranger.

To cut your hair, and throw the hair where birds can get it and build nests with it, you will have headaches.

From: Roland Steiner, "Superstitions and Beliefs from Central Georgia," *Journal of American Folk-Lore* 12 (1899): 261–71.

· *Popular Medicine* ·

(Unidentified)

To wear one earring on the ear next to a weak eye will give good eyesight.

An iron ring about the wrist will give strength.

A leather string tied about the wrist cures rheumatism.

A flannel rag round the wrist will cure pain in the arm.

To cure "biles," walk along and pick up the first little white flint rock you see, as it is found sticking in the ground. Rub the boil with the flint, then stick the flint in the ground again, in the same position as you found it. Turn around and leave it, walking backward for a few steps.

To cure chills and fever: After you have had three or four chills, take a piece of cotton string, tie as many knots in the string as you have had chills, go into the woods and tie the string around a persimmon bush, then turn around and walk away, not looking backward.

To wash your face in water in which eggs have been boiled will bring warts.

To take off a wart, take a grain of corn, eat out the heart or white kernel, strike or cut the wart till it bleeds, then take a drop of the blood, put it in the corn where the heart was taken out, and throw the grain to a chicken. The wart will go away.

To strengthen your wind in running, eat half-cooked corn bread.

Negroes believe that if one borrows a hat from a diseased person, and the wearer sweats round the forehead where the hat rests, he will take the disease.

Don't step over a child; it will stop the child from growing. Stepping over a grown person is a sign of death.

If you cut a mole on your body till it bleeds, it will turn into a cancer and kill you.

To eat a peach, apple, or plum that a bird has pecked is said to be poisonous.

To scratch the flesh with the fingernails till it bleeds is said to be poisonous.

The bite of a "blue-gummed Negro" is said to be poisonous.

If a pregnant woman raises her hands high above her head, as for instance to carry a water bucket on the head, it will cause the navel string of the child to tie about the neck and choke it to death. The child will be born dead. All children so born are supposed to have met their death in this way.

Don't drink water out of a bucket carried on a child's head; to do so will stop it from growing.

From: Roland Steiner, "Superstitions and Beliefs from Central Georgia," *Journal of American Folk-Lore* 12 (1899): 261–71.

· *Scots-English Charms and Remedies* ·

(Scots-English)

In many parts of our mountains generations have been born, grown to old age, and even died without the aid of a physician. The people have had to rely on home treatments and old women's remedies. These are mostly combinations or concoctions of the herbs, roots, and barks found in the neighborhood; one of the mountaineers said to me that he believed the Almighty put in each neighborhood a natural remedy for every sickness of that neighborhood. Some of these old remedies are:

Butterfly-root tea given hot cures pneumonia; boneset tea is also good for pneumonia.

Sourwood bark tea thickened with flour made into pills cures dropsy; another remedy for dropsy is made by steeping elder bark in vinegar in which rusty nails have been soaked.

Wild cucumber bark soaked in whiskey is good for liver trouble: Blood-root is also good for the liver.

Sampson snakeroot tea cures colic.

Lady's slipper tea is good for nervousness.

Balm of Gilead buds steeped in whiskey cures coughs.

Shop cinders and sulphur are good to renew the blood.

Dogwood bark and old field cinders are good to clear the complexion.

Pulverized wild-cherry bark taken before meals stimulates the appetite.

Tea made of sunflower seed, prickly pear, and green coffee cures gravel; spikewood root is also good for kidney troubles; and a hot greasy plate that has been used over meat or beans while cooking, placed over the region of the bladder, will remove the gravel and let the urine pass when all other remedies have failed.

Flax-seed tea cures acid in the blood.

Dried beef gall applied to a rising will bring it to a head; and a poultice made from the bark of sassafras roots will make a boil come to a head.

Smoke-dried leaves of life-everlasting cure toothache.

Seneca snakeroot tea is good for the hives, measles, and all diseases which must be "brought out"; it is also good for whooping cough. Red poke berries are good for thrash.

Hart leaves and bark from root of red alder are good to regulate the bowels, especially of teething children; cold water drunk off sliced cumphery roots is good for diarrhea.

Dried and powered butterfly-root dusted on a sore will stop proud flesh forming.

Poultice of Jemson leaves is good for the sore throat.

Charcoal and salt in equal proportions is a sure cure for scurvy.

Red-pepper pods applied to a felon will give relief.

The inside of a chicken gizzard dried and powdered is good for dyspepsia, and also to stop vomiting.

A bunch of cold keys put down the back will stop the nose bleeding.

Perhaps our medical friends can give us scientific reasons why these "herb remedies" are efficacious, but there are some accepted remedies which I fear would baffle their science, for instance: To cure whooping cough, the sufferer should eat a piece of bread baked by a woman whose maiden name was the same as that of her husband; but the woman must not give it to the sufferer, she must leave it where someone can get it for him, or better still, if the sufferer himself can steal it. To remove a wart, cut it until it bleeds and put a drop of the blood on a grain of corn and feed the corn to a duck. I fear our medical friends would call this "quackery."

To relieve the pangs of childbirth put the hat of the child's father under the bed. One of my correspondents writes that the trouble with this remedy up on his creek is that they can't always feel sure of the hat.

A very generally used remedy for the measles is a tea made from dried sheep dung. I have been struck with the prevalence of the faith in this remedy, and its use is by no means confined to the uneducated.

From: Haywood Parker, "Folk-Lore of the North Carolina Mountaineers," *Journal of American Folk-Lore* 20 (1907): 241–50.

· *The Evil-Eye Remedy* ·

(Scots-Irish)

Silver worn in one's shoes, or, by preference, salt, averts the influences exerted by "overlooking." These abandoned old women all exercise the power of "evil eye," and salt is the best preventive of all its consequences known.

From: J. Hampden Porter, "Folk-Lore of the Mountain Whites of the Alleghanie," *Journal of American Folk-Lore* 7 (1894): 105–17.

CHAPTER 12

The Supernatural

· Witches and Witchcraft ·

(Various)

A Bewitched Churning
(Unidentified)

I was working for a man," he said, "whose wife was regarded as a witch. One day I saw her put a very small quantity of milk into the churn and go to churning. There was not over a teacupful, or such a matter, of it. But after a while I saw her put some white powder into it. She got a big lot of butter. I noticed where she put the powder, and the first chance that I got I stole some of it and went home.

"I asked mother to let me have some milk. She thought I wanted it to drink, and gave it to me. But I put it in the churn, put in some of the powder, and I got more butter than she usually got from a whole churnful of milk.

"On my way back to the farm where I worked I met a very small, dark-haired, red-complected man that I had never seen before. He said to me, 'You have used some of my material, and now you must put your name in my book.'

"I asked him what he meant, and he said I had made butter with his material, and I'd got to put my name down in his book. I hated like the mischief to do it, but was afraid of him, and decided to do what he said. So, following his directions, I scratched my arm until the blood came, and with it I wrote my name in a little book which he handed to me. He then went away, seeming to feel satisfied, and I have never seen him since."

The old man told Mr. Howard that the witches had several times turned him into a horse and ridden him off to their night frolics.

He could remember distinctly looking at himself and thinking with pride what a fine horse he was.

He said that on one of these occasions they rode him through a lot of brier bushes, and the next morning his hands were full of briers. He also claimed to have learned the secrets of witchcraft, and declared that he could do anything with Mr. Howard that he pleased by simply thinking it, and offered to demonstrate his ability to do so by practical experiments.

But Mr. Howard frankly confesses that he has sufficient superstition in his nature to have inspired him with fear of the old man, and he begged him not to experiment upon him.

His host assured him that he could feel perfectly easy in his mind, as he would do nothing against the will of his guest.

Mr. Howard says that the old man's manner throughout these recitals was such as to inspire the belief that he was deeply in earnest in all that he related.

From: Henry M. Wiltse, "In the Southern Field of Folk-Lore," *Journal of American Folk-Lore* 13 (1900): 209–12.

A Bewitched Gun
(Unidentified)

"For many years," said he, "I made my living by hunting, and many deer, bear, turkeys, and all sorts of varmints to be found in these mountings have I killed.

"I was considered a powerful good shot with a rifle, and that I certainly was.

"One morning, howsom'ever, I went out, and the first thing I knew I had a fine shot at a big deer, which was standing stock-still, broadside toward me. I raised my gun, took good aim, and expected of course to drop him dead in his tracks. But I missed him, point-blank. He made a few jumps and then stood stock-still until I had wasted three shots on him, and hadn't cut a hair. Then he ran off.

"This sort of thing went on for several days. I had lots of powerful-fine close shots, but couldn't hit a thing.

"I told my wife that there was something awful wrong, either with me or with the gun. She told me I had better go to the witch doctor, as it was likely my gun was bewitched.

"I went to the witch doctor, who told me to go into the woods near a certain house, pick out a tree, and name it after the woman who lived there. He said she was a witch, and had bewitched my gun. He said after I had named the tree as he directed I must shoot at it, and listen to see if there was any noise made at the house—for if I hit the tree the witch would be hurt, and then my gun would be all right.

"I did as he said, and at the first crack of the gun I heard the woman cry out, as if she had been hit instead of the tree. I went to the tree and found that it was hit. From that time on my gun was as good as ever, and my shooting was as reliable as it had ever been."

From: Henry M. Wiltse, "In the Southern Field of Folk-Lore," *Journal of American Folk-Lore* 13 (1900): 209–12.

The Conjurer
(African)

Two miles from Grovetown, Georgia, lived an old widowed Negro woman, Sarah Davis, who had accumulated quite a sum of money. She was very close, and would neither lend nor give. A sharp Negro, learning that she was sick, put the following scheme in execution to get some of it. He went along the path that led to the spring, and found a convenient spot for his purpose, dug a hole, put in it a small bottle containing human hair, some graveyard dirt, and two small sticks; he covered up the holes, throwing leaves over the surface of the ground to conceal his work.

He then went into the house, where he found the old woman quite sick; her son and daughters were with her. After talking with her for some time, asking particularly the nature of her complaint, as to pain, etc., he plainly told her she was under a spell, or conjured. He told her the conjure was near her house, and that if she would give him ten dollars he would find it, break the spell, and cure her; if he did not find it, no pay. He asked that the son and daughter accompany him in the search, which proposition seemed fair enough. He told them he had with him a rod that could find it. He, with the son and daughter, began the search.

He did not go on the spring path when he began the search for the conjure, but went about the yard in opposite directions, holding in his hands the rod, a small piece of rod iron about twelve inches long; he held the rod firmly in both hands, a hand holding each end of the rod. After searching the yard thoroughly, with no success, he went towards the lot where the mules were kept, with no better luck; the rod would not turn. At last he turned his face toward the spring, and slowly walked along, no one speaking a word. When he neared the spot where he had put the bottle, the rod began to show signs of life; when he got within two feet of the spot, the rod acted very excitedly. He sent the son after a hoe and shovels, made a circle about four feet in diameter, and began digging. He gradually approached the bottle, then began very carefully to take away a little dirt at a time, till at last he unearthed the bottle; the son and daughter were speechless.

He took the bottle to the old woman, who was much relieved and paid the ten dollars, and then gave her some roots to chew. The bottle, after being broken, was buried in the middle of the public road. The old woman recovered, and, though the trick was exposed, still believes she was conjured, and cured by the doctor.

From: Roland Steiner, "Observations on the Practice of Conjuring in Georgia," *Journal of American Folk-Lore* 14 (1901): 173–80.

An African Wizard
(African)

Many years ago an old African, or Guinea Negro, who was a trainer of racehorses, and hanger-on of the sporting ring, claimed to be a conjurer and wizard, professing to have derived the art from the Indians after he arrived in this country from Africa. This power he never used criminally against anyone, but only in controlling riotous gatherings, commanding forgiveness from parties threatening him with personal violence; or he would cause runaway slaves to return to their masters, foretell the time they would appear and give themselves up, and compel their masters or overseers to pardon and forgive them for the offense of running away, even against their own threats of severe punishment when caught.

By rubbing any racehorse in a peculiar and secret way he would insure him to be a winner while under his training, and claimed to be able to make cards, dice, and other games subject to his will.

From: Roland Steiner, "Observations on the Practice of Conjuring in Georgia," *Journal of American Folk-Lore* 14 (1901): 173–80.

Conjure by Hat and Water
(African)

I give an illustration of conjure by hat and water. While Bill Marshall, a Negro, well known around Grovetown, Georgia, was riding in a wagon with another Negro, the latter's hat blew off. Bill Marshall picked it up, and handed it to the Negro, who in a few days was taken sick and died; his death was laid at the door of Marshall. Marshall went to a well to get some water; he drank out of the bucket; a Negro woman came after him, drank out of the same water, and died shortly after; the death was laid to Bill Marshall. I employed him to deaden timber in new ground; none of the Negroes would have anything to do with him, but said he was a bad man, a conjure doctor; one old Negro said, "Look at tree Bill cut, die in a week." I couldn't reason the question with them; Bill could get no place to stay or cook, so I had to discharge him. He is now living in a house he built far off from his fellows, and will be forced to follow "conjuring."

Some conjure by getting the excrement of the person to be conjured, boring a hole in a tree, and putting the excrement in the hole, and driving a plug in tight; this will stop one up, an action on the bowels can't be had unless the tree with the plug is found, the plug taken out, and the tree cut down and burned where it stands; the smallest trees are generally selected to prevent their being found.

Some conjure bags are made with snakeroot, needles, and pins, and tied up with pieces of hair of the person to be conjured in a bag of red flannel.

This mode of conjure does not produce death, but much suffering and pain.

Sol Lockheart found a conjure bag at his doorstep, he did not look into it, but picked it up with two sticks, and threw the bag and two sticks into the fire.

Conjure as graveyard dirt is taken from a grave one day after burial. Negroes rarely ever go near a graveyard in daytime, never at night.

One can be conjured by shaking hands with anyone, if he has rubbed his hands with graveyard dirt.

To sprinkle graveyard dirt about the yard, about a house, makes one sleepy, sluggish, and naturally waste away and perish until he dies.

Take heads of dried snake, "ground puppy," scorpion, or "toadfrog," pound them up, put in the water or victuals of anyone; the "varmints," when taken into one's stomach, turn to life, and slowly eat you up, unless you can get the conjure taken off.

Get a hair from the mole of your head, tie it around a new ten-penny nail, and bury it with the nail head down, point up, under the doorstep. This will "run one crazy."

From: Roland Steiner, "Observations on the Practice of Conjuring in Georgia," *Journal of American Folk-Lore* 14 (1901): 173–80.

The Men Who Became Birds
(African)

O nce upon a time there was a lady who had twelve children—eleven boys and one girl. The poor lady died, and her husband married again. His second wife was a witch, who was very bad. In the daytime she changed the eleven boys into birds, and allowed them to take their human form only at night. As to the girl, she changed her into a Negress. Her father did not know her any more, and put her out of his house. The witch treated her husband's children in that way because she wanted him to leave his money to her own children.

When the poor girl was put out of her father's house, she went to see her brothers and told them what had happened to her. They said that the next morning they would take her to another country. They made a bed with leaves; and the next day, when they were birds again, each one took hold of the bed in his beak, and they carried their sister far away into another country. They placed her in a forest, and built a pretty little hut for her. One day an old witch passed by the hut, and when she saw the young girl she asked her what she was doing there. The poor girl related her story, and the witch told her she would tell her how to make her brothers remain men all the time. She must make a shirt for each one of her brothers, and not sew the shirts but weave them, and stay without speaking until the shirts were ready. It took her a long time to do the work; and when she was nearly through—only one sleeve was missing to one shirt—her stepmother found out where she was and had her arrested as a witch. They were taking her in a cart to prison when her eleven brothers came flying around the cart. She immediately threw the shirts over them, and they became men again and rescued their sister. As one of the shirts had only one sleeve, the brother who had received that shirt had all his life, instead of an arm, a bird's wing.

From: Alcee Fortier, *Louisiana Folk-Tales* (Boston and New York: Houghton Mifflin Co., 1895).

Supernaturalism in Allegheny
(Scots-Irish)

Here supernaturalism is universal, and affords an explanation for everything that is not understood. Phantoms in brute or human forms haunt their houses, graves, ravines, streams, and forests. Only the fairer, more graceful, and benign creations of primitive fancy are absent. The people live in dread of spells and terrific appearances; their horses are hag-ridden, their cattle elf-shot, their families bewitched. Where incantations and charms are capable of doing harm, countercharms will be resorted to. In these parts the distinction between black and white magic is well established. The "Witch Doctor" represents the licensed necromancer of former times; a witch is what she ever was, but less powerful and not now exposed to persecution. There is no sorcerer, properly so called, yet the former functionary, who combines the character of a medicine and fetish man with his ordinary avocations, might, if evilly disposed, act the wizard's part. Anyone possessed of occult attainments, living differently from others, engaged in unprofitable and incomprehensible occupations, becomes a suspect. These singularities warrant the suspicion that he may have scoured a tin or pewter plate in some secret place, and given himself over to the devil by saying, "I will be as clear of Jesus Christ as this dish is of dirt."

From: J. Hampden Porter, "Folk-Lore of the Mountain Whites of the Alleghanie," *Journal of American Folk-Lore* 7 (1894): 105–17.

Lycanthropy
(Scots-Irish)

Lycanthropy is common with the worst witches, and they likewise transform themselves into deer and cats. So far as testimony alone can be relied upon to establish the truth of something said to have taken place, the following cases rest upon a sure foundation.

The sister-in-law of Dr. M———, during his absence, was "pressed to death" by the witch, Mrs. R———, sitting night after night upon her chest in the form of a wildcat. This sorceress had great celebrity in the section of country where she lived, and was dreaded by everybody. She declined to make my acquaintance, and repudiated and denounced my practices in unqualified terms. This was inconvenient, for it speedily became settled that destruction would overtake me in some cave or other, and laborers grew very shy of accompanying a person whom this sibyl had thus devoted. She was the only witch met with who had been seen to walk upon water and rise into the air. The unfortunate girl whom she destroyed saw her under her own form when she first came into the room, and then witnessed her transformation into a wildcat that immediately leaped upon the bed. A witch's familiar, when a cat, is always black, and all cats of this color are more or less possessed. Nevertheless, when a witch transforms herself into a cat it is not necessarily a black one, as the following relation will show.

Mr. H——— owned a mill among the Smoky Mountains in Georgia. Three of his millers died successively of some obscure disease that the doctors could not diagnose. All these men were unmarried, and lived in the mill itself. Their illnesses were brief, and it was observed that when attacked, they all vainly attempted to make some communication to their friends. This it was supposed had reference to the mysterious cause that hurried them to the grave. People began at once to feel a dread of these premises, and particularly of a long, low room off the entrance, in which these unfortunate men sat of an evening and slept. Nobody could be induced to take the place made vacant, and it seemed as if the establishment was to be abandoned when one of the neighbors who lived a short distance down the stream volunteered to run the mill. He ground his ax and came the same evening. While kindling a fire on the hearth a brindled cat glided out of the chimney, and without exciting any special attention on his part at this time, ensconced herself in a dark corner near the door. He soon had a cheerful blaze, and sat down by a table in front of it to read his Bible. But as time passed a feeling of uneasiness, of which he was conscious from the first, grew upon him, and gradually deepened into a kind of horror. It was utterly unconnected with any definite apprehension, or sense of real danger. Then the cat got up and wailed at the door, clawing to be let out. She rubbed against his legs, and looked up at him. Instantly an awful half-recognition of those eyes shot through his brain, and leaping up he seized the ax and struck at her, cutting off one foot. With a wild woman's scream the creature darted up the chimney and disappeared, while he, thoroughly unnerved, hastened home, and found his wife bleeding to death from a severed hand.

From: J. Hampden Porter, "Folk-Lore of the Mountain Whites of the Alleghanie," *Journal of American Folk-Lore* 7 (1894): 105–17.

Breaking a Witch's Spell
(Scots-English)

An animal killed by witchcraft should be burnt, partly because that is the best and most effectual way of destroying things that are infected, and also for the reason that in more than one way this may be made to affect the witch; she can be fascinated or punished. One of the parties implicated related the effects of fire in the case of a Tennesseean sorceress who had done much harm.

An incredulous and stupid person, such as exists in every community, borrowed a boiler from her and refused to return it. Then she came every night and danced on him till he nearly fainted. There was no doubt about this, because she permitted herself to be seen. Each day, also, one of his sheep reared up, gave two or three jumps, and fell dead. At length the "witch doctor" was called in, and he, being a pious man and a member of the church, advised his patient to try the effect of honesty and give back the boiler. This he did, but the witch laughed at him, and things went on as before.

It was now evident that her machinations were prompted by malice, and not resorted to from a sense of justice, so the doctor directed him to eviscerate the next sheep that died, to do this alone, and in perfect silence. Moreover, on no account to lend or give away any article, however trifling its value, until the effect of his charm had been fully tried.

Having taken out the lungs and heart, they were to be carried home, the kitchen cleared, and these organs laid upon a bed of live embers. While procuring them, the witch's granddaughter, "a right smart shoot of a girl, training for a witch herself," saw what he was doing as she passed through his field, and, anticipating the result, ran home, saying that her "Granny" would shortly be ill. Such was indeed the case, for no sooner had the sheep's vitals been placed upon the coals than her shrieks alarmed the neighborhood. A crowd gathered that seems to have had some inkling of what was going on, for a committee of women inspected the sufferer by force, and found her breast completely charred. The spell was broken before fatal consequences ensued, and from that time the persecutions and losses which had persisted so long came to an end.

From: J. Hampden Porter, "Folk-Lore of the Mountain Whites of the Alleghanie," *Journal of American Folk-Lore* 7 (1894): 105–17.

Hattie McGahee and Other Conjurers
(African)

A family of Negroes consisting of husband, wife, and son applied to me at my plantation near Waynesboro, Georgia, for work. The man and woman were well advanced in years and both of the pure Negro type. The woman asked that I would give them a house as far removed from others as possible, which request seemed to me rather odd, as most Negroes prefer living together, or near each other. They worked as well as the average Negro, and I had no cause to complain.

A few months after their arrival, when they were firmly established and were well acquainted with the neighborhood, it began to be rumored about that Hattie McGahee, the woman, was a root doctress, could relieve pains, cure diseases, foretell events, and bring about estrangement between husband and wife, or effect reconciliations. She had as assistants in the occult art a perfectly black dog and cat, which were regarded as evil spirits, perhaps as Satan himself.

Upon the same plantation were two Negroes, Joe Coleman and Henry Jenkins, both of whom were seeking to win the affections of a young Negress named Laura Jones. Henry Jenkins sought the assistance of Hattie McGahee, while Joe Coleman procured as adviser and friend a celebrated Negro root doctor called Hosey Lightfoot. The black cat or dog was brought into service by furnishing a few hairs which were burned with some sassafras sticks and as a powder administered in food to Laura. The plantation was divided as to the suitors for the hand of Laura, and Hattie declared open war against all those espousing the cause of Joe Coleman. Crossmarks and graveyard dirt, or small bundles of tied-up sticks, were found lying in the paths leading to the houses of the respective rivals, and many of the Negroes refused to work in the same field with Hattie and her husband.

Every headache or other pain, or even diseases common to the climate, were laid to the account of the different doctors. I once found a large pile of cotton lying in the field, which the Negroes refused to take out, claiming that Hattie McGahee had put a spell on it. Negroes would not even walk in the paths that Hattie used, fearing the effect of some spell. Matters were at a fever heat until a crisis was reached in the killing of Hattie McGahee's dog, which was ascribed to Joe Coleman and his friends. When the principals with their friends met to settle the difficulty personally, the result was that Henry Jenkins was fearfully mutilated with an ax and Joe Coleman suffered a fearful beating with sticks, while others of the respective parties escaped with more or less personal injury. Joe Coleman, the aggressor, was sent to the chain gang by the county court for six months. While he was serving out his term, Henry Jenkins recovered from his injuries, and married Laura. Shortly after the difficulty, the father of Joe Coleman was kicked by a mule and killed; his death was laid at the door of Hattie McGahee, the Negroes believing that she used some spell over the mule, making him kill Lewis Coleman, the father of Joe. Since I left Waynesboro, Henry Jenkins and another Negro had a difficulty, in which both were killed, about the same Laura Jones whom he married. I immediately discharged the whole McGahee family, saving the young son, who refused to go with his mother and father. Wherever she went, still pursuing the calling of a dealer in the occult science, trouble followed in her wake. Hattie could interpret dreams, was a weather prophet, and in short was completely proficient in her art.

Those following the profession of "conjure doctor" rarely remain in one place for a long time, and generally wish their homes far removed from other habitations. When their work becomes known and its effect felt, for the peace of all, master as well as man, it is necessary to remove them from the place.

In 1896, upon my plantation near Grovetown, Georgia, I secured as cook the services of a mulatto woman by the name of Jane Jackson, who was highly recommended. She and her husband lived in the yard. At the same time I employed as milkwoman Anna Bonney, whose husband, Jim Bonney, attended to the lot. An estrangement between Anna and Jane soon produced the following disastrous results. Anna would complain about Jane, Jane in turn would accuse Anna of taking the milk. One morning at breakfast, my brother and myself, upon drinking a little of the coffee in our cups, were made violently sick.

Of course Jane was questioned very closely in regard to it; but I soon became convinced that she was not the guilty party. We never could explain the coffee incident, having failed to analyze the coffee. A Negro told me that he thought powdered pecune root was put in the coffee, as it is a powerful emetic. Though Anna milked, Jane churned, and every effort to make butter failed. Jane said that Anna had put a spell on the milk. Anna retorted by saying that Jane put something in the milk to prevent the butter coming, so that she, Anna, could be discharged.

Chickens about the yard began to die, the water in the well had a peculiar taste, little bundles of sticks were found in the kitchen as well as in the cow lot, and graveyard dirt served its purpose in various ways and in many places. Having stopped using water out of the well, we had all the water used for drinking and culinary purposes brought from a spring that was a short distance from the house. Very soon sticks of various lengths, "devil's snuff," and graveyard dirt was found strewed along the path to the spring. Our milk cow was prematurely going dry, and a fine calf dying at the lot, together with the fact that Jim Bonney and his wife Anna were seen by a Negro, Steve Olley, at midnight making repeated circuits around the well, and motioning with their hands towards the house occupied by Jane Jackson.

Upon the Negroes telling me of the walk around the well, I determined to make a clean sweep of everybody, and discharged all hands in any way concerned in the matter. It was with great difficulty, while all this "cunjer" was going on, that I could get anyone to enter the yard in order to perform the slightest offices. Negroes would use neither ax nor hoes kept at the yard, but would bring their own, and take them away as soon as the work was finished. Some would not even pass through the yard. When a hen was put to setting, she rarely brought off chickens.

Shortly after the discharge of all parties, John Jackson, the husband of Jane Jackson, was seen, when passing on a path, to motion three times towards Anna Bonney's house. Anna was standing in the yard at the time the motions were made, and fell in convulsions. She was taken into the house, where she lingered for some weeks, and died. Her death was laid at the door of Jane Jackson. Before using the well, I had it thoroughly cleaned out, and red pepper thrown in, as well as into and under the house that was occupied by Jane Jackson, before I could get other Negroes to occupy the premises, or use the water from the well. It can be well understood from the foregoing, how this matter of "cunjer," in designing hands, can work evil to the innocent. Jane and Anna, with the assistance of their husbands, were fighting a battle royal against each other. Yet I and other innocent people had parts to play in this drama.

From: Roland Steiner, "Observations on the Practice of Conjuring in Georgia," *Journal of American Folk-Lore* 14 (1901): 173–80.

· *The Singing Bones* ·

(African)

Once upon a time there lived a man and a woman who had twenty-five children. They were very poor; the man was good, the woman was bad. Every day when the husband returned from his work the wife served his dinner, but always meat without bones.

"How is it that this meat has no bones?"

"Because bones are heavy, and meat is cheaper without bones. They give more for the money."

The husband ate, and said nothing.

"How is it you don't eat meat?"

"You forget that I have no teeth. How do you expect me to eat meat without teeth?"

"That is true," said the husband, and he said nothing more, because he was afraid to grieve his wife, who was as wicked as she was ugly.

When one has twenty-five children one cannot think of them all the time, and one does not see if one or two are missing. One day, after his dinner, the husband asked for his children. When they were by him he counted them, and found only fifteen. He asked his wife where were the ten others. She answered that they were at their grandmother's, and every-day she would send one more for them to get a change of air. That was true, every day there was one that was missing.

One day the husband was at the threshold of his house, in front of a large stone which was there. He was thinking of his children, and he wanted to go and get them at their grandmother's, when he heard voices that were saying:

> Our mother killed us,
> Our father ate us.
> We are not in a coffin,
> We are not in the cemetery.

At first he did not understand what that meant, but he raised the stone, and saw a great quantity of bones, which began to sing again. He then understood that it was the bones of his children, whom his wife had killed, and whom he had eaten. Then he was so angry that he killed his wife; buried his children's bones in the cemetery, and stayed alone at his house. From that time he never ate meat, because he believed it would always be his children that he would eat.

From: Alcee Fortier, *Louisiana Folk-Tales* (Boston and New York: Houghton Mifflin Co., 1895).

· Specters ·

(Various)

Ghosts
(Scots-Irish)

Mrs. S——— was accustomed to visit her sister's farm by a path that led along Trout Run. Here, at dusk one evening, she saw a small white dog trotting along in advance, but paid no attention to it until the form suddenly disappeared at a spot where there was no cover. This happened several times, and she put salt in her shoes and said an abundance of prayers. Then the specter no longer followed her.

Miss F———, who was not born on Christmas week, and therefore had no natural power of seeing spirits, related the apparition of her brother's first wife. This lady was devotedly attached to her husband, and when she was in the last stage of consumption could not die until he made an oath to remain single for the remainder of his life. Not long after he perjured himself, but the peace of that household was gone. Ever after there was "a sense of something moving to and fro" upon them all. His sister, in common with the rest, heard the sighs and sobs of the disconsolate ghost, she saw her dim figure floating through the dusk, and was chilled to the heart by its icy atmosphere as the spirit went by in passages or upon the stairs.

Mrs. H———, riding on a pillion behind her father from camp meeting, saw a tall white form rise beside the horse. It was not terrified, however, as often happens in such cases. Her father did not see the phantom, and was very deaf. She remained motionless from fear while the specter moved along beside them. Soon a running stream was reached, and it vanished upon its brink.

Mr. B———, going home one night by Crackwhip Furnace, then abandoned, beheld the likeness of a black bear in front, but it screamed horribly at him with a human voice. His horse was terrified, and when the thing came nearer and screamed again, he rode for his life. Half a mile away from the spot this same dreadful cry sounded in his ears shriller and more appalling than before.

Mr. C———, riding on the same road one dark autumnal evening, suddenly found his mare attacked by an invisible adversary. Blows were struck at her head, but the animal, though snorting, plunging, and rearing in terror, could not stir from the place; something met it at every turn. The rider tried to pray, but in vain. He was able to think the words, yet not to utter them. In his extremity the name of God at last burst from his lips. At once the horse sprang forward, and clasping its neck the pair dashed down hill into a brook. Whatever it was that beset them could not follow across flowing water, but a shriek that shook his heart swept by him as he fled.

From: J. Hampden Porter, "Folk-Lore of the Mountain Whites of the Alleghanie," *Journal of American Folk-Lore* 7 (1894): 105–17.

A Ghost's Revenge
(Scots-Irish)

Sometimes an apparition comes on a mission of justice; at others, ghosts revisit "the glimpses of the moon," inspired with the desire for vengeance. Before the separation of West Virginia from the mother state, Colonel ——— murdered one of his Negro women with aggravated circumstances of cruelty. The crime could not be proved against him, and his act remained unpunished by law. But when investigation was at an end, and it became evident that nothing would be done, a white dog made its appearance upon the estate. Numbers saw it, and knew it for a specter by its vanishing while in full view. This goblin brute hunted the man to death. It followed and went before him, came into his room, haunted the guilty being night and day, until he pined away, and, having made a confession, died.

From: J. Hampden Porter, "Folk-Lore of the Mountain Whites of the Alleghanie," *Journal of American Folk-Lore* 7 (1894): 105–17.

The Black Dog
(English)

In Botetourt County, Virginia, there is a pass that was much traveled by people going to Bedford County and by visitors to mineral springs in the vicinity. In the year 1683 the report was spread that at the wildest part of the trail in this pass there appeared at sunset a great black dog, who, with majestic tread, walked in a listening attitude about two hundred feet and then turned and walked back. Thus he passed back and forth like a sentinel on guard, always appearing at sunset to keep his nightly vigil and disappearing again at dawn. And so the whispering went with bated breath from one to another, until it had traveled from one end of the state to the other. Parties of young cavaliers were made up to watch for the black dog. Many saw him. Some believed him to be a veritable dog sent by some master to watch, others believed him to be a witch dog.

A party decided to go through the pass at night, well armed, to see if the dog would molest them. Choosing a night when the moon was full they mounted good horses and sallied forth. Each saw a great dog larger than any dog they had ever seen, and, clapping spurs to their horses, they rode forward. But they had not calculated on the fear of their steeds. When they approached the dog, the horses snorted with fear, and in spite of whip, spur, and rein gave him a wide berth, while he marched on as serenely as if no one were near. The party were unable to force their horses to take the pass again until after daylight. Then they were laughed at by their comrades to whom they told their experiences. Thereupon they decided to lie in ambush, kill the dog, and bring in his hide. The next night found the young men well hidden behind rocks and bushes with guns in hand. As the last ray of sunlight kissed the highest peak of the Blue Ridge, the black dog appeared at the lower end of his walk and came majestically toward them. When he came opposite, every gun cracked. When the smoke cleared away, the great dog was turning at the end of his walk, seemingly unconscious of the presence of the hunters. Again and again they fired and still the dog walked his beat. And fear caught the hearts of the hunters, and they fled wildly away to their companions, and the black dog held the pass at night unmolested.

Time passed, and year after year went by, until seven years had come and gone, when a beautiful woman came over from the old country, trying to find her husband who eight years before had come to make a home for her in the new land. She traced him to Bedford County and from there all trace of him was lost. Many remembered the tall, handsome man and his dog. Then there came to her ear the tale of the vigil of the great dog of the mountain pass, and she pleaded with the people to take her to see him, saying that if he was her husband's dog he would know her. A party was made up and before night they arrived at the gap. The lady dismounted, and walked to the place where the nightly watch was kept. As the shadows grew long, the party fell back on the trail, leaving the lady alone, and as the sun sank into his purple bed of splendor the great dog appeared. Walking to the lady, he laid his great head in her lap for a moment, then turning he walked a short way from the trail, looking back to see that she was following. He led her until he paused by a large rock, where he gently scratched the ground, gave a long, low wail, and disappeared. The lady called the party to her and asked them to dig. As they had no implements, and she refused to leave, one of them rode back for help. When they dug below the surface they found the skeleton of a man and the hair and bones of a great dog. They found a seal ring on the hand of the man and a heraldic embroidery in silk that the wife recognized. She removed the bones for proper burial and returned to her old home. It was never known who had killed the man. But from that time to this the great dog, having finished his faithful work, has never appeared again.

From: R. F. Herrick, "The Black Dog of the Blue Ridge," *Journal of American Folk-Lore* 13 (1910): 251–52.

· *The Devil* ·
(Various)

Why the Devil Never Wears a Hat
(African)

Here we find out why the devil never wears a hat, as told by one of African descent:

"De debbil, he am jes' chuck full ob fire an' steam an' brimstone, an' all dese jes' keep up a pow'ful workin' an' goin' on together; an' to keep from jes' nater'ly 'xplodin', he got a hole in de top o' he haid—a roun' hole—an' de steam an' fire jes' pour out 'n dere all de time. No cullud pusson ever see de debbil when de steam an' fire warn't rushin' out, 'n so 't warn't no use fur him to wear a hat."

From: Anne Weston Whitney, "Items of Maryland Belief and Custom," *Journal of American Folk-Lore* 12 (1899): 273–74.

Jack-o'-My-Lantern
(African)

Once dey wuz a man name Jack. He wuz a mighty weeked man, an' treat he wife an' chil'en like a dawg. He did n' do nuttin' but drink from mawin' tell night, an' 'twarn' no use to say nuttin' 'tall to 'im 'cause he wuz jes' ez ambitious ez a mad dawg. Well suh, he drink an' he drink tell whiskey could n' mek 'im drunk; but et las' hit bu'n 'im up inside; an' den de Debble come fur 'im. When Jack see de Debble, he wuz so skeart he leettle mo'n er drapt in de flo'. Den he bague de Debble to let 'im off jes' a leetle while, but de Debble say:

"Naw Jack, I ain't gwine wait no longer; my wife, Abbie Sheens, is speckin' yo'."

So de Debble start off pretty bris' an' Jack wuz 'bleeged to foller, tell dey come to a grog shop.

"Mr. Debble," said Jack, "don' yo' wan' a drink?"

"Well," said de Debble, "I b'leeve I does, but I ain't got no small change; we don' keep no change down dyah."

"Tell yo' wotcher do, Mr. Debble," said Jack. "I got one ten cent en my pocket; yo' change yo'sef inter nurr ten cent, an' we kin git two drinks, an' den yo' kin change yo'sef back agin."

So de Debble change hisse'f inter a ten cent, an' Jack pick 'im up; but stid o' gwine in de grog shop, Jack clap de ten cent in he pocketbook dat he hadn't took outen he pocket befo', 'cause he did n' wan' de Debble to see dat de ketch wuz in de shape ob a cross. He shet it tight, an' dyah he had de Debble, an' 'twarn' no use fur 'im to struggle, 'cause he could n' git by dat cross. Well suh; fus' he swar and threat'n Jack wid what he wuz gwine to do 'im, an' den he begun to bague, but Jack jes' tu'n roun' an' start to go home. Den de Debble say:

"Jack, ef yo'll lemme out o' hyah, I'll let yo' off fur a whole year, I will, fur trufe. Lemme go Jack, 'cause Abbie Sheens is too lazy to put de bresh on de fire, an' hit 'll all go black out ef I ain' dyah fo' long, to ten' to it."

Den Jack say ter hisse'f, "I gret mine to let 'im go, 'cause in a whole year I kin 'pent and git 'ligion an' git shet on 'im dat er way."

Den he say, "Mr. Debble, I'll letcher out ef yo' 'clar fo' gracious yo' won' come after me fur twel munt."

De den Debble promise befo' Jack undo de clasp, an' by de time Jack got he pocketbook open he wuz gone. Den Jack say to hisse'f, "Well, now I gwine to 'pent an' git 'ligion sho'; but 't ain' no use bein' in no hurry; de las' six munt will be plenty o' time. Whar dat ten cent? Hyah, 't is. I gwine git me a drink." When de six munt wuz gone, Jack 'lowed one munt would be time 'nuff to 'pent, and when de las' munt come, Jack say he gwine hab one mo' spree; an' den he would have a week er ten days lef' an' dat wuz plenty o' time, 'cause he done hearn o' folks 'penting on dey death bade. Den he went on a spree fo' sho', an' when de las' week come, Jack had 'lirium trimblins, an' de fus' ting he knowed dyah wuz de Debble at de do', an' Jack had to git outen he bade and go 'long wid 'im. After a while dey pas a tree full o' gret big red apples.

"Don' yo' wan' some apples, Mr. Debble?" said Jack.

"Yo' kin git some ef yo' wan' em," said de Debble, an' he stop an' look up in de tree.

"How yo' speck a man wid 'lirium trimblins to climb a tree?" said Jack. "Yo' cotch hole de bough, an' I'll push yer up in de crotch, an' den yo' kin git all yo' wants."

So Jack push 'im in de crotch, an' de Debble 'gin to feel de apples to git a meller one. While he wuz doin' dat, Jack whip he knife outen he pocket, an' cut a cross in de bark ob de tree, jes' under de Debble, an' de Debble holler:

"Tzip! Sumpi' nurr hut me den. Wotcher doin' down dyah, Jack? I gwine cut yo' heart out."

But he could n' git down while dat cross wuz dyah, an' Jack jes' sot down on de grars, an' watch 'im ragin' an' swarin' an' cussin'. Jack kep' 'im dyah all night tell 'twuz gret big day, an' den de Debble change he chune, an' he say:

"Jack, lemme git down hyah an' I'll gib yo' nurr year."

"Gimme nuttin'!" said Jack, an' stretch hisse'f out on de grars. Arfter a while, 'bout sun up, de Debble say:

"Jack, cut dis ting offen hyah an' lemme git down, an' I'll gib yo' ten year."

"Naw surree," said Jack, "I won' letcher git down less yo' 'clar fo' gracious dat yo' won' nuver come arfter me no mo'.'"

When de Debble fine Jack wuz hard ez a rock, he 'greed, an' 'clared fo' gracious dat he wouldn' nuver come fur Jack agin, an' Jack cut de cross offen de tree, and de Debble lef' without a word. Arfter dat Jack nuver thought no mo' 'bout 'pentin', 'cause he warn' feared ob de Debble, an' he did n' wan' to go whar dey warn' no whiskey. Den he lib on tell he body war out, an' he wuz' bleeged to die. Fus' he went to de gate o' heaven, but de angel jes' shake he hade. Den he wen' to de gate o' hell, but when wud come dat Jack wuz dyah, de Debble holler to de imps.

"Shet de do' an' don' let dat man come in hyah; he done treat me scanlous. Tell 'im to go 'long back whar he come frum."

Den Jack say:

"How I gwine fine my way back in de dark? Gimme a lantern."

Den de Debble tek a chunk outen de fire, an' say:

"Hyah, tek dis, and dontcher nuver come back hyah no mo'.'"

Den Jack tek de chunk o' fire an' start back, but when he come to a ma'sh, he done got los', an' he ain' nuver fine he way out sence.

From: William Wellis Newell, "The Ignis Fatuus, Its Character and Legendary Origin," *Journal of American Folk-Lore* 17 (1904): 39–60.

The Devil's Marriage
(African)

One day there was a pretty young girl, but she was very proud, and every time the young men came to court her, she found a pretext to send them away. One was too small, another was too tall, another had red hair; in short, she refused all her suitors. One day her mother said to her, "My daughter, you see that tall, tall tree in the middle of the river? I am going to put this pumpkin on the smallest branch at the top of the tree, and that young man who will be able to climb up and catch the pumpkin will be your husband."

The daughter said she had no objection, so they put a notice in the newspapers. The next week a crowd of young men presented themselves, and among them one who was beautifully dressed and exceedingly handsome. He was the Devil, but nobody knew him. The young girl told her mother, "I wish he would catch the pumpkin."

All the young men climbed on the tree, but no one could succeed in reaching the pumpkin. When the turn of the Devil came, in one minute he was up the tree, and had the pumpkin in his hand. As soon as he was down he said to the young girl, "Come now, come with me to my house."

The girl put on her best dress and went away with the Devil. On the road they met a man, who said to the Devil, "Give me my cravat and my collar which I had lent to you."

The Devil took off his cravat and his collar, and said, "Here, take your old cravat and your old collar." A little farther on, another man saw the Devil and told him, "Give me my shirt which I had lent you." The Devil took off his shirt and said, "Here, here, take your old shirt." A little farther, he saw another man, who said to him, "Give me my cloak which I had lent to you." The Devil took off his cloak, and said, "Here, here, take your old cloak." A little farther, another man asked for his trousers, then another one for his hat. The Devil took off the trousers and the hat, and said, "Here, here, take your old trousers and your old hat." He came down from his carriage and disappeared for a few minutes, then he returned as well dressed as before.

The young lady was beginning to be very much frightened when they met another man, who said, "Give me my horses which I had lent to you." The Devil gave him his four horses, and said to his wife, "Get down from the carriage and hitch yourself to it." She drew the carriage as far as the Devil's house, and was so frightened that her heart was almost in her mouth.

The Devil entered his garden, and said to his wife, "Remain here with my mother." As soon as he was gone the mother said to the young lady, "Ah! my daughter, you have taken a bad husband; you have married the Devil."

The poor girl was so sorry that she did not know what to do, and she said to the old woman, "Can you not tell me how I can run away?" The old woman replied, "Yes, wait until tomorrow morning; but come, let me show you something." She opened the door of a little room, and said, "Look, my daughter." The girl looked in the room, and what did she see? A number of women hanging from a nail. She was so frightened that she asked the old woman if she could not hide her somewhere until the next morning. The woman said, "Yes, but let me tell you how you can escape from here. When the Devil tells you to give one sack of corn to his rooster which wakes him up in the morning you will give him three sacks that he may eat more and not crow so early. Then you will go to the chicken house and take six dirty eggs. Take care not to take clean eggs; that will bring you bad luck."

The next morning the young lady gave the rooster three sacks of corn, she took her eggs, and ran away. When the rooster had finished eating his three sacks, he crowed, "Mr. Devil, awake quickly; someone has run away from the house!" The Devil got up quickly and started running after his wife. The poor girl looked behind her, and saw smoke and fire—indeed, the Devil himself. She took an egg and broke it: A high wooden fence arose in the middle of the road. The Devil had to return home to get his golden ax to cut down the fence. After he had broken down the fence he took his ax to his house.

The girl looked behind her; she saw smoke and fire—the Devil himself. She broke another egg: There grew up an iron fence. The Devil went home to get his golden ax, and had to take it back after breaking the fence.

The girl looked again; there was fire and smoke. She broke another egg: A great fire rose up in the road. The Devil went to get his jar of water to put out the fire, and then had to take the jar back.

The girl heard again a noise; it was fire and smoke. She broke another egg: A brick wall grew up. The Devil went to get his golden ax, and carried it back after breaking the wall.

The girl looked again: She saw fire and smoke. She broke another egg: A small river appeared, in which was a small canoe. She entered the canoe and crossed the river. The Devil was obliged to swim across.

The girl looked again; she saw fire and smoke. She broke another egg: A large river appeared. There was a big crocodile on the other side of the river warming himself in the sun. The girl sang, "Grandmother, I pray you, cross me over; grandmother, I pray you, save my life." The crocodile said, "Climb on my back, my little one, I shall save your life."

The Devil saw in what way the girl had crossed the river, so he said to the crocodile, "Cross me over, crocodile; cross me over." The crocodile replied, "Climb on my back; I shall cross you over." When he reached the middle of the river, he dived under the water, and the Devil was drowned.

When the girl had left her mother's house with her husband, her mother had said to her, "Well, my child, what do you wish me to do with your old white horse?" The girl said to her mother, "I don't care what you do; put him out in the pasture and let him die if he wants to." However, when she crossed the river on the crocodile's back, she saw her old horse in the pasture, and she said to him, "I pray you, old body, save my life!" The horse replied, "Ah, you want me now to save your life; did you not tell your mother to let me die, if I wanted? Well, climb on my back, I shall carry you to your mother."

The girl soon reached her mother's house. She got down from the horse and kissed him, then she kissed her mother. She remained at home after that, and did not wish to marry again, after having had the Devil for her husband.

From: Alcee Fortier, *Louisiana Folk-Tales* (Boston and New York: Houghton Mifflin Co., 1895).

Chapter 13

Nature

· *Animal Lore* ·

(Scots-English)

When the family moves, fire should be taken from the old home to start that in the new; but the cat should not be taken. Ashes should never be moved from the fireplace on Fridays, if so, something will be stolen from the house before the next Friday. If a young girl or maid be allowed to clean out the spring, it will go dry.

There are many signs of special significance, such as the belief that if the right hand itches you will shake hands with a stranger; if the left, you will soon handle money. This evidently gave rise to the expression, "He has an itching palm," meaning he is fond of money. Sneezing before breakfast means visitors, one for each sneeze. If a baby is allowed to see itself in a looking glass before it is six months old, it will die before it is a year old; and if by chance it does live, it will grow up "two-faced."

If a cat sits down among a crowd of girls, the one she looks at will marry first. When the guard dog lies down in the yard and rolls over on his back, a visitor may be expected from the direction his head points. If the nose itches, visitors may be expected; but it must not be rubbed up, for that would cause the visitors to lose their way. A measuring worm on one's clothes is a sign of approaching death, as the worm is taking measures for the shroud; the evil spell is broken, however, if the worm is knocked off before it finishes. The rolling onto the hearth of a burning log or "chunk" means company is coming, and if one spits on it and thinks of the persons desired to be seen, they will come; or any wish may be made and it will "come true." If you "cuss" or step over your pole, the fish will stop biting.

From: Haywood Parker, "Folk-Lore of the North Carolina Mountaineers," *Journal of American Folk-Lore* 20 (1907): 241–50.

· Cats ·

(Various)

Cats and Mice
(Unidentified)

It is very bad luck to kill a cat.

If a strange cat comes to the house, it is a sign of good luck.

To "move a cat," that is, to take a cat away with you, is bad luck. Negroes never move a cat.

A cat will suck a child's breath, and one must not be allowed to sleep in the same room with children.

It is bad luck to have a cat sleep in bed with you. A Negro told me that one night a cat almost drew all his breath away.

A black cat without a single white hair on it is said to be a witch. No Negro will keep a pure black cat in his house.

If you rub the hair of a black cat in the night, you will see the fire it has brought from hell.

Never give a black cat away, but lend it.

If you kill a mouse, the others will gnaw your clothes; if you shoot one with a gun, their friends will overrun the house and drive you from it. Mice are cats' food.

If a mouse eats a hole in a garment, and you darn it, you will have seven years' bad luck; to avoid this, you must make a square patch.

From: Roland Steiner, "Superstitions and Beliefs from Central Georgia," *Journal of American Folk-Lore* 12 (1899): 273–74.

The Origin of the Cat
(African)

When I stepped on the cat her limp and her cries were so piteous I took her to the kitchen to apologize with a saucer of cream and ask Mammy to care for her.

"Did *you* trod on dat cat? I certainly is might sorry, for it's bound to be unlucky for you if you hurt a cat."

I ventured the opinion that to kill a cat brought ill luck, but had not heard anything about accidentally hurting one.

"My mercy, chile, don't you know it is a *sin* to kill a cat? Duz you know anything about cats and how they come to be here on this earth?"

I acknowledged my ignorance, unless they were included in the general creation, and procession into the ark.

"Well, white folks don't know *nothing* 'cept what they reads out a books. Wa'n't *no* cats in *no* ark, and it's a sin to kill a cat, 'cause a cat is Jesus' right-hand glove. Jesus was down here once, on this here earth, walking round jest like a man. I 'spects you heerd about *that*, didn't you? It's all put down in the Bible, they tells me. I never *seen* it thar, fer I can't read nor write; don't know one letter from the next, but it's all writ down in the Bible, what God sent down from heaven in a bush all on fire right into Moses' hand. Yes, indeed, it is God's own truth, jest as I am telling you. When Jesus was here in this world, He went round constant visiting cullud folks. He always was mighty fond of cullud folks. So one day He was a-walking along and he come to a poor old cullud woman's house. When He went in the door and give her 'howdy,' she stand still and look at him right hard. Then she say 'Lord' (she never seen or heerd tell of Him before, but something in her just seemed to call his name), and she kept on a-looking and a-looking at Him hard, and she say over again, 'Lord, I is jest mizzable.' Then he say, 'Woman, what you mizzable fer?' Then she say, the third time, 'Lord, I is mizzable, fer the rats and the mice is a eating and a destroying everything I got. They's done eat all my cornmeal, and all my meat; they's done eat all my clothes. They's eat holes in my bed, and now they's jest ready to eat me myself, and I am that mizzable, I don't know no more *what* to do.'

"Jesus he look long time at her, mighty hard, and he say, 'Woman, behold your God!' and then He pulled off his right-hand glove, and flung it down on the floor. Soon as that glove touched that floor, it turned into a cat, right then and right thar, and it began a-catching all them rats, and all them mice, more'n any cat done since when it do its best. Indeed it did, made out of Jesus' right-hand glove, before that woman's own eyes—the four fingers for the legs, and the thumb for the tail—and that's the *truth* 'bout how cats got here. Guess you know *now* why it's a sin to kill a cat, and 'bliged to be unlucky to hurt one."

From: Marcia McLennan, "Origin of the Cat: A Negro Tale," *Journal of American Folk-Lore* 9 (1896): 71.

• *Snakes* •

(Unidentified)

It is good luck to kill the first snake seen in the spring.

If you find a snake in the yard about the house, kill him and then burn him. No mouse will come about the house.

Negroes believe that a black snake sucks cows.

Negroes will not kill a king snake, as he is the enemy of rattlesnakes and other poisonous snakes.

If a snake bites a man, he goes and eats some snakeweed; as the blood of a man is poisonous to a snake, he will die if he cannot get the weed.

When a king snake fights a rattlesnake and gets bitten, the king snake goes into the woods and gets a snakeroot leaf as antidote.

A "coach-whip" will run you down and whip you to death.

From: Roland Steiner, "Superstitions and Beliefs from Central Georgia," *Journal of American Folk-Lore* 12 (1899): 261–71.

· Birds ·

(Unidentified)

When a screech owl "hollers" about a sickroom, the sick person will in all probability die.

To stop a screech owl from "hollerin'," turn your left-hand pants pocket inside out, or take off the left shoe and turn the sole up, or throw "a chunk of fire" out the window.

If a screech owl flies into a room, it is a sign of sickness or death, or of some evil. If anyone kills the owl, some member of the family will be killed or hurt.

It is bad luck to kill a buzzard, a mockingbird, a bluebird, a bee-martin, or a thrush; the last two oppose and keep off hawks.

If a buzzard flies over your house, you are going to get a letter or hear good news.

Jaybirds go to hell on Friday, carrying a small stick as fuel for the Devil.

To keep hawks from catching chickens, put a white flint rock in the fire.

To break up a killdee's nest is a sign that you will break a limb.

From: Roland Steiner, "Superstitions and Beliefs from Central Georgia," *Journal of American Folk-Lore* 12 (1899): 261–71.

· Deer ·

(English)

El Moore is a good hunter, and a splendid good shot, too. But he got into a streak o' mighty ornery luck one time jes' on ercount er one er them thar white deer. He tole me all erbout hit with 'is own lips, an' El is a mighty truthful man.

He said he war out a' huntin' one mornin', an' he come onter a white deer, an' hit war not more 'n fifteen er twenty feet frum 'im.

He fired at hit, but never toch a hair. That deer jes' stood still untwel he'd a-wasted seven or eight shots on hit. Then hit run off, an' he tried his gun on a spot in a tree, an' the bullet went straight to ther mark.

He got his dander up then, an' laid fer thet white deer, an' he wasted a powerful lot more ammunition on hit, untwel fin'ly 'e plugged hit in ther shoulder.

But he was mighty sorry fer that, right then an' for a long time afterwards. He said hit made the sorrowfulest noise 'at he ever hearn in all of his life. An' from that day twelvemonth hit war unpossible fer El ter kill any kind er deer whatsomever. He could kill other kinds of varmints all right ernough, but kill a deer he couldn't.

From: Henry M. Wiltse, "In the Southern Field of Folk-Lore," *Journal of American Folk-Lore* 13 (1900): 209–12.

· Monkeys ·

(African)

There was a monkey which fell in love with a beautiful young girl. He dressed as a man and went to call on her. He was so well received that one day he took his best friend with him to see his ladylove. The young girl's father asked Mr. Monkey's friend some questions about his daughter's lover. The friend said that Mr. Monkey was good and rich, but there was a secret about him. The father wanted to know the secret, but the friend said he would tell him another day. Mr. Monkey was finally engaged to the young lady, and the night of the wedding he invited his friend to the supper. The latter was jealous of Mr. Monkey, and at the end of the supper began to sing. This was a song that made all monkeys dance, whether they wished to or not, so Mr. Monkey looked at his friend and beckoned him to stop singing. He continued, however, to sing, and all at once Mr. Monkey got up and began to dance. He jumped about so wildly that his tail came out of his clothes, and everyone saw that he was a monkey. The father understood the secret, and beat him dreadfully. His friend, however, ran off, dancing and singing.

From: Alcee Fortier, *Louisiana Folk-Tales* (Boston and New York: Houghton Mifflin Co., 1895).

· The Irishman and the Frogs ·

(Irish)

Once upon a time there was a drunken Irishman who was returning to his village and who passed by a little river where were many frogs. He heard the frogs say, "Brum, brum, brum!" "Ah!" said the Irishman, "you want my rum; I shall give you a little, but you must promise to give me back my jug. But tell me, is the water deep there?"

"Jou, jou, jou!" said the frogs. "Oh!" said the Irishman, "that is not very deep. Here is my rum." He threw his jug into the water and he waited a good while, then he said, "Well, gentlemen, send back my jug; it is late, I must go back home; they are waiting for me." But the frogs did not send back anything. Then the Irishman threw himself into the water that was very deep and came to his neck.

"Confounded liars," said the Irishman, "you told me the water would come to my knees (*genoux*), and it is up to my neck."

As he was drunk, he was drowned.

From: Alcee Fortier, *Louisiana Folk-Tales* (Boston and New York: Houghton Mifflin Co., 1895).

· The Rabbit ·

(African)

The glory of Brer Rabbit of the legends does not seem to cast any sacredness over the real rabbit that nibbles tender green things in gardens; *he* is shot, and snared, and poisoned as ruthlessly as if his fame was not celebrated by the slayers; but in a queer way he has honor paid him, beyond any of the beasts; alive he may be a pest, but dead he becomes a magician again. The right forefoot of a rabbit is one of the mightiest charms known to man. There is no calculating the number of dried rabbits' feet that are circulating in pockets through the South. A rabbit's stomach cures most diseases, especially the awful "conjure sickness," of which, as is well known, large numbers of Negroes die yearly. You must dry the charm, and powder it, and eat it.

Teething children, also, are helped by tying the skin of a rabbit's stomach around its neck.

From: Octave Thanet, "Folk-Lore in Arkansas," *Journal of American Folk-Lore* 5 (1892): 121–25.

· Brer Rabbit Tales ·
(African)

Compair Lapin and the Earthworm

Everybody knows that every year in the month of May Compair Lapin is sick; it is an earthworm which is in his neck, biting him and sucking his blood like a leech. That makes him weak, and for a month the worm holds on to him, hooked in his neck, before it falls. Rabbits believe that when they lie down in the grass the worms come out of the grass and climb on them. They are, therefore, very much afraid of worms, and if they see one, they runs as if they had a pack of hounds after them. If I tell you that, it is because I want to relate to you a story about Compair Lapin and the worm.

It was a day in spring, the little birds were singing, the butterflies were flying about from one flower to another. It seemed as if all animals were rendering thanks to God for his kindness to them. A little earthworm was the only one which was crying and complaining. He said he was so small he had neither feet, nor hands, nor wings, and was obliged to remain in his hole. The little birds, the lizards, and even the ants were troubling him and eating his little ones. If God would make him big and strong, like other animals, then he would be contented, because he would be able to defend himself, while now he was helpless in his hole. He cried and cried and said that he would be glad if he belonged to the Devil. Hardly had he spoken when he saw the Devil at his side.

"Well, I heard all you said; tell me what you want; I shall grant it to you, and you will belong to me when you die."

"What I want?—Yes.—I want strength, I want to become big, big, and beat everybody who will come to trouble and bother me. Give me only that and I shall be satisfied."

"That is all right," said the Devil; "let me go, in a short while you will be contented."

As soon as the Devil had gone, the worm found himself strong and big. The change had come suddenly, and his hole had become large and as deep as a well. The worm was so glad that he began to laugh and to sing. At that very moment Lapin passed, and he was terribly frightened. He ran until he was unable to go any farther, and, when he stopped, he whistled, "fouif." "Never," said he, "was I more frightened. I shall never sleep again as long as that big earthworm will remain in this country. If I had not been so foolish as to boast that I could beat the elephant, I should go to him. It is Bouki who told on me; but perhaps if I speak to him I shall be able to fix up matters. I must try to make them meet and fight, and perhaps I shall get rid of both at the same time. It would be a pretty fight. Let me go and see the elephant, or I won't be able to sleep tonight. Besides, the earthworm said that he would fix me. I can't live that way. Good gracious! what am I to do? Let me arrange in my head what I am going to tell the elephant in order to please him."

He went on until he met the elephant. He bowed very politely, and the elephant did likewise, and asked him how he was.

"Oh! I am very sick," said Compair Lapin; "another time I shall come to try my strength with you; I think I can beat you."

"You are a fool," said the elephant. "Go away, I don't want to harm you; I take pity on you."

"I bet you," said Compair Lapin, "that I can beat you."

"All right, whenever you want."

"A little later; but as I know that you are good, I had come to ask you a favor."

"What is it?"

"It is to help me, to give me a hand to carry lumber to build my cabin."

"Let us go right off, if you want."

Compair Lapin, who had carried his ax with him, cut down a big tree, and said to the elephant, "Take it by the big end. I shall raise the branches, and we shall carry the tree to the place where I wish to build my cabin."

The elephant put the tree on his shoulder without looking behind him, and Compair Lapin climbed into the branches, and let the elephant do all the work. When the latter was tired he would stop to rest a little, and Compair Lapin would jump down and run up to the elephant to encourage him. "How is that, compair, you are already tired; but that is nothing. Look at me, who have been working as much as you. I don't feel tired."

"What! that is mightily heavy," said the elephant.

"Let us go," said Lapin; "we have not far to go."

The big animal put the load again on his back and Compair Lapin appeared to be lifting the branches. Whenever the elephant would not be looking Lapin would sit on a branch and say, "A little farther; go to the right, go to the left."

At last they came to the hole of the earthworm, and Lapin told the elephant to put down the tree. He let it fall right upon the worm who was sleeping. The latter pushed out the tree as if it were a piece of straw, and coming out he began to insult the elephant. Compair Lapin went to hide in a place where he could see and hear all. The elephant lost patience and struck the worm with his trunk.

The worm then climbed up the back of the elephant, and there was a terrible fight for more than two hours, until they were nearly dead. The worm finally hid in his hole and the elephant lay down dying. Compair Lapin mounted upon him, pulled his ears, and beat him, and said to him; "Didn't I tell you I would beat you?"

"Oh! yes, Compair Lapin; I have enough; I am dying."

Lapin then left him, and, going into the worm's hole, he broke his head with a stick. "Now," said he, "I am rid of both of them."

A little later Compair Lapin met Compair Bouki and told him how he had made the elephant and the earthworm fight until they had killed each other. "You see, my friend, when two fellows are in your way, you must make them fight, then you will always save your skin."

From: Alcee Fortier, *Louisiana Folk-Tales* (Boston and New York: Houghton Mifflin Co., 1895).

Marriage of Compair Lapin

Tim, Tim! Bois sec. Cré coton! Compair Lapin is a little fellow who knows how to jump!

You all must remember, after they had thrown Compair Lapin into the briers, how quickly he had run away, saying that it was in those very thorns that his mother had made him. Now then, I will tell you that on the same day Miss Léonine went to meet him, and they started traveling.

They walked a long time, for at least a month; at last they reached the bank of a river which was very deep. The current was strong, too strong for them to swim over. On the other side of the river there was a pretty place: The trees were green and loaded with all kinds of fruits. Under the trees were flowers of every kind that there is in the world. When a person breathed there, it was as if a bottle of essence had been opened in a room.

Miss Léonine said, "Let us go to live there; besides, we cannot return to my father's. There, we shall be happy, and no one will bother us; but how shall we do to cross over to the other side?"

"Stop," said Compair Lapin, "let me think a moment," and then he began to walk and walk, until he saw a large piece of dry wood which had fallen into the water. "That is what I want," said he. He cut a tall pole, and then he mounted on the log and told Léonine to follow him. Poor Miss Léonine mounted also, but she was so much afraid that she was trembling dreadfully.

"Hold on well; you will see how we shall pass," and he pushed with his stick. The log began to go down the current; they were going like lightning, and Lapin kept on paddling. They sailed for half a day before they were able to reach the other side, for the current was so strong that the log was carried along all the time. At last it passed very near the shore. "Jump, jump," said Compair Lapin, and hardly had he spoken than he was on shore. Miss Léonine finally jumped also, and they found themselves on the other side of the river. They were very glad, and the first thing they did was to eat as much as they could of the good things they found there. Then they took a good rest.

They found a pretty place to pass the night, and the next day, at dawn, they took a good walk. As everything they saw was so fine, they thought they would remain there to live. When they had run away, they had not been able to take any money with them, so they were without a cent. But God had blessed them, for they had come to a place where they did not need much money. They had already been there a good while, and they were quiet and contented, and they thought that they were alone, when one day, they heard, all at once, a noise, a tumult, as if thunder was rolling on the ground.

"What is that, my lord? Go to see, Compair Lapin."

"I, no—as if I am foolish to go, and then catch something bad. It is better for me to stay quiet, and, in that way, nothing can happen to me."

The noise kept on increasing, until they saw approaching a procession of elephants. As they were passing quietly without attacking anyone, it gave Compair Lapin a little courage. He went to the chief of the elephants and told him that he asked his permission to remain in his country; he said that he came from the country of King Lion, who had wanted to kill him, and he had run away with his wife.

The elephant replied, "That is good; you may remain here as long as you want, but don't you bring here other animals who know how to eat one another. As long as you will behave well, I will protect you, and nobody will come to get you here. Come sometimes to see me, and I will try to do something for you."

Sometime after that, Compair Lapin went to see the king of elephants, and the king was so glad when Compair Lapin explained to him how he could make a great deal of money, that he named immediately Compair Lapin captain of his bank and watchman of his property.

When Compair Lapin saw all the money of the king it almost turned his head, and as he had taken the habit of drinking since they had dug in his country a well, of which the water made people drunk, he continued his bad habit whenever he had the chance.

One evening he came home very drunk, and he began quarreling with his wife. Léonine fell upon him and gave him such a beating that he remained in bed for three weeks. When he got up, he asked his wife to pardon him; he said that he was drunk, and that he would never do it again, and he kissed her. In his heart, however, he could not forgive Léonine. He swore that he would leave her, but before that he was resolved to give her a terrible beating.

One evening when Léonine was sleeping, Compair Lapin took a rope and tied her feet before and behind. In that way he was sure of his business. Then he took a good whip, and he whipped her until she lost consciousness. Then he left her and went on traveling. He wanted to go to a place where they would never hear of him anymore, because he was afraid that Léonine would kill him, and he went far.

When Miss Léonine came back to herself, she called; they came to see what was the matter, and they found her well tied up. They cut the ropes, and Léonine started immediately. She left her house, she traveled a long time, until she came to the same river which she had crossed with Compair Lapin upon the log. She did not hesitate, but jumped into the water. The current carried her along, and she managed, after a great many efforts, to cross over to the other side. She was very tired, and she had to take some rest; then she started to return to her father.

When her father saw her, he kissed her and caressed her, but his daughter began to cry, and told him how Compair Lapin had treated her. When King Lion heard that, he was so angry that all who were near him began to tremble.

"Come here, Master Fox; you shall go to the king of elephants, and tell him that if he does not send Compair Lapin to me as soon as he can, I shall go to his country to kill him and all the elephants and all the other animals, and everything which is in his country. Go quick!"

Master Fox traveled a long time, and arrived at last in the country where Compair Lapin was hidden. But he did not see him; he asked for him, but no one could give him any news of him. Master Fox went to see the king of elephants and told him what King Lion had said. The elephants hate the lions, so the king replied, "Tell your master that if he wishes me to break his jawbone, let him come. I shall not send anything or anybody, and first of all, get away from here quick. If you want good advice, I can tell you that you had better remain in your country. If ever Lion tries to come here, I shall receive him in such a manner that no one of you will ever return home."

Master Fox did not wait to hear anymore; but he had no great desire to go back to his country, for he thought Lion would kill him if he returned without Compair Lapin. He walked as slowly as he could, and all along the road he saw that they were making preparations for war. He thought that perhaps the elephants were going to attack King Lion. He went on his way, and on arriving at a prairie he saw Compair Lapin, who was running in zigzags, sometimes on one side of the road, sometimes on the other. He stopped whenever he met animals and spoke to them, and then he started again as rapidly as before. At last Master Fox and Compair Lapin met, but the latter did not recognize his old friend.

"Where are you going like that, running all the time?"

"Ah!" replied Compair Lapin, "you don't know the bad news. Lion has declared war against all elephants, and I want to notify all mules, horses, and camels to get out of the way."

"But you, why are you running so? They are surely not going to make a soldier of you?"

"No, you believe that. Ah, well, with all your cunning you know nothing. When the officers of the king will come to get the horses and mules for the cavalry to go to war, they will say, 'That's a fellow with long ears; he is a mule; let us take him.' Even if I protest, and say that I am a rabbit, they will say; 'Oh, no! look at his ears; you see that he is a mule,' and I should be caught, enlisted, and forced to march. It seems to me that I know you, but it is such a long time since I have seen you. May God help me, it is Master Fox, my old friend!"

"Yes, yes, it is I, my good fellow. Well! what do you say about all that bad business?"

"All that is for a woman," said Compair Lapin; "we must try, my friend, to have nothing to do with that war."

"But what shall we do?" said Master Fox. "They will force us into it."

"No, you must be King Lion's adviser, and I will be that of King Elephant, and in that way we shall merely look on and let them fight as much as they want."

"You know," said Master Fox, "Léonine has returned to her father; and as you were not married before the church, I believe that Lion is about to marry her to one of his neighbors. Does it not grieve you, Compair Lapin, to think of that?"

"Oh, no; *ça zié pas oua tcheur pas fait mal* (we feel no sorrow for what we do not see)."

The two cunning fellows conversed a long time, for they were glad to meet after such a long absence. As they were about to part, they saw two dogs, that stood nose to nose, growling fiercely, and then turned around rapidly and began to smell each other everywhere.

"You, Master Fox, who know everything, can you tell me why dogs have the bad habit of smelling each other in that way?"

"I will tell you, Compair Lapin, why they do that. In old, old times, when there was but one god, called Mr. Jupiter, all the dogs considered their lot so hard and unhappy that they sent a delegation to ask Mr. Jupiter to better their condition. When they arrived at the house of the god in heaven, all the dogs were so frightened that they ran away. Only one remained; it was Brisetout, the largest dog of the party. He was not afraid of anything, and he came to Mr. Jupiter, and spoke thus; 'My nation sent me to see you to ask you whether you think that we are going to watch over our masters all day and all night, bark all the time, and then be kicked right and left and have nothing to eat. We are too unhappy, and we want to know if you will allow us once in a while to eat one of the sheep of our masters. We cannot work like this for nothing. What do you say, Mr. Jupiter?'"

" 'Wait a moment; I shall give you such a reply that you will never wish to annoy me anymore. I am tired of hearing all sorts of complaints. I am tired, do you hear?'

"Then Mr. Jupiter spoke a language that no one could understand, and one of his clerks went out to get something. He told the dog to sit down. Brisetout remained on the last step of the staircase. He thought that Mr. Jupiter was going to give him a good dinner; but the first thing he knew, the clerk returned with another man. They took hold of Brisetout, they tied him well, then they took a tin pan in which they put red pepper and turpentine. They rubbed the dog all over with the mixture; it burnt him so much that he howled and bellowed. When they let him go, Mr. Jupiter told him; 'You will give my reply to your comrades, and each one that will come to complain will be received in the same manner; you hear?'

"Ah, no, Brisetout did not hear; he ran straight ahead without knowing where he was going. At last he arrived at a bayou, fell into it, and was drowned.

"Sometime after that, Mr. Jupiter did not feel well. He thought he would leave heaven and take a little trip to earth. On his way he saw an apple tree which was covered with beautiful apples. He began to eat some; and while he was eating, a troop of dogs came to bark at him. Mr. Jupiter ordered his stick to give them a good drubbing. The stick began to turn to the right and to the left, and beat the dogs so terribly, that they scattered about in a minute. There remained but one poor dog, who was all mangy. He begged the stick to spare him. Then Stick pushed him before Mr. Jupiter, and said, 'Master, that dog was so thin that I did not have the courage to beat him.' 'It is very well,' said Mr. Jupiter, 'let him go; but if ever any dog comes to bark at me again, I shall destroy them all. I don't want to be bothered by you, I say. You have already sent me a delegation, and I received them so well that I don't think they will like to come back to see me. Have you already forgotten that?' The poor lean dog replied, 'What you say is true, but we never saw again the messenger we sent you; we are still waiting for him.' Mr. Jupiter then said, 'I will tell you how you can find out the messenger you had sent to me: Let all dogs smell one another, and the one which will smell turpentine is the messenger.' "

"You see now, Compair Lapin, why dogs smell one another. It was all Mr. Jupiter's doing. Poor old fellow, he has now lost all his clients, since the pope ordered everybody to leave him, and he has had to close his shop. He left the heaven, and no one knows where he went to hide. You understand, Compair Lapin, people get tired of having always the same thing; so they took another religion, and I think that the one we have now is good."

"Thank you, thank you, Master Fox, for your good story; and in order to show you that I am your old friend, I will tell you what we can do. As I told you already, we must remain very quiet. As the elephants want to go to attack King Lion in his own country, they will make a bridge for the army to pass. When the bridge will be finished they will go straight ahead, without stopping anywhere, to attack King Lion, for they want to take him by surprise. Don't you tell that to anybody, you hear?"

Compair Lapin and Master Fox then shook hands, and they parted. Master Fox went on his way, and Compair Lapin went to the king of elephants and asked him to give orders to all the carpenters and black-smiths in the country to obey him. When all the workmen were assembled, Compair Lapin began to make the bridge, and soon finished it. On the side of the river which was in the country of the elephants, he made at the end of the bridge a large park. These were bars of iron planted in the earth; they were at least ten feet high, and so sharp that a fly could not touch one without being pierced through. Compair Lapin then covered the bars of iron with branches and brambles to make it appear like a patch of briers, in order that they might not know that it was a snare. Then he took four cows with their calves, and tied them in the very middle of the pit. Then he put in it red pepper, ashes, and tobacco snuff. Then he placed in the trap a great number of tubs of water, in which there was a drug that made people go to sleep right off. After he had finished all this, Compair Lapin said, "Now let King Lion come to attack us."

Master Fox was still traveling to render an account of his errand to King Lion; but he was so much afraid to return without Compair Lapin, that he concluded that it was better not to return at all. On his way he met a hen; he killed it, and covered an old rag with the blood. He tied his hind paw with the rag, and he began to limp, and jump on three feet. At last he met Bourriquet, to whom he said, "My dear friend, render me a little service; you see how sick I am. I pray you to go to King Lion, to tell him that I cannot come to see him. The elephants broke my legs because I had come to claim Compair Lapin."

"Oh, no!" said Bourriquet; "you were always against me with Compair Lapin. Go yourself."

"That is good," said Master Fox; "*c'est pas jis ein fois la bouche besoin manger* (I shall have my chance again, you will need me again). If you knew what I have seen and what I know, you would listen to me."

"Well, tell me all," said Bourriquet; "and I will go, since you cannot walk."

"That is all right; listen well. The elephants intend to come to attack King Lion in his country. They are making a bridge to cross the river, and as soon as the bridge will be finished they will come immediately to surprise Lion. If the king understood his business, he would hasten to attack the elephants in their own country, before they come to lift him up before he knows it."

As soon as Master Fox had finished speaking, Bourriquet galloped away and went to King Lion, to whom he said what Master Fox had related to him. The king was so glad that he ordered someone to give Bourriquet a little hay to eat. Bourriquet was not very much pleased, and he began grumbling. "Don't you know, Bourriquet," said the king's servant, *"qué ein choual donnin to doite pas gardé la bride* (that you must not look at the bridle of a horse which was given to you)."

"Well," said Bourriquet, "I had expected a better reward, but I'll take that anyhow, because *ein ti zozo dans la main vaut mié qué plein ti zozos quapé voltigé dans bois* (a bird in the hand is better than two in the bush)."

All at once they heard a dreadful noise. It was King Lion, who was starting for the war with all the animals which he could find: tigers, bears, wolves—all King Lion's subjects were there. As to Master Fox, he had run back to notify Compair Lapin that the enemies were coming.

Miss Léonine was with the army, and her father used to tell her all the time, "I am glad that you came; Compair Lapin will have to pay for all his tricks; you must treat him as he treated you."

King Lion was at the head of the army, and coming near the bridge he saw Master Fox, who was lying in the road with his leg broken.

"Oh! oh!" said Lion, "this is the way they treated you! They shall have to pay for all that."

"Make haste," said Master Fox; "don't wait till they come to attack you; pass the bridge immediately; that will throw them in confusion."

The army went on. They all ran to pass over the bridge, King Lion at the head, with his daughter. As soon as they arrived at the place where was the snare, and they saw the cows and their calves, King Lion and his troops killed them and began to eat them. Then they quarreled among themselves and began to fight. They scattered about the ashes, the red pepper, and the tobacco snuff, and were completely blinded. They fought terribly; they massacred one another; then those that were left drank the water in the tubs. Two hours later they were all sound asleep.

The elephants, which had remained prudently at a distance, hearing no more noise, came to the bridge. They killed all the animals that were left in Lion's army, and threw their bodies in the river. They flayed King Lion; they took his skin and sewed Bourriquet into it; then they tied some straw, covered with pitch, to Bourriquet's tail; they put fire to the straw, and they let him go to announce the news in Lion's country.

When Bourriquet passed on the bridge, he was galloping so fast that one might have thought that it was thunder that was rolling on the bridge, as if it were more than one hundred cartloads. When Bourriquet arrived in his country his tail was entirely consumed by the fire, but he said that he had lost it in a battle. Although he announced very sad news, no one could help laughing at him: He was so funny without his tail, and so proud of his glorious wound.

As soon as all was over at the bridge, Compair Lapin went to get Master Fox, and took him to the king of the elephants. He presented him to his majesty, and told him that Master Fox was his good friend, and if the king wanted to accept his services, they would both be his very faithful subjects. The king of elephants said to them, "I believe that you are two cunning rascals, and that in my war with King Lion, Master Fox *té galpé avec chévreil et chassé avec chien* (had been on both sides of the fence); but all right, he may remain here, if he wants. As for you, Compair Lapin, I want you to get married. Here is Miss White Rabbit; she is rich, and will be a good match for you. Tomorrow I want to dance at the wedding."

The next day all the people assembled, and celebrated with great splendor the marriage of Compair Lapin with Miss White Rabbit. Master Fox was the first groomsman. Three weeks after the wedding, Mrs. Compair Lapin gave birth to two little ones; one was white and the other as black as soot. Compair Lapin was not pleased, and he went to see the king of elephants.

"Oh! you know nothing," said the king; "you are married before the church, and I will not grant you a divorce. Besides, I must tell you that in the family of Mrs. Compair Lapin it happens very often that the little ones are black. It is when the ladies are afraid in a dark night; so console yourself, and don't be troubled."

Compair Lapin consented to remain with his wife until death should part them, and that is how he married after all his pranks.

As I was there when all that happened, I ran away to relate it to you.

From: Alcee Fortier, *Louisiana Folk-Tales* (Boston and New York: Houghton Mifflin Co., 1895).

When Brer Rabbit Saved the Pig

One winter, 'bout a week to Christmas, Brer Rabbit he have a pen full of powerful fat hogs, just honing for the smokehouse. Now you mightn't think it, sah, but Brer Rabbit was a mighty frolicsome chap when he was a young man, attending on the gals nigh 'bout every night.

Now Brer Bar and Brer Wolf have they mind on them hogs constant, but they feared Brer Rabbit got some trap set unbeknownst to theyselves.

One night Brer Rabbit, he go up to pay he 'dresses to Mr. Wolf's daughter. Now this yer Miss Wolf was a mighty prideful gal, and she keep Brer Rabbit waiting on the porch a powerful long time, while she get on her meeting clothes.

Well, whiles Brer Rabbit was a-waiting, all to once he hear he name round the corner the porch, and he cock up he ear, and sure 'nough dar he hear Brer Bar and Brer Wolf in cahoots for to steal he bestest pig.

Brer Rabbit he listen, and they lay out they plans, how they gwine dress off the pig, and leave it un'neath the black gum tree whilst they go for the cart, 'cause they 'spicious if they stop for to cut it up, Brer Rabbit gwine catch up with 'em.

Well, Brer Rabbit, he shake hisself and go in, and pay he 'spects to Miss Wolf, but right soon he say he 'bliged to say good night, and he clip it off to the black gum tree, and he hide hisself in the bushes. And sure 'nough, directly here come Brer Wolf and Brer Bar, with the pig done dressed for the smokehouse; they lay it down and cover it with brush, and strike out for the cart.

Then that bodacious Brer Rabbit, he go softly through the bresh, and just creep inside that pig and lay hisself down, and he lay out to keep he eye open and watch out for the cart, but 'fore he know hisself he fall asleep.

De firstest Brer Rabbit know, Brer Wolf and Brer Bar, they done lift the pig in the cart, and that ere Brer Rabbit on the inside the pig.

Then Brer Rabbit, he grow faintlike, and then he just turn in and groan harder and harder; and Brer Wolf and Brer Bar, they make sure it am ole Satan hisself in the pig, and they just strike out the cart and burn the wind for home, and Brer Rabbit, he drive the cart home, and hang the pig in the smokehouse.

From: Emma Backus, "Tales of the Rabbit from Georgia Negroes," *Journal of American Folk-Lore* 12 (1899): 108–15.

Brer Rabbit and the Tar Baby

"Didn't the fox *never* catch the rabbit, Uncle Remus?" asked the little boy the next evening.

"He come mighty nigh it, honey, sho's you bawn—Brer Fox did. One day atter Brer Rabbit fool 'im wid dat calamus root, Brer Fox went ter wuk en got 'im some tar, en mix it wid some turkentime, en fix up a contrapshun wat he call a Tar Baby; en he tuck dish yer Tar Baby en he sot 'er in de big road, en den he lay off in de bushes fer ter see wat de news wuz gwineter be. En he didn't hatter wait long, nudder, kaze bimeby here come Brer Rabbit pacin' down de road—lippity-clippity, clippity-lippity—dez ez sassy ez a jaybird. Brer Fox, he lay low. Brer Rabbit come prancin' 'long twel he spy de Tar Baby; en den he fotch up on his behime legs like he wuz 'stonished. De Tar Baby, she sot dar, she did, en Brer Fox, he lay low.

" 'Mawnin'!' sez Brer Rabbit, sezee, 'nice wedder dis mawnin',' sezee.

"Tar Baby ain't sayin' nuthin', en Brer Fox, he lay low.

" 'How duz yo' sym'tums seem ter segashuate?' sez Brer Rabbit, sezee.

"Brer Fox, he wink his eye slow, en lay low, en de Tar Baby, she ain't sayin' nuthin'.

" 'How you come on, den? Is you deaf?' sez Brer Rabbit, sezee. 'Kase if you is, I kin holler louder,' sezee.

"Tar Baby stay still, en Brer Fox, he lay low.

" 'Youer stuck up, dat's w'at you is,' says Brer Rabbit, sezee, 'en I'm gwineter kyore you, dat's w'at I'm a gwineter do,' sezee.

"Brer Fox, he sorter chuckle in his stummuck, he did, but Tar Baby ain't sayin' nuthin'.

" 'I'm gwineter larn you howter talk ter 'specttubble fokes ef hit 's de las' ack,' sez Brer Rabbit, sezee. 'Ef you don't take off dat hat en tell me howdy, I'm gwineter bus' you wide open,' sezee.

"Tar Baby stay still, en Brer Fox, he lay low.

"Brer Rabbit keep on axin' 'im, en de Tar Baby, she keep on sayin' nuthin', twel present'y Brer Rabbit draw back wid his fis', he did, en blip he tuck 'er side er de head. Right dar's whar he broke his merlasses jug. His fis' stuck en he can't pull loose. De tar hilt 'im. But Tar Baby, she stay still, en Brer Fox, he lay low.

" 'Ef you don't lemme loose, I'll knock you agin,' sez Brer Rabbit, sezee, en wid dat he fotch 'er a wipe wid de udder han', en dat stuck. Tar Baby, she ain't sayin' nuthin', en Brer Fox, he lay low.

" 'Tu'n me loose, fo' I kick de natal stuffin' outen you,' sez Brer Rabbit, sezee, but de Tar Baby, she ain't sayin' nuthin'. She des hilt on, en den Brer Rabbit lose de use er his feet in de same way. Brer Fox, he lay low. Den Brer Rabbit squall out dat ef de Tar Baby don't tu'n 'im loose he butt 'er cranksided. En den he butted, en his head got stuck. Den Brer Fox, he sa'ntered fort', lookin' des ez innercent ez wunner yo' mammy's mockin' birds.

" 'Howdy, Brer Rabbit,' sez Brer Fox, sezee. 'You look sorter stuck up dis mawnin',' sezee, en den he rolled on de groun', en laft en laft twel he couldn't laff no mo'. 'I speck you'll take dinner wid me dis time, Brer Rabbit. I done laid in some calamus root, en I ain't gwineter take no skuse,' sez Brer Fox, sezee."

Here Uncle Remus paused, and drew a two-pound yam out of the ashes.

"Did the fox eat the rabbit?" asked the little boy to whom the story had been told.

"Dat's all de fur de tale goes," replied the old man. "He mout, en den agin he moutent. Some say Jedge B'ar come 'long en loosed 'im—some say he did n't. I hear Miss Sally callin'. You better run 'long."

From: Henry Watterson, ed., *Oddities in Southern Life and Character* (New York: Houghton Mifflin Co., 1892).

Brer Rabbit and Brer Coon

Brer Rabbit an Brer Coon wuz fishermuns. Brer Rabbit fished fur fish an Brer Coon fished fur f-r-o-g-s.

Arter while de frogs all got so wile Brer Coon couldent ketch em, an he hadn't hab no meat to his house an de chilluns wuz hongry an de ole oman beat em ober de haid wid de broom.

Brer Coon felt mighty bad an he went off down de rode wid he head down wundering what he gwine do. Des den ole Brer Rabbit wuz er skippin down de rode an he seed Brer Coon wuz worried an throwed up his years an say-ed:

"Mornin, Brer Coon."

"Mornin, Brer Rabbit."

"How is yer copperrosity segashuatin, Brer Coon?"

"Porely, Brer Rabbit, porely. De frogs haz all got so wile I caint ketch em an I aint got no meat to my house an de ole oman is mad an de chilluns hongry. Brer Rabbit, I'se got to hab help. Sumthin' haz got to be dun."

Old Brer Rabbit look away crost de ruver long time; den he scratch hiz year wid his hind foot, an say:

"I'll tole ye whut we do Brer Coon. We'll git eber one of dem frogs. You go down on de san bar an lie down an play des lack you wuz d-a-i-d. Don't yer moobe. Be jes as still, jest lack you wuz d-a-i-d."

Ole Brer Coon mosied on down to de ruver. De frogs hear-ed em er comin an de ole big frog say-ed:

"Yer better look er roun. Yer better look er roun. Yer better look er round."

Nother ole frog say-ed:

"Knee deep, knee deep, knee deep."

An "ker-chug" all de frogs went in de water.

But Ole Brer Coon lide down on de san an stretched out jest lack he wuz d-a-i-d. De flies got all ober em, but he never moobe. De sun shine hot, but he never moobe; he lie still jest lack he wuz d-a-i-d.

Drectly Ole Brer Rabbit cum er runnin tru de woods an out on de san bar an put his years up high an hollered out:

"Hay, de Ole Coon is d-a-i-d."

De ole big frog out in de ruver say-ed:

"I don't bleve it, I don't bleve it, I don't bleve it."

An all de littul frogs roun de edge say-ed:

"I don't bleve it, I don't bleve it, I don't bleve it."

But de ole coon play jes lack he's d-a-i-d an all de frogs cum up out of de ruver an set er roun whare de ole coon lay.

Jes den Brer Rabbit wink his eye an say-ed:

"I'll tell yer what I'de do, Brer Frogs. I'de berry Ole Sandy, berry em so deep he never could scratch out."

Den all de frogs gun to dig out de san, dig out de san from under de ole coon. When de had dug er great deep hole wid de ole coon in de middle of it, de frogs all got tired an de old frog say-ed:

"Deep er nough—deep er nough—deep er nough."

An all de littul frogs say-ed:

"Deep er nough—deep er nough—deep er nough."

Ole Brer Rabbit was er takin er littul nap in der sun, an he woke up an say-ed:

"Kin you jump out?"

De ole big frog look up to de top of de hole an say-ed:

"Yes I kin. Yes I kin. Yes I kin."

An de littul frogs say-ed:

"Yes I kin. Yes I kin. Yes I kin."

Ole Brer Rabbit tole em:

"Dig it deeper."

Den all de frogs went to wuk an dug er great deep hole way down inside de san wid Ole Brer Coon right in de middle jest lack he wuz d-a-i-d. De frogs wuz er gittin putty tired an de ole big frog sung out loud:

"Deep er nough. Deep er nough. Deep er nough."

An all de littul frogs sung out too:

"Deep er enough. Deep er nough. Deep er nough."

An Ole Brer Rabbit woke up er gin and axed em:

"Kin yer jump out?"

"I bleve I kin. I bleve I kin. I bleve I kin."

Ole Brer Rabbit look down in de hole agin an say-ed:

"Dig dat hole deeper."

Den all de frogs gin to wuk throwin out san, throwin out san, clear till most sundown and dey had er great deep hole way, way down in de san, wid de ole coon layin right in de middle. De frogs wuz plum clean tired out and de ole big frog say-ed:

"Deep er nough. Deep er nough. Deep er nough."

An all de littul frogs say-ed:

"Deep er nough. Deep er nough. Deep er nough."

Ole Brer Rabbit peeped down in de hole agin and say:

"Kin yer jump out?"

An de ole frog say:

"No I caint. No I caint. No I caint."

An all de littul frogs say:

"No I caint. No I caint. No I caint."
Den Ole Brer Rabbit jump up right quick an holler out:
"RISE UP SANDY AN GIT YOUR MEAT!"
An Brer Coon had meat fer sepper dat nite.

From: A. W. Eddins, "How Sandy Got His Meat," *Texas Folklore Society Publications* 1 (1916): 47–49.

Brer Rabbit and Mr. Fox's Daughter

Mr. Fox, he have a mighty handsome daughter, and all the chaps was flying round her to beat all.

Brer Coon, Brer Wolf, Brer Rabbit, and Brer Possum was a courting of her constant, and they all ax Brer Fox for he daughter.

Now the gal, she favor Brer Rabbit in her mind, but she don't let on who her favor is, but just snap her eyes on 'em all.

Now Ole Brer Rabbit, he ain't so mighty handsome, and he ain't no proudful man, that's sure, but somehow it 'pears like he do have a mighty taking way with the gals.

Well, wen they all done ax Ole Man Fox for his daughter, he ax the gal, do she want Brer Wolf? And she toss her head and 'low Brer Wolf too bodaciously selfish; she say, "Brer Wolf's wife never get a bite of chicken breast while she live."

Then the ole man, he ax her how she like Brer Possum, and she just giggle and 'low "Brer Possum mighty ornery leetle ole man, and he 'longs to a low family anyhow." And Ole Man Fox, he 'low, "Dat's so for a fact," and he sound her 'fections for Brer Coon, but she made out Brer Coon pass all 'durance. Then the ole man he tell her Brer Rabbit done ax for her too, and she make out like she mighty took 'back, and 'low she don't want none of that lot.

Then Ole Brer Fox, he say that the gal was too much for him; but he tell the chaps to bring up the big stone hammer, and they can all try their strength on the big step rock what they use for a horse block, and the one what can pound dust out of the rock shall have the gal.

Then Brer Rabbit, he feel mighty set down on, 'cause he know all the chaps can swing the stone hammer to beat hisself, and he go off sorrowful like and set on the sandbank. He set a while and look east, and then he turn and set a while and look west, but may be you don't know, sah, Brer Rabbit sense never come to hisself 'cepting when he look north.

When it just come to hisself what he gwine to do, he jump up and clip it off home, and he hunt up the slippers and he fill them with ashes, and Lord bless your soul, the ole chap know just what them slippers do 'bout the dust out of the rock.

Well, the next morning they was all dar soon. Ole Brer Rabbit, the last one, come limping up like he mighty lame, and being so, he the last one on the land, 'cause he have last chance.

Now Brer Wolf, he take the big hammer and he fotch it down hard, and Brer Wolf mighty strong man in them days, but he ain't fetch no dust. Then Brer Coon and Brer Possum, they try, but Ole Man Fox he say, he don't see no dust, and Miss Fox she to 'hind the window curtain and giggle, and Old Man Fox he curl the lip and he say, Brer Rabbit, it you turn now. Brer Wolf he look on mighty scornful, and Brer Rabbit have just all he can do to fotch up the big hammer; it so hard he just have to stand on tiptoe in he slippers, and when the hammer come down, he heels come down sish, and the dust fly so they can't see the ole chap for the dust.

But Ole Brer Rabbit, he don't count that nothing but just one of his courting tricks.

From: Emma Backus, "Tales of the Rabbit from Georgia Negroes," *Journal of American Folk-Lore* 12 (1899): 108–15.

Why Mr. Dog Runs Brer Rabbit

One morning, Mr. Buzzard he say he stomach just hungry for some fish, and he tell Mrs. Buzzard he think he go down to the branch, and catch some for breakfast. So he take he basket, and he sail along till he come to the branch.

He fish right smart, and by sunup he have he basket plum full. But Mr. Buzzard am a powerful greedy man, and he say to hisself, he did, "I just catch one more." But while he done gone for his last one, Brer Rabbit he came along, clippity-clippity, and when he see basket plum full of fine whitefish he stop, and he say, "I 'clare to goodness, the old woman just gwine on up to the cabin, 'cause they got nothing for to fry for breakfast. I wonder what she think of this yer fish," and so he put the basket on he head, Brer Rabbit did, and make off to the cabin.

Direc'ly he meet up with Mr. Dog, and he ax him where he been fishing that early in the day, and Brer Rabbit he say how he done sot on the log 'longside of the branch, and let he tail hang in the water and catch all the fish, and he done tell Mr. Dog, the old rascal did, that he tail mighty short for the work, but that Mr. Dog's tail just the right sort for fishing.

So, Mr. Dog, he teeth just ache for them whitefish, and he go set on the log and hang he tail in the water, and it mighty cold for he tail, and the fish don't bite, but he mouth just set for them fish, and so he just sot dar, and it turn that cold that when he feel he gin up, sure's you born, Mr. Dog, he tail froze fast in the branch, and he call he chillens, and they come and break the ice.

And then, to be sure, he start off to settle Ole Brer Rabbit, and he get on he track and he run the poor ole man to beat all, and directly he sight him he run him round and round the woods and holler, "Hallelujah! hallelujah!" and the puppies come on behind, and they holler, "Glory! glory!" and they make such a fuss, all the creeters in the woods, they run to see what the matter. Well, sah, from that day, Mr. Dog he run Brer Rabbit, and when they just get gwine on the swing in the big woods, you can hear ole Ben dar just letting hisself out, "Hallelujah! hallelujah!" and them pups just gwine "Glory! glory!" and it surely am the sound what has the music dar, it surely has the music dar.

From: Emma Backus, "Tales of the Rabbit from Georgia Negroes," *Journal of American Folk-Lore* 12 (1899): 108–15.

Born to Luck

You hear, sah, how Brer Rabbit's left foot fetch you luck when you tote it constant in your pocket. It most surely do that, sah, 'cause that ole Brer Rabbit be just born to luck. Now this yer one time when the luck come to hisself.

Ole Miss Rabbit, she 'low she 'bliged to have a spring house; she say, Ole Miss Rabbit did, how Miss Fox and Miss Coon have the nice spring house, and she 'clare she plum broke down worritting herself trying to keep house, and no spring house.

Now Brer Rabbit, he promise and he promise, but Brer Rabbit don't have no honing to handle the mattocks, no sah, that he don't. Brer Rabbit is pow'ful dext'rous to work with he head, but Brer Rabbit ain't no half strainer to work with he hands.

But Ole Miss Rabbit, she kept worriting the old man constant; she 'low how she 'bliged to have that spring house, and she 'bliged to have it to once.

Well, when she rear and charge on the old man, that powerful that he can't put her off no more, then Brer Rabbit, he just go off to hisself, and study what he gwine do 'bout that ornery old spring house, but he can't see he way, till in come to he mind 'bout Ole Mammy Witch Wise, her what were the old woman what save up a bag of gold. Then, the night 'fore she die, she bury the bag where the creeters can't find it. That night she pass by all the creeters' houses and shake the bag, and they hear the chink of the gold, and in the morning Ole Mammy Witch Wise was dead and the gold was gone.

Well, sah, Brer Rabbit he go and see all the creeters, and he let on how he done have a token what tell him where Ole Mammy Witch Wise bury the gold, and that Ole Brer Rabbit, he bodaciously 'low how the token point to the bed in the spring what run 'long side he garden, and he say, Brer Rabbit do, if they all turn in and make a dam and hold the water back, they most surely find the gold.

Now Ole Brer Rabbit don't have no feelings that gold anywhere in them parts. Well, sah, the creeters they 'low to theyselves Brer Rabbit a mighty generous man to let them in, and they fetch they mattocks and they spades, and they dig, and Brer Rabbit he sit up on the dam and locate the spot, and he say to hisself that old spring house getting on mighty smart, when I 'clare 'fore the Lord, Brer Wolf's mattocks strike kerchink, an' out fly the gold, it most surely did, and the creeters they just jump in the hole and pick up the money. But Ole Brer Rabbit never lose he head, that he don't, and he just push the rocks out the dam, and let the water on and drown the latest one of them critters, and then he picks up the gold, and course Ole Miss Rabbit done get her spring house, but bless your soul, sah, that only just one they times when Ole Brer Rabbit have luck.

From: Emma Backus, "Tales of the Rabbit from Georgia Negroes," *Journal of American Folk-Lore* 12 (1899): 108–15.

Brer Rabbit and Medicine

Ole Brer Rabbit had a bad name for a partner, but one time he get Mr. Wolf to work a crop on shares with him, and they have a 'greement writ out on paper, how in the harvest they gwine divide half and half. Mr. Rabbit know Ole Mr. Wolf mighty good hand in the field, and sure to make a good crop. But when Ole Brer Rabbit set in to work, he get mighty tired, and the corn rows, they look so mighty long, and he 'gin to lag behind and work he brain.

Presen'ly he jump to the work, and make he hoe cut the air, and soon cotch up with Mr. Wolf, and he open the subject of the education in medicine, and he tell how he am a reg'lar doctor, and got his 'plomy in a frame to home, but he say he don't know how all the patients gwine get on. Now he turn over the farming, and Ole Mr. Wolf ax how much money he get for he doctoring, and when he hear so much, he tell Mr. Rabbit to go when he have a call, and put by the money, and in the fall put in the crop money and then divide. So that night Mr. Rabbit, he 'struct his chillens how they got for to run and call him frequent, and how they got to tell Mr. Wolf they wants the doctor.

And sure 'nough, Mr. Rabbit ain't more'n in the front row next day, when here come little Rab all out of breath and say, "Somebody send in great 'stress for the doctor." Mr. Rabbit make out like he can't go and leave Mr. Wolf to do all the work, but Mr. Wolf studying 'bout that big fee Brer Rabbit gwine turn in the company, and he tell him, "Go 'long, he can get on with the work." So Mr. Rabbit clips off in great haste, and he just go down on the edge of the woods, and what you 'spect he do? Well, sah, he just stretch hisself out in the shade of a swamp maple and take a nap, while Ole Mr. Wolf was working in the corn rows in the hot sun. When Mr. Rabbit sleep he nap out, he set up and rub he eyes, then he loony off down by the spring for a drink, then he come running and puffing like he been running a mile, and tell Mr. Wolf what a mighty sick patient he got, and make out like he that wore out he can't more 'n move the hoe.

Well, when they come back from dinner, Mr. Rabbit, he strike and make he hoe fly, but directly here come little Rab for the doctor, and Ole Mr. Rabbit, he take hisself off for 'nother nap, and matters goes on just dis yer way all summer. Ole Mr. Wolf, he have to do all the work, but he comfort himself with the 'flection, that he have half them big fees what Brer Rabbit turning in to the company money.

Well, when the fodder done pulled, and all the crop done sold, and they go for to count the money, Mr. Wolf ax Brer Rabbit where the doctor's fees what he gwine turn in. Brer Rabbit say they all such slow pay, he can't collect it. Then they fell out, and Mr. Wolf that mad, he say he gwine eat Brer Rabbit right there, and make an end of he tricks. But Mr. Rabbit beg that they take the trouble up to the court house to Judge Bar. So they loony off to the court house, and the old judge say it were a jury case, and he send Sheriff Coon out to fetch the jurymans, and he say, "Don' you fotch no mans here, 'cepter they be more fool than the parties in the case." But Sheriff Coon 'low he don' know where he gwine find any man what's more fool than Brer Wolf's in dis yer case, but he take out down the county, and by and by he seed a man rolling a wheelbarrow what ain't got nothing in it round the house and round the house, and he ax him, what he doing that for? And he say, he trying to wheel some sunshine in the house. Sheriff Coon say, "You is the man I wants to come with me and sot on the jury."

They go 'long, and directly they see a man pulling a long rope up a tall tree that stand 'longside a house; they ax him, what he gwine do? He say he gwine to haul a bull up on top of the house to eat the moss off the roof, and Sheriff Coon say, "I'll be bound you is my man for the jury, and you must go long with we all to the court." So they take their way back to the court house, then they have a great time taking evidence and argufying.

Ole Brer Wolf, he set up there, and 'sider every word of the evidence, but Ole Brer Rabbit he lean back and shut he eye, and work he brain on he own account. He settin' right close to the door; when the lawyer done get everybody worked up so they take no noticement, Brer Rabbit just slip softly out the back door, and he creep 'round the side of the cabin back to where ole Judge Bar set wid de bag of money on the floor, and what you 'spect? When they all talking, Ole Brer Rabbit just slide he hand in the crack, and softly slip out the bag of money, and take out home, and leave the case in the care of the court. That just like ole man Rabbit.

From: Emma Backus, "Tales of the Rabbit from Georgia Negroes," *Journal of American Folk-Lore* 12 (1899): 108–15.

Why People Tote Brer Rabbit Foot in Their Pocket

Well, sah, that's cause Ole Brer Rabbit done killed the last witch what ever live.

They tells how they done hang some of 'em, and burn some, till they get mighty scarce, but there was one ole witch what was risin' on five hundred years old, and 'cause she keep clear of all the folks what try to catch her, they done name her Ole Mammy Witch Wise.

Well, she do carry on to beat all them times, she 'witch all the folks, and she 'witch all the animals, and when they go to get their meal out some of the gardens, she just watch them animals, and they can't get in to save 'em, and they all nigh 'bout starved out, that they was, and they all hold a big consertation and talk over what they gwine do.

They was a mighty ornery lookin' set, just nigh 'bout skin an' bone, but when Ole Brer Rabbit come in, they 'serve how he mighty plump and fine order, and they ax him, however he so mighty prosp'rous and they all in such powerful trouble. And then he 'low, Brer Rabbit did, dat Ole Mammy Witch Wise can't 'witch him, and he go in the gardens more same as ever.

Why, Ole Mammy Wise don't 'low the animals get in the garden, she just want the pick of 'em herself, cause she don't have no garden that year; but when she set her mind on some Major Brayton's pease, she just put the pot on the fire, an' when the water bile smart, she just talk in the pot and say, "Bile pease, bile pease," and there they come, sure 'nough, for dinner; but you see if the animals done been troubling them pease, and there ain't no pease on the vine, then she call 'em in the pot.

So she just keep the creeters out till they nigh 'bout broke down, and they ax Brer Rabbit, can't he help 'em? Brer Rabbit scratch he head, but he don't say nothin', 'cause I tell you, when Ole Brer Rabbit tell what he gwine do, then you just well know that just what he ain' gwine do, 'case he's a man what don't tell what he mind set on.

So he don't make no promise, but he study constant how he gwine kill Ole Mammy Witch Wise. He know all 'bout how the old woman slip her skin every night, and all the folks done try all the plans to keep her out till the rooster crow in the morning, 'cause every witch, what's out the skin when the roosters crow, can't never get in the skin no mo'; but they never get the best of the Ole Witch Wise, and she rising five hundred years old. Brer Rabbit he got off hisself, and set in the sun on the sand bed and rum'nate. And you may be sure, when you see the old man set all to hisself on the sand bed, he mind just working. Well, sah, that night, he go in the garden and take a good turn of peppers, and tote them up to Ole Mammy Witch Wise house, and just he 'spect, there he find her skin in the porch, just where she slip it off to go on her tricks, and what you 'spect he do? Well, sah, he just mash them peppers to a mush, and rub 'em all inside the Ole Witch Wise skin, and then he set hisself under the porch for to watch.

Just 'fore crowing time, sure 'nough, there come the ole woman, sailing along in a hurry, 'cause she know she ain't got long, but when she go for to put on her skin, it certainly do bite her, and she say, "Skinnie, skinnie, don't you know me, skinnie?" But it bite more same than before, and while she fooling with it, sure 'nough the rooster done crow, and the ole woman just fall over in a fit. And in the morning Brer Rabbit notify the animals, and they gravel a place and burn her. And the colored people, they find out how Brer Rabbit get the best of the Mammy Witch Wise, and then they tell the white folks, and that why nigh 'bout all the rich white folks totes a rabbit foot in their pocket, 'cause it keeps off all the bad luck, and it do that, sure's yo' born.

From: Roland Steiner, "Observations on the Practice of Conjuring in Georgia," *Journal of American Folk-Lore* 14 (1901): 173–80.

• The Moon •

(Various)

The Dark of the Moon
(English)

The darkies do not make anything like so much of the moon as the whites. They are quite as superstitious in their fashion as the darkies; although none of their superstitions have the barbarous taint of the Negroes. They hold the "dark of the moon" to be especially ominous. No planting should be done then; and the meat of anything killed at that season will "cripse up in the pot."

From: Octave Thanet, "Folk-Lore in Arkansas," *Journal of American Folk-Lore* 5 (1892): 121–25.

Scots-English Moon Lore
(Scots-English)

The moon seems to exert a powerful influence on many agricultural and domestic affairs. All plants which produce fruit above ground must be planted in the light of the moon, not necessarily in a new moon; and all plants which produce fruit underground—potatoes and such—must be planted in the dark of the moon. Also the hogs must be killed in the dark of the moon, or the bacon and lard will shrink. Rails must be split and shingles and boards gotten in the dark of the moon to keep them from warping and splitting—and the boards or shingles must be put on when the horns of the new moon point down to keep them from cupping. Plant corn when the horns of the new moon point down and the ears will be heavy and grow low on the stalk; and sow wheat before the full moon in October. To prevent rotting, the worm fence should be laid in the light of the moon. To effectually kill the stumps, roots, and sprouts of trees, bushes, briars, etc., on land which is being cleared, they should be cut during the dark moon in August. Timber will last much longer if cut in the dark of the moon.

If the housewife would have her soap white and hard, she must make it in the light of the moon, and while the moon is on the increase; and while boiling the soap must be stirred one way only, and if stirred with a sassafras paddle it will have a pleasant odor and the maker will have good luck. If she would have her dyes well "set" so the colors will not "run," she must dye dark colors in the dark of the moon and *vice versa*.

The weather can be forecast by the moon. There will be as many snows during the winter as the moon is days old when the first snow comes. A new moon with horns pointing up indicates dry weather during that moon, if the horns tilt so as to spill the water it will be rainy. A common weather proverb runs:

> Circle around the sun,
> Will rain none,
> Circle around the moon,
> Will rain soon.

There are many signs and things besides the moon by which the weather may be forecast, and even partially regulated. For instance, if rain is needed in the spring or early summer, kill a black snake and hang it up with its belly to the sun, and the rain will come. The prevailing rains of a season will come from the same direction as comes the first rain of that season. If it does not rain on the first day of June it is not likely to rain for fifteen days, and rain on the first dog day means rain on each of the following forty days. If it rains while the sun is shining, the witches are dancing, and it will rain again next day.

From: Haywood Parker, "Folk-Lore of the North Carolina Mountaineers," *Journal of American Folk-Lore* 20 (1907): 241–50.

· *The Weather* ·

(Various)

Weather Signs I
(Unidentified)

When a peacock screams, it is a sign of rain.

When a hog squeals, it is a sign of cold weather.

When a whippoorwill cries, it is a sign of warm, clear weather. There is no more frost.

When a yellowhammer sings, it is a sign of warm weather.

The cooing of a turtledove is a sign of warm, clear weather.

When woodpeckers come in the spring, it is a sign of warm weather. Woodpeckers come south by night, and go north by day.

When birds come in numbers around the house, it is a sign of freezing weather.

When an alligator bellows, it is a sign of rain within twenty-four hours.

A rainbow is a sign of no more rain on that day.

When a storm is coming, buzzards fly high to get above it.

To hear fire make a noise like a woman walking in snow is a sign of snow.

From: Roland Steiner, "Superstitious and Beliefs from Central Georgia," *Journal of American Folk-Lore* 12 (1899): 261–71.

Weather Signs II
(Scots-English)

By due attention to signs and omens, the winter weather can be fore-told to a nicety: Frost will come just three months after you hear the first katydid. For each foggy day in August the winter will have a snow. It is a sure sign of coming snow to hear the fire "treading snow"—that is, making a noise similar to that made by walking on snow. A heavy "mast" means a severe winter. If the cat sits with her back to the fire, watch out for a cold snap.

I know the groundhog theory has been viciously attacked in some quarters, but the faith has not been shaken, for everybody knows that if the groundhog sees his shadow when he emerges from his hole on February 2, he will return to stay for six weeks that he may escape the severe weather to come.

A frequently quoted paraphrase of an old sailor's saying runs thus:

> Red clouds at night,
> A traveler's delight;
> Red clouds in the morning,
> A traveler's warning.

There are signs and omens affecting nearly all the agricultural and domestic affairs, and the prudent farmer and his good housewife should give due attention. If the good wife would keep the hawks from troubling her young chickens, she puts a white flint rock in the fireplace where it will keep warm. To make the guard dog stay at home and attend to his duties while she may go to help in the field or go for a neighborly visit, she cuts a bit of hair from the tip of his tail and buries it under the front doorsteps. Of course she wants her young cow to become a good milker—to insure this she carefully collects the milk first taken and pours it into a running stream; and she is always careful not to allow the milk, as it is drawn from the cow, young or old, to fall on the ground, for she knows that, if that happens, the cow will "hold up" her milk, and soon go dry; the good wife is also careful not to kill a toad for fear it will cause her cow to give bloody milk. If the butter will not come she heats a horseshoe and applies it to the bottom of the churn until an imprint is burnt thereon, and sometimes she may have to put it in the churn to drive away the troublesome witches. She never burns the eggshells, nor carries eggs into the house after dark, well knowing that if she does her hens will quit laying. The farmer is careful also not to burn the cobs from which the seedcorn is shelled, knowing that it will ruin his crop; but he is careful to bury them in a moist, swampy place, and a good crop is thus insured, regardless of seasons. Before buying a milk cow he examines carefully to see that she has small horns, small neck, slim tail, and a large "cowlick" between the thighs from udder up; these are signs of a good milker. He prefers the horse which has a Roman nose, broad forehead, and flowing mane and tail—such a horse is sensible and gentle; the dish-faced, white-eyed horse should be shunned; he is foolish and vicious.

From: Haywood Parker, "Folk-Lore of the North Carolina Mountaineers," *Journal of American Folk-Lore* 20 (1907): 241–50.

CHAPTER 14

Customs and Beliefs

· *Customs from Louisiana* ·

(African)

A custom which was quite interesting was the cutting of the last cane for grinding. When the hands had reached the last rows left standing, the foreman (*commandeur*) chose the tallest cane, and the best laborer (*le meilleur couteau*) came to the cane chosen, which was the only one in the field left uncut. Then the whole gang congregated around the spot, with the overseer and foreman, and the latter, taking a blue ribbon, tied it to the cane, and, brandishing the knife in the air, sang to the cane as if it were a person, and danced around it several times before cutting it. When this was done, all the laborers, men, women, and children, mounted in the empty carts, carrying the last cane in triumph, waving colored handkerchiefs in the air, and singing as loud as they could. The procession went to the house of the master, who gave a drink to every Negro, and the day ended with a ball, amid general rejoicing.

Shooting at the *papegai* was another great popular amusement. A rude bird representing a rooster was made of wood, and was placed on a high pole to be shot at. A calf or an ox was killed, and every part of the wooden bird represented a similar portion of the animal. All who wanted to shoot had to pay a certain amount for each chance. This sport is still a favorite one in the country, both with the whites and the blacks, but not so much so as before the war.

From: Alcee Fortier, *Louisiana Studies* (New Orleans: F. F. Hansell & Brothers, 1894).

· A Custom from Maryland ·

(Unidentified)

An interesting custom was formerly practiced by surveyors in marking out the boundaries of estates. It was usual for the surveyor, at a certain point, when surveying land, to give the smallest child in the party that followed him, whether black or white, a severe whipping. Trees, it was claimed, might be struck by lightning or otherwise destroyed, and stones might disappear, but the child, who was likely to outlive the others present, would never forget the spot where he received the whipping. A gentleman whose childhood home was in Calvert County writes of this custom as follows:

"I recollect when quite a small boy, perhaps five or six years old, I was staying at my uncle's when Mr. King was sent for to survey a lot of ground." Mr. King, he explains elsewhere, was the son of a surveyor, and father and son together had not only surveyed all the land in Calvert County, but much in the counties adjoining. "He had great difficulty," he continues, "in finding the starting point from an old deed which he had in his possession. After the starting point was found and the compass adjusted, he told me that in his younger days, the youngest boy around was severely whipped on that spot, so that all his life he would remember where the survey began. He cut a switch from a nearby tree, and told me that he would not be hard on me, but struck me a few licks gently that I might tell the place when I grew up; but I am afraid I could not find it now, it has been so long ago."

Another gentleman, who is a surveyor, writes of the same custom as having been practiced by his father and grandfather, who were surveyors in and around Baltimore.

From: Anne Weston Whitney, "Items of Maryland Belief and Custom," *Journal of American Folk-Lore* 12 (1899): 273–74.

· *Wedding Customs* ·

(German)

He calmly commented: "Them Polacks waste powder awful. Not only on Sunday, for fun, but down in the mine they use twice too much. And they can't blast the hardest coal, either.... And they're always gettin' careless and blowin' themselves to hell and everybody else. It's awful, it's awful," he said, but in a most philosophic tone.

He lowered his voice and pointed with his pipe stem: "Them people that live in the next house are supposed to be Cawcasians, but they haven't a marriage license. They let their little girl go for beer this afternoon, for them fellows explodin' powder over there. 'Taint no way to raise a child. That child's mother was a well-behaved Methodist till she married a Polack, and had four children, and he died, and they died, and some say she poisoned them all. Now she's got this child by this no-account white man. They live without a license, like birds. Yet they eat off weddin's."

"Eat off weddings?"

"Yes," he said. "These Bohunks and Lickerishes all have one kind of a wedding. It lasts three days and everybody comes. The best man is king. He bosses the plates."

"Bosses the plates?"

"Yes. They buy a lot of cheap plates. Every man that comes must break a plate with a dollar. The plate is put in the middle of the floor. He stands over it and bangs the dollar down. If he breaks the plate he gets to kiss and hug the bride. If he doesn't break it, the young couple get that dollar. He must keep on givin' them dollars in this way till he breaks the plate. Eats and plates and beer cost about fifty dollars. The young folks clear about two hundred dollars to start life on."

"And," he continued, "the folks next door make a practice of eatin' round at weddin's without puttin' down their dollars."

I began to feel guilty.

"It's a good deal like my begging supper and breakfast of you." He hadn't meant it that way. "No," he said, "you're takin' the only way to see the country. Why, man, I used to travel like you, before I was married, except I didn't take no book nor poetry nor nothin', and wasn't afeered of boxcars the way you are.... I been in every state in the Union but Maine. I don't know how I kept out of there.... I've been nine years in this house. I don't know but what I see as much as when I was on the go....

"That fellow Gallic over there that was shootin' that pistol at the sky killed a man named Bothweinis last year and got off free. It was Gallic's wedding and Bothweinis brought fifty dollars and said he was goin' to break all the plates in the house. He used up twelve dollars. He broke seven plates and kissed the bride seven times. Then the bride got drunk. She was only fifteen years old. She hunted up Bothweinis and kissed him and cried, and Gallic chased him down towards Shickshinny and tripped him up, and shot him in the mouth and in the eye.... The bride didn't know no better.... He was an awful sight when they brought him in. The bride was only a kid. These Bohunk women never learn no sense anyway. They're not smart like Cawcasian women, and they fade in the face quick."

He reflected: "My wife's a wonderful woman. I have been with her nine years, and she learns me something every day, and she still looks good in her Sunday clothes."

From: Vachel Lindsay, *A Handy Guide for Beggars* (New York: The Macmillan Company, 1916).

· *Names* ·

(Acadian)

The names of the children in Acadian families are quite as strange as the old biblical names among the early Puritans, but much more harmonious. For instance, in one family the boy was called Duradon, and his five sisters answered to the names of Elfige, Enyoné, Méridié, Ozéina, and Fronie. A father who had a musical ear called his sons Valmir, Valmore, Valsin, Valcour, and Valérien, while another, with a tincture of the classics, called his boy Deus, and his daughter Déussa.

From: Alcee Fortier, *Louisiana Studies* (New Orleans: F. F. Hansell & Brothers, 1894).

· Dances ·

(Acadian)

Having heard that every Saturday evening there was a ball in the prairie, I requested one of my friends to take me to see one. We arrived at eight o'clock, but already the ball had begun. In the yard were vehicles of all sorts, but three-mule carts were most numerous. The ball-room was a large hall with galleries all around it. When we entered it was crowded with persons dancing to the music of three fiddles. I was astonished to see that nothing was asked for entrance, but I was told that any white person decently dressed could come in. The man giving the entertainment derived his profits from the sale of refreshments. My friend, a wealthy young planter, born in the neighborhood, introduced me to many persons and I had a good chance to hear the Acadian dialect, as everybody there belonged to the Acadian race. I asked a pleasant looking man, *"Votre fille est-elle ice!"* He corrected me by replying, *"Oui, mademoiselle est là."* However, he did not say *mes messieurs* for his sons, but spoke of them as *mes garçons*, although he showed me his *dame*. We went together to the refreshment room, where were beer and lemonade, but I observed that the favorite drink was black coffee, which indeed was excellent. At midnight supper was served; it was chicken gumbo with rice, the national Creole dish.

Most of the men appeared uncouth and awkward, but the young girls were really charming. They were elegant, well-dressed, and exceedingly handsome. They had large and soft black eyes and beautiful black hair. Seeing how well they looked I was astonished and grieved to hear that probably very few of them could read or write. On listening to the conversation I could easily see that they had no education. French was spoken by all, but occasionally English was heard.

After supper my friend asked me if I wanted to see *le parc aux petits*. I followed him without knowing what he meant and he took me to a room adjoining the dancing hall, where I saw a number of little children thrown on a bed and sleeping. The mothers who accompanied their daughters had left the little ones in the *parc aux petits* before passing to the dancing room, where I saw them the whole evening assembled together in one corner of the hall and watching over their daughters. *Le parc aux petits* interested me very much, but I found the gambling room stranger still.

There were about a dozen men at a table playing cards. One lamp suspended from the ceiling threw a dim light upon the players, who appeared at first very wild, with their broad-brimmed felt hats on their heads and their long untrimmed sunburnt faces. There was, however, a kindly expression on every face, and everything was so quiet that I saw that the men were not professional gamblers. I saw the latter a little later, in a barn nearby where they had taken refuge: about half a dozen men, playing on a rough board by the light of two candles. I understood that these were the black sheep of the crowd and we merely cast a glance at them.

I was desirous to see the end of the ball, but having been told that the breakup would only take place at four or five o'clock in the morning, we went away at one o'clock. I was well pleased with my evening and I admired the perfect order that reigned, considering that it was a public affair and open to all who wished to come, without any entrance fee. My friend told me that when the dance was over the musicians would rise, and going out in the yard would fire several pistol shots in the air, crying out at the same time: *le bal est fini.*

From: Alcee Fortier, *Louisiana Studies* (New Orleans: F. F. Hansell & Brothers, 1894).

· Dress ·

(English)

Dress signified more to the men of the time of Elizabeth and James than it is easy for us moderns to imagine. Greatness declared itself by external display. The son of a rich merchant when he returned from his travels decked himself in gorgeous apparel, and formally made his appearance on the Exchange like a butterfly newly emerged. It was thus that his parents brought the young man out in the world. A sum equal in purchasing power to several thousand dollars in our time is said to have been spent on one pair of trunk hose. Men of the lowest ranks, desirous of appearing more than they were, impoverished themselves in buying expensive hats and hose; and it is recorded that women suffering for the necessaries of life sometimes contrived to adorn themselves with velvet. For the very reason that so much importance was attached to

dress, laws were made to repress inappropriate display in people of lower
rank. Even the severe Puritan moralists did not object to the pomp of
the great, but to the extravagant imitation of it by those who had no
right to such ostentation. It was with difficulty that men could conceive
of greatness without display. To refuse a bishop his vestments was to abate
something of his lofty rank.

Along with a love for external show went a scrupulous observance of
decorous and often pompous ceremonies. Englishmen in the sixteenth and
the early part of the seventeenth century never omitted to observe proper
formality, no matter how dire the emergency. One may see this exempli-
fied by reverting to some of the earliest events in American history. When
Gates arrived at Jamestown near the close of the "starving time," he
found only the gaunt ghosts of men clamoring to be taken from the scene
of so many horrible miseries. Instead of giving immediate attention to the
sufferings of the people, he caused the little church bell to be rung. Such
of the inhabitants as could drag themselves out of their huts repaired once
more to the now-ruined and unfrequented church with its roof of sedge
and earth supported by timbers set in crotches. Here the newly arrived
chaplain offered a sorrowful prayer, and then George Percy, the retiring
governor, delivered up his authority to Sir Thomas Gates, who thus found
himself in due and proper form installed governor of death, famine, and
desperation. When Gates abandoned the wrecked town with his starving
company, he fired a "peale of small shott," in order not to be wanting in
respect for a royal fort; and when De la Warr arrived, a few days later,
he made his landing with still greater pomp than that of Gates. There
was a flourish of trumpets on shipboard before he struck sail in front of
Jamestown. A gentleman of his party bore the colors of the governor
before him. The governor's first act when he set foot on American soil
was to fall on his knees and offer a long, silent prayer, which was probably
sincere though theatrical, after the manner of the age. He rose at length
and marched up into the ruined town. As he passed into the stockade by
the water gate, which was shabbily off its hinges, the color-bearer dropped
down before him and allowed the colors to fall at the feet of his lordship,
who proceeded to the tumbledown chapel, under the earthen roof of
which the authority over the colony was duly transferred to his hands
with such solemnities as were thought proper. Whenever Lord De la Warr
went to church at Jamestown he was attended by the councilors, captains,

and gentlemen, and guarded by fifty men with halberds, wearing De la Warr's livery of showy red cloaks. The governor's seat was a chair covered with green velvet. It was in the choir of the now reconstructed little church, and a velvet cushion lay on the table before him to enable him to worship his Maker in a manner becoming the dignity of a great lord over a howling wilderness. More than a quarter of the able-bodied men in Virginia were needed to get the governor to church and back again aboard the ship where he dwelt.

From: Edward Eglleston, *The Beginners of a Nation* (New York: D. Appleton and Co., 1896).

· *Dialects* ·

(English)

Everyone recalls the famous sentence of Sainte-Beuve: "I define a dialect," says he, "as an ancient language that has seen better days."

The fascination that the Arkansas dialect has always exercised over me comes from this very trait. In the speech of cow drivers and plowboys lingers the phrases that once were on the tongues of poets and courtiers. Herr von Rosen, Black's delightful German, learned his English from Pepys's *Diary*; and don't you remember how unique and charming were his "I did think," "I do want," and the like. The Arkansans use the same form of the verb. "I do plow, I did plow, I done plowed," is how we conjugate the verb; and it is to be noted that educated Southerners, who would not for the world say "I done," habitually use the second form, "I did." "I never did" is a special favorite; anyone familiar with Southern speech will recall the reiterated "I never did see"—always with the emphasis on the "did"—of common conversation. "I been" is good old English also. It occurs in Shakespeare, and Ben Jonson, and all the earlier English of Latimer and Jewel and Becon and the others. We pronounce it in the old way, as it is spelled, and we use it in the old way, instead of the past "was."

Our use of "like," in the place of "as," can show ancient warrant also. They say here, "Looks like I ben so puny I cudn't make out, nohow!" And they say in old English, "Yea, it looketh like we ben made a sport to our enemies!" Our common "mabbe" is probably a contraction of "mayhap" rather than of "may be." And "right" instead of "very" is as old as the day of Chaucer, to go back no farther.

I need not multiply instances. The same phenomena, if I may call it so, are to be found in the dialect of New England, as are many of the same phrases. For example—to give one out of a score—the expression "He faulted it" is as much Arkansan as Yankee. It was old English before the Puritans set sail for the New World.

From: Octave Thanet, "Folk-Lore in Arkansas," *Journal of American Folk-Lore* 5 (1892): 121–25.

· St. Patrick's Day ·

(Irish)

In the valley of Virginia there was for a generation a lively state of things between the sturdy Germans and the Irish, the latter assisted, little doubt, by the Scotch-Irish and the English. No one could deny the thrift and ability of the "Dutch," with their fine big barns, their fat flocks and herds, their overflowing garners, and their heaped-up feather beds. And though their more lively Celtic neighbors might find a narrow toehold for ridicule of their slow-witted men and their broad-waisted, barefooted women, they could not do better than imitate the steadfastness of the one and the housewifely virtues of the other.

But when these races came together in the first town of the valley, Winchester, their "national prejudices," says the old historian, "promised much disorder and many riots. It was customary for the Dutch on St. Patrick's Day to exhibit the effigy of the saint with a string of Irish potatoes around his neck, and his wife Sheeley with her apron loaded also with potatoes. This was always followed by a riot. The Irish resented the indignity offered to their saint and his holy spouse, and a battle followed. On St. Michael's Day the Irish would retort, and exhibit the saint with a rope of sauerkraut about his neck." Then the Germans would take up the challenge, "and many a black eye, bloody nose, and broken head was the result."

From: Arthur W. Spaulding, *The Men of the Mountains* (Nashville: Southern Publishing Association, 1915).

· New Year's Day ·

(African)

New Year's Day on the plantations was an occasion of great merriment and pleasure for the slaves. Its observance gave rise to scenes so characteristic of old times that I shall endeavor to describe them.

At daylight, on the 1st of January, the rejoicing began on the plantation; everything was in an uproar, and all the Negroes, old and young, were running about, shaking hands and exchanging wishes for the new year. The servants employed at the house came to awaken the master and mistress and the children. The nurses came to our beds to present their *souhaits*. To the boys it was always, "Mo souhaité ké vou bon garçon, fé plein l'argent é ké vou bienhéreux"; to the girls, "Mo souhaité ké vou bon fie, ké vou gagnin ein mari riche é plein piti."

Even the very old and infirm, who had not left the hospital for months, came to the house with the rest of *l'atelier* for their gifts. These they were sure to get, each person receiving a piece of an ox killed expressly for them, several pounds of flour, and a new tin pan and spoon. The men received, besides, a new jean or cottonade suit of clothes, and the women a dress and a most gaudy headkerchief or *tignon*, the redder the better. Each woman that had had a child during the year received two dresses instead of one. After the *souhaits* were presented to the masters, and the gifts were made, the dancing and singing began. The scene was indeed striking, interesting, and weird. Two or three hundred men and women were there in front of the house, wild with joy and most boisterous, although always respectful.

Their musical instruments were, first, a barrel with one end covered with an oxhide—this was the drum; then two sticks and the jawbone of a mule, with the teeth still on it—this was the violin. The principal musician bestrode the barrel and began to beat on the hide, singing as loud as he could. He beat with his hands, with his feet, and sometimes, when quite carried away by his enthusiasm, with his head, also. The second musician took the sticks and beat on the wood of the barrel, while the third made a dreadful music by rattling the teeth of the jawbone with a stick. Five or six men stood around the musicians and sang without stopping. All this produced a most strange and savage music, but, withal, not disagreeable, as the Negroes have a very good ear for music, and keep a pleasant rhythm in their songs. These dancing songs generally consisted of one phrase, repeated for hours on the same air.

In the dance called *carabiné*, which was quite graceful, the man took his *danseuse* by the hand, and made her turn around very rapidly for more than an hour; the woman waving a red handkerchief over her head and everyone singing,

> Madame Gobar, en sortant di bal,
> Madame Gobar, tignon li tombé.

The other dance, called *pilé Chactas*, was not as graceful as the *carabiné*, but was more strange. The woman had to dance almost without moving her feet. It was the man who did all the work: turning around her, kneeling down, making the most grotesque and extraordinary faces, writhing like a serpent, while the woman was almost immovable. After a little while, however, she began to get excited and, untying her neckerchief, she waved it around gracefully, and finally ended by wiping off the perspiration from the face of her *danseur* and also from the faces of the musicians who played the barrel and the jawbone, an act which must have been gratefully received by those sweltering individuals.

The ball, for such it was, lasted for several hours, and was a great amusement to us children.

From: Alcee Fortier, *Louisiana Studies* (New Orleans: F. F. Hansell & Brothers, 1894).

· Religions ·

(African)

Seeking Jesus
(African)

Right after the war a great many Negroes came into the interior of Georgia from the Sea Islands of South Carolina and Georgia. They brought with them a religious festival or custom called "Seeking Jesus."

They would congregate in a cabin, all the lights and fires would be put out, when one among the number would call out, "Where is Jesus?" Someone would answer: "Here is Jesus." They would rush to the part of the cabin where the answer was given, and, of course, not finding him there, would say, "He ain't here." Then another voice would cry out in the darkness from another part of the cabin: "Here is Jesus." Another rush would be made, when the statement, "He is not here," would again be made. The calls and answers would be repeated for hours, sometimes all night. The women and men would become excited and frantic, would tear their hair, and scream and pray until the meeting was broken up in a religious frenzy.

From: Roland Steiner, "Seeking Jesus," *Journal of American Folk-Lore* 14 (1901): 172.

Voodoo as a Religion
(African)

The religion of the Voodoo was based on sorcery, and, being practiced by very ignorant people, was, of course, most immoral and hideous. It is, fortunately, fast disappearing, the Negroes becoming more civilized. The dances of the Voodoo have often been described, and were, according to the accounts, perfect bacchanalia. They usually took place at some retired spot on the banks of Lake Pontchartrain or of Bayou St. John.

Although this sect is nearly extinct, the Negroes are still very much afraid of their witchcraft. The Voodoo, however, do not always succeed in their enchantments, as is evidenced by the following amusing incident.

One of my friends, returning home from his work quite late one evening, saw on a doorstep two little candles lit, and between them four nickels, placed as a cross. Feeling quite anxious as to the dreadful fate which was to befall the inhabitants of the house, the gentleman blew out the candles, threw them in the gutter, put the nickels in his pocket, and walked off with the proud satisfaction of having saved a whole family from great calamities. This is how the Creoles fear the Voodoo!

The Negroes are also very much afraid of the will-o'-the-wisp, or *ignis fatuus*. They believe that on a dark night it leads its victim, who is obliged to follow, either into the river, where he is drowned, or into the bushes of thorns, which tear him to pieces, the Jack-o'-lantern exclaiming all the time, "Aïe, aïe, mo gagnin toi,"—"Aïe, aïe, I have you."

The old Negro who was speaking to me of the *ignis fatuus* told me that he was born with a caul, and that he saw ghosts on All Saints' Day. He also added that he often saw a woman without a head, and he had the gift of prophecy.

From: Alcee Fortier, *Louisiana Studies* (New Orleans: F. F. Hansell & Brothers, 1894).

Part III

Midwestern and Prairie Folktales

CHAPTER 15

Legends and Legendary Figures

· *The Boot Hill Cemetery* ·

(Unidentified)

The citizens of Dodge City seemed proud of their fat graveyard in the "Boot Hill" Cemetery, where there were eighty-one graves, all the occupants having died with their boots on—in other words, killed, except one, who died a natural death. A fine record for a town only one year old—that is dating from the time she became a center for cattlemen, buffalo hunters, and railroad crews.

From: Charles A. Stringo, A *Lone Star Cowboy* (Santa Fe: 1919).

· *The Troubadour* ·

(Swedish)

Roll out!"
    Silence.
"Roll out, ye roundheads! 'Tis daylight in the swamps!"
    The slogan of the little Irish "cookee" bored through the fetid air within the huge log cabin where lay a hundred Scandinavians, and like a bugle call it stirred the slumbering men to action. Frowsy heads popped from rude bunks—flaxen heads, with wide blue eyes beneath the thatch—

and then, in a wondrous hurry and flurry, the camp's complement of lumberjacks began falling into their heavy mackinaw garb.

We Sybarites who dwell within the city's walls, where a cold shower and half a grapefruit start us on our daily round of carking care, know not the morning toilet of the lumberjack. Monday, Tuesday, Wednesday, Thursday—ever so many days in a row—he foregoes the pleasure of the morning bath. Liquid in some form he must have, even if it be a bottle of lemon extract or a dipperful of patent medicine, but, being a sturdy Viking, he looks not on the water when it is white against the porcelain, and welcomes not the ruddy glow that is born of the Turkish towel when it moveth itself aright. As Tom Gray might have said, had he written his elegy in a lumber camp:

> Let not Ambition mock their useful toil,
> Their homely joys and destiny obscure,
> Nor Grandeur wear, regardless of the soil,
> The long-enduring flannels of the poor.

It was late in January, and old King Cold was master of the great, grim pineries. I stepped to the door of the spacious stockade, and opened it. The frost struck me a stinging slap in the face, and with lungs and nostrils burning I recoiled.

On every side rose the tall pines of northern Wisconsin, each tree as straight and clean-cut as a Roman pillar. Over near the cook's camp, which looked like a distant mountain when viewed through the frost fog, the shantyboss was trying to reduce a dry, dead stump to kindling. From the stables came the fervent and altogether unique oaths of the early-rising teamsters, who were feeding and harnessing their horses, while eight patient oxen, denied the stable privileges, chewed their cuds out in the open air, chained in a row to a long log. Oxen often perish in the pineries, but not with gout.

Very busy was the cook. From his domain came the odor of frying sausages and the sweetly solemn sound of flapjacks falling on the massive range. A famous chef was Gaston, and one who boasted, in his idle moments, of a classy pedigree. His father, it seems, had ridden in the death cart to the guillotine, swearing and sneering at the rabble, and his great-uncle had been with the Old Guard of Napoleon's *Grand Armée* on that disastrous trip to and from Moscow, freezing to death just before they reached the river Beresina. The lumberjacks, who were obliged to eat Gaston's dishes day after day, were about equally divided as to his end, some praying that he might go the way of his father, and others favoring the freezing process.

"Take it!"

This was the breakfast horn. Out of the sleeping quarters tumbled the still drowsy herd—swampers, loaders, "road monkeys," teamsters, saw-yers—all in one mad scramble blent. Some paused briefly at the rude washstands to wash hands and faces, some compromised by washing hands, and some "beat the barrier" entirely, reasoning, not unwisely, that he who eats his flapjacks while they are hot may live to wash another day.

Oleson and I watched them filing in to the feast. We didn't eat at the first table because time was not the essence of our respective contracts. I was a hunting guest of the foreman's, and didn't have to work. Oleson couldn't work. He had consumption.

All of us were sorry for Oleson. For seven years he had been in the employ of the great lumber syndicate, the foreman told me. From swamper to sawyer, from sawyer to loader, from loader to cruiser, from cruiser to scaler, Oleson had blazed a lightning trail—until the curse came.

"He's practically a pensioner now," the foreman explained, "but he thinks he's as good as ever. They all do."

And so, on this bitter January morning, I stood in the doorway of the sleeping quarters and gazed pityingly at the stricken descendant of Eric the Red. This I could do without fear of detection, because, now that the malady had progressed almost to the last degree, Oleson had a way of looking only at the pines and the snow and the ever-nearing sky.

A chest that had lost its convex curve heaved fretfully between two of the widest shoulders that I had ever seen on mortal man. Tall and straight, like the pines he loved, he seemed the reincarnation of the first Norseman, but the gray was in his face, where the red beard should have been, and his blue eyes were too large, and they glittered.

"Maester Yackson," he remarked, "Ay don't know vy it ban, but Ay can't eat dese har flapyacks anymore. Ay vonder ef my stomach ban going back on me. Ay got no appetite ever sence Ay ban catching dis har cold on lungs."

I was silent.

"Let's go over to office," he suggested. "Ay got little song Ay ban fixing op yesterday, and maybe yu skol care to hear it."

We crossed the frozen clearing to the "office," and Oleson pulled a
scrap of paper from his pocket—a scrap of paper crowded to the edges
with a song. For Oleson was a troubadour. Where he learned to sing, and
how he learned, I never asked him, and I cannot ask him now. I had
come to the camp with a right robust idea of my own intellectual superiority, because I was just out of school and could tell, almost to an inch,
how far Mr. Hector, deceased, had been dragged around the walls of Troy.
Oleson, I suspect, didn't know whether Hector was a Trojan hero or a
hard-hitting outfielder, but Oleson could sing.

He had a high tenor voice that was very likely a baritone before he
got the "cold on his lungs," and he could make verses—quaint little
ballads of the pine woods and songs of his home beyond the sea.

"Listen, Maester Yackson," he said. "How yu tenk dis ban for new
song?

> "Ay ban tenking lots of yu,
>   Little Steena Yohnson,
> Ay ban sure yu love me true,
>   Little Steena Yohnson.
> Oder geezers lak to play
> In yure yard, but yu skol say,
> 'Ay don't lak yu fallers, nay!'
>   Little Steena Yohnson.
>
> "Some day yu skol be my vife,
>   Little Steena Yohnson;
> Ay ban glad, Ay bet yure life,
>   Little Steena Yohnson.
> Ay ban vork lak nigger, too,
> Yumping round vith logging crew,
> Ay skol building home for yu,
>   Little Steena Yohnson.
>
> "Maybe ve skol saving dough,
>   Little Steena Yohnson;
> Back to Sveden ve skol go,
>   Little Steena Yohnson;

Back var dis har midnight sun
Shining like a son of a gun!
Skol yu tenk dis har ban fun,
    Little Steena Yohnson?"

As the last notes died away, the singer broke into a fit of hollow coughing. When it was over I held him and gave him my handkerchief.

That night, in the main camp, Oleson sang again. It was a weird night, turbulent and terribly cold without, stuffy and strangely silent within. An enormous sheet-iron stove, red hot from end to end, throbbed in the center of the room, and the dim forms of twice fifty lumberjacks were ranged in a hollow square against the walls of Norway pine.

"Tillie!" clamored the rude toilers. "Seng Tillie!"

Right proudly smiled the troubadour from his throne at the far end of the room—he sat alone on a dry-goods box, between two yellow kerosene lights—and then he chanted:

"Little Tillie Oleson
    Ban my little pearl;
God ant never making
    Any nicer girl.
Dis har Qveen of Sheba
    She ban nice to see;
But little Tillie Oleson
    Ban gude enough for me.

"Ay ban yust a svamper
    Vorking op in Voods;
Ay ant ever having
    Much of dis vorld's goods.
Ay know lots of ladies
    Var Ay used to be;
But little Tillie Oleson
    Ban gude enough for me.

"Ven ve sit by fireplace
    Op at Tillie's house,

> She ban cuddling near me
> Yust lak little mouse.
> After ve ban married
> Happy ve skol be;
> Yas, little Tillie Oleson
> Ban gude enough for me."

A burst of applause filled the smoky room, but Oleson heard it not. Looking straight ahead, he sang ballad after ballad, while the north wind blared a glorious orchestration and the stars blinked down through their frozen eyelashes. Ballad after ballad he sang, with his gray, gaunt face uplifted and his soul in his high, silvery voice, and his audience floating with him through the moaning crests of the pines.

> "Ay ban sure yu love me true—
> Little—Steena—Yohnson—
> Ay skol—building home—for yu—"

The north wind was wailing now, as it charged across the clearing, a rude accompaniment to a dying song; for the troubadour pitched from his pine platform and lay crumpled up on the floor.

From: William F. Kirk, "A Swedish Troubadour," *Cosmopolitan Magazine* 47, no. 1 (July 1909): 254–56.

· *Paul Bunyan* ·

(Unidentified)

The legends of Paul Bunyan are widely distributed throughout the lumber districts of the North. The tales in our little collection have come from lumber camps in the northern peninsula of Michigan and from the Saginaw Valley in the southern peninsula, from Langlade County and from camps along the Flambeau and Wisconsin rivers in Wisconsin, from northern Minnesota, and from camps as far west as Oregon, Washington, and British Columbia. It is quite apparent that the lumberjacks in their slow migration westward have carried the tales freely from camp to camp into all of the lumbering states of the North and into the forests of Canada.

The antiquity of the tales is more difficult to determine than the extent of their distribution. It seems certain, however, from the circumstances that they have been passed down from one generation of lumbermen to another for a long period of time, that these stories of Paul Bunyan date well back into the early days of lumbering in Michigan, and that they were carried from Michigan to Wisconsin about the middle of the last century. It seems certain too that many of the tales now included in the Bunyan cycle were narrated long before Bunyan became the lumberman hero. Similar tales, lacking, of course, the local color of the Bunyan yarns, are to be found in the extravagant stories of Baron Munchausen and of Rabelais as well as in folktales from more-settled parts of the United States of America. An extremely interesting study, so complex, however, that we have not yet completed it, is the tracing of the Old World originals of the Bunyan stories to determine just to what extent the American tales are new and to what extent they were brought from France and England by early pioneers.

Whether Paul Bunyan ever lived or is as mythical as Sairey Gamp's Mrs. Harris we have not yet succeeded in definitely finding out. All lumberjacks, of course, believe, or pretend to believe, that he really lived and was the great pioneer in the lumber country; some of the older men even claim to have known him or members of his crew, and in northern Minnesota the supposed location of his grave is actually pointed out. A half-breed lumberman whom Miss Stewart interviewed asserted positively that there *was* a Paul Bunyan and that the place where he cut his hundred million feet from a single forty is actually on the map. We have found in several localities characters still living about whose prowess as lumbermen exaggerated stories are already being told; it is probable that the tales will continue to be told, with additions, after these local heroes have died. In a similar manner, we believe, did Paul Bunyan come into existence. He was probably some swamper or shacker or lumberjack more skillful and more clever than average, about whose exploits grew a series of stories; after his death his fame probably spread from camp to camp, more tales were added to those told about him, and thus, gradually, he became in time an exaggerated type of the lumberjack, and the hero of more exploits than he could possibly have carried out in his lifetime.

The Bunyan stories are usually told in the evening around the fires in the bunkhouses. The older narrators speak in the French-Canadian dialect, and the stories are often full of the technical jargon of the woods. Usually the stories are told to arouse the wonder of the tenderfoot or simply as contributions in a contest in yarning. They are always of a grotesque and fabulous type, and they are all more or less closely related to the exploits of Bunyan and his lumbering crew. "That happened," says the narrator, "the year I went up for Paul Bunyan. Of course you have all heard of Paul." And so the tale begins. It is matched by a bigger yarn, and the series grows. Often the scene of the exploits narrated is quite fictitious, like the Round River, which is in section thirty-seven, or the Big Onion River, three weeks this side of Quebec. Often too the lumberjacks will tell of events that they say occurred on another lumbering stream than the one they are working on; thus the men of the Flambeau camps will tell of the deeds of Paul Bunyan on the Wisconsin River or on the Chippewa River. Sometimes the storytellers will take Bunyan abroad and will tell of his doings, for example, among the big trees of Oregon, or they will tell of what happened when Paul was a boy on his father's farm. Usually, however, the tales are supposed to have occurred in the "good" days of lumbering, some forty or fifty years back when the country was new, and in localities not far from the camps in which the yarns are told.

But to our tales. Bunyan was a powerful giant, seven feet tall and with a stride of seven feet. He was famous throughout the lumbering districts for his physical strength and for the ingenuity with which he met difficult situations. He was so powerful that no man could successfully oppose him, and his ability to get drunk was proverbial. So great was his lung capacity that he called his men to dinner by blowing through a hollow tree a blast so strong that it blew down the timber on a tract of sixty acres, and when he spoke, the limbs sometimes fell from the trees. To keep his pipe filled required the entire time of a swamper with a scoop shovel. In the gentle art of writing Bunyan had, however, no skill. He kept his men's time by cutting notches in a stick of wood, and he ordered supplies for camp by drawing pictures of what he wanted. On one occasion only did his ingenuity fail; he ordered grindstones and got cheeses. "Oh," says Paul, "I forgot to put the holes in my grindstones."

Bunyan was assisted in his lumbering exploits by a wonderful blue ox, a creature that had the strength of nine horses and that weighed, according to some accounts, five thousand pounds; twice that, according to others. The ox measured from tip to tip of his horns just seven feet, exactly his master's height. Other accounts declare that the ox was seven feet—or seven ax handles—between his *eyes*, and *fourteen* feet between his horns. Originally he was pure white, but one winter in the woods it snowed blue snow for seven days (that was the winter of the snowsnakes) and Bunyan's ox from lying out in the snow all winter became and remained a brilliant blue. Many of the Bunyan legends are connected with the feats performed by the ox. Bunyan's method of peeling a log was as follows: He would hitch the ox to one end of the log, grasp the bark at the other end with his powerful arms, give a sharp command to the animal, and, *presto*, out would come the log as clean as a whistle. On one occasion Paul dragged a whole house up a hill with the help of his ox, and then, returning, he dragged the cellar up after the house. Occasionally, as might have been expected from so huge a creature, the ox got into mischief about camp. One night, for example, he broke loose and ate up two hundred feet of towline.

One favorite tale connected with the blue ox is that of the buckskin harness. One day old Forty Jones of Bunyan's crew killed two hundred deer by the simple process of tripping a key log which supported a pile of logs on a hillside above the place where the animals came to drink. The skins were made into a harness for the blue ox. Some days later while the cook was hauling a log in for firewood, it began to rain, the buckskin began to stretch, and by the time the ox reached camp the log was out of sight around a bend in the road with the tugs stretching back endlessly after it. The cook tied the ox and went to dinner. While he was eating, the sun came out boiling hot, dried the buckskin harness, and hauled the log into camp. Another version of this tale is reported to us by Professor Beatty of the University of Wisconsin, who heard the story when he was a boy in Canada. Whether Professor Beatty's version is simply a detached member of the Bunyan story cycle or whether, conversely, it existed originally as an independent tale and was later connected with the blue ox, we do not know. The latter explanation seems the probable one.

One tale of the blue ox had best be told in the words of the lumberjack who sent it to a friend of Miss Stewart's, in a letter written with very evident care and with every other word capitalized.

Paul B Driving a large Bunch of logs Down the Wisconsin River When the logs Suddenly Jamed. in the Dells. The logs were piled Two Hundred feet high at the head, And were backed up for One mile up river. Paul was at the rear of the Jam with the Blue Oxen And while he was coming to the front the Crew was trying to break the Jam but they couldent Budge it. When Paul Arrived at the Head with the ox he told them to Stand Back. He put the Ox in the old Wisc. in front of the Jam. And then Standing on the Bank Shot the Ox with a 303 Savage Rifle. The Ox thought it was flies And began to Switch his Tail. The tail commenced to go around in a circle And up Stream And do you know That Ox Switching his tail forced that Stream to flow Backwards And Eventually the Jam floated back Also. He took the ox out of the Stream. And let the Stream And logs go on their way.

Most of the exploits of Paul Bunyan center at Round River. Here Bunyan and his crew labored all one winter to clear the pine from a single forty. This was a most peculiar forty in that it was shaped like a pyramid with a heavy timber growth on all sides. The attention of skeptics who refuse to believe in the existence of the pyramid forty is certain to be called by the storyteller to a lumberman with a short leg, a member, the listener is solemnly assured, of Bunyan's crew, who got his short leg from working all winter on one side of the pyramid, and who thus earned the nickname of "Rockin' Horse." From this single forty Bunyan's crew cleared one hundred million feet of pine, and in the spring they started it down the river. Then began the difficulty, for it was not until they had passed their old camp several times that they realized that the river was *round* and had no outlet whatever. According to another version this logging occurred on a lake with no outlet.

Bunyan's crew was so large that he was obliged to divide the men into three gangs; of these one was always going to work, one was always at work, and the third was always coming home from work. The cooking arrangements for so many men were naturally on an immense scale. Seven men with seven wheelbarrows were kept busy wheeling the prune stones away from camp. The cookstove was so extensive that three forties had to be cleared bare each week to keep up a fire, and an entire cord of wood was needed to start a blaze. One day as soon as the cook had put a loaf of bread into the oven he started to walk around the stove in order to remove the loaf from the other side, but long before he reached his destination the bread had burned to a crisp. Such loaves were, of course, gigantic—so big, in fact, that after the crew had eaten the insides out of them, the hollow crusts were used for bunkhouses, or, according to a less-imaginative account, for bunks. One legend reports that the loaves were not baked in a stove at all but in a ravine or dried riverbed with heat provided by blazing slashings along the sides.

Such a stove as Bunyan's demanded, of course, a pancake griddle of monstrous size. As a matter of fact, Bunyan's cook, Joe Mufferon, used the entire top of the stove for a griddle and greased it every morning by strapping hams to the feet of his assistant cooks and obliging them to skate about on it for an hour or so. Of this famous tale there are several versions. According to one the cook mixed his batter in a sort of concrete mixer on the roof of the cookshanty and spread it upon the stove by means of a connecting hose. A version from Oregon shows the influence of local conditions upon the Bunyan tales; from this version we learn that two hundred *Japanese* cooks with bacon rinds or bear steak strapped to their feet skated upon the stove before the cook spread his batter. In a Minnesota version Bunyan employs his twenty-four daughters for the same menial task. By mistake one day the nearsighted cook put into the batter several fingers of blasting powder instead of baking powder, and when the mixture was spread upon the griddle, the cookees made a very rapid ascent through the cookshanty roof and never returned to camp.

Paul Bunyan's ingenuity in keeping his men supplied with food and drink appears best in the pea-soup lake story, of which there are several versions, and in the wondrous tale of the camp distillery. Near the Round River camp was a hot spring, into which the tote-teamster, returning one day from town with a load of peas, dumped the whole load by accident. Most men would have regarded the peas as a dead loss, but not so Paul. He promptly added the proper amount of pepper and salt to the mixture and had enough hot pea soup to last the crew all winter. When his men were working too far away from camp to return to dinner, he got the soup to them by freezing it upon the ends of sticks and sending it in that shape. According to another version of the pea-soup lake story Paul deliberately made the pea soup; he dumped the peas into a small lake and heated the mess by firing the slashings around the shore. In a Wisconsinized version of the Michigan tale the peas have become, for some reason, beans. A much exaggerated version of this story comes from northern Wisconsin. According to this account the tote-teamster was driving across a frozen lake when a sudden thaw overtook him. The teamster saved himself, but the ox was drowned. Bunyan dammed up the lake, fired the slashings around the shore, and then, opening the dam, sluiced down the river to his laboring crew an abundance of excellent hot pea soup with oxtail flavor.

The legend of the establishment of the camp distillery is one of the most entertaining of the Bunyan tales. Paul had trouble in keeping any liquor in camp because the men sent to town for it drank it all up on the way back. The following is Mr. Douglas Malloch's versified account of how he solved the difficulty:

> One day the bull-cook parin' spuds
> He hears a sizzlin' in the suds
> And finds the peelin's, strange to say,
> Are all fermentin' where they lay.
> Now Sour-face Murphy in the door
> Was standin'. And the face he wore
> Convinced the first assistant cook
> That Murphy soured 'em with his look.
> And when he had the peelin's drained
> A quart of Irish booze remained.
> The bull-cook tells the tale to Paul
> And Paul takes Murphy off the haul
> And gives him, very willingly,
> A job as camp distillery.

Some of the tales of the camp exploits concern members of Paul Bunyan's crew rather than the hero himself. One of the men, for example, had two sets of teeth, and, walking in his sleep one night, he encountered the grindstone and chewed it to bits before he was fully aroused to what he was doing. In the adventure of another member of the crew we have the familiar tale of the man who jumped across the river in three jumps. The crew sometimes showed ingenuity on their own account as when they rolled boulders down the steep sides of the pyramid forty, and running after them ground their axes to a razor edge against the revolving stones.

Connected very frequently with the Bunyan tales are accounts of fabulous animals that haunted the camp. There is the bird who lays square eggs so that they will not roll down hill, and hatches them in the snow. Then there is the sidehill dodger, a curious animal naturally adapted to life on a hill by virtue of the circumstance that it has two short legs on the uphill side. Of this creature it is said that by mistake the female dodger once laid her eggs (for the species seems to resemble somewhat the Australian duckbill) wrong end around, with the terrible result that the little dodgers, hatching out with their short legs *down*hill, rolled into the river and drowned. The pinnacle grouse are birds with only one wing, adapted by this defect for flight in one direction about the top of a conical hill. There is little doubt that these animal stories existed outside the Bunyan cycle, and are simply appended to the central group of tales.

The story of Bunyan's method of paying off his crew at the end of the season shows the hero's craftiness. Discovering in the spring that he had no money on hand, Bunyan suddenly rushed into camp shouting that they had been cutting government pine and were all to be arrested. Each man thereupon seized what camp property lay nearest his hand and made off, no two men taking the same direction. Thus Bunyan cleared his camp without paying his men a cent for their labor.

Not all of the Bunyan stories are concerned with Bunyan's life in the Round River or the Big Onion camps. There are several accounts of his exploits far from the forests of the north-central states. It is said that when he was once dredging out the Columbia River, he broke the dredge, and, sticking it into his pocket, walked to the nearest blacksmith shop in South Dakota, had it repaired, and returned to the Oregon camp before dark. Besides his blue ox Bunyan had, according to some versions, so many oxen that their yokes, piled up, made twenty cords of wood. One day he drove all of these animals through a hollow tree which had fallen across a great ravine. When he reached the other side, he found that several of the oxen had disappeared, and, returning, he discovered that they had strayed into a hollow limb. Occasionally one hears some account of Paul Bunyan's boyhood exploits on his father's farm. It is said that on one occasion he and his father went out to gather a huge watermelon which was growing on a sidehill above a railroad track. They carelessly forgot to prop the melon up before they severed the stem with a crosscut saw, and as a result it broke loose, rolled downhill, burst open on striking the rails, and washed out two hundred feet of track. This tale and similar ones do not seem to belong strictly to the Bunyan cycle, but to be, rather, like the animal fables, mere appendages.

From: K. Bernice Stewart and Homer A. Watt, "Legends of Paul Bunyan Lumberjack," *Wisconsin Academy of Sciences, Arts, and Letters Transactions* 18, part 2 (1916): 639–51.

· *Johnny Appleseed* ·

(Unidentified)

John Chapman was born at Springfield, Massachusetts, in the year 1775. Of his early life but little is known, as he was reticent about himself, but his half sister, who came west at a later period, stated that Johnny had, when a boy, shown a fondness for natural scenery and often wandered from home in quest of plants and flowers and that he liked to listen to the birds singing and to gaze at the stars. Chapman's penchant for planting apple seeds and cultivating nurseries caused him to be called "Appleseed John," which was finally changed to "Johnny Appleseed," and by that name he was called and known everywhere.

The year Chapman came to Ohio has been variously stated, but to say it was one hundred years ago would not be far from the mark. An uncle of the late Roscella Rice lived in Jefferson County when Chapman made his first advent in Ohio, and one day saw a queer-looking craft coming down the Ohio River above Steubenville. It consisted of two canoes lashed together, and its crew was one man—an angular, oddly dressed person—and when he landed he said his name was Chapman, and that his cargo consisted of sacks of apple seeds and that he intended to plant nurseries.

Chapman's first nursery was planted nine miles below Steubenville, up a narrow valley, from the Ohio River, at Brilliant, formerly called Lagrange, opposite Wellsburg, West Virginia. After planting a number of nurseries along the riverfront, he extended his work into the interior of the state—into Richland County—where he made his home for many years.

Chapman was enterprising in his way and planted nurseries in a number of counties, which required him to travel hundreds of miles to visit and cultivate them yearly, as was his custom. His usual price for a tree was "a fip penny-bit," but if the settler hadn't money, Johnny would either give him credit or take old clothes for pay. He generally located his nurseries along streams, planted his seeds, surrounded the patch with a brush fence, and when the pioneers came, Johnny had young fruit trees ready for them. He extended his operations to the Maumee country and finally into Indiana, where the last years of his life were spent. He revisited Richland County the last time in 1843, and called at my father's, but as I was only five years old at the time I do not remember him.

My parents (in about 1827–1835) planted two orchards with trees they bought from Johnny, and he often called at their house, as he was a frequent caller at the homes of the settlers. My grandfather, Captain James Cunningham, settled in Richland County in 1808, and was acquainted with Johnny for many years, and I often heard him tell, in his Irish-witty way, many amusing anecdotes and incidents of Johnny's life and of his peculiar and eccentric ways.

Johnny was fairly educated, well-read, polite and attentive in manner, and chaste in conversation. His face was pleasant in expression, and he was kind and generous in disposition. His nature was a deeply religious one, and his life was blameless among his fellowmen. He regarded comfort more than style and thought it wrong to spend money for clothing to make a fine appearance. He usually wore a broad-brimmed hat. He went barefooted not only in the summer, but often in cold weather, and a coffee sack, with neck and armholes cut in it, was worn as a coat. He was about five feet, nine inches in height, rather spare in build but was large-boned and sinewy. His eyes were blue, but darkened with animation.

For a number of years Johnny lived in a little cabin near Perrysville (then in Richland County), but later he made his home in Mansfield with his half sister, a Mrs. Groome, who lived on the Leesville road (now West Fourth Street) near the present residence of R. G. Hancock. The parents of George C. Wise then lived near what is now the corner of West Fourth Street and Penn Avenue and the Groome and Wise families were friends and neighbors. George C. Wise, Hiram R. Smith, Mrs. J. H. Cook, and others remember "Johnny Appleseed" quite well. Mrs. Cook was, perhaps, better acquainted with "Johnny" than any other living person today, for the Wiler house was often his stopping place. The homes of Judge Parker, Mr. Newman, and others were ever open to receive "Johnny" as a guest.

But the man who best understood this peculiar character was the late Dr. William Bushnell, father of our respected fellow townsman, the Honorable M. B. Bushnell, the donor of this beautiful commemorative monument, and by whose kindness and liberality we are here today. With Dr. Bushnell's scholastic attainments and intuitive knowledge of character he was enabled to know and appreciate Chapman's learning and the noble traits of his head and heart.

When upon his journeys, "Johnny" usually camped out. He never killed anything, not even for the purpose of obtaining food. He carried a kit of cooking utensils with him, among which was a mush pan, which he sometimes wore as a hat. When he called at a house, his custom was to lie upon the floor with his kit for a pillow and, after conversing with the family a short time, would then read from a Swedenborgian book or tract, and proceed to explain and extol the religious views he so zealously believed, and whose teachings he so faithfully carried out in his everyday life and conversation. His mission was one of peace and good will and he never carried a weapon, not even for self-defense. The Indians regarded him as a great "Medicine Man," and his life seemed to be a charmed one, as neither savage men nor wild beast would harm him.

Chapman was not a mendicant. He was never in indigent circumstances, for he sold thousands of nursery trees every year. Had he been avaricious, his estate instead of being worth a few thousand might have been tens of thousands at his death.

"Johnny Appleseed's" name was John Chapman—not Jonathan—and this is attested by the muniments of his estate, and also from the fact that he had a half brother (a deaf mute) whose Christian name was Jonathan.

Chapman never married and rumor said that a love affair in the old Bay State was the cause of his living the life of a celibate and recluse. Johnny himself never explained why he led such a singular life except to remark that he had a mission—which was understood to be to plant nurseries and to make converts to the doctrines taught by Emanuel Swedenborg. He died at the home of William Worth in St. Joseph Township, Allen County, Indiana, March 11, 1847, and was buried in David Archer's graveyard, a few miles north of Fort Wayne, near the foot of a natural mound. His name is engraved as a senotaph upon one of the monuments erected in Mifflin Township, Ashland County, this state, to the memory of the pioneers. Those monuments were unveiled with imposing ceremony in the presence of over six thousand people September 15, 1882, the seventieth anniversary of the Copus tragedy.

During the War of 1812 Chapman often warned the settlers of approaching danger. The following incident is given: When the news spread that Levi Jones had been killed by the Indians and that Wallace Reed and others had probably met the same fate, excitement ran high and the few families which comprised the population of Mansfield sought the protection of the blockhouse, situated on the public square, as it was supposed the savages were coming in force from the north to overrun the country and to murder the settlers.

There were no troops at the blockhouse at the time and as an attack was considered imminent, a consultation was held and it was decided to send a messenger to Captain Douglas, at Mount Vernon, for assistance. But who would undertake the hazardous journey? It was evening, and the rays of the sunset had faded away and the stars were beginning to shine in the darkening sky and the trip of thirty miles must be made in the night over a new-cut road through a wilderness—through a forest infested with wild beasts and hostile Indians.

A volunteer was asked for and a tall lank man said demurely, "I'll go." He was bareheaded, barefooted, and unarmed. His manner was meek and you had to look the second time into his clear, blue eyes to fully fathom the courage and determination shown in their depths. There was an expression in his countenance such as limners try to portray in their pictures of saints. It is scarcely necessary to state that the volunteer was "Johnny Appleseed" for many of you have heard your fathers tell how unostentatiously "Johnny" stood as "a watchman on the walls of Jezreel," to guard and protect the settlers from their savage foes.

The journey to Mount Vernon was a sort of Paul Revere mission. Unlike Paul's, "Johnny's" was made on foot—barefooted—over a rough road, but one that in time led to fame.

"Johnny" would rap on the doors of the few cabins along the route, warn the settlers of the impending danger, and advise them to flee to the blockhouse.

"Johnny" arrived safely at Mount Vernon, aroused the garrison, and informed the commandant of his mission. Surely, figuratively speaking,

> The dun-deer's hide
> On fleeter feet was never tied,

for so expeditiously was the trip made that at sunrise the next morning troops from Mount Vernon arrived at the Mansfield blockhouse, accompanied by "Johnny," who had made the round-trip of sixty miles between sunset and sunrise.

About a week before Chapman's death, while at Fort Wayne, he heard that cattle had broken into his nursery in St. Joseph Township and were destroying his trees, and he started on foot to look after his property. The distance was about twenty miles and the fatigue and exposure of the journey were too much for "Johnny's" physical condition, then enfeebled by age; and at the eventide he applied at the home of a Mr. Worth for lodging for the night. Mr. Worth was a native Buckeye and had lived in Richland County when a boy and when he learned that his oddly dressed caller was "Johnny Appleseed" gave him a cordial welcome. "Johnny" declined going to the supper table but partook of a bowl of bread and milk.

The day had been cold and raw with occasional flurries of snow, but in the evening the clouds cleared away and the sun shone warm and bright as it sank in the western sky. "Johnny" noticed this beautiful sunset, an augury of the spring and flowers so soon to come, and sat on the doorstep and gazed with wistful eyes toward the west. Perhaps this herald of the springtime, the season in which nature is resurrected from the death of winter, caused him to look with prophetic eyes to the future and contemplate that glorious event of which Christ is the resurrection and the life. Upon reentering the house, "Johnny" declined the bed offered him for the night, preferring a quilt and pillow on the floor, but asked permission to hold family worship and read "Blessed are the poor in spirit, for theirs is the kingdom of Heaven," "Blessed are the pure in heart, for they shall see God," etc.

After he had finished reading the lesson, he said prayers—prayers long remembered by that family. He prayed for all sorts and conditions of men; that the way of righteousness might be made clear unto them; and that saving grace might be freely given to all nations. He asked that the Holy Spirit might guide and govern all who profess and call themselves Christians and that all those who were afflicted in mind, body, or estate, might be comforted and relieved, and that all might at last come to the knowledge of the truth and in the world to come have happiness and everlasting life. Not only the words of the prayer, but the pathos of his voice made a deep impression upon those present.

In the morning "Johnny" was found in a high state of fever, pneumonia having developed during the night, and the physician called said he was beyond medical aid, but inquired particularly about his religious belief, and remarked that he had never seen a dying man so perfectly calm, for upon his wan face there was an expression of happiness and upon his pale lips there was a smile of joy, as though he was communing with loved ones who had come to meet him and to soothe his weary spirit in his dying moments. And as his eyes shone with the beautiful light supernal, God touched him with his finger and beckoned him home.

Thus ended the life of the man who was not only a hero, but a benefactor as well; and his spirit is now at rest in the Paradise of the Redeemed, and in the fullness of time clothed again in the old body made anew, will enter into the Father's house in which there are many mansions. In the words of his own faith, his bruised feet will be healed, and he shall walk on the gold-paved streets of the New Jerusalem of which he so eloquently preached. It has been very appropriately said that although years have come and gone since his death, the memory of his good deeds live anew every springtime in the beauty and fragrance of the blossoms of the apple trees he loved so well.

"Johnny Appleseed's" death was in harmony with his unostentatious, blameless life. It is often remarked, "How beautiful is the Christian's life"; yea, but far more beautiful is the Christian's death, when "the fashion of his countenance is altered," as he passes from the life here to the life beyond.

What changes have taken place in the years that have intervened between the "Johnny Appleseed" period and today! It has been said that the lamp of civilization far surpasses that of Aladdin's. Westward the star of empire took its way and changed the forests into fields of grain and the waste places into gardens of flowers, and towns and cities have been built with marvelous handiwork. But in this march of progress, the struggles and hardships of the early settlers must not be forgotten. Let us not only record the history, but the legends of the pioneer period; garner its facts and its fictions; its tales and traditions; and collect even the crumbs that fall from the table of the feast.

Today the events which stirred the souls and tried the courage of the pioneers seem to come out of the dim past and glide as panoramic views before me. A number of the actors in those scenes were of my "kith and kin" who have long since crossed over the river in their journey to the land where Enoch and Elijah are pioneers, while I am left to exclaim:

> "Oh, for the touch of a vanished hand
> And the sound of a voice that is still."

While the scenes of those pioneer days are vivid to us on history's page, future generations may look upon them as the phantasmagoria of a dream.

At seventy-two years of age—forty-six of which had been devoted to his self-imposed mission—John Chapman ripened into death as naturally and as beautifully as the apple seeds of his planting had grown into trees, budded into blossoms, and ripened into fruit. The monument which is not to be unveiled is a fitting memorial to the man in whom there dwelt a comprehensive love that reached downward to the lowest forms of life and upward to the throne of the Divine.

From: A. J. Baughman "Historical Sketch of the Life and Work of 'Johnny Appleseed,' " *The Firelands Pioneer*, New Series 8 (December 1900): 702–11.

· Tales of Father Marquette ·

(French)

Father Marquette and the Man-Eater

Until it was worn away by the elements a curious relief was visible on the bluffs of the Mississippi near Alton, Illinois. It was to be seen as late as 1860, and represented a monster once famous as the "piasa bird."

Father Marquette not only believed it but described it as a man-eater in the account of his explorations, where he mentions other zoological curiosities, such as unicorns with shaggy mane and land turtles three feet long with two heads, "very mischievous and addicted to biting."

He even showed a picture of the man-eater that accorded rudely with the picture on the rocks. It was said to prey on human flesh, and to be held in fear by the Indians, who encountered it on and near the Mississippi. It had the body of a panther, wings like a bat, and head and horns of a deer. Father Marquette gave it a human face.

The sculpture was undoubtedly made by Indians, but its resemblance to the winged bulls of Assyria and the sphinxes of Egypt has been quoted as confirmation of a prehistoric alliance of Old and New World races or the descent of one from the other.

It has also been thought to stand for the totem of some great chief— symbolizing, by its body, strength; by its wings, speed; by its head, gentleness and beauty. But may not the tradition of it have descended from the discovery of comparatively late remains, by primitive man, of the winged saurians that crawled, swam, dived, or flew, lingering on till the later geologic period? The legend of the man-eater may even have been told by those who killed the last of the pterodactyls.

From: Charles M. Skinner, *Myths & Legends of Our Own Land*, vol. 2 (Philadelphia and London: J. B. Lippincott Co., 1896).

The Sun Fire at Sault Sainte Marie

Father Marquette reached Sault Sainte Marie in company with Greysolon Du Lhut, in August 1670, and was received in a manner friendly enough, but the Chippewas warned him to turn back from that point, for the Ojibways beyond were notoriously hostile to Europeans, their chief— White Otter—having taken it on himself to revenge, by war, his father's desertion of his mother. His father was a Frenchman. Inspired by his mission, and full of the enthusiasm of youth and of the faith that had led him safely through a host of dangers and troubles, Marquette refused to change his plans, and even ventured the assertion that he could tame the haughty Otter and bring him to the cross.

At dawn he and his doughty henchman set off in a war canoe, but on arriving in White Otter's camp and speaking their errand, they were seized and bound, to await death on the morrow. The wife of the chief spoke, out of the kindness of her heart, and asked mercy for the white men. However, it was to no avail. The brute struck her to the ground. That night his daughter, Wanena, who had seen Du Lhut at the trading post and had felt the stir of a generous sentiment toward him, appeared before the prisoners when sleep was heaviest in the camp, cut their bonds, led them by an obscure path to the river, where she enjoined them to enter a canoe, and guided the boat to the Holy Isle. This was where the Ojibways came to lay offerings before the image of the manitou, whose home was believed to be there. There the friendly red men would be sure to find and rescue them, she thought, and after a few hours of sleep she led them into a secluded glen where stood the figure rudely carved from a pine trunk, six feet high, and tricked with gewgaws. As they stood there, stealthy steps were heard, and before they could conceal themselves White Otter and eight of his men were upon them. Du Lhut grasped a club from among the weapons that—with other offerings—strewed the earth at the statute's feet and prepared to sell his life dearly. The priest drew forth his crucifix and prayed. The girl dropped to the ground, drew her blanket over her head, and began to sing her death song.

"So the black coat and the woman stealer have come to die before the Indian's god?" sneered the chief.

"If it be God's will, we will die defying your god and you," replied Marquette. "Yet we fear not death, and if God willed he could deliver us as easily as he could destroy that worthless image." He spoke in an undertone to Du Lhut, and continued, confidently, "I challenge your god to withstand mine. I shall pray my God to send his fire from the sky and burn this thing. If he does so will you set us free and become a Christian?"

"I will; but if you fail, you die."

"And if I win, you must pardon your daughter."

White Otter grunted his assent.

The sun was high and brought spicy odors from the wood; an insect hummed drowsily, and a bird-song echoed from the distance. Unconscious of what was being enacted about her, Wanena kept rocking to and fro, singing her death song, and waiting the blow that would stretch her at her father's feet. The savages gathered around the image and watched it with eager interest. Raising his crucifix with a commanding gesture, the priest strode close to the effigy, and in a loud voice cried, in Chippewa, "In the name of God, I command fire to destroy this idol!"

A spot of light danced upon the breast of the image. It grew dazzling bright and steady. Then a smoke began to curl from the dry grass and feathers it was decked with. The Indians fell back in amazement, and when a faint breeze passed, fanning the sparks into flame, they fell on their faces, trembling with apprehension, for Marquette declared, "As my God treats this idol, so can he treat you!"

Then, looking up to see the manitou in flames, White Otter exclaimed, "The white man's God has won. Spare us, O mighty medicine!"

"I will do so, if you promise to become as white men in the faith and be baptized." Tamed by fear, the red men laid aside their weapons and knelt at a brook where Marquette, gathering water in his hands, gave the rite of baptism to each, and laid down the moral law they were to live by. Wanena, who had fainted from sheer fright when she saw the idol burning, was restored, and it may be added that the priest who Christian-ized her also married her to Du Lhut, who prospered and left his name to the city of the lake. News of the triumph of the white men's God went far and wide, and Marquette found his missions easier after that. Du Lhut alone, of all those present, was in the father's secret. He had perpe-trated a pious fraud, justified by the results as well as by his peril. A burning glass had been fastened to the crucifix, and with that he had destroyed the idol.

Trading thus on native ignorance a Frenchman named Lyons at another time impressed the Indians at Dubuque and gained his will by setting a creek on fire. They did not know that he had first poured turpentine over it.

From: Charles M. Skinner, *Myths & Legends of Our Own Land*, vol. 2 (Philadelphia and London: J. B. Lippincott Co., 1896).

· Wild Bill Hickock ·

(Various)

The Tale of Wild Bill Hickock
(Unidentified)

In the month of May 1837, there was born, in LaSalle County, Illinois, a boy who was afterward named James Butler Hickock, and who eventually became known as "Wild Bill." LaSalle County at that time was very thinly populated, being termed the frontier of the West.

The Hickocks were a representative family of the sturdy pioneer type, which sought fortune in the far western country, which promised great agricultural possibilities. The boy grew up in these primitive parts, which no doubt had great influence in shaping his future destiny. Schools were few and far apart and of but short duration, so the children of the place and period were left to devise other plans of entertainment and amusement.

Young Hickock found his greatest pleasure in roaming through the woods, playing and mimicking the acts of hunters and Indians, and at an early age he contrived to secure an old flintlock pistol with which he practiced incessantly until he became a wonderful shot for a boy.

Hickock was not very obedient to his parents, and he often practiced truancy from school, making excursions into the woods, and when punished by his parents he would take a few potshots at the pigs and chickens in retaliation. In consequence, he did not receive much education, his only interest in that line being the reading of books of adventure. Thus his life passed until he was about fourteen years of age, when he became the owner of a modern rifle and pistol. From now on his time was spent almost entirely with these arms, hunting in the woods or practicing marksmanship.

Tiring of his uneventful life at home, he decided to go farther into the great West and carve out for himself a name as a desperado or hero, saying before he started that "he would beat anything that Kit Carson or any other man ever done." Two years' experience as a driver on a canal boat seemed to have satisfied his ambitions; so he returned, remaining at home until he was eighteen years of age. Then the Missouri-Kansas border warfare attracted his attention. In due time he arrived at Leavenworth and joined Jim Lane's antislavery band of armed men. His wonderful feats of marksmanship attracted the attention and admiration of the entire command. Here he was given the name of "Shanghai Bill." He served under Lane for two years and then retired, becoming stagedriver for the Overland Stage Company in 1857. Here he gained the reputation of being a reckless driver, yet few accidents happened to him. He was a man to fear as a gunman, and was the victor in many fights in drunken saloon brawls. Hickock's route was on the Santa Fe Trail, and in 1859 he quitted the service of the Stage Company, securing employment as a driver of freight wagons to Santa Fe.

While thus employed he met with an adventure which almost proved fatal to him. One evening while some distance from camp he saw a large cinnamon bear with her two cubs, whose flight the mother was protecting. Hickock advanced upon them, armed only with a pair of pistols and a large bowie knife. When at close range he fired both pistols at the mother bear, inflicting a wound that only infuriated her. Roaring and growling, she cast herself at Hickock, who met her advance with his knife. Then followed a bloody fight between man and beast. Young Hickock finally succeeded in forcing the knife into a vital spot with his last remaining strength. Together they fell on the blood-soaked soil. Hickock was shortly afterward found by his companions, nearer dead than alive. He was now incapacitated for further work, lying abed helpless for several months.

While convalescing, the Overland Stage Company offered him employment as hostler, or horse wrangler, at the Rock Creek Station, on the Oregon Trail, which was then an important relay station, where fifty or more horses were kept. This was in the spring of 1861. Hickock with a companion lived in a dugout located in the banks of the creek about midway between the East and West stations. McCanles was at this time owner of the stations, but soon after sold them to the Overland Stage Company, who sent Horace Wellman to be stationmaster. Here in the East station house was the tragedy enacted that gave Hickock the name of "Wild Bill."

Passing over this event, in which he did not receive a wound, "Wild Bill," after a few other adventures of a minor nature, joined the Union army at Leavenworth and was appointed brigade wagon master. This duty took him down through Missouri in Sedalia, and in March 1862, we find him a sharpshooter in the battle of Pea Ridge, under General Curtis.

"Wild Bill" continued to give as a scout, spy, and sharpshooter, a most remarkable service to this division of the Union army, throughout the entire war; his record perhaps being unequaled in the annals of the army of the West.

After the close of the war, Hickock, accompanied by a young Indian whom he had befriended, and the Indian's beautiful sister, proceeded to the Niobrara River, where he pursued the occupation of trapping and trading among the Sioux. Returning to Springfield, Missouri, in 1865, he took up his favorite occupation of gambling. Here he killed the notorious Dave Tutt, in a duel on the public square. He now joined Generals Carr and Primrose, in company with Buffalo Bill, as a scout in an expedition against the Cheyennes under Black Kettle. This Indian was killed by Wild Bill in a personal encounter, in which Bill received dangerous wounds in return that caused his removal to Fort Hays.

While recovering, Hickock visited his old home in Illinois and acted as guide for the Vice Presidential party, hunting buffalo, on the plains. In 1869 he was elected marshal of Hays City, Kansas, which was perhaps the most lawless town of the plains, and whose population of two thousand souls was largely made up of the worst cutthroats and blacklegs of the plains country. Over a hundred gambling dens and innumerable saloons and resorts of vice filled the pine-shack town. No other man had been able to preserve order, but "Wild Bill," after sending a few booted desperadoes to the graveyard, earned the respect of every inhabitant, mostly through their fear of his unerring hand, which seemed to take deadly aim instantly, and shot to kill quicker than any other hand ever could.

Here he had an encounter with several drunken soldiers from Fort Hays, killing four, but they finally caused him to secrete himself in the hills, to save his life. Finally, to evade the order of arrest issued by General Sheridan, he went to Junction City.

Here he organized a "Wild West" show, with which he toured the East. This venture proved unsuccessful; so he returned to Abilene, then the most notorious "cattle town" of the Southwest, and became its marshal. Here, as in Hays City, Wild Bill finally restored law and order, by the extinction of a few of its leading characters. His life as marshal was crowded with many events in which he was the successful gunman, taking as toll perhaps the lives of a dozen desperate characters.

He joined Buffalo Bill's Wild West show in 1873, but as before, this life proved to be too much of a hollow sham, so in time he appeared in the Black Hills, where gold had been recently discovered, and where mining camps with their full quota of bad men and women, gambling and vice, flourished in their highest states. Here Wild Bill was at home, and for the next year or so with a few companions prospected in the mountains of this region, despite the dangers from Indians, with whom he had several encounters.

Returning in the spring of 1876 to Cheyenne, he met a lady whom he had admired for many years. A wedding and a honeymoon trip to the East followed. Returning to Kansas City, he led a party of gold hunters to Deadwood, in the Black Hills. Here he resided, plying his favorite vocations, principally gambling, until the latter part of July, when he was treacherously shot from behind by Jack McCall, whom he had beaten in a game of cards a few days previously, and whose brother he had killed when marshal of one of the border towns of Kansas.

He was buried on the hillside by his friend Colorado Charley. McCall was given a trial by judge and jury, but perhaps it was improvised for the occasion, maybe similar to the trial given "Wild Bill" for the murder of McCanles, for McCall was acquitted, but was later arrested at Yankton, tried, convicted, and hanged.

Thus passed away one of the most remarkable characters of the plains; a man who was over six feet in height, deep-chested and compactly built, with eyes gray, clear, and calm as those of a woman, belying the power and danger behind them. He was lithe of form, muscular and wiry of build. His hair, auburn in hue, fell in ringlets down over his shoulders. His upper lip was covered with a thin, drooping, sandy-brown mustache. The mode of dress he affected gave him the appearance of being more a gentleman of fortune than the desperate character "Wild Bill," who was known all over the Western country as the quickest man to draw a gun; and who shot to kill, waiting for explanations afterward. To these facts, perhaps, he could attribute his long career as a death dealer to men who crossed his path.

Mrs. Agnes Lake, whom Wild Bill married, was the widow of a circus man. Her daughter afterwards married John Robinson, the old circus man.

From: Charles Dawson, *Pioneer Tales of the Oregon Trail and Jefferson County* (Topeka: Crane and Co., 1912).

How Wild Bill Got His Name
(Unidentified)

The real name of Wild Bill was James Butler Hickock. He was eighteen years old when he first saw the West as a fighting man under Jim Lane, finally settling down in the year 1861 as station agent for the Overland at Rock Creek Station, about fifty miles west of Topeka. He was really there for a guard for the horse band, for all that region was full of horse thieves and cutthroats. It was here that occurred his greatest fight, the greatest fight of one man against odds at close range that is mentioned in any history of any part of the world.

Two border outlaws by the name of the McCanles boys, leading a gang of hard men, intended to run off with the stage company's horses. When they found that they could not seduce Bill to join their number, he told them to come and take the horses if they could; and on the afternoon of December 16, 1861, ten of them rode to his dugout to do so. Bill was alone, his stableman being away hunting. He rushed into the dark interior of his dugout and got ready his weapons—a rifle, two six-shooters, and a knife.

The assailants proceeded to batter in the door with a log, and as it fell in, Jim McCanles, who must have been a brave man to undertake so foolhardy a thing against a man already known as a killer, sprang in at the opening. He of course was killed at once. This exhausted the rifle, and Bill picked up the six-shooters from the table and in three quick shots killed three more of the gang as they rushed in at the door. Four men were dead in less than that many seconds; but there were still six others left, all inside the dugout now, and all firing at him at a range of three feet. It was almost a miracle that under such surroundings the man was not killed. Bill was now crowded too much to use his firearms and took to the bowie, thrusting at one man and another as best he might. It must have been several minutes that all seven of them were mixed in a mass of shooting, thrusting, panting, and gasping humanity. Then Jack McCanles swung his rifle barrel and struck Bill over the head, springing upon him with his knife as well. Bill got his hand on a six-shooter and killed McCanles just as he would have struck.

After that no one knows what happened, not even Bill himself. "I just got sort of wild," Bill said when describing it. "I thought my heart was on fire. I went out to the pump then to get a drink, and I was all cut and shot to pieces."

They called him Wild Bill after that, and he had earned the name. There were six dead men on the floor of the dugout. He had fairly whipped the ten of them, and the remaining had enough and fled from that awful hole in the ground. Bill followed them to the door. His own weapons were exhausted or not at hand by this time, but his stableman came up just then with a rifle in his hands. Bill caught it from him and, cut as he was, fired and killed one of the desperadoes as he tried to mount his horse. The other wounded man later died of his wounds. Eight men were killed by the one. It took Bill a year to recover from his wounds.

From: Charles Dawson, *Pioneer Tales of the Oregon Trail and Jefferson County* (Topeka: Crane and Co., 1912).

• *Billy the Kid* •

(Unidentified)

A crowd of strangers were playing cards under a cottonwood tree nearby. The cook informed me that they were "Billy the Kid" and his Lincoln County, New Mexico, Warriors.

When the cook rang the supper bell these strangers ran for the long table. After being introduced, I found myself seated by the side of good-natured "Billy the Kid." Henry Brown, Fred Waite, and Tom O'Phalliard are the only names of this outlaw gang that I can recall.

When supper was over I produced a box of fine Havana cigars, brought from Chicago as a treat for the boys on the ranch. They were passed around. Then one was stuck into my new $10 meerschaum cigar holder, and I began to puff smoke towards the ceiling.

Now "Billy the Kid" asked for a trial of my cigar holder. This was granted. He liked it so well that he begged me to present it to him, which I did. In return he presented me with a finely bound novel which he had just finished reading. In it he wrote his autograph, giving the date that it was presented to me.

During the next few weeks "Billy the Kid" and I became quite chummy.

After selling out the band of ponies, which he and his gang had stolen from the Seven River warriors, in New Mexico, he left the Canadian river country, and I never saw him again.

Two of his gang, Henry Brown and Fred Waite—a half-breed Chicasaw Indian—quit the outfit and headed for the Indian Territory.

During his long stay around the LX ranch, and Tascosa, "Billy the Kid" made one portly old capitalist from Boston, Massachusetts, sweat blood for a few minutes.

Mr. Torey owned a large cattle ranch above Tascosa. On arriving from the East he learned that "Billy the Kid" and gang had made themselves at home on his ranch, for a few days—hence, he gave the foreman orders not to feed them, if they should make another visit. This order reached the "Kid's" ears.

While in Tascosa "Billy the Kid" saw old man Torey ride up to the hitching rack in front of Jack Ryan's saloon. He went out to meet him, and asked if he had ordered his foreman not to feed them.

Mr. Torey replied yes, that he didn't want to give his ranch a bad name by harboring outlaws.

Then the "Kid" jerked his Colts pistol and jabbed the old man several times in his portly stomach, at the same time telling him to say his prayers, as he was going to pump him full of lead.

With tears in his voice Mr. Torey promised to countermand the order. Then war was declared off.

Thus did Mr. Torey, a former sea captain, get his eyeteeth cut in the ways of the wild and wooly West.

This story was told to me by "Billy the Kid" and Steve Arnold, who was an eyewitness to the affair. But the "Kid" said he had no intention of shooting Mr. Torey—that he just wanted to teach him a lesson.

On arriving in Fort Stanton, Charlie Wall and I separated. I continued on to Lincoln, where I laid over a few days. Pat Garrett and Mr. Poe had already arrived in Lincoln from Las Cruces.

The next day after my arrival the sheriff held an auction to sell "Billy the Kid's" saddle and pistol.

The deputy county clerk and I were the only bidders for the Colts 41 caliber, double-action pistol, which the "Kid" held in his hand at the time of his death.

My last bid was $13, what I thought it was actually worth. The deputy clerk bid $13.50 and got it. I heard that he afterwards sold it for $250 on the strength of it's past history.

While laying over in Lincoln I learned the true account of "Billy the Kid's" death from the three men who had a hand in the affair. These men being Pat Garrett, John W. Poe, and "Kip" McKinnie.

Many stories have been circulated about the underhanded manner in which Garrett murdered the "Kid." Therefore I will here give the true account of it.

About July 1, 1881, Pat Garrett received a letter from a Mr. Brazil stating that the "Kid" had been seen lately around Fort Sumner.

The sheriff answered the letter telling Mr. Brazil to meet him at the mouth of the Tayban Arroyo, on the Pecos River, after dark on July 13.

Now Garrett took his two deputies, John Poe and "Kip" McKinnie, and started horseback, for the meeting place.

These three officers watched and waited during the whole night of July 13, but Mr. Brazil failed to show up.

On the morning of the 14th they rode up the Pecos River. When opposite Fort Sumner the sheriff sent Mr. Poe into that abandoned fort, where lived many Mexican families, to see if anything could be learned about the "Kid" having been there.

Then Garrett and McKinnie rode six miles up the river to Sunny-side, to keep in hiding until the arrival of Mr. Poe.

About night John Poe reached Sunny-side and reported to Garrett that he couldn't find out a thing of importance about the "Kid." Then the sheriff said they would ride into Fort Sumner, after dark, and see Pete Maxwell, a wealthy sheepman, and the son of the famous Land Grant Maxwell. The "Kid" was in love with Pete Maxwell's sister, hence Garrett thinking that Pete might have seen him hanging around their home.

It was dark when the officers started on their six-mile journey.

Arriving in Fort Sumner their horses were tied in an old orchard. Then they walked into Pete Maxwell's large, grassy yard. The residence was a long adobe building fronting south, with a covered porch the full length of the adobe house. Garrett knew the room in which Pete generally slept. The door of this room was open. The sheriff told his two deputies to lie down on the grass, while he went in to talk with Pete.

Now the sheriff lay over on Mr. Maxwell's bed and began questioning him about the "Kid." No one outside of Mr. Garrett was to know what Pete told him.

In the rear of the Maxwell dwelling lived an old Mexican servant, who was a warm friend to the "Kid."

Previous to the arrival of the sheriff and his deputies, "Billy the Kid" had entered this old servant's adobe cabin. The old man had gone to bed.

"Billy the Kid" lit the lamp; then pulled off his boots and coat and began reading the newspapers, which had been brought there for his special benefit.

After glancing over the papers the "Kid" told the old man to get up and cook him some supper, as he was very hungry, having just walked in from the sheep camp.

The old servant told him that he didn't have any meat in the house. Then the "Kid" replied, "I'll go and see Pete and get some." Now he picked up a butcher knife from the table and started, barefooted and bareheaded.

In walking along the porch of Pete's room, "Kip" McKinnie saw him coming, but supposed he was one of the servants.

When nearly opposite Pete's room "Kip" raised up and his spur rattled, which attracted the "Kid's" attention. Pulling his pistol he asked in Spanish, "*Quien es? Quien es?*" (Who's there, who's there?)

Not getting an answer he backed into Pete's room and asked, "Pete, who's out there?"

Maxwell didn't reply. Now the "Kid" saw strange movements in the bed and asked, "Who in the h——l is in here?"

With the pistol raised in his right hand, and the butcher knife in his left, he began fighting across the room. Pete whispered in the sheriff's ear, "That's him Pat."

By this time the "Kid" had backed to the dim moonlight coming through the south window, which shone directly on him, making him an easy target for the sheriff. Bang! went Garrett's Colts pistol, and down went a once mother's darling, shot through the heart.

After the first shot, the sheriff cocked the pistol and it went off accidentally, putting a hole in the ceiling.

The next day Billy Bonney, alias "Billy the Kid," was buried by the side of his chum, Tom O'Phalliard, in the old military cemetery.

A few months later Pat Garrett had the body dug up to see if the "Kid's" trigger finger had been cut off, but it had not.

A man in the East was showing the front finger of a man, preserved in alcohol. He claimed it was "Billy the Kid's trigger finger." The news-papers had sensational accounts of it.

Years later when the United States Government employed Will Griffin to remove all dead bodies of soldiers in the Fort Sumner graveyard, to the National Cemetery in Santa Fe, the graves of "Billy the Kid" and Tom O'Phalliard were the only ones left.

Mr. Griffin, who is still a resident of Santa Fe, says at the time he moved the soldiers bodies there was a board slab marking the "Kid's" grave. Now that old cemetery is an alfalfa field, and those two outlaw graves may have been obliterated.

From: Charles A. Siringo, *A Lone Star Cowboy* (Santa Fe: 1919).

CHAPTER 16

Pirates and Buried Treasure

· *The Pot of Gold* ·

(Unidentified)

Most historic spots have a story of romance, valor, superstition, or lost treasure. So, it will not be amiss to relate of Rock Creek Station the legend or tale of the "pot of gold." Whether or not there was a pot of gold buried—whether it was ever found—there exists no way of knowing, and it's for you to decide.

Imagine a big kettle of cast iron, standing three or four inches off the ground on three legs, deep enough in which to hide a water bucket, having an iron lid covering the top, and filled to the brim with gold—nothing but gold, in nuggets, chunks, dust, and coined pieces of every existing mintage prior to the sixties; and then think that it lies buried somewhere in the hills close to Rock Creek Station, on the old Oregon Trail.

Thus runs the legend. McCanles brought a tidy sum of money with him from North Carolina, and this was daily added to by his incomes until it became necessary to adopt more than ordinary means for safeguarding it. There were no banks in that country in those days. The country was new, and there was danger from Indians and outlaws. McCanles determined to conceal his money by burying it. The big iron pot was used for the primitive underground bank. It was buried under the puncheon floor of the bedroom of his east ranch, and there he nightly poured a golden stream into the fast-filling receptacle. Then came his preparations for leaving the country and the sale of the stations, which necessitated the removal of the pot and its burial at some other place. Mrs. McCanles, his widow, said many times that her husband, under her protection, removed the pot and reburied it somewhere close to the station a few nights before they vacated the stationhouse. McCanles was gone only one hour, so the spot selected by him could not be very far away. Following the reburial, McCanles was busy for a few months, and then, just as he was on the eve of his departure, he was killed by Wild Bill.

Only a few days before he was killed he informed Mrs. McCanles of his intention to confide to her in a day or so the exact location of the pot of gold, hinting vaguely that two boulders marked its hiding place. But McCanles reckoned not that death would seal his lips. Perhaps his attempt to speak to his son in his dying moments was to reveal the secret place of the pot of gold.

Many men have searched days and months all over the hills, from the ranch to the McCanles home at the mouth of Rock Creek, but if any were successful in their hunt for the buried treasure silence sealed their lips. Opinions and beliefs are much divided, some believing that James Leroy McCanles might have found it soon after his brother's death; others that this or that man found it, while the greater part believe it yet remains to be found. And some believe that the whole thing is nothing more than a mythical story of a Pot of Gold.

From: Charles Dawson, *Pioneer Tales of the Oregon Trail and Jefferson County* (Topeka: Crane and Co., 1912).

CHAPTER 17

Portents, Charms, and Remedies

· Folk Cures from Kansas ·

(Unidentified)

The folk cures enumerated in this article were collected in two counties in the state of Kansas. These two counties, Douglas and Coffey—the former north, the latter south of the east central portion of the state—afford, we may well believe, typical lore of at least the whole eastern portion of the state.

The minor portion of these cures, which were collected in Coffey County, were obtained from two families of colored people. The majority of the superstitions, however, which were collected in Douglas County, were obtained from people who declared they knew no superstitions and believed none; namely, students in attendance at the University of Kansas during the year 1890. These students came from nearly every county in the state; hence this collection more nearly represents a state lore than at first sight appears.

It was my first intention to make merely a collection of wart cures. Occasionally persons whom I interrogated volunteered a cure for some other malady. These few incidentally collected remedies are also included in this paper.

In classifying these remedies it seems expedient to bring them into groups according to the disease which they are intended to cure.

Warts. On account of the suddenness of their appearance and disappearance without apparent cause, warts have given rise, among the common folk, to a large number of superstitions and remedies. The belief that warts are produced by contact with toads is widespread. Helvetius long ago said that "every popular delusion becomes the mother of a noxious and numerous progeny." Preeminently is this true in regard to the belief that warts can be transferred, by fair means or foul, from one to another, as the following beliefs will show.

Pick the wart with a pin, and collect in brown paper the blood that flows from the wound; make a parcel of the paper and throw it into the road without looking where it falls. If the bundle is picked up, the wart will be transferred to the person who found the bundle.

Cut a straw into very small lengths; rub the circumference of the wart with each length, then wrap the lengths together and throw them into the street. Whoever finds them will relieve you of your warts.

Into a red calico bag put "hearts" from grains of corn; "run down the road"; throw away the bag, not looking where it falls; run home again, and if anyone picks up the bag your warts will go away.

Tie stones in a rag; throw them into the road; if the stones are picked up the wart will go away.

Another version, probably of this same remedy, is as follows: Rub the wart with seven pebbles; wrap the pebbles in a paper and throw them away; if the parcel is picked up the wart will go away.

Rub the wart with a corncob; tie up the cob in paper; throw it in the street; if the parcel is picked up the wart will disappear.

A wart may be wished away to another. This takes on more specific forms in the following:

If you see anyone asleep in church say to yourself, "When you awake, take these warts."

If you have a wart and see a man riding on horseback in the rain (or, as another version runs, "riding on a gray horse") say, "Take these along," rub the wart and it will leave you.

Pick the wart with a pin, give the pin away, and the wart will also be given away.

At Delphos, Kansas, lives a young man who gallantly procured his sweetheart's warts by purchase.

The efficacy of the cures in the following group depends upon two conditions, namely, the instrument employed in removing the wart should in some instances be stolen, and it must in nearly all cases, after being used according to prescribed directions, be buried. The burying, however, is only a means to an end, for the disintegration, decay of the instrument is the result to be attained before the removal of the wart can be effected.

Tie a red thread around your finger; untie the thread and bury it. "When the thread rots the wart will go away."

Rub the wart with a dishrag and throw the rag away, taking care not to see where it falls; when the rag has decayed the wart will disappear.

According to another version, the dishrag should be buried in the cellar.

Steal a dishcloth, rub the wart with it, and then bury the cloth under the eaves of the house. If you tell no one and no one finds out your theft, your wart will go away.

Steal a bean and boil it so that it cannot germinate; rub the wart with the "insides of the two halves" of this cooked bean and bury them. When they have disintegrated, the wart will be cured.

Cut a bean into halves; rub the wart with one half of the bean; bury that half; throw the other half into the fire and the wart will disappear.

Cut a sour apple in two portions; rub the wart with each portion and bury them. When the apple has decayed the wart will be gone.

Cut a cranberry in halves; rub the wart with each half and bury them under a stone and your wart will be removed.

Rub the wart with salt and tie up the salt in a bag; bury the bag under a stone. According to another version, the salt should be stolen.

Rub the wart with a piece of salty bacon; bury the pork with a spade, and, if you tell no one, your wart will go away.

Cut as many notches in a stick as you have warts; bury the stick and your warts will be cured.

If you find a bone on the ground, notice the position in which the bone is lying; rub the wart with this bone and replace it in its former position and your wart will soon disappear.

Rub the wart with the wishbone of a chicken; throw away the bone at night, and, if you fail to find it in the morning, your wart will surely go away.

Rub the wart with a dishcloth; run around the house three times and the wart will be cured.

Tie a blue silk thread around your wart and the wart will be gone in three days.

Write on the stove with a piece of chalk the number of your warts. When the number has burned off the stove your warts will be gone.

Make crossmarks on a piece of paper; carry the paper in your pocket and your wart will go away.

Spit on a toad and your wart will leave you.

Wash your hands in water that has been standing in a stump. Another version of this same cure runs as follows:

> Oats, rye, barleycorn, shorts,
> Stump-water, stump-water, cure these warts.

Toothache. In order to cure the toothache cut your fingernails on Friday.

Another "sure cure" is to wash behind your ears every morning.

Hydrophobia. "The hair of the dog that bit you will cure hydrophobia."

Rheumatism. The skin of an eel, if worn about the leg, will cure rheumatism.

The skin of a black cat worn in one's clothing will cure rheumatism.

Carry a potato in one's pocket to cure rheumatism.

The Negro sometimes sleeps with a young dog in order to transmit rheumatism to the dog.

Headache. Headache may be prevented by wearing in one's hat the rattles of a rattlesnake.

The skin of a snake worn around one's hat crown will cure the headache.

A Sty. A sty may be cured by rubbing it with a gold ring, a silver spoon, or one's finger moistened with saliva.

Nosebleed. Wear a red string or red beads around the neck to prevent the nosebleed.

Wear a string of gold beads around your neck and your nose cannot bleed.

Hold your hands above your head and your nose will cease bleeding.

Hold a silver spoon against the back of the neck to stop the nosebleed.

Shingles. The blood of a black cat will cure shingles.

Palsy. "Never let a chicken die in your hands" and you will not have palsy.

Asthma. Bore a hole in the wall the height of the child's head; when the child grows above the hole it will be cured of asthma.

Cramps. You may always prevent cramps in the feet by turning your shoes upside down every night beside your bed.

From: Gertrude C. Davenport, "Folk-Cures from Kansas," *Journal of American Folk-Lore* 11 (1898): 129–32.

CHAPTER 18

The Supernatural

· Ghosts ·

(Various)

The Ghost Story
(Unidentified)

Without attempt to uphold the beliefs of the superstitious, a ghost story is chronicled. Nearly every community has in its story lore some weird tale of people or things that assumes the aspect of the supernatural. Seemingly, all people, regardless of their beliefs, relish the relation of such tales; so the story is submitted on its own merits, just as it was told, leaving the reader to draw his own conclusions. An old settler gives the story, as follows:

Wife and I with our bunch of towheaded youngsters were headed westward, traveling by ox team, in a canvas-topped wagon, bound for Nebraska, in response to the solicitations of my father, who had settled there a few years previously. Crossing the Missouri River in the early days of spring, at St. Joseph, we joined one of the first caravans of emigrants going westward over the Old Oregon Trail. Traveling over the wonderful prairies and through the rich valleys of eastern Kansas, we had our ideas of the Great American Desert rudely but pleasantly shattered. In due time we reached our destination, and encamped on the tract of land that had been selected for us, which was a well-timbered and well-watered body of land, lying along a spring-fed stream, that ran back into a valley which was flanked on the sides by frowning bluffs capped by ledges of sandstone. As the first tints of green began to appear to bedeck the landscape it was a wonderful sight to witness the unfolding of such picturesque scenery, the like of which we had never seen before.

Our new home lay about halfway between the Old Trail and the Little Blue River, but this is all I will tell you, for ghosts and their haunts should not be too definitely located, as it might spoil their charms or the veracity, if there be any.

We immediately commenced the building of a home, and, with the aid of my relatives and neighbors, contrived to erect a habitable log cabin, a one-room affair with a loft above, a clapboard roof, a mud-and-stick chimney, and a stone fireplace at one end.

Compared with our previous places of habitation and modes of living this seemed at first to be very primitive and almost unendurable, but before long we grew to regard this homely little log cabin as the coziest place it had been our pleasure to reside in.

With the coming of the warm days of spring, we broke out the little flats of land along the creek bottom, and planted them with corn, potatoes, melons, etc. Gardens were made, and we entered into the cultivation of our promising crops, hoping to reap an abundance for our needs. Nature had by now fully bedecked the whole panorama with a wonderful profusion of foliage, blossom, and color. Our little world seemed to be filled to overflowing with promise and happiness. Strawberry time had come. The hillsides were apparently covered with the patches of this red luscious fruit. One Sabbath morning, wife and I, light of heart, arm in arm, set out to roam the hillsides to gather a pailful of strawberries. We were soon in the midst of a profusion of strawberries, so plentiful, full and ripe on all sides of us, that we ran here and there, trampling under foot many berries, in our greed to secure the nicest ones.

Our pail was soon full to the brim, and our fingers and lips stained from picking and eating, till we were forced to desist, for want of further capacity. Then, feeling the tire of contented satisfaction, we sat down upon a convenient rock, lazily viewing the surrounding scenery, resting before we would attempt our homebound journey. With half-closed eyes lying back on the big shaded ledge of stone, my thoughts were dwelling on the incidents of the short past, in which we had left the comforts of civilization and had taken up our abode in this the land of promise, thinking how content we were; and just as I began to conjecture the future, I was aroused by the exclamation of the wife, who was now pointing across the rock-walled ravine to a springy spot, shaded by scattered clumps of underbrush. Brushing aside the sleepy tangles of my eyes, I noted the cause of her excitement, which I first thought might be Indians. Underneath and in the tangles of leaf and stem, quite in contrast to the rich background of green, were berries—strawberries of great size and blood-red color, rivaling even the choicest of the tame ones we had seen in the gardens of our Eastern homes.

Leaving our already filled pail, we hastened over to view the wonderful sight. Picking and eating the first few that we came to, we decided to take some home in my old hat and in the wife's apron; so, with many ejaculations of wonder and surprise, we filled these articles, and as I strode through a thick tangle of brush in leaving the patch, my foot caught on an object which threw me to the ground, and on turning over, seeking to arise, I found at my feet the skull of a human being. Leaping to my feet, I rushed out of the thicket almost completely unnerved at my ghastly find. Wife witnessing my stumble and following movements, ran back towards me, inquiring with alarm the cause of this unusual action. Together we walked back, and I pointed to the eyeless bare skull that was apparently grinning at us from his moldy moss-covered retreat from which my foot had ruthlessly torn him but a moment before. Proceeding into the thicket to investigate more fully, we found that underneath the leafy and molding foliages of the past seasons which had covered their bodies like that of the "Babes in the Wood" were the bones of many other persons. In fact, our strawberry patch had been the burial ground of the unknown dead. Wife and I, stilled by the presence of the dead, stood with bowed heads, silently offered up prayers to Him on high, who alone could give the solution of this mystery.

Glancing up, I met the gaze of my wife, and with one accord my old hat was overturned and the corners of her apron were dropped and the berries spilled on the ground. For we both knew, without further questioning, what had caused the berries to be so big and red.

Then we made a thorough search thereabout for the bones of the unknown dead, faithfully gathering the bones as they lay, endeavoring to give each skull its own and full complement of bones. Finally we felt that this duty had been performed, and the result was twelve skeletons, which we judged were a party of emigrants, men, women, and children.

After considerable labor, a grave was dug and the bones placed within, and filled up with earth and stones covering the top to mark and protect the grave. Thoroughly tired by our toil, we wended our way homeward, conscious that we had fulfilled our duty to those poor unfortunate beings by giving them at least a burial. After the supper meal was partaken and we had gathered on the doorstep in the twilight of the evening, we began to feel content and at peace with all fellow beings; then there came an uncanny, weird moan or cry, like that of woman or child in the depth of anguish or despair. Listening in awe, I awaited the repetition of that mournful sound. Soon it came, now in the fringe of trees about the cabin, then in the waist-high corn. Swiftly recalling the incidents of the day, I tried to assure myself that it was not real, that this was but the result of a befuddled mind, just imagination; but the children were now questioning us as to the cry, and upon receiving noncommittal answers, and perhaps reading our faces, they grew frightened and began to cry.

To assert myself and to allay their fears I arose and said to the wife, "Hand me my rifle and I will go down there and shoot that old owl, tree toad, or whatever it may be." Leaving the wife and children on the porch, I proceeded to search about in the growing corn, around the barn, and all through the nearby underbrush, but without result, although I seemed to be following the voice from point to point. Finally it seemed to be at the cabin. Hastening there, I found that my family had fled within and had barred the door. Undaunted, I continued the search, following the clues from whence I heard the voice. After vain attempts which led me to the roof, around and underneath the cabin, I contracted the same feelings of the rest of the family, and called for admittance. There was not much sleep for us that night, for we could hear the cries of our unearthly visitor at frequent intervals, till the early dawn of the morning. Night after night we had much the same experience until we grew accustomed to it and were but little disturbed. Our neighbors joined with us on several occasions to find the mysterious visitor, but despite the most exacting vigils and search, we gave it up, for not one single object or reason could be found that might be suspected of making the nightly occurring sounds, which the neighbors dubbed "The Lost Woman Ghost."

The summer wore on, succeeded by the bountiful autumn harvests. We should have been happy and content, but the "nightly visitor" had worn on our nerves, so after the harvest had been gathered, I was only too glad to sanction the wife's suggestion that we go and live with my father down on the Little Blue River, for the winter, as it was too lonesome away up here by ourselves.

We spent the long winter down there, hunting and trapping, returning occasionally to see if everything was all right at our homestead, but never staying overnight, so we did not know if our unwelcome guest had departed or not. With the opening days of spring, we moved back, for our crops must be planted and tended, and the first night of our return was celebrated by the usual performance of the unseen voice.

Of course this was annoying, but what could we do? Then there was no harm resulting, so we settled down, accepting the situation as best we could. Strawberry time came again, and we started out once more to search the hillsides and ravines for the big red berries. Our wanderings brought us to the burial place of the unknown party of people that we had found just one year ago. Here we stood for a moment with bared heads in reverence, swiftly recalling the incidents of their past as we knew of them, praying that we might in some way learn who they were, so that their relatives might know of their fate, and as we realized the improbability of this, we turned away with dimmed eyes, and continued to ascend the hill.

Upon reaching the top, we sat down upon a large flat boulder to rest. The whole panorama lay spread out at our feet, and across the ravine to our right was a hillside almost mountainous in appearance, cut and intersticed by irregular, rock-filled canyons or gorges, down which trickling spring-fed streams flowed, the rock-strewn hillside being covered with straggling growths of dwarfed oaks and hackberry trees, with the hill itself rising high to the blue skyline, capped with a heavy ledge of brown sandstone, irregularly set, cracked and fissured deeply with dark recesses underneath the many overhanging shelves, which suggested ideal retreats for wild animal life. As we searched with our eyes every part of its face for some new wonder of formation, a ghastly sight came to our vision— the skeleton of a human being. On closer investigation we found it to be that of a woman, huddled in a crouched, squatting position, back against the wall of a cavernlike place, seemingly as though she had taken refuge here, only to be found, and had raised her arms to ward off the blow that had stilled her life. Tenderly we gathered up the bones and carried them down to the burial place, and interred them with the rest, whom we judged to have been her companions. The afternoon was spent in the search for others that might be lying unburied on the hillsides, but the search proved fruitless; our only other find being a few piles of fire-warped wagon irons and charred woodwork, near which lay bones of oxen, many having the wooden yokes still around their necks. A few arrows were found scattered about in these piles of bones, so we knew that this was the work of Indians.

In the twilight of that evening I sat upon the broad doorstep of our cabin, thinking of all these things, the part that we had played, and who these people might be; then came the thought, could there be any connection between them and the ghostly visitor? If so, perhaps it would give me answer tonight. Though I waited and meditated long into the night I was in one way disappointed, for the voice came not—not alone that night, but never afterwards. So to me the mystery has deepened as the years have gone by. Was this the spirit of the murdered woman beseeching me to bury her bones beside those we had previously buried, who no doubt had met a similar fate? I hope so, and if this gave rest to the Soul, let it be the end.

From: Charles Dawson, *Pioneer Tales of the Oregon Trail and Jefferson County* (Topeka: Crane and Co., 1912).

The House Accursed
(Unidentified)

Near Gallipolis, Ohio, there stood within a few years an old house of four rooms that had been occupied by Herman Deluse. He lived there alone, and, though his farming was of the crudest sort, he never appeared to lack for anything. The people had an idea that the place was under ban, and it was more than suspected that its occupant had been a pirate. In fact, he called his place the Isle of Pines, after a buccaneers' rendezvous in the West Indies, and made no attempt to conceal the strange plunder and curious weapons that he had brought home with him, but of money he never appeared to have much at once. When it came his time to die he ended his life alone, so far as any knew—at least, his body was found in his bed, without trace of violence or disorder. It was buried and the public administrator took charge of the estate, locking up the house until possible relatives should come to claim it, and the rustic jury found that Deluse "came to his death by visitation of God."

It was but a few nights after this that the Reverend Henry Galbraith returned from a visit of a month to Cincinnati and reached his home after a night of boisterous storm. The snow was so deep and the roads so blocked with windfalls that he put up his horse in Gallipolis and started for his house on foot. "But where did you pass the night?" inquired his wife, after the greetings were over. "With old Deluse in the Isle of Pines," he answered. "I saw a light moving about the house, and rapped. No one came; so, as I was freezing, I forced open the door, built a fire, and lay down in my coat before it. Old Deluse came in presently and I apologized, but he paid no attention to me. He seemed to be walking in his sleep and to be searching for something. All night long I could hear his footsteps about the house, in pauses of the storm."

The clergyman's wife and son looked at each other, and a friend who was present—a lawyer, named Maren—remarked, "You did not know that Deluse was dead and buried?" The clergyman was speechless with amazement. "You have been dreaming," said the lawyer. "Still, if you like, we will go there tonight and investigate."

The clergyman, his son, and the lawyer went to the house about nine o'clock, and as they approached it a noise of fighting came from within— blows, the clink of steel, groans, and curses. Lights appeared, first at one window, then at another. The men rushed forward, burst in the door, and were inside—in darkness and silence. They had brought candles and lighted them, but the light revealed nothing. Dust lay thick on the floor except in the room where the clergyman had passed the previous night, and the door that he had then opened stood ajar, but the snow outside was drifted and unbroken by footsteps. Then came the sound of a fall that shook the building. At the same moment it was noticed by the other two men that young Galbraith was absent. They hurried into the room whence the noise had come. A board was wrenched from the wall there, disclosing a hollow that had been used for a hiding place, and on the floor lay young Galbraith with a sack of Spanish coins in his hand. His father stooped to pick him up, but staggered back in horror, for the young man's life had gone. A postmortem examination revealed no cause of death, and a rustic jury again laid it to a "visitation of God."

From: Charles M. Skinner, *Myths & Legends of Our Own Land*, vol. 2 (Philadelphia and London: J. B. Lippincott Co., 1896).

The Haunted House
(Irish)

For many years there stood near the banks of Big Sandy, above the old mail station, a big log house that was reputed to be haunted. No one would venture to go through the woods nearby or to approach it after the shades of the evening had fallen. Many were the tales of the apparitions or ghostly sounds heard by some belated wayfarer. The story *de resistance* was of the headless man, who would emerge from the house at about sundown, carrying a basket on his shoulder. No one ever ventured to stay long enough to see where he went or what he did with the basket, so the belief in specters deepened. Finally, Jake Dein, who had bought the house and premises, decided to move it up to his place of abode on the old stage station, which was accomplished with the aid of the neighbors. This brought a quietus of the alleged acts of the ghostly visitors.

The history of the house and its former occupant reveals the following: James Conway, a sort of wild Irishman, who was connected with the life along the Oregon Trail, and who was an inveterate drinker, married a comely-looking woman, and decided to settle down to the simple life. Building himself what was termed at that time one of the finest houses in the settlement, the next few years promised to bring about the realization of their dreams. Like many who attempt to go back to the soil and live down the follies of their early days, Conway gradually resumed his old ways, to the displeasure of his wife. One day when returning from Meridian after a drunken debauch, his team became unmanageable and ran away. When found, the tongue of the wagon was protruding through his body, and he was buried nearby the house. In a few months the body of his wife was found alongside the railroad tracks, just above Powell. How she had met her death was only conjecture, as there were no marks on her body, nor any witnesses. As they did not have any children, the place fell into a bad state of repair. Weeds and underbrush grew up, and it became ideal in every respect for the haunts of superstitious creations.

One solution for the headless man was that Jake Dein annually cribbed his corn in the deserted house, and he would often go over and get a basket of corn therefrom late in the evening or early in the morning to feed his livestock. Perhaps some excited person mistook Dein for the ghost. So the story, like the house, passes away, becoming but a dimly marked incident in the pioneer history of Jefferson County.

From: Charles Dawson, *Pioneer Tales of the Oregon Trail and Jefferson County* (Topeka: Crane and Co., 1912).

· *The Coffin of Snakes* ·

(French)

No one knew how it was that Lizon gained the love of Julienne, at L'Anse Creuse (near Detroit), for she was a girl of sweet and pious disposition, the daughter of a God-fearing farmer, while Lizon was a dark, ill-favored wretch, who had come among the people nobody knew whence, and lived on the profits of a taproom where the vilest liquor was sold, and where gaming, fighting, and carousing were of nightly occurrence. Perhaps they were right in saying that it was witchcraft. He impudently laid siege to her heart, and when she showed signs of yielding he told her and her friends that he had no intention of marrying her, because he did not believe in religion.

Yet Julienne deserted her comfortable home and went to live with this disreputable scamp in his disreputable tavern, to the scandal of the community, and especially of the priest, who found Lizon's power for evil greater than his own for good, for as the tavern gained in hangers-on the church lost worshippers. One Sunday morning Julienne surprised the people by appearing in church and publicly asking pardon for her wrongdoing. It was the first time she had appeared there since her flight, and she was as one who had roused from a trance or fever-sleep. Her father gladly took her home again, and all went well until New Year's Eve, when the young men called d'Ignolee made the rounds of the settlement to sing and beg meat for the poor—a custom descended from the Druids. They came to the house of Julienne's father and received his welcome and his goods, but their song was interrupted by a cry of distress—Lizon was among the maskers, and Julienne was gone. A crowd of villagers ran to the cabaret and rescued the girl from the room into which the fellow had thrust her, but it was too late—she had lost her reason. Cursing and striking and blaspheming, Lizon was at last confronted by the priest, who told him he had gone too far; that he had been a plague to the people and an enemy to the church. He then pronounced against him the edict of excommunication, and told him that even in his grave he should not rest; that the church, abandoned by so many victims of his wiles and tyrannies, should be swept away.

The priest left the place forthwith, and the morals of the village fell lower and lower. Everything was against it too. Blight and storm and insect pest ravaged the fields and orchards, as if nature had engaged to make an expression of the iniquity of the place. Suddenly death came upon Lizon. A pit was dug near his tavern and he was placed in a coffin, but as the box was lowered it was felt to grow lighter, while there poured from it a swarm of fat and filthy snakes. The fog that overspread the earth that morning seemed to blow by in human forms, the grave rolled like a wave after it had been covered, and after darkness fell a blue will-o'-the wisp danced over it. A storm set in, heaping the billows on shore until the church was undermined, and with a crash it fell into the seething flood. But the curse had passed, and when a new chapel was built the old evils had deserted L'Anse Creuse.

From: Charles M. Skinner, *Myths & Legends of Our Own Land*, vol. 2 (Philadelphia and London: J. B. Lippincott Co., 1896).

· *The Nain Rouge* ·

(Unidentified)

Among all the impish offspring of the Stone God—all his wizards and witches—that made Detroit feared by the early settlers, none were more dreaded than the *Nain Rouge* (Red Dwarf), or Demon of the Strait, for it appeared only when there was to be trouble. In that it delighted. It was a shambling, red-faced creature, with a cold, glittering eye and teeth protruding from a grinning mouth. Cadillac, founder of Detroit, having struck at it, presently lost his seigniory and his fortunes. It was seen scampering along the shore on the night before the attack on Bloody

Run, when the brook that afterward bore this name turned red with the blood of soldiers. People saw it in the smoky streets when the city was burned in 1805, and on the morning of Hull's surrender it was found grinning in the fog. It rubbed its bony knuckles expectantly when David Fisher paddled across the strait to see his love, Soulange Gaudet, in the only boat he could find—a wheelbarrow, namely—but was sobered when David made a safe landing.

It chuckled when the youthful bloods set off on Christmas Day to race the frozen strait for the hand of buffer Beauvais's daughter Claire, but when her lover's horse, a wiry Indian nag, came pacing in it fled before their happiness. It was twice seen on the roof of the stable where that sour-faced, evil-eyed old mumbler, Jean Beaugrand, kept his horse, Sans Souci—a beast that, spite of its hundred years or more, could and did leap every wall in Detroit, even the twelve-foot stockade of the fort, to steal corn and watermelons, and that had been seen in the same barn, sitting at a table, playing seven-up with his master, and drinking a liquor that looked like melted brass. The dwarf whispered at the sleeping ear of the old chief who slew Friar Constantine, chaplain of the fort, in anger at the teachings that had parted a white lover from his daughter and led her to drown herself—a killing that the red man afterward confessed, because he could no longer endure the tolling of a mass bell in his ears and the friar's voice in the wind.

The *Nain Rouge* it was who claimed half of the old mill, on Presque Isle, that the sick and irritable Josette swore she would leave to the devil when her brother Jean pestered her to make her will in his favor, giving him complete ownership. On the night of her death the mill was wrecked by a thunderbolt, and a red-faced imp was often seen among the ruins, trying to patch the machinery so as to grind the devil's grist. It directed the dance of black cats in the mill at Pont Rouge, after the widow's curse had fallen on Louis Robert, her brother-in-law. This man, succeeding her husband as director of the property, had developed such miserly traits that she and her children were literally starved to death, but her dying curse threw such ill luck on the place and set afloat such evil report about it that he took himself away. The *Nain Rouge* may have been the Lutin that took Jacques L'Espérance's ponies from the stable at Grosse Pointe, and, leaving no tracks in sand or snow, rode them through the air all night, restoring them at dawn quivering with fatigue, covered with foam, bloody with the lash of a thornbush. It stopped that exercise on the night that Jacques hurled a font of holy water at it, but to keep it away the people of Grosse Pointe still mark their houses with the sign of a cross.

It was lurking in the wood on the day that Captain Dalzell went against Pontiac, only to perish in an ambush, to the secret relief of his superior, Major Gladwyn, for the major hoped to win the betrothed of Dalzell; but when the girl heard that her lover had been killed at Bloody Run, and his head had been carried on a pike, she sank to the ground never to rise again in health, and in a few days she had followed the victims of the massacre. There was a suspicion that the *Nain Rouge* had power to change his shape for one not less offensive. The brothers Tremblay had no luck in fishing through the straits and lakes until one of them agreed to share his catch with St. Patrick, the saint's half to be sold at the church door for the benefit of the poor and for buying masses to relieve souls in purgatory. His brother doubted if this benefit would last, and feared that they might be lured into the water and turned into fish, for had not St. Patrick eaten pork chops on a Friday, after dipping them into holy water and turning them into trout? But his good brother kept on and prospered and the bad one kept on grumbling. Now, at Grosse Isle was a strange thing called the rolling muff, that all were afraid of, since to meet it was a warning of trouble; but, like the *feu follet*, it could be driven off by holding a cross toward it or by asking it on what day of the month came Christmas. The worse of the Tremblays encountered this creature and it filled him with dismay. When he returned his neighbors observed an odor—not of sanctity—on his garments, and their view of the matter was that he had met a skunk. The graceless man felt convinced, however, that he had received a devil's baptism from the *Nain Rouge*, and St. Patrick had no stauncher allies than both the Tremblays, after that.

From: Charles M. Skinner, *Myths & Legends of Our Own Land*, vol. 2 (Philadelphia and London: J. B. Lippincott Co., 1896).

· *Werewolves of Detroit* ·

(French)

Long were the shores of Detroit vexed by the Snake God of Belle Isle and his children, the witches, for the latter sold enchantments and were the terror of good people. Jacques Morand, the *coureur de bois*, was in love with Genevieve Parent, but she disliked him and wished only to serve the church. Courting having proved of no avail, he resolved on force when she had decided to enter a convent, and he went to one of the witches, who served as devil's agent, to sell his soul. The witch accepted the slight commodity and paid for it with a grant of power to change from a man's form to that of a werewolf, or *loup garou*, that he might the easier bear away his victim. Incautiously, he followed her to Grosse Pointe, where an image of the Virgin had been set up, and as Genevieve dropped at the feet of the statue to implore aid, the wolf, as he leaped to her side, was suddenly turned to stone.

Harder was the fate of another maiden, Archange Simonet, for she was seized by a werewolf at this place and hurried away while dancing at her own wedding. The bridegroom devoted his life to the search for her, and finally lost his reason, but he prosecuted the hunt so vengefully and shrewdly that he always found assistance. One of the neighbors cut off the wolf's tail with a silver bullet, the appendage being for many years preserved by the Indians. The lover finally came upon the creature and chased it to the shore, where its footprint is still seen in one of the boulders, but it leaped into the water and disappeared. In his crazy fancy the lover declared that it had jumped down the throat of a catfish, and that is why the French Canadians have a prejudice against catfish as an article of diet.

The man-wolf dared as much for gain as for love. On the night that Jean Chiquot got the Indians drunk and bore off their beaver skins, the wood witches, known as "the white women," fell upon him and tore a part of his treasure from him, while a werewolf pounced so hard on his back that he lost more. He drove the creatures to a little distance, but was glad to be safe inside the fort again, though the officers laughed at him and called him a coward. When they went back over the route with him they were astonished to find the grass scorched where the women

had fled before him, and little springs in the turf showed where they had
been swallowed up. Sulfur water was bubbling from the spot where the
wolf dived into the earth when the trader's rosary fell out of his jacket.
Belle Fontaine, the spot was called, long afterward.

From: Charles M. Skinner, *Myths & Legends of Our Own Land*, vol. 2 (Philadelphia and
London: J. B. Lippincott Co., 1896).

CHAPTER 19

Customs and Beliefs

· Wedding and Marriage Customs ·

(Various)

Customs on Marriage
(Greek)

In Greece the women are kept in almost-oriental seclusion. In the past the number of men has been considerably larger than the number of women, and matrimony was regarded as the inevitable career of every woman.

The Greek boy has been taught to believe that he must support his sister, provide her with a liberal marriage portion, and care for her after her husband's death if she is left without means. The result of this training is that "the sacred tradition that brothers must see their sisters settled in life before they themselves marry" has become well established.

From: Grace Abbott, A Study of Greeks in Chicago (Chicago: University of Chicago Press, 1909).

Customs on Marriage
(German)

The engagement of a very wealthy young couple had been rumored for some time. On a certain day, the brother of the groom-to-be made his appearance at our house, in the capacity of *Hochzeitsbitter* or *Brautbitter* (that is, the person who invites guests to the wedding). He was mounted on a thoroughbred. The bridle and saddle were gayly decorated with many ribbons. The hat of the *Hochzeitsbitter* was also adorned with a mass of bright-colored ribbons, varying in length from one half to two yards. So numerous were these streamers that the hat itself was invisible. In the stiff March breeze, which was augmented by the speed at which the horse traveled, the horse and rider were one splendid confusion of colors. It was with the greatest difficulty that the rider retained possession of his head-covering. In addition to these ribbons, the hatband was studded with coins and paper money. While approaching the house, the *Hochzeitsbitter* uttered short piercing cries and discharged a heavy pistol. After entering the house he delivered his invitation by reciting, in an awkward manner, a short poem, which in a long drawn-out way bade those present to attend the ceremony at a certain time and place. His mission ended, he sped on, uttering shouts and discharging his pistol, as at his approach.

The wedding ceremony took place in a small country church. Crowds of invited guests, from far and near, attended. After the simple, brief ceremony everyone hastened to his horse or conveyance. The bride and groom rode in a new spring wagon, drawn by two thoroughbreds. The *Hochzeitsbitter* officiated as driver of this wagon. After he had gotten a fair start, the whole crowd dashed after this wagon at a dead run. The home of the groom's father, where the celebration was to be continued, was five miles away. Up and down the rolling prairie the mad chase took its course. Everyone attempted to overtake and, if possible, to pass the bridal pair. Suddenly the whole racing procession came to an abrupt halt. It was discovered by us who were in the rear, that a strong chain had been stretched across the road. It was the work of the small boy. The groom cast a handful of small coins among the youngsters. The chain was lowered and the mad chase resumed, to be checked a second and third time in like manner. Finally, with foam-bedecked horses, we reached the home of the groom's father.

A sumptuous feast was awaiting us. After this had been thoroughly enjoyed, the dishes of the table at which the bride had eaten were quickly cleared away. The tablecloth was seized by the married women, and a lively scramble ensued in an attempt to ensnare one of the girls with the tablecloth. Finally one of the young women was caught. The blushing maid was led back in triumph, amid the congratulatory shouts of all those present, who hailed her as the next bride-to-be. Later in the afternoon the whole party adjourned to a nearby meadow. Here the bride and groom took their stand at one end of the spacious field, the groom holding a broom in his hand. The young men all retired to the opposite side of the meadow. A footrace followed, the winner seizing the broom in triumph, which victory symbolically designated him as the next groom-to-be. In the evening there came a dance, which lasted until daybreak. The following night occurred the charivari in its most deafening form.

It may not be out of place to explain some of these peculiar practices. There is no doubt that many of them date back many, many years in the history of our race. That they should survive in the land where they originated is not so surprising. But that they should prevail in an entirely foreign environment, surrounded by strange customs, is indeed noteworthy. The voluntary isolation of these people in a measure explains their existence.

The ribbons which adorn the hat of the *Hochzeitsbitter* are the contributions of those persons whom he has invited. The coins and paper money on his hatband come from the same source. The money becomes a part of the bride's dowry. The giving of the ribbons, I take it, is a survival of a custom of giving much more valuable gifts. At the bride's home, or wherever the ceremony is continued, the *Hochzeitsbitter* always wears his decorated hat, which in itself shows how many persons have been invited. The guests bring presents to the wedding, and it is the duty of the *Hochzeitsbitter* to receive and arrange them. Besides these duties, he has others, the chief of which is the entertainment of the guests. He is a very busy person and in his odd attire a most striking figure. Not only the *Hochzeitsbitter* is decorated with ribbons on the wedding day, but also the guests adorn themselves. The buggy whip always bears a long ribbon in order that everyone may know the persons are going to the wedding as invited guests.

The chase which I described is no doubt a survival of a very old custom. It doubtless dates back to the time when men secured their wives by a chase; that is, they took them by force. This is, of course, not realized by those who participate in the race from the church. All that this chase means to them is that if anyone succeeds in passing the bridal pair, the guests are given license to play all sorts of pranks at the place where the celebration is continued. The obstructions which the small boys placed in the way of the procession, and the accompanying ransom paid by the groom, most probably are a remnant of the time when women were secured by purchase.

I stated that the *Brautbitter* delivered his invitation in poetic form. I have been fortunate enough to collect a few of these poems. They are now getting rare and rather hard to obtain. The practice seems to be dying out, as the younger generations are succeeding the old. The poems are usually handed down by word of mouth. The persons who now possess them have, as a rule, served in the capacity of *Brautbitter* themselves. When a young man has to perform this duty, he seeks some old man who knows such a poem, and with much labor learns it from him. Like most things that come down to us by word of mouth, there are doubtless many things in these poems at the present time which may, with certainty, be regarded as interpolations. As will be seen, they are in High German. Although these people use only the Low German dialect in their daily intercourse, they always write in High German, and what poetry they may have is in High German. It is the language of the church and school, and whatever elements of culture may come to them in German come to them through the High-German medium.

The following is one poem recited by the *Brautbitter:*

> *Hier bin ich her gesandt,*
> *Werde ein Brautbitter genannt.*
> *In diesem Hause bin ich wohl bekannt.*
> *Hier nehme ich meinen Hut und Stab*
> *Und setze meinen Fuss darein*
> *Dass ich möchte willkommen sein.*
> *Sollt' ich nicht willkommen sein,*
> *So bitte ich um eine Flasche Wein.*
> *Ein Flasche Wein ist mir zu viel,*
> *Ein kleiner Schnaps macht auch Pläsier.*
> *Ich bin noch jung an Jahren,*
> *Habe noch nicht viel erfahren,*

Was ich erfahren hab' und weiss
Das will ich Euch sagen mit Fleiss.
Ich soll ein Kompliment bestellen
Von Junggesellen ———— und Jungfrau ————
Sie haben sich vor einigen Wochen
Verlobt und versprochen,
Dass sie nächsten Sonntag Hochzeit halten.
Dazu lade ich Euch ein,
Herr und Frau, Söhne und Töchter, Gross und Klein,
Die im Hause zu finden sein.
Ich möchte, dass ihr sie besucht und ehrt
Und die Mahlzeiten verzehrt.
Zehn Kühe, zwanzig Ochsen, dreissig Gänsebraten,
Vierzig Schweinebraten, die werden schön geraten.
Und ein Fass Wein ist noch nicht über den Rhein.
Und wenn die Musikanten die Saiten lassen erklingen,
So kann ein jeder nach seinem Belieben tanzen und
    springen.
Und gutes Kartenblatt,
Damit ein jeder sein Vergnügen hat.
Nun kränzelt mein schön Hütlein
Mit vielen schönen Bändlein.
Habe ich meine Rede nicht gut gemacht,
So habe ich sie doch zu Ende gebracht.

The following is a rather free prose translation of this poem:

Hither I have been sent, I am called the *Brautbitter*. In this
house I am well known. Here I take off my hat and rest my staff
and enter in. I trust I may be welcome. Should I not be welcome,
then I ask for a flask of wine. A flask of wine is too much for
me, a drink of brandy gives pleasure too. I am still young in years,
have not had much experience. What I know, however, I tell you
with diligence. I am sent to deliver the compliments of
Mr. ————and Miss ————. They became engaged a few weeks
ago, and promised to get married next Sunday. To the wedding
I invite you, lord and lady, sons and daughters, great and small,

as they are in this house. I wish that you visit them and do them honor and consume the feast. Ten cows, twenty oxen, thirty roast geese, forty roast pigs will be well prepared. And a barrel of wine is not yet over the Rhine. And when the musicians strike up the strings, then may each one after his liking dance. Also good card games will be prepared, that each one may have his pleasure. Now decorate my pretty hat with many a fine ribbon. Have I not said my speech well, I have at least brought it to a close.

From: William G. Bek, "Survivals of Old Marriage-Customs Among the Low Germans of West Missouri," *Journal of American Folk-Lore* 23 (1910): 60–67

· *Patriotism* ·

(Greek)

The patriotism of the Greek is one of his most prominent characteristics and takes very often the exceedingly boastful form usually credited to "Yankees" in English novels. They are always ready to tell you of the superiority of the Greek soldier over any other and the men who have been to college in Greece speak of American schools and American scholarship with almost German contempt. A small Greek boy was sure that he won the affection of his Irish schoolteacher by showing her pictures of "the Athens." Most of them feel it their duty to spread the fame of their noble race whenever possible. Approving of Hull House, they succeeded in convincing the Bulgarians, for a time at least, that it was intended for the Greeks alone, and the first Greek boy who went through the juvenile court felt that he had added to the glory of the Greek name and dignified that worthy American institution, as well. While somewhat exasperating at times, this enthusiastic devotion to their mother country is after all a most desirable characteristic and one which the Anglo-American should readily appreciate.

From: Grace Abbott, *A Study of Greeks in Chicago* (Chicago: University of Chicago Press, 1909).

· The Last Great Sun Dance ·

(Native American)

The sun dance was a great public ceremonial rite held so sacred and so dear by Sioux sun worshippers that we know little more of its real significance than of the Druid rites at Stonehenge that awed and swayed the early Britons, less than we know of Aztec fire worship. It was a rite held but once a year—always in the full of a spring moon, usually in June, when the green grass was well up and the ponies fat and strong and ready for whatever desperate foray the excitement of the dance might inspire.

The last great sun dance, which assembled all of the Ogallalas or Lakota Sioux, and a third of the Brulés, and I believe the last actual dance ever held, occurred at Red Cloud's agency on White Clay Creek in Southern Dakota, either in the spring of 1880 or 1881, I cannot be certain which.

I had ridden over to the agency on a day's business, and just as I was about to saddle and start for home, the agent, Dr. McGillicuddy, told me the sun dance was about to begin, and that it would probably be the last great sun dance the Sioux would ever hold; that, in addition to his ten thousand Ogallalas, two thousand of Spotted Tail's Brulés from the Rosebud Agency had arrived to attend the dance, and that three army officers (Major John Bourke and Lieutenants Waite and Goldman) were due that evening, specially detailed to study and report upon its mysteries and significance, and invited me to remain and see the ceremony, which I was only too glad—then—to do.

Among the many different objects worshipped, undoubtedly the sun as a divinity was the very keystone of the Sioux's religion. Whether the sun was held to be *Wakantanka*, or the Great Spirit, in person, or whether the sun was worshipped as most highly emblematic of *Wakantanka*, I never could learn. Certain it is that it was to the sun alone that the Sioux warrior appealed, by devout sacrifice, fasting, or feast, in his most dire dilemmas and when about to engage in his most desperate enterprises.

And since plainly the sun is all-powerful to give or to deny, the maker of heat and light, the giver of the generous warmth, and the shedder of the copious tears that makes the grass to grow that fattens alike the buffalo and the ponies, and that, later, serves to ripen the wild plum and the sarvis berry, the maize, the gooseberry, and the turnip—why indeed should not Sioux sufferers supplicate his charity and largess, and Sioux adventurers into perils beseech his aid?

Of the inner significance of the various ceremonies incident to the dance we know little.

Certain, however, it is that no cultsman, civilized or pagan, ever bent before the throne of his spiritual allegiance with more of profound faith and reverence, or took more pains to purify the body by cleansing and to exalt the spirit by fasting before supplicating and sacrificing to his deity, than did the Sioux sun dancer.

Any could participate in the sun dance proper, but few did. Motives for participation in the last extreme rites were various.

Parents having a child mortally ill often made a vow to *Wakantanka* that if the child's life were spared they would dance the next sun dance.

A like vow was made by a warrior having a deadly enemy—as recompense for aid in safely putting the enemy where he could do no more harm.

Sioux in deadly peril of flood or famine so vowed—as pledge for help to escape their peril.

Young bucks yet untried in war so vowed and danced—to prove their courage.

For a year the Indian Bureau had been struggling to destroy the tribal relation of these people, to clip the authority of the chiefs, to induce them to till the soil and build houses, and thus to wean them from their nomadic habits and teach them the value of peace and industry.

And that, in some ways, they were not so slow to "catch on" was proved effectively when General James R. O'Bierne came out as the special agent of the Indian Bureau and called a council of the chiefs of the tribe to tell them what the Great Father proposed to do for them. After an eloquent eulogy of peace and the comforts and prosperity it brings, and a grim picture of the distresses entailed by war, he told them that to every head of a family who would abandon his tepee and build a house of one room, the Great Father would present a cooking stove, with a heating stove thrown in for a house of two rooms; that they would be given wagons, plows, hoes, scythes, rakes, etc.

Evidently the interpreter had translated *scythe* as "a knife that cuts grass," for immediately O'Bierne finished, up rose an old chief named No Flesh and asked:

"What does the chief say we are to get?" and the interpreter repeated the offer.

"You tell the chief to tell the Great Father," answered No Flesh, "that we don't want *knives* that cut grass—nothing the white man has thrown aside—*we want wagons that cut grass.*"

And mowing machines No Flesh's people got!

This year the Sioux must dance and sacrifice with no guests present but Spot's band of Brulés. Of the other guests from time immemorial usually bidden to this ceremony, the Omahas and Pawnees were already so nearly shut in by and absorbed into the settlements to the southeast that only the memory lingered in the minds of the elders of their approaching cavalcades, bright with glitter of arms and brilliant with every color of the rainbow, outlined against the white walls of the Niobrara bluffs, or a thread of many colors winding through the somber pines that crested their summits; while the Cheyennes left within the United States since Dull Knife's last fight at Fort Robinson were few and scattered, the Nez Percé well-nigh extinct, and the Blackfeet, Crees, Mandans, and Gros Ventres were pressed back, within narrow reservation lines, tight up against the Canadian border, a full moon's journey distant.

The tepees of the tribe were strung out for miles along the valleys of White Clay and Wounded Knee, more thickly clustered into villages at irregular intervals about the lodge of one or another of the sub-chiefs that owned their fealty.

At twilight of this eventide criers were out in every village, with weightier news and orders than any their soft monotones had conveyed since the issuance of Sitting Bull's call to arms and to assembly on the Little Big Horn—criers who paused at points of vantage through the villages, called for attention, and cried the stirring news that, by order of Red Cloud and his elder counselors, the time for the sun dance had come, and that on the following morning the entire tribe would assemble on the great flat two miles south of the agency, and there pitch their tepees in the vast circle prescribed by sun dance traditions.

The scene the next morning was like a savage derby day. For hours, indeed throughout the livelong day, a broad stream of primitive humanity swept past the agency buildings, filling the valley from rim to rim, *en route* to Sun Dance Flat—as since it has been known—a stream that ebbed and flowed a bit but never stopped till the entire tribe, with all their wealth of lodges, weapons, implements, and domestic chattels, freighted on *travois* or on the backs of ponies, had reached the designated camping site; a stream gay of temper as in its colors, all keen for the feasts and agog for the excitement of the coming ceremony.

With the valley too narrow to allow for a perfect circle with so many tepees pitched close together in a single row, an ellipse was formed parallel with the general course of the stream, with a length north and south of something over a mile, and a breadth at the center of nearly three quarters of a mile, with, at the extreme north end, a broad entrance or opening in the otherwise solid ellipse of the tepees.

All this work of removal and arrangement of the lodges was conducted with perfect discipline under the direction of the chiefs or their lieutenants, aided by specially designated armed bailiffs who were quick to punish breaches of discipline or disobedience of orders with no light hand.

A second day was allowed for settling this horde of people, making place for Spot's Brulés, who had come in the day before, correcting the tepee alignment and restoring order.

On the next day, the third, a small band of not more than ten or twelve of the most noted warriors of the tribe were named by the chiefs to go out into the hills and select the *Wahkan* (mystery) tree, to be cut and used as the sun pole (center) of the great sun dance tepee later to be built.

For this emprise the participants decked themselves as for battle, with all the gauds of their savage war equipment, mounted their best war ponies, and then circled the camp, each chanting the personal deeds that had won him the honor to make one of the *Wahkan* tree hunters.

And then they rode out into the hills. Toward evening they returned, and, having found a satisfactory tree, they cut out a broad square of sod near the center of the camp, exposing the generous brown loam beneath, as the site for the sun pole—the center of the sun lodge.

The doings on Sun Dance Flat the first and second days were told us, for none of us visited the Flat until the third day—and then I know at least one of the little party was none too glad he had come.

The "political" situation at the agency was then under tense strain. As a part of his efforts to stop the Sioux from plundering neighboring ranch-horse herds, and to maintain better order on the reservation, Dr. McGilli-cuddy had recently organized a police force of a hundred young bucks, and had made a magnificent young warrior named Sword their captain. Red Cloud, and indeed the entire tribe, bitterly objected to the organization of this force, and had threatened active hostility toward it. Indeed,

Sword's police had made themselves specially obnoxious by backing up the doctor in his opposition to unreasonable demands by the visiting Brulés. So it was very much of a problem whether it would be safe for us to go to the dance.

But when, the morning of the third day, Dr. McGillicuddy and Major Bourke discussed the wisdom of making our contemplated visit to the dance, both agreed a bold front was likely to permanently settle the Brulés's grouch and the Ogallalas's resentment of the doctor's police organization, more likely than to stay tight at the agency, and leave them suspicious we were afraid of them. Indeed, any available defenses at the agency were so poor we were as well off at one place as another.

So two ambulances were soon brought and we trotted off up the creek toward the sun dance, with half of Sword's police ahead of us and half behind in a fairly well-formed column of twos.

Coming to the sun dance camp, the scene was one never to be forgotten. The camp lay on a broad, level bench of the valley, probably a mile and a half long, a green wall of cottonwoods lining the stream to the west, while in the south and east rose tall bluffs thickly covered with pines. The tepees were pitched in a single row to form a vast ellipsoid, in its breadth occupying the entire width of the valley and nearly filling it from end to end. The center of the ellipsoid was entirely open, like the parade ground of a big garrison.

Here were no divisions of class. The tepees of the rich and of the poor hobnobbed side by side—here a magnificent tall lodge covered with splendid buffalo robes painted with the totem of the family, there a miserable low hut little better than a temporary *wickiup*, ill-covered with fragments of rent and worn canvas.

And in and out among the tepees swarmed the Sioux host, a moving frame of brilliant colors enclosing the bright green of the central plain, the dark blue and bright red of broadcloth blankets and leggings, and the golden yellow of buckskin prevailing.

When well within the circle, Sword asked the doctor to stop the ambulances a few minutes. He then proceeded to put his police through a mounted company drill of no mean accuracy, good enough to command the commendation of Major Bourke and Lieutenants Waite and Goldman.

The drill finished, and without the least hint to us of his purpose, Sword suddenly broke his cavalry formation and, at the head of his men, started a mad charge, in disordered savage mass, straight at the nearest point of the line of tepees to the west; and, come within twenty yards of the line, reined to the left parallel to the line, and so charged round the entire circle, his men shouting their war cries and shooting as fast as they could load and fire over the heads of their people, sometimes actually through the tops of the lodges.

It was Sword's challenge to the tribe! One hundred challenging twelve thousand!

And luckily for us all the bluff was not called. The tribe ducked to cover within their tepees like rabbits to their warrens.

Altogether it made about the most uncomfortable ten or fifteen minutes I ever passed, for we had nothing to do but sit idly in our ambulances, awaiting whatever row his mad freak might stir.

At length, the circuit finished, Sword drew up proudly before us and saluted, his horses heaving of flank and dripping of sides, and spoke to Changro.

Then Louis interpreted:

"Sword he say now Sioux be good Injun—no bother police anymore! They know they eat us up quick, but then Great Father send heap soldier eat them up!!"

And so it proved, for to the performance of the duties required of the police by the agent, there was never again active opposition.

After a quick turn about the camp we drove back to the agency. Arrived there, all drew a deep breath, and then drank deep to an impromptu toast, suggested by Inspector Conley the moment his glass was filled:

"Here's to the pretty d——d good luck that we-uns still wears our hair!"

The fourth morning we were out at the camp bright and early and spent the day there—and a busy day indeed it proved for the tribe and their visitors.

At dawn of this morning a tepee two or three times the size of the largest ordinarily used was set up within the circle, due east of the point chosen for the sun pole, and nearer to the line of the tepees than to the pole. This was in effect a great medicine lodge, within which all the candidates for the dance were that morning assembled by the medicine men, and therein kept closely secluded, none being permitted to enter except certain designated attendants.

For the three preceding days all the candidates had been purifying themselves for the ceremony by a very rigorous fast and an almost uninter-rupted succession of sweatbaths.

Of nourishment for these days, and indeed through the remaining four days of the dance, the dancers partook of little except the frequent nibbling of white sage leaves, bound like wreaths or great bracelets about their wrists, and occasionally renewed. The floor of the medicine lodge, moreover, was strewn thickly with white sage, and indeed sage seemed to play an important part throughout the dance, for the dancers were frequently rubbing their breasts with handfuls of the herb. Why, we could only conjecture—perhaps from an exaggerated value set upon its medicinal virtues.

Their sweatbath was as effective as it was primitive. It was simply a *wickiup*, a low hut built by sticking the thick ends of brush or slender boughs into the earth about a circle six or eight feet in diameter and interlacing their tops. This hive-shaped frame was thickly covered with buffalo robes till tight as a drum. Large, hot stones, heated in a nearby fire, were rolled into the hut; the bathers, naked, then entered with a vessel of water and sat down about the heated stones, while one of their number began dipping the "bush" of a buffalo tail in the water and sprinkling the stones. Thus the lodge was kept densely filled with steam, and there the bathers sat and took it as long as they could stand it, then ran out and plunged into and refreshed themselves in the nearest stream or pool and resumed the steaming process.

About nine o'clock in the morning practically the entire tribe mounted and assembled outside the circle. None were left in the tepees except the old and infirm and youngsters too small to ride. At a signal from the chief medicine man, and led by the men who had selected the *Wahkan* tree, all started at best speed of their ponies as mad a charge upon the tree (a mile distant) as ever upon an enemy in war—up a steep slope, across a rocky, timbered hogback, down into and through a ravine, upon the farther slope of which stood the chosen "mystery tree."

About the tree the tribe was soon so densely massed that we could see little of ceremonies that occupied more than an hour.

Then the medicine men pressed the throng back and four young warriors, honored by selection as the fellers of the tree, approached the tree, and each in turn first proudly told the story of his most daring deeds in battle, and then struck the tree one heavy blow with an ax, each striking it on the opposite sides representing the four cardinal points of the compass; the first blow falling, if my memory rightly serves, on the east side.

This done, a young squaw, held, we were told, to be of unblemished reputation, dressed in a beautiful white tanned (unsmoked) fawnskin tunic, covered with concentric rows of elk teeth (these teeth then a standard currency of the tribe, having a value of a dollar each), sprang forward, grasped the ax, and quickly finished the felling of the tree.

Next the four men who first struck the tree proceeded to trim it neatly of all branches, until it remained a graceful length of springy poplar, perhaps ten inches in diameter at the base. Then the pole was *travoised* back to camp, with greatest care not to manhandle it, for to touch it or even to travel in advance of it seemed either a breach of the ritual or an offense threatening heavy penalty or hazard of some sort.

Upon reaching the summit of a low hillock, near and overlooking the Sun Flat, the mass of the tribe stopped, and a few elders advanced with the sun pole and set it firmly in its chosen place.

Then ensued the wildest charge conceivable—all the mounted warriors galloping through the broad north entrance of the circle and rushing at top speed upon the sun pole, until, under pressure of converging lines, many horses and riders went down, not a few to serious injury. Finally out of the heaving, struggling, panting, bleeding mass at last a young warrior was borne out in honor, as having been the first to strike the pole.

The chiefs and their aides soon had the rout untangled, and all were ordered to their tepees, save a large band (chiefly squaws), that quickly set about the erection of the sun dance lodge proper.

This lodge as built was circular in form and, I should think, more than two hundred feet in diameter. Two rows of posts, forked at the top, were set about this circle about fifteen or twenty feet apart, the outer posts probably eight feet high, the inner about ten feet. The spaces between the outer circle of posts were then closely filled in by sticking thick pine boughs in the ground, thus making a tight enclosure, with no opening save the main entrance on its eastern side. Shelter was then furnished by stretching robes and tepee cloths above the spaces between the outer and inner posts—and the lodge was done, ready for the next day's ceremonies in the great central circle about the sun pole, open to the sky, and about one hundred and fifty feet in diameter.

The next morning, the fifth, we reached the lodge at dawn and found it packed to overflowing, the dancers gathered in the central ring, naked above the waist, but covered below by red and blue blankets belted about the loins, all wearing sage "wristlets."

As well as I can remember, there were forty-odd dancers, none past middle life, a few comparative youths, and one squaw. We were told the squaw and her husband were dancing as the fulfilment of a vow to endure its punishment if the life of a sick child were spared.

The space within the lodge beneath the shelter was crowded with the tribe, all tricked out in their bravest finery. Many of the richer of the squaws were dressed in golden yellow or snow white fawn- or buckskin tunics, soft as velvet, falling halfway between knees and feet, some of the tunics with broad yoke or stole-shaped decoration of a solid mass of turquoise blue beads, edged with a narrow row of red beads, and some more or less covered with rows of elk teeth—some of these latter representing hundreds of dollars in value, and going to prove that Eve's daughters had an inconvenient knack of making themselves a most extravagant luxury long before the first *modiste* wrought in silks, laces, and velvets. The brilliant colors and rich beadwork of the men's costumes and the barbaric magnificence of their feathered warbonnets are too well known to take space here.

There was one costume, however, that deserves mention, as does also the wearer, Little Big Man, the proudest of them all, who, while owning a scant five feet in height, had the breadth and depth of chest, and length and power of arms, of a giant, and who had the reputation of being one of the most desperate and ruthless warriors of the tribe. Someone had presented him, or perhaps, indeed, he had won in the Custer fight, a captain's blouse, in very good condition, and just as we entered the lodge, Little Big Man, proudly wearing this uniform coat, fell in behind us. Camp stools had been brought for Mrs. McGillicuddy and Mrs. Blanchard, the trader's wife, and when they were seated at the inner edge of the circle and we grouped near them, Little Big Man squatted upon the ground beside them, evidently bent upon winning their admiration. Presently, apparently thinking he was not creating the sensation justly his due, he rose, unbuttoned, and removed his blouse, and so stood beside them, completely naked to the waist, his broad breast and great, sinewy arms showing a dozen or more scars of deadly tussles in which, to be here alive, he must have bested the enemy, each scar emphasized by a dab of red paint streaming like blood beneath it. After himself alternately admiring these scars and looking to the ladies for approval, he gravely resumed his blouse and his seat.

And then a funny thing happened. Scarcely was he seated, when a tall, handsome young squaw stepped in front of him, bent quickly, and scooped up a double handful of sand and threw it in his face. Instantly he pulled a six-shooter and fired to kill her, but, blinded by the sand, and his arm knocked up by another Indian, the ball flew high above the heads of all— and then for five minutes the lodge rang with such peals of derisive laughter that Little Big Man slunk away into the crowd and was not seen by us again at the sun dance.

Changro explained the cause of the incident lay in Little Big Man's evil tongue, that in camp gossip the night before he had besmirched this young woman's character, and that she thus took the first opportunity to give him the lie in the good old tribal way.

Just as the sun rose above the horizon, the dance in his honor began.

The dancers were ranged in separate rows, eight or ten dancers to the row. They stood shoulder to shoulder, facing east, a little wooden whistle in the mouth of each.

At the boom of a great medicine tom-tom, each extended his arms forward and upward toward the sun, hands open and palms turned out- ward, bent slightly at the knee, and began a slow but steady rising on the ball of the foot and dropping back on the heels, which was the only movement of the "dance" proper, his eyes gazing unblinkingly upon the sun, a pipe of each whistle accompanying each "step" of the dance. And so they whistled and gazed and danced for hours, and days indeed, till noon of the third succeeding day, their arms occasionally rested by drop- ping them to the sides, their eyes by a medicine man standing behind each row holding inclined forward above their heads a long wand, from the top of which a small feather dangled at the end of a long string, and as the feather was blown about by the wind, each dancer closely followed its every shift by movement of head and eyes.

Only at long intervals, and when exhausted well-nigh to the point of falling in their tracks, were the ranks broken and the dancers given a brief rest, a mouthful of broth, and fresh sage armlets.

Throughout this dance no word was spoken to or by the dancers, as far as we could see; they were left to rapt mental concentration upon the subject of whatever vow or prayer had moved them to this sacrifice to their deity.

Throughout the continuation of the sun dance proper, which was largely confined to the south side of the great central ring, an endless succession of other ceremonies was going on, some of which are still clear to me, but many of which I no longer can recall.

About noon of this day the "Buffalo Dance" began, and lasted through the better part of the afternoon. Bar a great herd of several thousand buffalo then still ranging far to the northwest of the Black Hills, this magnificent animal, which for generations had furnished the tribe their most highly prized food and clothing supply, had forever disappeared from the plains, fallen before the mercenary rifles of white robe hunters, who took pelts by hundreds of thousands, and left carcasses to rot and bones to whiten where their quarry fell. That they were all dead and gone and disappeared for good and all, no Sioux could then be made to believe; for had they not always found them migratory, as were they themselves? Had not their ancestors long generations back *travoised* westward from the very foothills of the Appalachians, following the slow drift of the buffalo toward the setting sun? Often, to be sure, they disappeared from some favorite campsite, like the French Lick, but never more than a few days' journey was needed to locate untold thousands of these great black beauties, comfortably settled on fresh range.

Apparently this dance was an appeal for a return of the prolific herds.

It was opened by a long invocation, addressed apparently to the sun by an aged medicine man. Then he attached to a rope hanging from the top of the *Wahkan* pole first the figure of a man, about eighteen inches in length, and beneath it the figure of a buffalo bull, each cut out of pieces of rawhide. These figures were fashioned with extraordinary fidelity to every detail of every outline of man and animal, and, indeed, were startlingly complete. When so attached, these figures remained swinging about fifteen feet above the ground. Next, heralded by the low-toned, booming notes of the tom-tom, entered at a sharp trot a chief, mounted, at the head of forty or fifty dismounted warriors, all stripped and painted as for war, each armed with rifle or pistol, and circled three times around the pole from left to right, who, as they ran, loaded and fired as rapidly as possible at the pendent figures, chanting as they ran. The third circuit finished, the chief led his men to the west of the ring and grouped them facing the pole.

Thereafter in rapid succession so entered, ran, shot, and chanted other squads, until probably five hundred warriors were so assembled. By this time both figures were bullet-riddled, but still hanging where first placed.

Then the entire band, made up of the several squads, started trotting about the pole, massed so closely about it that many were firing practically straight up in the air, so straight it was simply a miracle that none in or about the lodge were killed or hurt by the actual rain of bullets certainly falling near about us. Really, one might almost as well have been under direct fire.

"Boys," called Conley, hunching his head down deep between his shoulders, "I surely neve' had no use fer them slickers on top o' a stick tenderfeet holds over their haids in a rain, but if they've got airy one g'aranteed bum-proof, mama! but wouldn't she come handy now! An' th' hell of it is if airy one o' us gets winged, we won't know which o' them lead rainmakers we ought to kill! Wish we was all prairie dogs an' close to ou' holes!"

Sentiments I am certain every one of us cordially echoed, for during the hour or more this buffalo dance lasted, there was scarcely a moment we were not directly threatened with the receipt of a heavier load of lead than we could walk off with.

Finally, when a ball cut the rope between man and buffalo, and the latter fell to the ground, instantly the dance ceased, and a warrior was seized and borne aloft in honor from the ring, apparently as the potter of the buffalo, though how they could tell whose shot brought down the image was past understanding.

Toward evening we all drove back to the agency for supper.

About nine o'clock Conley, Changro, and I rode back to the sun dance, and there remained throughout the night; and there too in and about the lodge, stayed the entire tribe, feasting on stewed dog and coffee, stuffing themselves hour after hour to a surfeit none but a savage could stand, discussing the ceremony, boasting how well some kinsman dancer was enduring his fast and dance, and betting that he would honorably acquit himself in the final torture of the "tie-up" to the sun pole, yarned, laughed, and amused themselves as did the old Roman audience while slippery, dark red patches in the arena were being sprinkled with sand, in preparation for the entry of the next group of gladiators.

And throughout the slow-dragging hours of the night the dance went on, with few brief intervals of rest, the monotonous drone of the feeble whistles keeping time to the pad-pad, pad-pad of dropping heels, the eyes of every dancer fixed fast upon the moon—for, as sister to the sun, she next to him held their reverence.

As for ourselves, little attention was paid to us by the Sioux—a few were surly, but most indifferent.

To us the scene was weird and awful past adequate description.

In the central ring, dimly lighted by the moon and stars, the thin, wasted, haggard forms of the fasting dancers looked like pale ghosts of demons, prey-hunting in a spirit land.

Beneath the shadow of the shelter, half lighted by many little camp fires over which dogs were stewing, beef roasting, and coffee boiling, the tribe was gathered, grouped closest about the fires, whose flickering flames tinted the bronze of the savage Sioux faces to such a sinister shade of red as made the merriest of them something to shudder at.

The following day was almost wholly given up—in so far as the side ceremonies were concerned—to a rite nearly akin to, if not identical with, Christian baptism. Babies born within the year were brought by their fathers and mothers to an old medicine man, who, taking each child in turn, held it up toward the sun, and then laid it at the foot of the sun pole. Next he drew a narrow-bladed knife, extended its point first east, next west, then north and south, and then proceeded to pierce the child's ears. This finished, and the child restored to its mother, a grandfather or father of the family made an address, in which he besought for the child the friendship of the tribe and their best wishes for its health, for its success in chase and war if a man child, for its happy marriage if a girl, ending by humbly begging the poor of the tribe to come and receive as free gifts all the largess the family were able to bestow, a charitable offering or sacrifice in behalf of favor for the child.

While the address was in progress, the squaws were piling near the pole all the goods the family could afford, and, in the cases of several exceptionally fond parents, evidently far more than they could afford—yards of blue and red broadcloth, calicoes, moccasins, tunics, leggings, some newly made for this offering, some taken then and there from the wearers' persons, provisions, *parflèches*, saddles, and a few arms. One loving mother, a really beautiful young squaw, stripped off and added to her pile a superb fawnskin tunic, ornamented with not less than two or three hundred elk teeth worth a dollar apiece.

Many added one or more horses to their offering. I remember Trader Blanchard told me that the week before the sun dance he sold sixty thousand yards of various cloths, besides many other goods, for offerings at this dance!

The elder's speech finished and the gifts gathered, a stampede and greedy scramble for this wealth ensued, in which it seemed to me rich vied with poor for the prizes. But it was a good-natured struggle—the first to lay hands on was the one to have—and there was little disputing over first rights. The horse gifts made no end of fun, for they were turned loose in the ring without even a bit of rope on, and not a few were unbroken broncos, resentful of manhandling, and yet only to be taken by *coup de main*. Young bucks lit all over each offered horse-like flies, only to be kicked or tossed galley west, until at length some lucky one got a stout grip on mane with one hand and nostrils with the other, thus choking the struggling prize to surrender.

At noon of the succeeding day the hour of supreme sacrificial trial had arrived for all who had vowed to undergo it—the "tieing up" to the sun pole—of whom, according to my recollection, there were only nine, and it found them wan, thin, and exhausted of body, but still strong of spirit.

Four-plait rawhide ropes hung from the top of the pole, the lower half of each unbraided and twisted into two strands, a loop at the end of each.

Each candidate in turn was laid at the foot of the sun pole. The chief medicine man then drew his narrow-bladed knife, extended it toward each of the four cardinal points of the compass, bent over the candidate, and passed the blade beneath and through a narrow strip of flesh on each breast (the puncture being scarcely more than a half-inch in breadth), stuck a stout, hardwood skewer through each of the two openings so made, and, lastly, looped each of the two ends of one of the hanging ropes over each of the two skewers—torture the candidates endured without plaint or the flinching of a muscle.

This finished, the candidate was helped to his feet and given a long, stout staff—to help him in his terrible task of rending his own flesh till the skewers were torn from their lodgment in his breast!

Some pulled slowly but steadily and strongly backward, aided by their staffs, until the skin of their breasts were drawn out eighteen inches, while that of their backs was tight as a drum head. Others jumped and bucked on their ropes like a bronco suffering the indignity of his first saddle.

Yet no cry escaped their lips; no eye showed pain!

On they struggled, and yet on, blood flowing freely from their wounds, until worn nature could do no more, and one after another fell fainting on his leash!

To fail of breaking loose was a lasting disgrace, only to be partially redeemed by heavy presents to the tribe. And thus it happened that as each fell his nearest and dearest ran up and fiercely beat and kicked him to rouse him to new effort.

The spirit and courage to break loose all had, but only one still owned store of strength sufficient for the awful task.

After struggling until so weak they could no longer be made to rise, eight were bought off by presents, and their skewers cut loose by the medicine man.

The ninth man, the husband by the way, of the one squaw dancer, after repeatedly falling in a faint, at last roused himself, cast aside his staff, staggered up to the pole, and, commanding every last remaining grain of strength, bounded violently away from the pole, bounded with such force that his body swung on the rope free of the ground so hard that when he again hit the ground he was free of the rope! A plucky and a strong one indeed was he—tied to the pole nearly an hour and a half!

And this man's squaw was well worthy of her lord, for, while not herself tied up, she submitted herself to sacrificial torture, in the severe scarifying of her arms, undertaken by none of her fellow dancers!

Thus was the vow of this brave pair honestly and dearly paid.

So sacrificed the Sioux to the sun, as the chief of their many deities.

While we know little enough of the details of their cult, we know much to their credit, socially and morally, they certainly owed to it: We know it for a religion broad enough in scope, sound enough in ethics, and strong enough in its hold upon its adherents to have made them a "good" people as we first found them; a kindly, loving people among their own kith and kin; a charitable people, always free givers to the poor, and generous helpers of any in distress, whether of their own or of hostile blood; a truthful people that hated a forked tongue, to whom it was harder to lie than for the average "Christian" to tell the truth; a race of virtuous, honest wives and devoted mothers; a race of iron-hearted men that condemned to a life at the most menial tasks any guilty of poltroonery; a race that never stole, except as they took spoils, won in the manly game of war at hazard of their lives; a race lofty in its thought and eloquent in its expression; a race of stoics that bore most terrible pain with all the patient fortitude ever shown under torture by the most heroic Christian martyr; happy fatalists who went chanting to their death, placid in the certainty of their conviction of enjoying immortality in the Happy Hunting Grounds of the Great Spirit.

Surely, in the light of such results, a religion worth owning and a deity worth praying to, let whomsoever may sneer at it as pagan!

And why not the sun as deity? Why not the one supreme potentiality of all nature, that, obviously alike to savage and to sage, holds the means to make or mar our destinies? Why not the sun, the very keystone to the great cosmic work of the Creator?

Who that has reveled and bathed in the sun's warm rays and shivered under cloud, that has observed earth's generous largess when kissed by sunlight and her chill poverty when the sun long denies himself, can offensively cry pagan of a sun worshipper?

From: Edgar Beecher Bronson, *Cowboy Life on the Western Plains* (New York: Grosset & Dunlop, 1910).

· *Good Friday Celebration* ·

(Greek)

On Halsted Street, south of Harrison, almost every store for two blocks has Greek characters on the windows, and recalling one's long-forgotten college Greek, one learns that the first coffeehouse is the "Cafe Appolyon," and that their newspaper *The Hellas* is published next door. A block west on Blue Island Avenue one finds the "Parthenon Barber Shop" and the Greek drugstore. If an American were to visit this neighborhood on the night of Good Friday, when the stores are draped with purple and black, and watch at midnight the solemn procession of Greek men march down the street carrying their burning candles and chanting hymns, he would probably feel as though he were no longer in America, but after a moment's reflection he would say that this could be no place but America for the procession was headed by eight burly Irish-American policemen and along the walks were "Americans" of Polish, Italian, Russian Jewish, Lithuanian, and Puritan ancestry watching, with mingled reverence and curiosity, this celebration of Good Friday, while those who marched were homesick and mourning because "this was not like the Tripolis."

From: Grace Abbott, *A Study of Greeks in Chicago* (Chicago: University of Chicago Press, 1909).

· *Religion* ·

(Czech)

From the domain of Roman Catholic Austria to unpledged Nebraska is a step of many thousands of miles. The difference in the religious attitude of many Czechs who have taken that long step is as great and is likewise analogous.

The Bohemians of the state may be roughly classified into three general groups: Roman Catholics, Protestants, and Liberal Thinkers. There are forty-four towns and villages in Nebraska in which Bohemian Catholic churches and priests are located. Parochial schools are maintained in connection with some of the churches as, for instance, the building in Dodge where 140 children attend the instruction of Sisters of Our Lady.

There are some twenty Bohemian Protestant churches in the state, being mainly Methodist and Presbyterian.

The Liberal Thinkers are more recently organized, there being but five societies in Nebraska.

From: Professor Šárka B. Hrbkova, "Bohemians in Nebraska," *The Bohemian Review* 1, no. 6 (July 1917): 11.

Part IV

Western
Folktales

Chapter 20

Legends and Legendary Figures

· *The Coming of the White Man* ·

(Native American)

I
t appears that an old woman living near the ancient Indian village
of Ne-Ahkstow, about two miles south of the mouth of the Great
River (the Columbia), had lost her son. She wailed for a whole year,
and then she stopped. One day, after her usual custom, she went to the
seaside, and walked along the shore towards Clatsop. While on the way
she saw something very strange. At first it seemed like a whale, but, when
the old woman came close, she saw that it had two trees standing upright
in it. She said, "This is no whale; it is a monster." The outside was all
covered over with something bright, which they afterwards found was
copper. Ropes were tied all over the two trees, and the inside of the
Thing was full of iron.

While the old woman gazed in silent wonder, a being that looked like
a bear, but had a human face, though with long hair all over it, came
out of the Thing that lay there. Then the old woman hastened home in
great fear. She thought this bearlike creature must be the spirit of her
son, and that the Thing was that about which they had heard in the
Ekanum tales.

The people, when they had heard the strange story, hastened with bows and arrows to the spot. There, sure enough, lay the Thing upon the shore, just as the old woman had said. Only instead of one bear there were two standing on the Thing. These two creatures—whether bears or people the Indians were not sure—were just at the point of going down the Thing (which they now began to understand was an immense canoe with two trees driven into it) to the beach, with kettles in their hands.

As the bewildered people watched them they started a fire and put corn into the kettles. Very soon it began to pop and fly with great rapidity up and down in the kettles. The popcorn (the nature of which the Clatsops did not then understand) struck them with more surprise than anything else—and this is the one part of the story preserved in every version.

Then the corn-popping strangers made signs that they wanted water. The chief sent men to supply them with all their needs, and in the meantime he made a careful examination of the strangers. Finding that their hands were the same as his own, he became satisfied that they were indeed men. One of the Indians ran and climbed up and entered the Thing. Looking into the interior, he found it full of boxes. There were also many strings of buttons half a fathom long. He went out to call in his relatives, but, before he could return, the ship had been set on fire. Or, in the language of Charlie Cultee, "It burnt just like fat." As a result of the burning of the ship, the Clatsops got possession of the iron, copper, and brass.

Now the news of this strange event became noised abroad, and the Indians from all the region thronged to Clatsop to see and feel of these strange men with hands and feet just like ordinary men, yet with long beards and with such peculiar garb as to seem in no sense men. There arose great strife as to who should receive and care for the strange men. Each tribe or village was very anxious to have them, or at least one of them. The Quienaults, the Chehales, and the Willapas, from the beach on the north side, came to press their claims. From up the river came the Cowlitz, the Cascades, and even the far-off Klickitat. The different tribes almost had a battle for possession, but, according to one account, it was finally settled that one of the strange visitors should stay with the Clatsop chief, and that one should go with the Willapas on the north side of the Great River. According to another, they both stayed at Clatsop.

From this first arrival of white men, the Indians called them all "*Tlehon-nipts,*" that is, "Of those who drift ashore." One of the men possessed the magical art of taking pieces of iron and making knives and hatchets. It was indeed to the poor Indians a marvelous gift of Tallapus, their god, that they should have a man among them that could perform that priceless labor, for the possession of iron knives and hatchets meant the indefinite multiplying of canoes, huts, bows and arrows, weapons, and implements of every sort. The ironmaker's name was Konapee. The Indians kept close watch of him for many days and made him work incessantly. But, as the tokens of his skill became numerous, his captors held him in great favor and allowed him more liberty. Being permitted to select a site for a house, he chose a spot on the Columbia which became known to the Indians, even down to the white occupancy of the region, as "Konapee."

From: William Dennison Lyman, *The Columbia River* (New York and London: G. P. Putnam's Sons, 1909).

· *The Beeswax Ship* ·

(Native American)

The next legend of the prehistoric white man is that of the "Beeswax Ship." This, too, has a real confirmation in the presence of large quantities of beeswax at a point also near Nekahni Mountain, just north of the mouth of the Nehalem River. Some naturalists claimed at one time that this substance was simply the natural paraffin produced from the products of coal or petroleum. But more recently cakes of the substance stamped with the sacred letters, "I.H.S.," together with tapers, and even one piece with a bee plainly visible within, may be considered incontestable proof that this is indeed beeswax, while the letters, "I.H.S." denote plainly enough the origin of the substance in some Spanish colony.

An interesting point in connection with this is the historical fact that on June 16, 1769, the ship *San José* left La Paz, Lower California, for San Diego, and was never heard from again. Some have conjectured that the *San José* was the "Beeswax Ship," driven far north by some storm or mutiny. As to the peculiar fact that a ship should have been entirely loaded with beeswax it has been conjectured that some of the good padres of the Spanish missions meant to provide a new station with a large amount of wax for the sake of providing tapers for their service, the lighted candles proving then, as they do now, a matter of marvel and wonder to the natives, and, with other features of ceremonial worship, having a great effect to bring them into subjection to the Church.

The Indian legend runs on to the effect that several white men were saved from the wreck of the "Beeswax Ship," and that they lived with them. But having infringed upon the family rights of the natives, they became obnoxious, and were all cut off by an attack from them. One story, however, asserts that there was one man left, a blue-eyed, golden-haired man, that he took a Nehalem woman, and that from him was descended a fair-complexioned progeny, of which a certain chieftain who lived at a beautiful little lake on Clatsop plains, now known as Culliby Lake, was our Quiaculliby.

From: William Dennison Lyman, *The Columbia River* (New York and London: G. P. Putnam's Sons, 1909).

· *The Donner Party* ·

(Unidentified)

Though it comes not within the scope which the writer of this volume proposed to himself, in undertaking to relate any events not having any connection with the Irish race in California, yet, because there were several Irish families among the sufferers at Donner Lake, and these the most deserving and undespairing of the whole party, it seems not to be out of place to give a brief account of that dreadful occurrence in this volume. The Donner party were principally from Tennessee, from counties bordering on the Cumberland River, and though ostensibly a party of native Americans, had at least one-third of its members of Irish birth or origin. For instance, there were the Murphys, most of whom survived, and the Breens, the Dolans, and Hallorins, one of whom did most of the praying and kept the only daily journal of those terrible days, always ending his entries in his little logbook with a prayer that the merciful God would soon come to their relief. One of the Murphys—a Mary—who survived, gave the name Marysville to the metropolis of Yuba County; her brother William is City Attorney, and a distinguished lawyer of said burgh. In the organization of the Donner party, a serious mistake was made in the election of a brute like Reed as captain, who was so unfeeling as to murder one of the party, named Snyder, for a slight disobedience of rules. After this instance of barbarous cruelty, the so-called captain ought either to have been executed as a murderer, or at least degraded from his position. He was driven off or left the party soon after the murder of Snyder. Then again, when the party ran short of food, the two Indian guides who volunteered to extricate them from their predicament, were murdered and devoured by the entire party. The survivors plundered their dead companions' property, and seemed more anxious to save it than their lives. So accustomed did the wretches become to the use of human flesh, that when relief came, they preferred the flesh of their fellowmen to that of beef or mutton. There was even one named Keisburgh, who, it was suspected, murdered several of his companions to devour them. For over three months the whole party suffered from cold and hunger and sickness. When a death occurred, the flesh was instantly torn from the skeleton and devoured by the survivors.

The following is an extract from one of the newspapers of that date, April 10, 1847:

The bones of those who had died and been miserably devoured by those who survived were lying around their tents and cabins. The bodies of men, women, and children, with one half the flesh torn from them, lay on every side. A woman sat by the side of the body of her husband, who had just died, cutting out his tongue to eat it. The heart she had already cut out of his breast and broiled and eat it. The daughter was seen eating the flesh of her father, which she smoked to preserve it for future use; the mother that of her children; the children that of their parents. The emaciated, wild, and ghastly appearance of the survivors added horror to the scene. Language cannot describe the awful change that a few weeks of dire suffering had wrought in the minds of the wretched beings. Those who, but one month before, would have shuddered at the thought of eating human flesh or of killing their relatives or companions to preserve their own lives, now looked upon the opportunity these acts afforded them of escaping the most dreadful of deaths as a Providential interference on their behalf! Calculations were coldly made, as they sat gloomily around

their fires in camps, for the next meals of human flesh! Various
expedients were devised to prevent the dreadful crime of murder,
but they finally resolved to kill those who had the least claims to
longer existence. . . . Some sunk into the arms of death cursing
God for their miserable fate, brought on by themselves, while the
last whisperings of others were prayers and praise to the Almighty.
After the few first days but one, the all-absorbing thought prevailed of self-preservation. The fountains of all natural affection
were dried up. Even the wild Indians, having visited their camp
with hostile intentions, pitied them, and instead of destroying
them, as they could have easily done, divided their own scanty
food with them. When the party sent to relieve them with ordinary food arrived, so barbarous had those wretches become that
they preferred the putrid human meat to that of cereals and animal food sent to relieve them. The day before relief arrived one
of the party took a child, four years old, to bed with him, and
eat it before morning. The next day another child was devoured
in the same manner.

Some clung to their property till death, which, it is thought, many of
them could have escaped, had they not clung to it with desperation.

Let us contrast the conduct of the Donner party with that of the
Murphy-Miller party, caught in the selfsame predicament, three years before, and the reader will see how superior the organization, how indomita-
ble the courage, and how confiding and trustful in God's mercies was the
character of the latter when compared with the former. Instead of cursing
and blaspheming God's providence, as happened by the majority, but not
all, in the Donner party, there was the most perfect resignation and confidence in the Divine assistance, that not one, for a moment, in the darkest
hour, despaired. Instead of plotting the murder of their fellowmen, as was
done in the instance of the two Indian guides, and most probably in
several other instances, all the men of the Murphy-Miller party went off
in search of supplies, exposing themselves to the danger of perishing of
want in order that those in the camp should not run short of provisions.
In a word, there was no discord, no idleness, no blasphemous reprouches
among the Murphy-Miller party, as was evidently the case among the
Donner immigrants. Hence, though situated in exactly the same circumstances, the former were saved and reached their destination in good

order, while the latter were demoralized and well-nigh entirely destroyed. After the Donner calamity became known and published it was feared that immigration to the country would be retarded at the recital of such unnatural occurrences. But no; for in less than a year after the discovery of gold in fabulous quantities in California was circulated on the wings of the press, from all parts of the United States, and, it may be said, from all over the civilized earth, a stream of immigration set in so continuous, so large, and so irresistible that not a hundred Donner Lake misfortunes could check its onward course. There were other accidents on a smaller scale than the Donner, many were massacred by Indians and disguised robbers, and along the whole route there were evidences of suffering, disease, murder, and treachery. But such was the hurry people were in to reach the "gold diggings" and to become rich that they scarce looked at the horrors before their eyes, so blind were they to every other pursuit, or dead to every feeling save that of getting gold.

From: Dr. Quigley, *The Irish Race* (San Francisco: A. Roman & Co., 1878).

· *Battles with Indians* ·

(English)

One of the most extraordinary individual experiences connected with the Steptoe retreat was that of Snickster and Williams. Some of the survivors question the correctness of this, and others vouch for its accuracy. It perhaps should not be set down as proven history. Snickster and Williams were riding one horse, and could not keep up with the main body. The Indians, therefore, overtook and seized them before they reached the Snake River. In a rage because of having been balked of their prey, the Indians determined to have some amusement out of the unfortunate pair, and told them to go into the river with their horse and try to swim across. Into the dangerous stream, two thousand feet wide, almost ice cold, and with a powerful current, they went. As soon as they were out a score of yards, the Indians began their fun by making a target of them. The horse was almost immediately killed. Williams was struck and sank. Snickster's arm was broken by a ball, but diving under the dead horse, and keeping himself on the farther side till somewhat out of range, and then boldly striking across the current, which foamed with Indian bullets, he reached the south side of the river and was drawn out, almost dead, by some of Timothy's Nez Percé Indians.

From: William Dennison Lyman, *The Columbia River* (New York and London: G. P. Putnam's Sons, 1909).

· *The Shattered Cabin* ·

(Unidentified)

A t the mouth of the Horseshoe Creek, lodged on a little rocky island, is a shattered cabin. We camp near this, and while we are engaged in preparing an appetizing meal of fish and venison, a grizzled prospector appears coming down the trail. After the manner of the mountains, he makes himself at home and camps with us for the night. In the course of his conversation he narrates many stories of this wild region and of the prospecting and hunting adventures that have happened in it. Finally he tells us the story of the lost cabin, a story that certainly contains all the elements of a romance. It appears that some years ago two young fellows from the East, cousins, had come to the Stehekin to prospect. The old man who told us the story was then the only prospector in the canyon, and he soon made friends with the two adventurers. From broken pieces of conversation and finally some confidences on the part of one of the boys, he learned something of their story. They had been bosom friends all their lives, but had fallen in love with the same girl. The poor girl, not knowing which she did like best, told them that the only thing was for both to leave her for two years, and at the end of the time she would decide in favor of the one that had showed himself the braver and more successful man. Each kept his destination a perfect secret, but to their astonishment, within a month after, they found each other in Spokane. They concluded that it was the appointment of fate, and so went together to the wild country of Chelan, to seek a fortune.

After they had been there a short time they found a mutual distrust springing up, and finally, by the advice of the old man, they agreed to separate. George was to stay below. He was the more sullen and selfish of the two, and it was due to him that they had fallen out. Harry was of a frank and generous nature, and when it became evident that they must part he insisted that he should help build a cabin for George. And the cabin that they built was the very one that we now saw lodged against the rocks. Harry went up the canyon toward the Skagit Pass, and there in the lonely grandeur of the glaciers he plied his pick and shovel.

A few months later there came a mighty chinook, the warm wind of the Cascades, which strips the peaks of snow within a day, transforms the creeks into raging torrents, and sends floods down every dry gulch. The night after the wind began to blow the old miner came to George's cabin, and in the intense darkness of the cloudy night they listened to the hurtling of the storm and the roar of the rapidly growing river. About midnight there came suddenly a succession of rifle shots near at hand, and in a few minutes a thunder and roar of water beyond anything that they had heard. Rushing out they saw that the water was already surrounding the cabin and they had to run in the darkness for their lives. Stumbling among the rocks they reached at last land high enough for safety, while the floods went tearing by. With the first light they looked out to see that the cabin had gone adrift, but sadder to tell, they soon found Harry—mangled, tortured, at the point of death—just strong enough to tell them that from his situation he had seen that a fearful flood was coming and he was trying to save George. But he had fallen in the darkness and crashed upon the rocks, and even in his suffering he had fired his rifle as a warning, hoping that it might be heard and save, and so it did. And the faithful fellow died content. "We tell the tale as it was told us." But the poor old wreck of a cabin took on something of a new significance as it leaned up against the rocks, while the restless river sobbed and frothed about it.

From: William Dennison Lyman, *The Columbia River* (New York and London: G. P. Putnam's Sons, 1909).

· The Adventure of Alexander Ross ·

(Unidentified)

Equally illustrative of the life of the fur traders is the account given by Alexander Ross of one of his many adventures in the Columbia country. In 1814 Ross went from Okanogan to Yakima to secure horses. With him were four other whites and three Indian women. The Yakima Valley was then as now a paradise of the Indians. There the tribes gathered by the thousands in the spring to dig camas, to race horses, and to gamble, as well as to form alliances and make plans for war.

When the little company of traders reached the encampment, they discovered to their astonishment that it was a veritable city. Six thousand men, women, and children, with ten thousand horses, and uncounted dogs and many shackled bears and wolves were strewn across the plain.

It was a dangerous situation for the traders, for it became plain to them that the Indians were unfriendly. But assuming an air of careless bravado, Ross proceeded to display his store of trinkets for the purpose of starting a traffic in horses. Assuming a very hilarious manner the Indians would seize and drive away the animals as fast as the white men got them. Then the Indians began to deprive them of clothes and food. Finally they made ready to seize their three women as slaves. Ross managed to have the women escape temporarily, but then the savages were worse than ever.

Matters reached a crisis when an obstreperous chief named Yaktana snatched a knife from the hands of one of the Canadians. A desperate struggle was just at the point of breaking out, which would inevitably have resulted in the death of all the white men, when a sudden intuition flashed through the quick mind of Ross, and rushing between the combatants he handed his own knife, a much more elegant one, to Yaktana, saying in a friendly tone, "This is a chief's knife. Take it and give back the other." There was an instant revulsion. Yaktana was so much flattered that he turned at once into a staunch supporter of the shrewd trader. Food was brought. The horses were restored. Equipment was provided. The three women were regained, and the company made their way without further trouble to Okanogan.

From: William Dennison Lyman, The Columbia River (New York and London: G. P. Putnam's Sons, 1909).

· The Legend of San Felipe ·

(Spanish)

At the first conquest the Spanish brought with them many padres (priests), who went out to all the pueblos. Many died and many were killed, and at last came the great rebellion (1680). When the Spanish made the second conquest they found but two priests left. One of these went very far away— *quiza* to Moqui—but the other made a church in Cochiti and stayed there. (The truth is, they found *no* survivors, though there is an unconfirmed Spanish story that one priest was left alive at Moqui.) The Indians of the northern pueblos were very much enemies of the Spanish, and most of all the people of Cochiti, San Ildefonso, and Santo Domingo were angry with them. In a little while the *principales* of those pueblos held a *junta* in Cochiti, and made it up to kill the padre and drive out the Spanish. The sacristan of Cochiti was a good Christian, and when he heard this he went running by night to the convent and told the padre, "Padre, I am your friend. They are making to kill you, but I will save you if I can. But you must go immediately. I will go with you as far as I can and get home before day, for they will kill me if they know."

So the sacristan carried the padre across the river on his back, and then they took the *camino real* (highway) past Santo Domingo, and where Algodones now is. Here the sacristan said, "I go no farther. This is the road, and you must save yourself." It was already near day, and the padre saw he must hide. There was a little island on the river with cottonwoods very thick on it, and he went to hide there until another night.

Now, by the grace of God, on that very day the pueblo of San Felipe was to make a great hunt; and already before the sun had come the sentinels were going to all the high places to watch for game, and one was on the top of the mesa just below that island. When it grew more day, he saw something black moving among the cottonwoods, and thought, "Good luck! For already I see a bear!" but in truth it was the padre getting a drink. The sentinel made his hunt signal, and in a very little all the hunters were around the island. When they found it was no bear, but the padre from Cochiti, they were astonished, but he told them all that had happened. Then at once the *principales* held council on the island; and when all had spoken, they said, "We will save him and take him to our pueblo." Then they took off his black robes and put upon him the shirt and *calzoncillos* and moccasins of one of the Indians, and painted his face and hands. But when they were coming to the town they met many of the Cochiteños hunting for him and asking, "Have you met the priest?" They said "No, we have not met him"; but even then one of the Cochiteños recognized him in his paint, and they demanded him with injurious words. Refusing, there was a great fight, which lasted even to the pueblo, but they of San Felipe came safely inside with the padre. Then the Cochiteños went away for help, and next day came again with many more of their own pueblo and of Santo Domingo, surrounding the town and wounding some. So, as the enemy were many, the people of San Felipe retreated to the top of the mesa, and made a fort there. The others besieged them for many days, and soon the water and the food which they had carried up with them began to be very little; and then the water was all gone. And when they knew no more how to live without water, the old men made a *junta* and brought the padre to it. When he had heard all, he hunted for paper; and at last he found a very little piece in his wallet. Upon this he made a writing with charcoal, and told the sacristan to put the paper in a certain spot, with the writing upward, and stones on it that it might not blow away. Then he made prayer for three days, night and day; and afterward sent the sacristan to bring the paper again. And in truth there was now also a writing on the other side. Who wrote it? *Quien sabe?* But we think the saints. When he had read the new writing, he told the sacristan to bring him a piece of topaz (volcanic glass), and this he broke upon a rock till it was sharp like a knife. And when the people had brought all their *tinajas* and gourds, he made his arm bare and cut it with the stone knife, and held it stretched out; and from the wound ran streams of water, the same as a clear river, and filled all the vessels. When all were full it ceased to run; and all the people fell down and gave thanks to God. A great while the enemy remained, but always when the water jars were empty, the padre filled them again with pure water from his arm, till at last the Cochiteños were tired and went away. Then the people came down again to the pueblo, taking the padre in great honor, and they were in peace, for after that there was no more war. But to this day we make a sacred *fiesta* for the Day of the Padre; and God has been very good to us for that, more than to any of the pueblos that killed their priests. No, we do not know his name. It is very long ago, and that has been lost.

From: Charles F. Lummis, *A New Mexico David* (New York: Charles Scribner's Sons, 1905).

· Stories of Father Junipero ·

(Spanish)

The Founding of San Diego

I have spoken of San Diego as one of the great new cities, and great it is, but altogether new it certainly is not, for it was founded by a Spanish missionary, known as Father Junipero, more than one hundred years ago.

These old Spanish missionaries were great men in their day; brave, patient, and very self-sacrificing in their attempts to settle the wild countries and civilize the Indians.

This Father Junipero walked all the way from Mexico City to San Diego, although he was more than fifty years old; and finally, after he had spent nearly a quarter of a century in founding missions up and down the coast of California, he walked all the way back to Mexico, where he died.

When it is added that he was a lame man, that he was more than threescore and ten years of age, and that he traveled all the distance on this last journey on foot and alone, with neither arms nor provisions, trusting himself entirely to Providence, one can hardly fail to remember his name and speak it with respect.

From: Joaquin Miller, *True Bear Stories* (Chicago and New York: Rand McNally & Co., 1900).

Father Junipero's Lodging

Father Junipero, founder of the California missions, was on one of his errands of inspection and encouragement. Friar Palou, of the Franciscans, was his companion, and they were plodding over the unpathed country toward Monterey, a full day's distance from the settlements, when night came upon them. The air was chill, there was no shelter, but their health was sound and their courage warm.

"Well, brother," said the padre, "we can go no farther tonight. God is good. He will not let us come to harm. We have a loaf for supper and a cloak for a bed. The stars are coming out and the snakes are going in. We shall sleep in peace."

"We shall sleep in peace, brother," replied Palou. "Let us say our prayers. For I am heavy with the day's journey."

As if the flowerbells had tolled for vespers, the two knelt on the hillside and offered up their thanks and their petitions, asking that heaven would shelter them through the dark hours by its loving kindness and bless their work of spreading the gospel. As they arose from their knees the keen eye of Father Junipero caught a twinkle of light a half mile ahead, and he gave a little cry of surprise. "It must be white men," he said, for it is not the red light of an Indian fire. Yet who would have thought of finding our people in this wilderness?"

Friar Palou held aloof, and his face was pale. "It is not our people," he said. "There is no house or cabin all the way from San Juan to Monterey. Alas! Alas! It is the Devil who seeks us, far from our churches. He tempts us with a hope of shelter when there is none."

"Be of better faith. We will go forward. Surely a house may have been built here since we last crossed this country."

"If your faith is strong I will follow, though I shall keep tight hold on my crucifix, and constantly repeat the Virgin's name."

A walk of a few minutes brought them to the light. It was shining, white and calm, from the window of a small, neat, adobe house, all set about with flowers. The door stood open, and the sturdy figure of a man was dark against the luminous interior as he peered into the night. When the travelers had come in sight he showed no surprise; on the contrary, he stepped from the doorway with a grave courtesy, motioned them to enter, and said: "Good friends, you are wayworn and hungry. Be pleased to become our guest. You are welcome."

With hearty thanks for this unexpected hospitality the missionaries walked into the plain but clean, sweet-smelling room. It was simply furnished and everything was distinct in a soft yet brilliant light of candles. A saintly faced, lovely lady greeted them and motioned them to places at a table where a supper of bread, herbs, and wine had been prepared, and a gentle, sunny-haired boy held his mother's hand, leaned his rosy cheek against her, and smiled at them. The grave, kindly man who had made them welcome—he with the brown face and hands, the simple dress and honest way of an artisan—served the food and drink, and all spoke of the work on which the fathers were traveling. It seemed to them as if on earth there could be no other home like this, so sweet and gracious were their hosts, so low and musical their voices, so pure the air and feeling of the place. When the repast was ended they would have begged to rest on straw outside the house; but before they had put this request into words an inner door had been thrown open and they were ushered into a white chamber holding two beds, warmly though daintily covered, and with pleasant "good nights" the family withdrew, leaving the fathers to their rest.

"We spoke truly when we said we should sleep in peace," quoth Palou.

"It is as if God had turned our steps here. Brother, there is such a peace in my soul as I have never felt before. It is well with the world, for heaven is kind to men."

Tired though they were, they prayed long and earnestly before they slept. In the morning, before day had broken, they awoke without a call, were bidden to another simple meal, and presently resumed their journey, after many thanks to the man, the woman, and the child for their goodness. They solemnly invoked the blessing of God on all three, and bowed low and stood awhile in silence when the family asked a blessing on them—silent because they were strangely moved and thrilled.

They had been on their way not many minutes when they encountered a muleteer of the country, who looked at them curiously. "Good day to your reverences," he cried. "You look as happy and well fed and freshened with sleep as if you had breakfasted with his excellency the governor and had lain on goose feathers all night."

"We have fared notably," said Palou, "for we stopped at the house yonder, and so kind a family can be found nowhere else."

"At what house, pray? There is no house for miles and miles. Even the savages come into this part of the land but seldom."

Said Father Junipero, "It is plain that you, like ourselves, have not been here for some time. The house we have just left is yonder, by those trees—or—that is——— Why! Look, brother! It is gone."

The dawn was whitening, and the morning star threw down one long beam on the place where that house had been; a beam such as fell from the star of Bethlehem, so that a silver mist brooded upon the site.

"Kneel!" commanded Junipero. "A miracle has been done. Now I know that the cottage was built by angels, and they who served us were Joseph, Mary, and Jesus. God smiles upon our work. From this hour we dedicate ourselves to it with new vigor and a firmer faith."

From: Charles M. Skinner, *American Myths & Legends*, vol. 2 (Philadelphia and London: J. B. Lippincott Co., 1903).

CHAPTER 21

Pirates and Buried Treasure

· *Pirate Joe* ·

(Spanish)

Pirates? Why of course we have had pirates!" said old Uncle Poncho, as the young boys gathered about him, jangling among themselves, some claiming that California had never had a real pirate, and others that there had been plenty of them. Uncle Poncho settled it, for Uncle Poncho's word was law. He continued: "We have had plenty of pirates, and good ones too, for that matter. The first one, you know, was Sir Francis Drake with his *Golden Hind* that I told you boys about the other day. We cannot claim him altogether, for he came here before our missions were established, and consequently did little harm to us; but later there was one fine, brave, sassy fellow that came here to Monterey first, and then followed down the coast to San Juan Capistrano, and then disappeared forever. Do you want me to tell you about him and Pirate Joe? If you do, you have all got to be mighty still."

"Oh, yes, Uncle, we'll be pious if you say so, if you'll just keep a-talking about the pirates."

The old man was in his element. He knew every bit of history, romance, fable, and fiction told of this glorious Western state, and if he sometimes mixed the knowledge, it was due to the nature of the audience.

"Well, boys, this pirate's name was Buchar."

"Why, I thought you said it was Joe?" broke in one of the fellows.

"Now, see here, young man, I want no more of that. Your job is to listen, and I'll come to the 'Joe' part.

"As I said before, this man's name was Buchar; he was a Frenchman, and you spell it B-o-u-c-h-a-r-d," slowly spelt out the old man. "He came from that South American province, Buenos Aires, and the ruler had given him a letter of marque, that is, a regular permit to poach on other countries' commerce or ships at sea.

"It was on the afternoon of November 20, 1818, that a sentinel stationed off Point Pinos out there," waving his hand toward the point, "reported two vessels in sight headed for Monterey. One was a little thing, but the other one was big, and black as thunder. The sentinel called her *'frigata negra'* (black frigate), and the other one *'frigata chica'* (little frigate). The Spaniards had been looking a month for these pirates, and there had been so many cries of 'Wolf, wolf, wolf!' that Governor Sola hardly knew whether to prepare the guns or not.

"But when the sentinel announced that the one ship, instead of looking like a great white swan and floating a well-known flag, came like a great black hawk and floated an unknown banner, there was no further time lost. Sola sent his men, on the run, under Ensigns Manuel Gomez and José Estrada, down to the shore battery; while he saw that the women and children were hustled off at once into the interior. They were sent to the Mission of Soledad with all the provisions they could gather together.

"Like hawks of unrest, the two vessels sailed around all day, just out of hailing distance; and when night closed in good and dark, about eleven o'clock, the *'chica'* came quietly pushing her nose right into the harbor and cast anchor. Our men were on watch, and as soon as they found she was settled, they hailed her. Making a trumpet of his hands, one of our men shouted, 'Ship ahoy! What ship is that, and where do you hail from?' "

Uncle Poncho suited the action to the words, and every boy sprang to his feet at the terrible shout he gave.

"And will you believe me? The impudent, daring devils sent back an answer in English: 'We can't understand.'

"Our men repeated the inquiry, adding the order to send a boat ashore with the ship's papers. But the stranger said that they would attend to all formalities in the morning.

"Now, as for the ships, they proved in the morning to be *La Gentila*—that was the *'frigata negra'*—and the *Santa Rosa Libertad*—the *'frigata chica.'* Both were in command of Captain Hippolyte Bouchard, the bucca-neer. The black vessel carried thirty-eight heavy guns and two *violentes,* or light howitzers; the little one carried twenty-six guns, and her officer was Lieutenant Pedro Condé; together their force of men was two hundred and eighty-five—men of all nations, colors, and kinds. Now, there are some later so-called historians who say there were three hundred and fifty men on board, but two hundred and eighty-five is enough for me, and every one of them had two wives. I'll tell you about them later. So you can see, boys, what big ships they must have been to carry all those people, and the tons and tons of gold and silver and jewels and valuable stuff that the pirates got from every ship they boarded and every town they looted."

The old man loved to make the stories big and watch the effect upon his listeners.

"At the first streak of light on the following morning the saucy little beggar of a *Libertad* began dropping balls right down in Monterey's lap, and that was the only formality that she sent in the morning in reply to the questions of the night before, as to who she was, and where she came from. The unfriendly salute was returned by the Spanish sending a terrific fire of six- and eight-pounders straight at the two vessels, which now lay close together and very close in. The fire continued on both sides for about two hours, when six boatloads of men were seen to go from the little frigate out to the black one; and that was evidence that we had done mighty good work with our balls on the *Santa Rosa,* for she sent up a white flag and begged for suspension of firing.

"The Spaniards told them to send an officer ashore at once; and they replied that the officer had gone over to *La Gentila.* But this time our people would not stand any foolishness, but replied, 'Send a responsible officer at once, or firing will be resumed.'

"That brought a boat with three men; one was the second officer, Joseph Chapman, and the other two were black men—one named Fisher, and the other a native of Buenos Aires, without a name. The breakers were high, and the sea rough; and when near shore the boat capsized, and the two Negroes struck back toward the ship, but could not make it, the nameless native being drowned.

"A lot of *vaqueros* dashed down to the water and began lassoing the other two struggling men. The Negro was easy work and soon lay high and dry on the sand; but when the lasso fell over Joe Chapman's neck, he just trod water and pulled that horse and rider clean into the surf, and the fellow had to hollo for assistance; another *vaquero* landed a *reata* over Joe's shoulders just as he had cleared himself of the first one, and he just caught that lasso and pulled the man and horse right into the water; but a third *vaquero* was quicker, and landed his lasso before Joe got rid of the second one, and so together the two *vaqueros* hauled the big fellow onto the shore limp as a rag.

"Now, boys, there is a man named Foster that says the lassoing business occurred at the Ortega rancho, down near Santa Barbara; and I'm inclined to believe him, for he knows a great deal more about Spanish events as they occurred than the Americans that came after him and have to get their facts from such as he.

"When Pirate Joe recovered sufficiently he began a long series of excuses and lies, as Governor Sola called them, and for his pains was promptly locked up in the guardhouse. When Bouchard saw his representatives marched off to the guardhouse, he sailed his big, black ship right down upon the little town and demanded its surrender.

"But Sola stoutly refused to surrender, and answered that the Spaniards would fight till the last drop of blood was shed, and never give up.

"Matters remained that way during the day and next night. All night it drizzled and rained; and at about eight o'clock the following morning, the black frigate was seen to send out nine boats loaded down with men and arms; four of them carried small cannon, and they all headed straight for Point Potreros. Sola sent his twenty-five men down to the shore to prevent their landing, but as the ship and the fort had both recommenced firing, the situation was full of danger for the few men on shore, and Governor Sola ordered Estrada to spike the battery guns and retreat with all the men to the presidio; for it was evident that so small a garrison as was stationed at Monterey could not withstand the attack of three or four hundred men."

"But, Uncle Poncho, you said there were but two hundred and eighty-five, and now you say three or four hundred," piped up one of the younger boys.

"Well," acknowledged the storyteller, "Governor Sola said in his report that there were three or four hundred when he began to retreat, and I— and I don't know just who is right; but when there is a lot of people after you they look more than if they are just on a ship out in the water." And all were satisfied with the explanation.

"The pirates sacked the presidio, carried off two eight-pound guns, and spiked all the others. Then they looted all the houses nearby and killed all the cattle that they wanted.

"While two of the pirates were looting General Castro's father's property, they came suddenly upon a pretty young girl who was trying to catch a horse. When she saw them she fell upon her knees and prayed them to do her no harm. They asked her name and why she was there alone. She explained that her mother had left a most cherished book at the home when they departed so hastily, and that she had returned for it; and as proof she showed the book—it was a prayer book.

"One of the men laughed and said she was a good girl, and sent the other man to catch her horse. As she knelt there at the door of her own deserted home, the man came to her, and, calling her Señorita Castro, for such she was, kissed her on the forehead, and when the other men brought the horse he helped her to mount. Then he swore a terrible oath and said, 'My girl, you are more brave than some of your people were on the beach when we landed. You shall go back. Ride fast! for there are others of Bouchard's men who would not treat you so well. My name is Pedro Condé; and I already have two wives on board my ship, or I would have taken you there.'

"You can imagine that Señorita Castro rode like the wind to the next rancho, for that last sentence nearly scared her to death."

"I wouldn't 'a been afraid," said one of the small boys. "I would have asked to go with him; but then she was only a girl."

Poncho continued his story:

"The pirates got about five thousand dollars' worth of plunder and then set fire to the town and departed for Santa Barbara. On the way they stopped at the beautiful old rancho of the Ortegas, where Stephen C. Foster says Pirate Joe was lassoed, and the pretty Señorita Guadalupe begged for his life and offered to give surety for his good behavior. 'He is such a handsome, strong señor, it would be a pity to kill so powerful a man,' pleaded the charming daughter of Ortega. And so it came that Pirate Joe was allowed to live, and he made good; he turned out to be the handiest man in all California.

"He was known as 'José el Ingles,' for Señorita Ortega didn't like to hear him called 'Pirate Joe'; but in reality he was not an Englishman, but was born in Massachusetts, and he spoke the English language. Like all really first-class pirates, he could speak lots of different languages; he spoke

French and Spanish and English, and quickly learned a lot of Indian, so that when he gave an order it was something like this: 'Mon Dieu! *ventura! vamos! trae los bueyes* go down to the playa and come as quick as you can *puede, mite ma.*' And Father Sanchez said that Joe could get more work out of the Indians in his unintelligible tongue than all the majordomos put together.

"When the pirate ship lost Joe it lost a good man, and California gained a better one; for the longer Joe stayed here the better he got.

"The Ortega rancho was one of the largest places in California—it appeared like a small mission—and when the pirates landed at Refugio and marched up to attack the place, they expected strong resistance; but instead of that, the beautiful old home was deserted. The pirates looted it and then burned it.

"What was worse, Bouchard deliberately cut the throats of three fine stallions imported by Señor Ortega from Mexico. Perhaps that was in revenge for the Spaniards having captured three of the pirates. There is no telling how they rate those men. The captives gave their names as Lieutenant William Taylor of Boston, Martin Romero of Paraguay, and a Negro who called himself Matéo José Pascual.

"Another historian tells us that, when Bouchard and eighty of his men were climbing the steep *cuesta de Santa Inés*, Carrillo drove them back by rolling great heavy stones down upon them, killing five and severely wounding two more. I am awfully glad if he did," continued the old man, "for the Spaniards seemed to be getting the worst of it, so far.

"The pirate ships stopped at Santa Barbara and gave her such a good scare that it cheated her out of proper growth. Here Bouchard offered to exchange prisoners, and when Guerra finally consented, in the name of humanity, to do so, what do you think, boys?—the only prisoner Bouchard had taken in all that time was one good-for-nothing, drunken man, named Molina, of Monterey, whom everybody was glad to be rid of; and we had to give back the one from Boston, the one from Paraguay, and the Negro, Pascual.

"Santa Barbara was known to be a strongly fortified presidio, and the pirates were glad enough to leave her alone. They glanced at San Pedro, but saw nothing there but a few caches of hides; so they sailed on to the grand old mission of San Juan Capistrano. But the Padres were ready for them there; they had sent all the sacred vessels and church ornaments, carefully packed in boxes, away up in the hills to Pala. They had driven the stock far inland and hidden all things of value. When the pirates landed there was nothing for them. The women and children had fled to distant ranchos, and the mission was quite a heap of ruins from the earthquake of 1812, which you remember about; and so the place had an air of desolation that checked the pirates. The only thing they could find was the Padres' storehouse of good old wines. They drank like pirates, and then boarded their vessels and sailed away, and were never heard from again. That's the story of our pirates," concluded Uncle Poncho.

"But about Pirate Joe?" respectfully asked the fellow who had first interrupted the old man.

"Oh, yes, you want to know some more about him, do you? Well, he became one of our most respectable citizens. He could do anything, from shoeing a kicking mule to completing a fine piece of surgery. He was a carpenter, a blacksmith, a shipbuilder, a doctor, and he could mend drums splendidly. For the most part he lived at Mission San Gabriel and was an especial favorite of Father Sanchez. He built a wonderful gristmill there, which is known as 'El Molino Viéjo' today, and he built another one at Santa Inés. Besides that, he helped get out all the timbers for the Church of Our Lady of the Angels."

"And did he marry the beautiful señorita?" asked another.

"Yes, he did. In 1822, he was duly baptized in the little Mission Church of San Buenaventura and named 'José Juan Chapman'; the same year he and the beautiful Señorita Guadalupe Ortega were married in the chapel of Santa Inés and later went to live at Los Angeles. But the most wonderful thing he ever did was in 1831: He entirely constructed a sixty-ton schooner at San Gabriel, fitting each piece to its proper place, and then had it carted down to San Pedro, where it was put together. And every board fitted just exactly. It was launched amid great festivities, and christened *Guadalupe*.

"Senor José Juan lived until 1849, and died an honored man. He was a great pirate."

From: A. S. C. Forbes, *Mission Tales in the Days of the Dons* (London: A. C. McClurg & Co., 1909).

CHAPTER 22

Superstitions

· *Superstitions on Death* ·

(Spanish)

I shall now give a brief list of a few popular superstitions about the dead:

1. They (i.e., ghosts) appear to good people only, never to the wicked.
2. If a person dies on a beautiful day, he has gone to heaven; if on a stormy day, he goes to hell.
3. A person who crosses a funeral procession will die within the year following.
4. If one is in continual dread of someone who has died, or one whose ghost has been seen, it is sufficient to say to him, "Go to h——," and one is troubled no more.
5. If two persons call for God's judgment on any dispute or quarrel, they die at the same time.
6. If one does not desire to be molested by the ghost of a dead person, it is sufficient to visit the dead body and touch its toes. There will be no apparitions and no fear whatever.
7. If the vice or custom of some dead person is commented upon, or even barely mentioned, it is necessary to offer up a prayer for him; otherwise he will come at night and pull the toes of those who ridicule him.
8. Ghosts speak to those to whom they appear.

9. Persons who see a ghost or spirit, forever lose their senses.

10. If a person dies and leaves money hidden, he returns to disclose the secret to one of his family.

11. If anyone chews gum in bed, he is masticating the bones of the dead.

12. If a person spills salt, any quantity whatsoever, he has to come back after death to pick it all up with his eyelids.

13. To be strong and have no fear of the dead, it is necessary to pray to St. Gertrude.

14. God is not pleased to hear people speak of the dead. If the dead are laughed at, evil may follow.

15. When a candle is burning to the end, someone is dying.

From: Aurelio M. Espinosa, "New-Mexican Spanish Folk-Lore," *Journal of American Folk-Lore* 23 (1910): 395–418.

· Dwarfs ·

(Spanish)

Dwarfs (*los duendes*) are individuals of small stature, who frighten the lazy, the wicked, and in particular the filthy. The New Mexican idea about dwarfs is embraced in the above statement. The people express much uncertainty about the origin, whereabouts, and doings of dwarfs. A young lady from Santa Fe, however, seemed to have some definite ideas about their life. She pictured them as living together in a certain lonely place, where they inhabited underground houses, went out secretly to steal provisions and clothing, especially at night, and often even went to the cities to buy provisions. In the caves they prospered and lived with their families. Most of the people, however, profess ignorance about dwarfs. They have only the general idea of their being evil spirits that terrorize the wicked, lazy, or filthy, as I have already stated.

The following story is one well known: A family once moved from one place to another, and, on arriving at the new house, the mother was looking for the broom to sweep. Her daughter, a lazy and careless girl, had forgotten it in the old home. Presently a dwarf appeared, descending slowly from the roof with the broom in his hand, and, presenting it to the lady, he said, "Here it is!"

A confused idea also exists in some localities with respect to the dwarf as a wandering soul. I have not been able to obtain any definite information on this point, but the idea of a dwarf being a suffering soul from purgatory is found in modern Spanish literature.

From: Aurelio M. Espinosa, "New-Mexican Spanish Folk-Lore," *Journal of American Folk-Lore* 23 (1910): 395–418.

· Axolotl ·

(Mexican)

The most curious and incomprehensible superstition of the Mexican people, and one which has the widest dissemination, concerns the curious lizard called the *axolotl,* a name by which it was known to the Aztecs, although I do not feel prepared to say that they had the superstition concerning it.

The *axolotl* frequents damp, slimy places, near pools or tanks of water, and all kinds of refuse ("*basura*").

It will enter the person of a woman, at certain times, and will remain just as long as would a human fetus.

Young girls, at their first change of life, are especially exposed, and will manifest all the symptoms of pregnancy.

It is within the limits of probability, although I am not sufficiently posted in medical matters to assert that such is the case, that a badly nourished girl would be susceptible to cold, rheumatism, and dropsy at such a critical moment in her life, and that imagination could supply any features that might be lacking to make the romance complete. There are several remedies: One calls for a liberal fomentation with hot goat's milk; and in the other, a young man appears to marry the girl. Often when women were bathing in the waters of the Rio Grande itself, or in some of the great "*acequias,*" mischievous boys would yell "*Axolotl!*" and cause a scampering of all the bathers.

From: John G. Bourke, "Popular Medicine, Customs, and Superstitions of the Rio Grande," *Journal of American Folk-Lore* 7 (1894): 119–46

· *The Evil Eye* ·

(Mexican)

The evil eye, or blight—*mal ojo*, meaning bad eye, or simply *ojo*—is a spell cast upon children by people who look at them steadily, and generally speak kindly to them. If you can find the man who has "*echado el ojo*" upon a child, make him fill his mouth with water and eject it into the child's mouth. The child will recover at once.

If you cannot find out who has cast the "*ojo*" on a child, take the herb called "*Yerba de Cristo*," boil it in water, and wash the infant from head to foot with the decoction. Then take a raw egg, and make with it, while in the shell, the sign of the cross three times on the baby's breast, in the name of the Father, Son, and Holy Ghost. Break the egg, throw away the shell, put both yolk and white on a plate under the child's cradle. The egg will cook, the child will get well, and the villain who cast the evil eye will be afflicted with bleary eyes!

United States Commissioner Walter Downs told me that he had seen a horse which the Mexicans asserted had been hurt by the "*ojo*" (evil eye). The man accused of casting the spell admitted his guilt, but said that he would cure the animal at once. He filled his mouth with water, spat upon the horse's neck, and rubbed and patted the place until dry.

Mr. Downs said that the horse got well, which was, of course, all the better for the reputation of the charlatan.

Maria Antonia confirmed all that I had learned about the method of cure by having the culprit eject water from his own mouth into that of the child.

She said too that any "*Juez*" in the Rio Grande Valley would commit a man accused of such a crime as casting the evil eye; but since so many "Americanos" were coming down to that country, some of the judges thought it to be more prudent to enter a charge of being a tramp, disorderly conduct, or something else of that general character.

From: John G. Bourke, "Popular Medicine, Customs, and Superstitions of the Rio Grande," *Journal of American Folk-Lore* 7 (1894): 119–46.

CHAPTER 23

Portents, Charms, and Remedies

· *Portents on Dreams* ·

(Spanish)

Most of the superstitions concerning sleep are about children. Some are as follows:

1. When children smile or laugh in their sleep, they see angels or are conversing with their guardian angel.
2. A sleeping child must not be caressed, because it causes him to die (his bile bursts).
3. If children fall asleep immediately after a violent fall or accident of any kind, they die.
4. If little girls play with their dolls in bed, or sleep with them, the Devil (*el mashishi*) appears to them in their sleep.
5. If children play with fire, they urinate while sleeping.
6. If one places the right hand over the heart of a person who is sleeping, the latter talks in his or her sleep and reveals all his or her secrets.

The superstitions and beliefs concerning dreams are many and various. Some dreams are interpreted literally, others not. Deaths, illness, or other misfortunes are announced by dreams.

1. When one is desirous of having a dream, it is sufficient to place one's shoes or stockings near the pillow, and a dream is sure to come.
2. If a person dreams that a certain one has died, it means that a friend or relative is dying or will die, but not the one dreamed about.
3. If one dreams of blood, a terrible misfortune is about to happen.
4. If one dreams that one's teeth are falling, a relative has died.
5. If one dreams of lean meat, a child will soon die.
6. If one dreams of fat meat, an old person will soon die.
7. If one dreams of a funeral, a wedding will soon follow.
8. If one dreams of a wedding, death is announced.
9. If one dreams of wealth, poverty will come.
10. If one dreams of a black cat or black dog, an enemy is approaching.

From: Aurelio M. Espinosa, "New-Mexican Spanish Folk-Lore," *Journal of American Folk-Lore* 23 (1910): 395–418.

· Remedies from New Mexico ·

(Spanish)

Here we are concerned with the popular superstitious remedies, which are evidently based on mere ignorant superstition. The following is a brief list of some of them:

1. *For tuberculosis.*—The milk of the she-ass or the flesh of the bitch.
2. *For constipation in children.*—An egg is broken against their stomach.
3. *For the toothache.*—Human excretion, or that of a hen.
4. *For any female disease.*—Ashes and urine are mixed together with garlic, and this is applied to all parts of the body by making crosses with it.
5. *For violent fever.*—The windows and doors are closed, and the patient is well wrapped.
6. *For chapped hands.*—They are washed with the urine of a male child.
7. *For wounds or cuts.*—They are carefully bandaged with rags of men's clothing.

8. *To stop bleeding of the nose.*—A wet key or coin is pressed to the forehead.

9. *For warts.*—One takes a small rag and makes a knot in it. Then one goes to a roadcrossing and throws it away. The first person who happens to pass by will grow a wart, and the other one loses it.

10. *For sunstroke.*—A glass of water is placed on the patient's head. When the water boils, the ailment is gone.

11. *For hordeolum.*—The penis of a baby is rubbed against the eye.

12. *To make hair grow.*—It is cut during full moon.

13. *For dog bites.*—Burn the bite with hair taken from the dog's snout.

14. *To cut the umbilical cord.*—An egg is buried in the wall on the 2nd of February (the day of Our Lady of Candelaria).

15. *For stench in the mouth.*—The patient must cross the river thrice before sunrise, and the gums are burned with three blue stones.

16. *For hectic children.*—The children are wrapped up for a while with a cow's stomach.

17. *For any pain in the eye.*—A warm raisin is put in the ear.

18. *For pain in the bile.*—The patient should be dressed in a red calico garb.

19. *For heart trouble.*—The drinking of water mixed with ants or lice.

20. *To facilitate the afterbirth.*—The patient drinks water boiled with a man's old hat, or blows thrice into the hollow of her hand.

21. *For colds.*—Water is warmed with three large blue stones, and the patient is bathed with it.

22. *When horses have the colic,* they are wrapped with the skirts of a woman who has just given birth to a male child.

23. *For cramps.*—Human excretion.

24. *For insanity.*—The insane are cured by swallowing the heart of a crow that has just been killed. The heart of the crow must still be warm.

25. *For hiccough.*—The person affected should drink nine draughts of water without breathing.

26. *For tonsilitis.*—The patient's fingers are pulled until they crack.

From: Aurelio M. Espinosa, "New-Mexican Spanish Folk-Lore," *Journal of American Folk-Lore* 23 (1910): 395–418.

· Remedy for El Ojo ·

(Spanish)

El ojo is an illness, a serious fever, which people say is caused by excessive affection towards children. If a woman sees a child and caresses it much, she may, after looking at it, if the child also sees her, make it seriously ill, a violent fever following. This superstition is called *hacer ojo* (to have a secret and mysterious influence by winking; illness following on the part of the child). No one is to blame for this mysterious influence, since it happens without the knowledge of anyone. Death is sure to follow, if a remedy is not applied. The remedies are the following. The woman who has caused the harm (*la que le hizo ojo al niño*) takes the child in her arms; then, taking water in her mouth, she gives the child to drink with her mouth. The child is then put to sweat either in bed or under the woman's arm, and it soon recovers. A second remedy is to take the sweepings from the four corners of a room, boil them in water, and then take a little of this water in the mouth and spit it upon the child's face. There is a third remedy; but this is one that should be applied only in case the child has a violent fever, and when it is not certain whether or not it is *el ojo*. The child is well wrapped up and put to bed. An egg is emptied out on a plate and placed on a chair near the head of the bed where the child is sleeping. If the child has *el ojo*, an eye will soon appear formed on the egg, and the child will quickly recover.

When a friend visits, and a little child is present who is very pretty and attractive, the visitor, through fear of causing *el ojo*, pays no attention to the child, and says to it, "*Quñate de aquí, Dios te guarde!*" ("Go away, and may God help you!") Strings of coral are also placed about children's necks, so that they may be safe from *el ojo*.

From: Aurelio M. Espinosa, "New-Mexican Spanish Folk-Lore," *Journal of American Folk-Lore* 23 (1910): 395–418.

CHAPTER 24

The Supernatural

· Witches and Witchcraft ·

(Various)

Los Brujos
(Spanish)

Los brujos ó brujas are mischievous individuals who practice evil on their neighbors, often for little or no cause. Generally, however, it is on their enemies that witches practice the evil doings which they are able to perform. No one is born a witch. Witchcraft is a science, a kind of learning which may be learned from other witches. Anyone who is a witch can give his or her powers to another one; though an individual, by practicing evil, may, on agreement with the Devil, become a witch. New Mexicans speak of a witch as being "in agreement with the Devil" (*pactado con el diablo* or *patau con el diablo*).

Belief in witchcraft of one sort or another is found among practically all primitive peoples, and has survived in all countries until comparatively recent times. In New Mexico this belief is still widespread. People, young and old, have a terrible superstitious fear of witches and their evil doings. Numerous stories cling around their beliefs, and these are often confused and sometimes even contradictory. The means of doing harm which the witches have at their disposal are various, but in practically all their methods they bring into play their power of being transformed into any animal whatsoever. A lady once visited with a lady friend whom she did not know to be a witch. Both retired in the evening and went to sleep in the same bed. About midnight (the hour when witches go forth from their homes to practice mischief and take revenge on their enemies) the visitor saw her friend get up from the bed and light a candle. Presently she produced a large dish, placed it on a table, pulled out both of her eyes, and, putting them in the dish, flew out through the chimney, riding on a broomstick. The visitor could no longer stay in the house of the witch, but dressed in haste and ran to her home.

The owl, called in New Mexico *tecolote*, is very much feared, and is supposed to be the animal whose form the witches prefer to take. The hoot of the owl is an evil omen; and the continuous presence of an owl at nightfall near any house is a sure sign that witches are approaching with evil intentions, or that some evil is about to visit the house.

In a certain village in northern New Mexico, which was considered a favorite rendezvous for witches, a certain house had been surrounded for various nights by owls and foxes (the fox is another animal whose form witches like to take). Fearing harm from witches, since the hooting of the owls and the howling of the foxes had become almost insufferable, men went out to meet them with bows and arrows. The owls and foxes disappeared in all directions, with the exception of one old fox, which had been wounded near the heart by an arrow. No one dared to approach the wounded fox, however; and the next morning it was discovered that an old lady, a witch, living nearby, was in her deathbed, with an arrow wound near the heart.

I have never heard of the soul of the person leaving the body and entering into the animal in question, the body remaining lifeless until the retransformation takes place, as is the belief in Chili. In New Mexico the general belief is that complete transformation of body and soul takes place at will; and in case of no transformation, the witch usually leaves the eyes behind.

On another occasion a man was riding on a fast horse and saw a fox. He started in pursuit; and after a long chase, when the fox was very tired and was already dragging its tongue along the ground, a sudden transformation took place. At a sharp turn of the road the fox stopped, and the rider did the same. To his amazement, he at once perceived a gray-haired woman sitting on a stone and panting in a terrible manner. Recognizing in her an old woman who was his neighbor, and whom he had suspected of being a witch, he went his way and troubled her no more.

A witch may have a person under the influence of some evil, illness, or even vice, at will. The unfortunate individual who is beset by witches is also pursued and molested by devils and other evil spirits who help the witches. The general name for any evil or harm caused by a witch is, in New Mexico, *maleficio* (spell, enchantment, harm), and the verb is *maleficiar* (to do harm, to bewitch). *Estar maleficiau* (to be under the spell or influence of a witch) is the greatest of evils, and hard to overcome. A witch, however, may be compelled by physical torture to raise the spell or cease doing harm; but this method is not advisable, since sooner or later the witch will again take revenge. In some instances, it is said, innocent old women have been cruelly tortured in attempting to force them to cure imaginary or other wrongs of which they were accused. On one occasion a witch was roped and dragged until she restored health to one she had *maleficiau*. One of the more common evils which witches cause is madness or insanity; and the person may be restored, as a rule, by causing the witch to endure great physical pain. All kinds of physical ills are said to be caused by witches. A certain woman suffered great pain in the stomach, and it was feared that she was *maleficiada*. Some living creature was felt to move about within her stomach; and he relatives became alarmed, and attributed the trouble to an old woman who was suspected of being a witch. She was purposely called in to visit the sick one as a *curandera* (popular doctor); and, fearing violence, she approached the *maleficiada* and instantly caused a large owl—the cause of her illness—to come out of her stomach.

The ideas and beliefs of the New Mexican lower classes about witchcraft are not always clear. Conflicting stories are frequently told; and when questioned in detail about this or that particular belief, their answers are confused and uncertain. The *brujas* (generally women) are women who are wicked (*pautadas con el diablo*) and non-Christian. By confessing their sins to a priest, repenting, and abandoning their devilish ways, they may become good Christian women. A certain witch desired to forsake her evil ways and save her soul, since those who die witches cannot expect salvation. She confessed to a priest, and gave him a large bundle in the shape of a ball, which consisted largely of old rags, and pins stuck into it—the source and cause of her evil powers. The priest took the diabolical bundle and threw it into a fire, where, after bounding and rebounding for several minutes in an infernal manner, it was consumed, and the compact with the Devil ceased (*ya no estaba pautada con el diablo*).

It is not always easy to determine who is, and who is not, a witch. In case any woman is suspected of being a witch, there are ways of ascertaining the truth. If the witch is visiting in any house, a broom with a small cross (made from straws of the same broom) stuck to it is placed at the door. If the woman is a witch, she will never leave the room until the broom and cross are removed. Another way, which is very similar to this one, is to place the broom behind the door, with a cross made from two needles. It is a significant fact that the broom and cross play an important part in witchcraft in New Mexico. A comparative study of this problem may reveal some very interesting facts. The broom plays an important role in the witchcraft of all countries. So far as the cross is concerned, it is in every respect a most important element in the folklore of New Mexico. A third way of determining if a woman is a witch or not is to spy her while sleeping, for all witches sleep with their eyes open. Of a vigilant and careful person, it is said, "*Es como los bruios duerme con los ojos abiertos.*" Furthermore, any man or boy named John or John the Baptist may catch a witch by putting on his clothes wrongside out, or by making with his foot a circle around the witch. Other strange beliefs similar to these are current in various localities, and nearly all start with the idea that the one who can catch a witch is one named John or John the Baptist (*Juan Bautista*). There are some charms used against witches. The cores of red peppers burned on Fridays will keep away the witches and their evil doings. Another preventive is to urinate in the direction of their homes.

To some persons, to relatives and particular friends, the witches do no harm, though they are absolutely incapable of doing any good. From such people, witches do not conceal the fact that they are witches, though as a rule great secrecy prevails. To these confidential friends they often tell their evil intentions or threats of vengeance. A certain woman in New Mexico who was suspected of being a witch always carried with her, concealed under her clothes, a bundle of rags with pins, and a small toad wrapped up in rags, which she would often show to her friends, caressing it with her hand.

New Mexicans also believe that a witch may take the form of a black dog. A black dog, however, may represent the Devil or some other evil spirit. A certain woman in Santa Fe was often beaten in her bed by a black dog that no one but herself could see. This was supposed to be a witch; and her neighbors say that it was a witch, the wife of a man with whom the woman who was beaten had had illicit relations.

From: Aurelio M. Espinosa, "New-Mexican Spanish Folk-Lore," *Journal of American Folk-Lore* 23 (1910): 395–418.

Witchcraft
(Mexican)

Maria Antonia was emphatic in her expression of belief that there were lots of *brujas* (witches) around, who took delight in doing harm to you personally, or in spreading sickness among your cattle, blighting your crops, or ruining your fruit trees.

Everybody believed in witches; there might be some fool "Americanos" who would say they did not, but she was sure that they were only talking for talk's sake. However, what the "Americanos" did concerned her but little. She had been told that many "Americanos" were not "Christianos." She wouldn't talk to a man who was so wickedly stupid that he refused to believe what every one of good sense knew to be so." "Don't you believe in *brujas, mi capitan*? "Why, surely, *comadrecita*—do you not see that I am different from those fool gringos who come down here pretending to know more than their grandparents did? What I am anxious to learn is, what is the cure, or the best preventive, so that I may run no danger of being '*maleficiado*' myself."

The best remedy, Maria Antonia said, was to offer to San Antonio, or another powerful patron who works miracles in that particular line, a "*milagro*" of silver made in the form of the limb of the livestock or the fruit tree which had been bewitched. She had never known that to fail, but then there were other remedies, too, which I might as well learn.

There are not only witches in the world, but a class of people whom she styles "*gente de chusma*," who seem to be allied to our fairies. They fly about from place to place on the winds. They have sold their souls to the Devil and must never think of God when they die. Their souls fly about from place to place. They will not enter a house where there is mustard. You must take mustard—that in a bottle will do—and make with it a cross upon the wall, alongside of the bed upon which you are to sleep.

Once there was a man down here (Rio Grande City, Texas) who owed a washerwoman five dollars and refused to pay her. Now this washerwoman was a witch, and she filled this man full of worms, but Maria Antonia was called in just in time and gave him a strong emetic and a strong purge, and then dosed him with a decoction of *yerba de cancer*, *yerba gonzalez*, and *guayuli*, and expelled thirteen worms (*gusanos*) with green heads and white bodies.

To keep away witches: Smoke, drink, or chew powdered *mariguan* every morning. This herb is also given secretly in the food of admirers who have grown insensible to the charms of cast-off and despairing sweethearts.

To cure a man who has been rendered impotent by witchcraft: Take out from the lamp hanging in front of the Blessed Sacrament a few drops of oil, put upon a clean rag, and anoint the genitalia. Drop a little more of the oil upon a pan of live coals, saying, "I do this in the name of the Father, Son, and Holy Ghost." Then seek the woman who is beloved, and all obstacles will disappear, but the witch who has caused all the trouble will die at once.

To cure a man who has fallen violently in love, through witchcraft: Take a shilling's worth of sweet oil, and another of brandy made in Parras (state of Coahuila); mix, and give in doses of a large spoonful until the patient has vomited freely; then give him some beef tea, made hot, but without salt, fat, or tallow. The patient will break out into a profuse sweat, and will vomit again—but he must now be careful of himself, lest he take cold. Let him now eat what he pleases, and go to sleep. When he wakes up in the morning, he will be completely cured of his infatuation.

To keep witches away from you at night: When about to retire, kneel down and say the following prayer, in a low voice:

> *Cuatro esquinas tiene mi casa.*
> (My house has four corners.)
> *Cuatro angeles que la adoran.*
> (Four angels adore it.)
> *Lucas, Marcos, Juan, y Mateo.*
> (Luke, Mark, John, and Matthew.)
> *Ni brujas, ni hechiceras.*
> (Neither witches, nor charmers.)
> *Ni hombre malhechor.*

(Nor evil-doing man.)
(Must harm me, understood.)

En el Nombre del Padre.
(In the Name of the Father.)
Y del Hijo, y del Espiritu Santo.
(And of the Son, and of the Holy Ghost.)

Recite the above three times, and witches can neither harm you nor enter your house.

I have two sets of prayers to counteract witchcraft: One to San Cipriano, printed in Saltillo, in 1888, in the press of Ignacio C. de la Peña. It is too long to be copied entire, but includes an invocation for preservation from sudden death, lightning, earthquake, fire, calumny, evil tongues, bad thoughts, and all enemies visible and invisible, and for all who are bewitched (*maleficiados*) or likely to be. The second, entitled *Novena de San Ramon Non-nato*, Mexico, 1889, does not specify witchcraft in direct terms.

The last punishment inflicted for witchcraft within the limits of the United States was that imposed by Judge Sam Stewart of Rio Grande City (Fort Ringgold), Texas, in 1876.

As nearly as I can arrange the story from my notes and my recollection of the judge's account, it was about like this: A young man of good Mexican family was slowly wasting away under the attack of a disease, the exact nature of which quite baffled the local medical talent. All the medicines on sale in the *Botica del Aguila* (Eagle Drug Store) had been sampled to no purpose, and the sick man's condition had become deplorable. The physicians, who disagreed in everything else, concurred upon the one point that he had but a few days longer to live. At this juncture, a friend suggested to the mother that she call in one of the numerous old hags, who, under the name of *curanderas*, combine in equal portions a knowledge of kitchen botany, the black art, humbuggery pure and simple, and a familiarity with just enough prayers and litanies to give a specious varnish to the more objectionable features of their profession. The *curandera* responded promptly, and made her diagnosis almost with a glance of the eye.

"Your son," she said to the grief-stricken mother, "has neither consumption nor paralysis. The doctors can't tell what ails him, but I can see it all, and with the power of God can soon make him well again."

"What is the matter with him, then, my dear little friend?"

"Black Thomas cats. When I came into the room, the floor was a foot deep with Thomas cats which had jumped out of your son's throat, but they became frightened when they saw me and scampered back again. I'll soon get rid of them all."

Her intentions may have been good, but she got rid of nothing. Her *remedios* produced no effect, and the patient kept on sinking.

Just then a rival *curandera* came up to the mother and said, "That woman is deceiving you. She don't know what she's talking about. Why your son never has been troubled by Thomas cats—but I can tell you at once what ails him."

"Tell me, then, in the name of God."

"It is bullfrogs. I can see them jumping over each other and running into and out from his mouth."

To make a long story short, the first *curandera* would not give up the case, but insisted on holding on to what, in the language of today, would be called a decidedly soft snap, and the town, as is usual in such cases, taking up a quarrel in which it didn't have the slightest interest, became divided into the two bitterly hostile factions of the "bullfroggers" and the "Thomas-catters." The street became blocked with a crowd of partisans and excitement ran high. Judge Stewart surrounded the whole gang and had them run down to court, where he dismissed all but the ten *curanderas* (for there were ten altogether), who were loudly proclaiming their influence with witches.

"Have you ever seen any witches?" he asked of the first.

"Oh yes, indeed, many times. Why only last Wednesday, the witches picked me up at midnight and took me out on the Corpus Christi road, and up above the clouds, where they played *pelota* (football) with me, and when they got tired of that, they dropped me into a mesquite thicket, and here you see my clothes all torn to rags to prove that I am telling the truth."

From: John G. Bourke, "Popular Medicine, Customs, and Superstitions of the Rio Grande," *Journal of American Folk-Lore* 7 (1894): 119–46.

Witchcraft in New Mexico
(Spanish)

Our witchology is full, detailed, and graphic. Every *paisano* in New Mexico can tell you their strange habits, their marvelous powers, and their baleful deeds. They never injure the dumb animals, but woe to the human being who incurs their displeasure! Few, indeed, are bold enough to brave their wrath. If a witch ask for food, wood, clothing, or anything else, none dare say her nay. Nor dare anyone eat what a witch proffers; for, if he do, some animal, alive and gnawing, will form in his stomach. By day the witches wear their familiar human form; but at night, dressed in strange animal shapes, they fly abroad to hold witch meetings in the mountains, or to wreak their evil wills. In a dark night you may see them flying through the sky like so many balls of fire, and there are comparatively few Mexicans in the territory who have not seen this weird sight! For these nocturnal sallies the witches wear their own bodies, but take the legs and eyes of a coyote or other animal, leaving their own at home. Juan Perea, a male witch, who died here in San Mateo some months ago, met with a strange misfortune in this way: He had gone off with the eyes of a cat, and during his absence a dog knocked over the table and ate up Juan's own eyes; so the unfortunate witch had to wear cat's eyes all the rest of his life.

Before they can fly, witches are obliged to cry out, "*Sin Dios, sin Santa Maria!*" (Without God and without the Holy Virgin) whereupon they mount up into the air without difficulty. If you are on good terms with a witch you may persuade her to carry you on her back from here to New York in a second. She blindfolds you and enjoins strict silence. If you utter a word you find yourself alone in some vast wilderness, and if you cry, "God, save me!" you fall from a fearful height to the ground—but are luckily never killed by the fall. There are several courageous people in the territory who have made journeys thus upon the backs of witches. At least they are ready to swear so, and they find ten thousand believers to one skeptic. One striking peculiarity about New Mexico witches is that anyone named Juan or Juana (John or Jane) can catch them, and that no one else can, except a priest with holy water. To catch a witch, Juan draws a nine-foot circle on the ground, turns his shirt inside out, and cries, "*Veuga, bruja!*" (Come, witch!) whereupon the witch has to fall inside the circle, and Juan has her completely in his power. This ability to catch witches, however, is seldom exercised, for, let Juan once catch a witch, and all the other witches in the country join hands and whip him to death.

And now, having briefly outlined the nature of witches here, let me give you some veracious anecdotes of their exploits, religiously believed throughout this section. Lorenzo Labadie, a man of prominence in New Mexico, once unknowingly hired a witch as nurse for his baby. He lived in Las Vegas. Some months afterward there was a ball at Puerta de Luna, a couple of hundred miles south, and friends of the family were astonished to see the nurse and baby there. "Where is Señor Labadie and his family?" they asked. The nurse replied that they were at a house a few miles distant, but too tired to come to the ball. The friends went there next day and found the Labadies had not been there. Suspecting the nurse to be a witch, they wrote to Don Lorenzo, who only knew that the nurse and baby were in his house when he went to bed, and there also when he woke up. It being plain, therefore, to the most casual observer, that the woman was a witch, he promptly discharged her.

From: "Folk-Lore Scrapbook," *Journal of American Folk-Lore* 1 (1888): 167–68.

Three Witches
(Spanish)

If the Puritans had had as much to say about the rest of the vast area now covered by the United States as they did in their narrow New England strip, I should not be writing this. Such witches as they had, they promptly assisted to a more merciful world; but the real home of witchcraft on this continent was as far outside their jurisdiction as their knowledge. No such merciless censors as they were to be found in the arid area which Spain had colonized in the great Southwest long before a Caucasian foot had touched Plymouth Rock; and in the bare, adobe villages which began to dot the green valleys of what is now New Mexico, witchcraft was an institution which none cared to molest. Physically, there were no braver people than these Spanish-speaking pioneers who made the first settlements in the New World. Their whole life was one heroic struggle with wild beasts and wilder men, with suffering, privation, and danger. The colonists of the Atlantic coast, perilous as was their undertaking, had never such gruesome foes as the Spaniards fought here for three centuries. None but brave men would have opened such a wilderness, and none but brave ones could have held it. History records no greater heroisms than the unwritten ones which the rocky mesas of New Mexico witnessed almost daily.

But with all their courage in facing material danger, these simple, uneducated folk shrank from the mysterious and the unknown like children from the dark. Indeed, they *were* children. Their superstitions entered into every phase of daily life. And such wonderfully curious superstitions! An American child today would be ashamed to believe the stuff that brave men had faith in then. Though our own forefathers were perhaps quite as superstitious as they, a few generations brought enlightenment. But while we have been climbing to the height of civilization, this out-of-the-way corner of the nation—so different from all the rest in physical appearance, in customs and manners, in ideas and ambitions—has been very nearly at a standstill.

During the forty years that New Mexico has been under our flag, she has changed for the better, but the change is little more than skin-deep. The ideas and the customs of the great majority of her people are almost as un-American as the ideas and customs of the Zulus. Her sparsely settled area of 122,000 square miles holds more that is quaint and wonderful, more of the Dark Ages, more that the civilized world long ago outgrew, than all the rest of the country put together; and today one of the most wonderful things within her bare, brown borders is the survival and prevalence of witchcraft.

There are not now nearly as many witches in New Mexico as there were a few years ago, but there are enough—if popular belief is accepted. Of course I am speaking now from the New Mexican standpoint, to which the small, educated class looks back with indulgent incredulity, but in which the common people believe as sincerely as did the Puritans when they burned poor old women at the stake "because they were witches." Of the little Mexican hamlets in the more secluded corners of the territory, there are few which cannot still boast a resident witch, in whose malignant powers the simple villagers have firmest faith, and the story of whose alleged doings would fill a large volume.

I had the probably unprecedented privilege, a short time ago, of photographing three live witches as they stood in the door of their little adobe house—Antonia Morales and Placida Morales, sisters, and Villa, the daughter of Placida, and not more than seventeen years old. All three live in the little village of San Rafael, which lies beside the beautiful Gallo Spring in the fertile valley behind that great, black lava flow which, centuries ago, ran down the valley of the *Rio Puerco*—"Dirty River"—from the now-extinct craters of the Zuñi Mountains. Their house is about in the center of the straggling village. Only a few hundred feet away stands the little Presbyterian mission schoolhouse, where thirty or forty Mexican children are learning to read and write, to speak English, and to "do sums," under the charge of two young ladies from the East. The little church is even closer.

But a majority of the people believe more heartily in the witches than they do in the school. The town is much in awe of these three lone women. No one cares to refuse when they ask for food or other favors. They will do almost anything rather than incur the displeasure of the *brujas*, as the witches are called. Anyone can tell you direful tales of what befell those who were rash enough to offend them. Queer reading these witch stories make in this day and country. Here are some of the remarkable tales which I hear from the believing lips of "the oldest inhabitants":

Francisco Ansures, a good-looking young Mexican, whose adobe house is one of the six that constitute the little village of Cerros Cuates, had the misfortune four years ago to offend one of the witches. I say his misfortune, for he did not know, until the penalty came upon him, that he had offended, and to this day is not aware what particular evil he did to her. But the witch knew, and punished him for his deed, whatever it may have been.

She said nothing at the time, but waited patiently till one day she had a chance to give him a cup of coffee. He drank the decoction unsuspectingly. In a few minutes thereafter he was horrified to see that his hair had grown two feet in length, and that his rough overalls had turned to petticoats. Still worse, when he cried out in dismay, his pleasant tenor voice had become a squeaky treble.

In a word, he had been turned into a woman—at least, that is what he says, and what his industrious little wife maintains to this day. They declare that he remained a woman for several months, and recovered his proper sex only by paying a male witch who lived in the Cañon de Juan Tafoya to turn him back again.

A witch named Marcelina—a poor, withered little woman about fifty years old—was stoned to death in San Mateo, thirty miles north of San Rafael, in 1887, because she had "turned Don José Patricio Mariño into a woman, and made Señor Montaño very lame."

Montaño is still lame; but not nearly so much so as before he helped to kill poor old Marcelina. That pious act not only relieved his feelings, but soothed his distorted muscles also. Mariño is again a man—and one of very good standing in San Mateo—having hired another witch to retransform him into a man's shape.

In the Pueblo Indian town of Zia, less than ten years ago, lived a witch who was quietly but perseveringly causing all the children of the place to die one after the other. At last the people could stand it no longer, and arose in a mass to wipe her out, but found their efforts vain. The priest refused to come from his home in a neighboring town to help them, so they enlisted the sacristan—one of their own number—who had charge of the church. He marched at the head of the mob, carrying a jar of holy water, which he had taken from the church. As they came near, the poor old woman fled, with the mob in howling pursuit. Just as they were about to overtake her, she suddenly turned herself into a dog, and soon distanced them. They got their horses and ran her down; but she changed again to a coyote and ran faster than ever.

It took the riders nearly all day to catch up with her again; and then the coyote became a cat in the twinkling of an eye, and ran up a tall tree. They tried in vain to shake her down; but when the sacristan arrived he threw some holy water up the tree so that it splashed on her, and down she tumbled like a rock, changing back to her human shape as she dropped.

The crowd fell upon her with clubs and hatchets and beat her head and body fearfully; but still she lived and groaned, though any one of her hundred wounds was enough to kill a strong man.

"Untie the knot! Untie the knot!" she kept screaming, and at last a man who was not too infuriated to hear, stooped down and untied a queer little knot which he found in one corner of her blood-soaked blanket. The instant that was loosed her spirit took its flight.

Nicolas Mariño, brother of Patricio, once saw a big ball of fire alight in the arroyo which runs through the town of San Mateo. 'Coulas, as he is familiarly called, is a brave man; and though he knew this must be a witch, he started in pursuit. Just as he reached it, the ball of fire turned into a big rat, which ran off through the grass. When he caught up with the rat, it changed to a huge dog, which growled savagely, sprang clear over his head, and disappeared among the willows.

Juana Garcia, a woman of San Mateo, had a daughter named Maria Acacia, who was taken suddenly sick in the evening. As Juana went outside to gather some herbs for medicine, she saw an unknown animal prowling about the house, and caught it. No sooner did she get her hands on it than it turned into a woman, whom she recognized as Salia, the witch daughter of Witch Marcelina.

"Cure my daughter," cried Juana, "or I will have you killed!"

Salia promised, and was allowed to go. But when morning came Maria was no better. Juana went straight to Salia's house and demanded, with natural indignation:

"Why didn't you cure my daughter, as you promised you would?"

"Pooh! I don't believe she is sick," answered Salia. "We'll go and see."

The witch was a better walker than the mother, and reached the house first. When Juana arrived she found Maria making *tortillas*—a Mexican bread, shaped like a flapjack, cooked on a hot stone, and so durable that it is often carried for days at the pommel of the traveler's saddle. The witch had gone, and the girl was as well as ever.

"What did she do to you?" asked the astonished mother.

"She just took some ashes from the fireplace, and rubbed them on my arms, and I got up well," replied Maria.

Juan Baca is one of the best-known characters among the common people in this part of the country. He is a member of the Order of the Penitentes—that strange brotherhood of fanatics who whip their bare backs through Lent to expiate the sins of the year, bear huge crosses, fill themselves with the agonizing needles of the cactus, and wind up on Good Friday by crucifying one of their number.

His wife once refused coffee to Salia, who went away angry. Next day a sore formed on Señora Baca's nose, and small, white pebbles kept dropping therefrom. Juan knew what was the matter, and going to Salia's house, he said:

"Look, you have bewitched my wife. If you don't cure her at once, I will hang you."

"It is well," answered Salia; "I will cure her."

Juan went home contented. But his wife grew worse instead of better; and taking his long reata, with its easy slipping noose at one end, he went again to Salia's.

"I have come to hang you," said he.

"No, don't! I'll come right over!" cried Salia; and over she went with him. She gave the sick woman a little black powder, and rubbed her nose once. Out came a sinew four inches long, and instantly the nose was as well as ever.

These are only samples—I could tell you a hundred more—of the stories implicitly believed by thousands of people in this far-off corner of the United States. Their superstitions as to the general traits of the witches are no less curious and foolish. It is believed that the witches can do anything they wish, but that they never wish to do a good act unless bribed or scared into it. They never injure dumb brutes, but confine their evil spells to human beings who have, knowingly or unwittingly, incurred their wrath.

At night they go flying to the mountains to meet other witches; and hundreds of ignorant people declare that they have seen them sailing through the dark sky like balls of fire. Before leaving home they always exchange their own legs and eyes for those of a dog, cat, or coyote; cry out *"Sin Dios y sin Santa Maria,"* which signifies, "Without God and without the Virgin Mary"; and then fly off. Juan Perea, a male witch who died in San Mateo in 1888, once met with a singular misfortune. He had taken the eyes of a cat for one of his nocturnal rambles, leaving his own eyes on the table. During his absence a dog knocked the table over and ate the eyes; and the unlucky witch had to finish his days with the green eyes of a cat. Luckily, the dog did not eat his legs, which were old and tough, or I don't know how he would have got along.

Anyone named Juan (John) can catch a witch by going through a curious rigmarole. He draws a large circle on the ground, seats himself inside it, turns his shirt wrongside out, and cries, "In the name of God I call thee, *bruja*," and straightway whatever witch is near must fall helpless inside his circle. Everyone who lives here can tell you that a Juan has this power; but he seldom uses it, for he knows that if he does so all the witches in the country will fall upon him and beat him mercilessly to death.

Another curious superstition prevalent here is that if you stick a couple of needles into a broom so that they form a little cross, and put it behind the door when a witch is in your house, the witch cannot get out of that door until a dog or a person has passed out ahead.

This superstition was employed on one occasion to tease a woman who passed for a witch. Not very long ago, this reputed witch visited the house of some refined and educated Spanish friends of mine in San Mateo, and one of the young ladies made the needle experiment.

The witch started several times to go out, but each time paused at the door for someone else to precede her. All roguishly hung back, and she was there nearly all day. At last a child went out, and the witch rushed out after. Probably she had noticed the trick, and wished to keep up the deceptive reputation of witchcraft.

The sign of the cross, or the spoken name of God or one of the saints, stops a witch at once. I know people here who assert that they were being carried on a witch's back, thousands of miles a minute, to some distant destination; but that when they became alarmed, and cried, "God save me!" they instantly fell hundreds of feet—without being hurt—and found themselves alone in a great wilderness.

School and church are gradually killing off these strange and childish superstitions, but they die hard, and it will be many a year before New Mexico will be bereft of her last reputed witch.

From: Charles F. Lummis, A New Mexico David (New York: Charles Scribner's Sons, 1905).

· Specters ·

(Various)

Ghosts
(Spanish)

A certain evening during Holy Week the Penitentes entered the church in Taos for the purpose of flogging themselves. After flogging themselves in the usual manner, they left the church. As they departed, however, they heard the floggings of a Penitente who seemed to have remained in the church. The elder brother (*hermano mayor*) counted his Penitentes, and no one was missing. To the astonishment of the other Penitentes, the one in the church continued his flagellation, and they decided to return. No one dared to reenter the church, however; and while they disputed in silence and made various conjectures as to what the presence of an unknown Penitente might mean, the floggings became harder and harder. At last one of the Penitentes volunteered to enter alone; but, as he opened the door, he discovered that the one who was scourging himself mercilessly was high above in the choir, and it was necessary to obtain a lighted candle before venturing to ascend to the choir in the darkness. He procured a lighted candle and attempted to ascend. But, lo! he could not, for every time he reached the top of the stairs, the Penitente whom he plainly saw there, flogging himself, would approach and put out his candle. After trying for several times, the brave Penitente gave up the attempt, and all decided to leave the unknown and mysterious stranger alone in the church. As they departed, they saw the mysterious Penitente leave the church and turn in an opposite direction. They again consulted one another, and decided to follow him. They did so; and, since the stranger walked slowly, scourging himself continuously and brutally, they were soon at a short distance from him. The majority of the flagellants followed slowly behind; while the brave one, who had previously attempted to ascend to the choir, advanced to the side of the mysterious stranger and walked slowly by him. He did not cease scourging himself, though his body was visibly becoming very weak, and blood was flowing freely from his mutilated back. Thus the whole procession continued in the silence of the night, the stranger leading the Penitentes through abrupt paths and up a steep and high mountain. At last, when all were nearly dead with fatigue, the mysterious Penitente suddenly disappeared, leaving his good companion and the other Penitentes in the greatest consternation. The Penitentes later explained that this was doubtless the soul of a dead Penitente who had not done his duty in life—a false Penitente—and God had sent him back to earth to scourge himself properly, before allowing him to enter heaven.

From: Aurelio M. Espinosa, "New-Mexican Spanish Folk-Lore," *Journal of American Folk-Lore* 23 (1910): 395–418.

The Weeping Woman
(Spanish)

The myth of The Weeping Woman (*La Llorona*) is peculiar to Santa Fe. A strange woman dressed in black, dragging heavy chains and weeping bitterly, is often seen after midnight walking about the dark streets or standing at the windows and doors of private houses. Vague ideas are expressed about her, but many state that she is a soul from purgatory, desiring to communicate with someone, or obliged to atone for her sins by dragging chains and weeping. That any soul from purgatory or heaven can come down to earth to communicate with relatives and friends is a widespread belief in New Mexico; and it is not strange that any apparition, real or imaginary, is looked upon as a wandering soul. When The Weeping Woman is heard weeping at the door, no one leaves the house; and finally she departs, continuing her sad lamentations and dragging heavy chains. There are also some who state that the *llorona* is an infernal spirit wandering through the world and entering the houses of those who are to be visited by great misfortunes, especially death in the family; and a few say that she is nothing more than an old witch (*una vieja bruja*).

From: Aurelio M. Espinosa, "New-Mexican Spanish Folk-Lore," *Journal of American Folk-Lore* 23 (1910): 395–418.

The Phantom Train of Marshall Pass
(Unidentified)

Soon after the rails were laid across Marshall Pass, Colorado, where they go over a height of twelve thousand feet above the sea, an old engineer named Nelson Edwards was assigned to a train. He had traveled the road with passengers behind him for a couple of months and met with no accident, but one night as he set off for the divide he fancied that the silence was deeper, the canyon darker, and the air frostier than usual. A defective rail and an unsafe bridge had been reported that morning, and he began the long ascent with some misgivings. As he left the first line of snowsheds he heard a whistle echoing somewhere among the ice and rocks, and at the same time the gong in his cab sounded and he applied the brakes.

The conductor ran up and asked, "What did you stop for?

"Why did you signal to stop?

"I gave no signal. Pull her open and light out, for we've got to pass No. 19 at the switches, and there's a wild train climbing behind us."

Edwards drew the lever, sanded the track, and the heavy train got under way again; but the whistles behind grew nearer, sounding danger signals, and in turning a curve he looked out and saw a train speeding after him at a rate that must bring it against the rear of his own train if something were not done. He broke into a sweat as he pulled the throttle wide open and lunged into a snowbank. The cars lurched, but the snow was flung off and the train went roaring through another shed. Here was where the defective rail had been reported. No matter. A greater danger was pressing behind. The fireman piled on coal until his clothes were wet with perspiration, and fire belched from the smokestack. The passengers too, having been warned of their peril, had dressed themselves and were anxiously watching at the windows, for talk went among them that a mad engineer was driving the train behind.

As Edwards crossed the summit he shut off steam and surrendered his train to the force of gravity. Looking back, he could see by the faint light from new snow that the driving wheels on the rear engine were bigger than his own, and that a tall figure stood atop of the cars and gestured frantically. At a sharp turn in the track he found the other train but two hundred yards behind, and as he swept around the curve the engineer who was chasing him leaned from his window and laughed. His face was like dough. Snow was falling and had begun to drift in the hollows, but the trains flew on; bridges shook as they thundered across them; wind screamed in the ears of the passengers; the suspected bridge was reached; Edwards's heart was in his throat, but he seemed to clear the chasm by a bound. Now the switch was in sight, but No. 19 was not there, and as the brakes were freed, the train shot by like a flash. Suddenly a red light appeared ahead, swinging to and fro on the track. As well be run into behind as to crash into an obstacle ahead. He heard the whistle of the pursuing locomotive yelp behind him, yet he reversed the lever and put on brakes, and for a few seconds lived in a hell of dread.

Hearing no sound now, he glanced back and saw the wild train almost leap upon his own—yet just before it touched it the track seemed to spread, the engine toppled from the bank, the whole train rolled into the canyon and vanished. Edwards shuddered and listened. No cry of hurt men or hiss of steam came up—nothing but the groan of the wind as it rolled through the black depth. The lantern ahead had disappeared too. Now another danger impended, and there was no time to linger, for No. 19 might be on its way ahead if he did not reach the second switch before it moved out. The mad run was resumed and the second switch was reached in time. As Edwards was finishing the run to Green River, which he reached in the morning ahead of schedule, he found written in the frost of his cab window these words: A FRATE TRAIN WAS RECKED AS YU SAW. NOW THAT YU SAW IT YU WILL NEVER MAKE ANOTHER RUN. THE ENJINE WAS NOT OUNDER CONTROL AND FOUR SEXSHUN MEN WOR KILLED. IF YU EVER RUN ON THIS ROAD AGAIN YU WILL BE RECKED. Edwards quit the road that morning, and returning to Denver found employment on the Union Pacific. No wreck was discovered next day in the canyon where he had seen it, nor has the phantom train been in chase of any engineer who has crossed the divide since that night.

From: Charles M. Skinner, *American Myths & Legends*, vol. 2 (Philadelphia and London: J. B. Lippincott Co., 1903).

· *The River of Lost Souls* ·

(Spanish)

In the days when Spain ruled the western country an infantry regiment was ordered out from Santa Fe to open communication with Florida and to carry a chest of gold for the payment of the soldiers in St. Augustine. The men wintered on the site of Trinidad, comforted by the society of their wives and families, and in the spring the women and camp followers were directed to remain, while the troops set forward along the canyon of the Purgatoire—neither to reach their destination nor to return. Did they attempt to descend the stream in boats and go to wreck among the rapids? Were they swept into eternity by a freshet? Did they lose their provisions and starve in the desert? Did the Indians revenge themselves for brutality and selfishness by slaying them at night or from an ambush? Were they killed by banditti? Did they sink in the quicksands that led the river into subterranean canals?

None will ever know, perhaps; but many years afterward a savage told a priest in Santa Fe that the regiment had been surrounded by Indians, as Custer's command was in Montana, and slain, to a man. Seeing that escape was hopeless, the colonel—so said the narrator—had buried the gold that he was transporting. Thousands of doubloons are believed to be hidden in the canyon, and thousands of dollars have been spent in searching for them.

After weeks had lapsed into months and months into years, and no word came of the missing regiment, the priests named the river *El Rio de las Animas Perdidas*—the River of Lost Souls. The echoing of the flood as it tumbled through the canyon was said to be the lamentation of the troopers. French trappers softened the suggestion of the Spanish title when they renamed it Purgatoire, and "bullwhackers" teaming across the plains twisted the French title into the unmeaning "Picketwire." But Americo-Spaniards keep alive the tradition, and the prayers of many have ascended and do ascend for the succor of those who vanished so strangely in the valley of Las Animas.

From: Charles M. Skinner, *American Myths & Legends*, vol. 2 (Philadelphia and London: J. B. Lippincott Co., 1903).

· The Flood at Santa Fe ·

(Spanish)

Many are the scenes of religious miracles in this country, although French Canada and old Mexico boast of more. So late as the prosaic year of 1889 the Virgin was seen to descend into the streets of Johnstown, Pennsylvania, to save her image on the Catholic church in that place, when it was swept by a deluge in which hundreds of persons perished. It was the wrath of the Madonna that caused just such a flood in New Mexico long years ago. There is in the old Church of Our Lady of Guadalupe, in Santa Fe, a picture·that commemorates the appearance of the Virgin to Juan Diego, an Indian in Guadalupe, old Mexico, in the sixteenth century. She commanded that a chapel should be built for her, but the bishop of the diocese declared that the man had been dreaming and told him to go away. The Virgin came to the Indian again, and still the bishop declared that he had no evidence of the truth of what he said. A third time the supernatural visitor appeared, and told Juan to climb a certain difficult mountain, pick the flowers he would find there, and take them to the bishop.

After a long and dangerous climb they were found, to the Indian's amazement, growing in the snow. He filled his blanket with them and returned to the episcopal residence, but when he opened the folds before the dignitary, he was more amazed to find not flowers, but a glowing picture painted on his blanket. It hangs now in Guadalupe, but is duplicated in Santa Fe, where a statue of the Virgin is also kept. These treasures are greatly prized and are resorted to in time of illness and threatened disaster, the statue being taken through the streets in procession when the rainy season is due. Collections of money are then made and prayers are put up for rain, to which appeals the Virgin makes prompt response, the priests pointing triumphantly to the results of their intercession. One year, however, the rain did not begin on time, though services were almost constantly continued before the sacred picture and the sacred statue, and the angry people stripped the image of its silks and gold lace and kicked it over the ground for hours. That night a violent rain set in and the town was nearly washed away, so the populace hastened the work of reparation in order to save their lives. They cleansed the statue, dressed it still more brilliantly, and addressed their prayers to the Virgin with more energy and earnestness than ever before.

From: Charles M. Skinner, *American Myths & Legends*, vol. 2 (Philadelphia and London: J. B. Lippincott Co., 1903).

· Monsters ·

(Spanish)

The Bugaboo or Bugbear

There is no definite idea in the minds of the people of New Mexico about the bugaboo or bugbear (*el coco*). It is considered as a wild, ugly-looking man or animal that frightens bad boys. The children are frightened at the very name of *el coco*, and all fear it. Such expressions as *te come el coco; ahí viene el coco; si no callas, llamo al coco pa que te coma*; etc, are very common. By extension of meaning, any terrible-looking person who frightens others is called *el coco*, and hence the expression *meterle el coco á una persona* (to scare a person).

El coco is also often called *el agüelo*, a myth which must not be confused with, though it is apparently the source of, the custom which exists in New Mexico about another *agüelo*. During Christmas week an old man called *el agüelo* visits houses and makes the children play and pray. Those who cannot say their prayers he whips and advises them to learn them quickly. The origin of the name *agüelo* in this interesting custom is undoubtedly taken from *el coco*—"bugaboo."

The children, of course, who are frightened at all times of the year with the mythical *coco* or *agüelo*, do not differentiate between the mythical one and the real *agüelo* of Christmas time, who makes them dance, say their prayers, and give him cakes and sweets.

From: Aurelio M. Espinosa, "New-Mexican Spanish Folk-Lore," *Journal of American Folk-Lore* 23 (1910): 395–418.

The Monster Viper

This is a Spanish-Indian myth. The belief is that the Pueblo Indians of New Mexico have in each pueblo a monster viper (*el viborón*) in a large subterranean cave, which is nourished with seven living children every year. I know absolutely nothing about the origin of this myth, and have had no time to study it; but I am inclined to believe that this is a pure Indian myth, probably of Aztec origin. The interesting thing about it is that the Indians themselves have very vague ideas concerning it, some even denying it. The belief among the New Mexicans of this Indian myth is widespread, and the gradual disappearance of the New Mexico Pueblo Indians is explained by the myth in question. In the pueblo of Taos it is said that an Indian woman, when her turn came to deliver her child to the monster viper, fled to her Mexican neighbors, and thus saved her child.

From: Aurelio M. Espinosa, "New-Mexican Spanish Folk-Lore," *Journal of American Folk-Lore* 23 (1910): 395–418.

The Evil One

The myth about the evil one, *la malora*, also called *malogra* (literally, "the evil hour"), is indeed interesting, both from the purely folklore side as well as from the philological side. How *mala hora*—the evil hour, ill fate, bad luck—came to be thought of as a definite, concrete, individual wicked spirit is interesting from more than one point of view. This myth is a well-known one. *La malora* is an evil spirit which wanders about in the darkness of the night at the crossroads and other places. It terrorizes the unfortunate ones who wander alone at night, and has usually the form of a large lock of wool or the whole fleece of wool of a sheep (*un vellón de lana*). Sometimes it takes a human form, but this is rare; and the New Mexicans say that when it has been seen in human form, it presages ill fate, death, or the like. When it appears on dark nights in the shape of a fleece of wool, it diminishes and increases in size in the very presence of the unfortunate one who sees it. It is also generally believed that a person who sees *la malora*, like one who sees a ghost (*un difunto*), forever remains senseless. When asked for detailed information about this myth, the New Mexicans give the general reply, "It is an evil thing" (*Es cosa mala*).

From: Aurelio M. Espinosa, "New-Mexican Spanish Folk-Lore," *Journal of American Folk-Lore* 23 (1910): 395–418.

· The Devil ·

(Various)

El Diablo
(Spanish)

In New Mexican Spanish the Devil is known by various names—*el
mashishi, el diablo, el malo*. There is little difference in the meaning of
these names. All three are epithets of the Devil. The Devil does not play
such an important part in popular superstition anywhere. He is rather a
literary personage, one more frequently encountered in genuine literature
than in popular tradition. The witches and all other evil spirits are in
agreement with the Devil—*pautaus con el diablo*—but other than this
general belief and the frequency of the word *diablo* in oaths and exclama-
tions, the Devil is not an important factor in New Mexican Spanish
folklore, and he is not even feared. The simple sign of the cross will scare
away any devil or other evil spirit which may dare to appear, so the New
Mexicans do not worry about the Devil. He once caused humanity to fall,
but now his power has become much weakened: *No le vale con San Miguel*
(He has been conquered by St. Michael). Another very common epithet
for the Devil, in addition to the three already given, is *aquel gallo* (that
old rooster); and in a certain riddle he is called *pata galán* (pretty legs).

From: Aurelio M. Espinosa, "New-Mexican Spanish Folk-Lore," *Journal of American Folk-
Lore* 23 (1910): 395–418.

Captain Above and the Devil
(Native American)

One of the old mission Padres has fully described the religious beliefs
of the Hasanias Indians. Father Isidro de Espinosa was very much
grieved for them because they had "not the true faith," since in general
they were of very good disposition, good to look upon, "well made, and
much whiter than the Mexicans and Tlascaltecans, and naturally politic
and of good understanding." He was very much surprised by their answers
and could not but admire their ingenuity and loyalty in giving reasons
for all their rites and superstitions in which their fathers had bred them.

He stated that in all that numerous nation, comprising many tribes of the same idiom and more than fourteen or fifteen dialects, all believed that there is a great captain in the sky, who is called "*Caddi Ayo*" or "Captain Above," and that he directs all lives and destinies.

These Indians believe "that in the beginning of the world there was only one woman, and this woman had two daughters—one a virgin. . . . One day when the two sisters were alone without their mother, when the elder was leaning upon the lap of the younger, and the latter was examining her head, they were seized from before and this is what happened. There appeared suddenly a deformed and gigantic man of ferocious aspect, with horns so high that you could not see them, and this was *Cuddaja*— devil or demon—and, seizing the elder sister, he tore her to pieces with his nails, and chewed and swallowed her. Meanwhile the virgin climbed to the top of a very high tree, and when the devil had finished eating the sister, he raised his eyes to look for the maiden, and, seeing her, tried to force her to descend, but not being able, he commenced (with his teeth and nails) to cut down the tree.

(When they told me this, I asked why, if his horns were so high, he did not use them at this time, but they were unable to answer me.) The girl, seeing her danger, let herself fall into a deep pond of water at the foot of the tree, and diving in the water she went out very far and made her escape to where her mother was. The giant, in the meantime, began to agitate the water to prevent her swimming out so as to make her a prisoner; but she made sport of him and finally succeeded in escaping to her mother and told her all that had happened. They went together to the site where the other daughter had died, and, following the track of blood that the devil had made when eating her, they found in an acorn shell a little drop of blood, and, covering it with another shell of the same kind, the mother put it in her bosom and took it to her house, where she put it in a little earthen jar, and covering it well, put it in a corner. In the night she heard a noise like something gnawing in the jar, and going to investigate she found that from the drop of congealed blood had grown a child as large as her finger. She covered it again, and the following night, hearing the same noise, she found the child had grown to the stature of a large man. She was very much pleased. And when he took his bows and arrows and asked for his mother, they told him all the devil had done and he went out to look for him. When he found him he shot him so far with the point of his arrow that he never appeared again. He came to his grandmother and aunt and said to them: "It is not good to be upon the earth," and told them that he would now ascend to the "Cachao" (their name for heaven). He has been there ever since governing the world. And this *Caddi Ayo*, or Captain Above, is the first or highest deity they worship, and they believe that he is able to reward the good and punish the evil which they commit.

From: Adina DeZavala, "Religious Beliefs of the Teajas or Hasanias Indians," *Publications of the Folk-Lore Society of Texas* 1 (1916): 39–43.

CHAPTER 25

Nature

· *Story of the Texas Wild Horses* ·

(Unidentified)

It is interesting to think that the scrawny, tawny-colored horses of southwest Texas are remote descendants of the ancient Arabian stock, but such, I think, is the case, and I believe you will agree when I have called your attention to a few historical facts. The Mohommedans began their conquest in A.D. 632 and by 732 had extended their dominion across Africa, through Spain, and into France. We are told that these Moslems introduced horses and horseback riding into Europe, and made chivalry possible. Let us now skip a few centuries and come up almost eight hundred years to the exploration of the Spaniards—Cortez and Pizzaro—in America. These men brought with them horses from Spain— evidently ancient Arabian stock—and allowed these horses to escape on the western prairies. They grew and multiplied until they became numberless. Nor was their role in history played out, as all can testify who have read the story of Philip Nolan and his ill-fated expedition. Thus we see that the inferior Spanish mustang is a descendant of the Andalusian horses and more remotely of the ancient Arabian stock. Their wild nature and dwarfed size are due to their survival for four hundred years in a wild state and in a new and semidesert environment.

Wild horses are gregarious in nature, going in small herds, each herd led and protected by a stallion. Each stallion has his own range on which other herds are not permitted to trespass. The life is patriarchal, tribal, and nomadic. According to my narrator, the colts remained with the herd until they were a year old. When they had reached any degree of maturity they were driven out by the stallion, as drones from a hive. The fillies were promptly adopted by a neighboring herd, while the horse colts were left in bunches of five or six to shift for themselves as they might. These bays rambled about on the range together for a year, by which time they were able-bodied, active, and fractious. On some morning the young stallion would return to a herd, choosing one led by a weak horse. The leader of a herd becomes jealous of a stranger and charges after one of the newcomers. When he is thus led away, the young horses rush into the herd; the old stallion will allow himself to be led but a short distance away, and soon returns. He continues the fight until he is killed, whereupon the young stallions divide the herd among themselves, each taking four or five mares, or they fight for supremacy to extermination, for no herd has more than one stallion.

The stallion is the protector, and will fight for the colts when they are young. He will stand still in the sun with the colt leaning against him. The horses range twenty-five miles from their watering place, and return for water every two days. A whinny is the signal for the start to the water hole, and they return in a run, with mane and tail flying. They cut figure 8's on their way, picking up loose stock enroute. They get to water at about ten or eleven o'clock in the morning. They drink until they are inflated to a capacity limit. Immediately after watering, any cowhorse can run up on them in twenty minutes. After drinking they stand about in the shade and sleep for an hour, and then graze slowly away. Night finds them five or six miles from the watering place. They lie down in the early part of the night, but get up and begin to graze about twelve, continuing until ten o'clock the next day.

There are several ways of catching the mustangs. Strange as it may seem, it is possible for two men to capture them on foot. This is naturally the most tedious way and may require two weeks' time. As stated before, the mustangs have a definite range, which they refuse to leave, or to which they instinctively return when forced off. The mustang catchers take advantage of this habit. One man starts following the herd. At first he is unable to get within less than half or three-quarters of a mile, but he continues after them hour after hour. At intervals he is relieved by mustang catcher number two. At last the herd becomes accustomed to the men and allows them to get much closer. The catcher selects then a tree with a heavy top and dense foliage. It is necessary to select this tree in the path which the horses take. Then the man conceals himself in the top of the tree with a rope, one end of which he has tied to the tree trunk. The second man seeks to get the herd to pass under the tree, in which case the rope is dropped over the head of one horse, and he becomes a prisoner.

When the catchers have horses to ride, the process is much shorter. Anything that destroys the unity of the herd is very disconcerting to the mustang, and makes the capture much easier. Sometimes domesticated horses are turned loose in the herd for this purpose. The most effective means is to catch one mustang, clog him, and then set him free. The animal might be clogged by means of a wooden block fastened to the leg, or by taking a wagon rod about three feet long and bending it around the fore ankle. This was an inhuman practice, resulting sooner or later in the death of the animal, but the catchers did not value the horses and paid no attention to the sacrifice. After one is caught, four or five may then be captured in one day. When a choice one is found he is roped, thrown, blindfolded, saddled, and ridden on the spot and considered "broken."

The quickest, though most uncertain way, of catching the mustang is the method known as creasing. That is to say, the horse is shot in such a way as to render him unconscious, and while in this condition is made a captive. You may wonder just how this is done. On the top of the horse's neck just in front of the shoulders is a very sensitive nerve center. If a bullet can be put through this fleshy part of the neck, all is well. The horse falls insensible, and while in this state is tied securely by the catcher. The horse regains consciousness to find himself a captive. He suffers no permanent injury, and a small crease on top of the neck is all that remains to tell the story. It is still possible to find domesticated mustangs bearing this mark of a former wild state.

Such are the stories of the wild horses. These horses are fast disappearing and all that remains is a vast number of yellow, brown, and dun-colored horses with a black stripe down the back and bulging eyes. There are many stories about these horses, and folklorists should get busy and gather them now. They will soon be a part of America's past, and so far in the background as to be useless from a historical if not a legendary point of view.

From: W. Prescott Webb, "Wild Horse Stories of Southwest Texas," *Publications of the Folk-Lore Society of Texas* 1 (1916) 58–61.

· *Bears* ·

(English)

Bill Cross and His Pet Bear

When my father settled down at the foot of the Oregon Sierras with his little family, long, long years ago, it was about forty miles from our place to the nearest civilized settlement.

People were very scarce in those days, and bears, as said before, were very plenty. We also had wolves, wildcats, wild cattle, wild hogs, and a good many long-tailed and big-headed yellow California lions.

The wild cattle, brought there from Spanish Mexico, next to the bear, were most to be feared. They had long, sharp horns and keen, sharp hoofs. Nature had gradually helped them out in these weapons of defense. They had grown to be slim and trim in body, and were as supple and swift as deer. They were the deadly enemies of all wild beasts; because all wild beasts devoured their young.

When fat and saucy, in warm summer weather, these cattle would hover along the foothills in bands, hiding in the hollows, and would begin to bellow whenever they saw a bear or a wolf, or even a man or boy, if on foot, crossing the wide valley of grass and blue camas blossoms. Then there would be music! They would start up, with heads and tails in the air, and, broadening out, left and right, they would draw a long bent line, completely shutting off their victim from all approach to the foothills. If the unfortunate victim were a man or boy on foot, he generally made escape up one of the small ash trees that dotted the valley in groves here and there, and the cattle would then soon give up the chase. But if it were a wolf or any other wild beast that could not get up a tree, the case was different. Far away, on the other side of the valley, where dense woods lined the banks of the winding Willamette River, the wild, bellowing herd would be answered. Out from the edge of the woods would stream, right and left, two long, corresponding surging lines, bellowing and plunging forward now and then, their heads to the ground, their tails always in the air and their eyes aflame, as if they would set fire to the long gray grass. With the precision and discipline of a well-ordered army, they would close in upon the wild beast, too terrified now to either fight or fly, and, leaping upon him one after another, with their long, sharp hoofs, he would, in a little time, be crushed into an unrecognizable mass. Not a bone would be left unbroken. It is a mistake to suppose that they ever used their long, sharp horns in attack. These were used only in defense, the same as elk or deer, falling on the knees and receiving the enemy on their horns, much as the Old Guard received the French in the last terrible struggle at Waterloo.

Bill Cross was a "tender foot" at the time of which I write, and a sailor, at that. Now, the old pilgrims who had dared the plains in those days of '49, when cowards did not venture and the weak died on the way, had not the greatest respect for the courage or endurance of those who had reached Oregon by ship. But here was this man, a sailor by trade, settling down in the interior of Oregon, and, strangely enough, pretending to know more about everything in general and bears in particular than either my father or any of his boys!

He had taken up a piece of land down in the pretty Camas Valley where the grass grew long and strong and waved in the wind, mobile and beautiful as the mobile sea.

The good-natured and self-complacent old sailor liked to watch the waving grass. It reminded him of the sea, I reckon. He would sometimes sit on our little porch as the sun went down and tell us boys strange, wild sea stories. He had traveled far and seen much, as much as any man can see on water, and maybe was not a very big liar, for a sailor, after all. We liked his tales. He would not work, and so he paid his way with stories of the sea. The only thing about him that we did not like, outside of his chronic idleness, was his exalted opinion of himself and his unconcealed contempt for everybody's opinion but his own.

"Bill," said my father one day, "those black Spanish cattle will get after that red sash and sailor jacket of yours some day when you go down in the valley to your claim, and they won't leave a grease spot. Better go horseback, or at least take a gun, when you go down next time."

"Pshaw! Squire. I wish I had as many dollars as I ain't afeard of all the black Spanish cattle in Oregon. Why, if they're so blasted dangerous, how did your missionaries ever manage to drive them up here from Mexico, anyhow?"

Still, for all that, the very next time that he saw the old sailor setting out at his snail pace for his ranch below, slow and indolent as if on the deck of a ship, my father insisted that he should go on horseback, or at least take a gun.

"Pooh, pooh! I wouldn't be bothered with a horse or a gun. Say, I'm goin' to bring your boys a pet bear some day."

And so, cocking his little hat down over his right eye and thrusting his big hands into his deep pockets almost to the elbows, he slowly and lazily whistled himself down the gradual slope of the foothills, waist deep in the waving grass and delicious wild flowers, and soon was lost to sight in the great waving sea.

Two things may be here written down. He wouldn't ride a horse because he couldn't, and for the same reason he wouldn't use a gun. Again, let it be written down also that the reason he was going away that warm autumn afternoon was that there was some work to do. These facts were clear to my kind and indulgent father; but of course we boys never thought of it, and laid our little shoulders to the hard work of helping father lift up the long, heavy poles that were to complete the corral around our pioneer log cabin, and we really hoped and half believed that he might bring home a little pet bear.

This stout log corral had become an absolute necessity. It was high and strong, and made of poles or small logs stood on end in a trench, after the fashion of a primitive fort or stout stockade. There was but one opening, and that was a very narrow one in front of the cabin door. Here it was proposed to put up a gate. We also had talked about portholes in the corners of the corral, but neither gate nor portholes were yet made. In fact, as said before, the serene and indolent man of the sea always slowly walked away down through the grass toward his untracked claim whenever there was anything said about portholes, posts, or gates.

Father and we three little boys had only got the last post set and solidly "tamped" in the ground as the sun was going down.

Suddenly we heard a yell; then a yelling, then a bellowing. The yelling was heard in the high grass in the Camas Valley below, and the bellowing of cattle came from the woody river banks far beyond.

Then up on the brown hills of the Oregon Sierras above us came the wild answer of the wild black cattle of the hills, and a moment later, right and left, the long black lines began to widen out; then down they came, like a whirlwind, toward the black and surging line in the grass below. We were now almost in the center of what would, in a little time, be a complete circle and cyclone of furious Spanish cattle.

And now, here is something curious to relate. Our own cows, poor, weary, immigrant cows of only a year before, tossed their tails in the air, pawed the ground, bellowed, and fairly went wild in the splendid excitement and tumult. One touch of nature made the whole cow world kin!

Father clambered up on a "buck-horse" and looked out over the stockade; and then he shouted and shook his hat and laughed as I had never heard him laugh before. For there, breathless, coatless, hatless, came William Cross, Esq., two small wolves, and a very small black bear! They were all making good time, anywhere, anyway, to escape the frantic cattle. Father used to say afterwards, when telling about this little incident, that "it was nip and tuck between the four, and hard to say which was ahead." The cattle had made quite a "roundup."

They all four straggled in at the narrow little gate at about the same time, the great big, lazy sailor in a hurry for the first time in his life.

But think of the coolness of the man, as he turned to us children with his first gasp of breath, and said, "Bo—bo—boys, I've bro—bro—brought you a little bear!"

The wolves were the little chicken thieves known as coyotes, quite harmless, as a rule, so far as man is concerned, but the cattle hated them and they were terrified nearly to death.

The cattle stopped a few rods from the stockade. We let the coyotes go, but we kept the little bear and named him Bill Cross. Yet he was never a bit cross, despite his name.

From: Joaquin Miller, *True Bear Stories* (Chicago and New York: Rand McNally & Co., 1900).

How to Tree a Bear

Away back in the "fifties" bears were as numerous on the banks of the Willamette River, in Oregon, as are hogs at nut time in the hickory woods of Kentucky, and that is saying that bears were mighty plenty in Oregon about forty years ago.

You see, after the missionaries established their great cattle ranches in Oregon and gathered the Indians from the wilderness and set them to work and fed them on beef and bread, the bears had it all their own way, till they literally overran the land. And this gave a great chance for sport to the sons of missionaries and the sons of new settlers "where rolls the Oregon."

And it was not perilous sport, either, for the grizzly was rarely encountered here. His home was farther to the south. Neither was the large and clumsy cinnamon bear abundant on the banks of the beautiful Williamette in those dear old days, when you might ride from sun to sun, belly deep in wild flowers, and never see a house. But the small black bear, as indicated before, was on deck in great force, at all times and in nearly all places.

It was the custom in those days for boys to take this bear with the lasso, usually on horseback.

We would ride along close to the dense woods that grew by the riverbank, and, getting between him and his base of retreat, would, as soon as we sighted a bear feeding out in the open plain, swing our lassos and charge him with whoop and yell. His habit of rearing up and standing erect and looking about to see what was the matter made him an easy prey to the lasso. And then the fun of taking him home through the long, strong grass!

As a rule, he did not show fight when once in the toils of the lasso; but in a few hours, making the best of the situation like a little philosopher, he would lead along like a dog.

There were, of course, exceptions to this exemplary conduct.

On one occasion particularly, Ed Parish, the son of a celebrated missionary, came near losing his life by counting too confidently on the docility of a bear which he had taken with a lasso and was leading home.

His bear suddenly stopped, stood up, and began to haul in the rope, hand over hand, just like a sailor. And as the other end of the rope was fastened tightly to the big Spanish pommel of the saddle, why of course the distance between the bear and the horse soon grew perilously short, and Ed Parish slid from his horse's back and took to the brush, leaving horse and bear to fight it out as best they could.

When he came back, with some boys to help him, the horse was dead and the bear was gone, having cut the rope with his teeth.

After having lost his horse in this way, poor little Ed Parish had to do his hunting on foot, and, as my people were immigrants and very poor, why we, that is my brother and I, were on foot also. This kept us three boys together a great deal, and many a peculiar adventure we had in those dear days "when all the world was young."

Ed Parish was nearly always the hero of our achievements, for he was a bold, enterprising fellow, who feared nothing at all. In fact, he finally lost his life from his very great love of adventure. But this is too sad to tell now, and we must be content with the story about how he treed a bear for the present.

We three boys had gone bear hunting up a wooden canyon near his father's ranch late one warm summer afternoon. Ed had a gun, but, as I said before, my people were very poor, so neither brother nor I as yet had any other arms or implements than the inseparable lasso.

Ed, who was always the captain in such cases, chose the center of the dense, deep canyon for himself, and, putting my brother on the hillside to his right and myself on the hillside to his left, ordered a simultaneous "Forward march."

After a time we heard him shoot. Then we heard him shout. Then there was a long silence.

Then suddenly, high and wild, his voice rang out through the treetops down in the deep canyon.

"Come down! come quick! I've treed a bear! Come and help me catch him; come quick! Oh, Moses! come quick, and—and—and catch him!"

My brother came tearing down the steep hill on his side of the canyon as I descended from my side. We got down about the same time, but the trees in their dense foliage, together with the compact underbrush, concealed everything. We could see neither bear nor boy.

This Oregon is a damp country, warm and wet; nearly always moist and humid, and so the trees are covered with moss. Long, gray, sweeping moss swings from the broad, drooping boughs of fir and pine and cedar and nearly every bit of sunlight is shut out in these canyons from one year's end to the other. And it rains here nearly half of the year; and then these densely wooded canyons are as dark as caverns. I know of nothing so grandly gloomy as these dense Oregon woods in this long rainy season.

I laid my ear to the ground after I got a glimpse of my brother on the other side of the canyon, but could hear nothing at all but the beating of my heart.

Suddenly there was a wild yell away up in the dense boughs of a big mossy maple tree that leaned over toward my side of the canyon. I looked and looked with eagerness, but could see nothing whatever.

Then again came the yell from the top of the big leaning maple. Then there was a moment of silence, and then the cry: "Oh, Moses! Why don't you come, I say, and help me catch him?" By this time I could see the leaves rustling. And I could see the boy rustling too.

And just behind him was a bear. He had treed the bear, sure enough!

My eyes gradually grew accustomed to the gloom and density, and I now saw the red mouth of the bear amid the green foliage high overhead. The bear had already pulled off one of Ed's boots and was about making a bootjack of his big red mouth for the other.

"Why don't you come on, I say, and help me catch him?"

He kicked at the bear, and at the same time hitched himself a little farther along up the leaning trunk, and in doing so kicked his remaining boot into the bear's mouth.

"Oh, Moses, Moses! Why don't you come? I've got a bear, I tell you."

"Where is it, Ed?" shouted my brother on the other side.

But Ed did not tell him, for he had not yet got his foot from the bear's mouth, and was now too busy to do anything else but yell and cry "Oh, Moses!"

Then my brother and I shouted out to Ed at the same time. This gave him great courage. He said something like "Confound you!" to the bear, and getting his foot loose without losing the boot he kicked the bear right on the nose. This brought things to a standstill. Ed hitched along a little higher up, and as the leaning trunk of the tree was already bending under his own and the bear's weight, the infuriated brute did not seem disposed to go farther. Besides, as he had been mortally wounded, he was probably growing too weak to do much now.

My brother got to the bottom of the canyon and brought Ed's gun to where I stood. But, as we had no powder or bullets, and as Ed could not get them to us, even if he would have been willing to risk our shooting at the bear, it was hard to decide what to do. It was already dusk and we could not stay there all night.

"Boys," shouted Ed, at last, as he steadied himself in the forks of a leaning and overhanging bough, "I'm going to come down on my laz rope. There—take that end of it, tie your laz ropes to it and scramble up the hill."

We obeyed him to the letter, and as we did so, he fastened his lasso firmly to the leaning bough and descended like a spider to where we had stood a moment before. We all scrambled up out of the canyon together and as quickly as possible.

When we went back next day to get our ropes we found the bear dead near the root of the old mossy maple. The skin was a splendid one, and Ed insisted that my brother and I should have it, and we gladly accepted it.

My brother, who was older and wiser than I, said that he made us take the skin so that we would not be disposed to tell how he had "treed a bear." But I trust not, for he was a very generous-hearted fellow. Anyhow, we never told the story while he lived.

From: Joaquin Miller, *True Bear Stories* (Chicago and New York: Rand McNally & Co., 1900).

· *The Basilisk* ·

(Spanish)

The well-known myth of the basilisk (*el basilisco*)—a myth which is found in nearly all countries—is widely extended in New Mexico. It does not differ entirely from that of Spain or Chili, but there is one element which distinguishes it from the basilisk myths of other countries. In all countries where the myth appears, it is believed that the basilisk is born from an egg laid by a cock. According to the New Mexican belief, the basilisk is said to be born from an old hen. There is no egg connected with the myth at all. After a hen is seven years old, she no longer lays eggs, and she may give birth to a basilisk. A hen which is known to be more than seven years of age should be killed, lest she give birth to a basilisk. Not only in this respect is the New Mexican myth different from that of Spain and Chili; the basilisk in New Mexico is not like a snake; it is not a serpent or reptile; it has a shapeless, ugly form, resembling a deformed chick, and is of black color. So it is described by a New Mexican, who, after going to a chicken house, whither he was attracted by the cackling of a hen, found a basilisk, fortunately dead.

Any female bird or fowl may give birth to a basilisk. Everywhere in New Mexico the myth is the same. As to the deadly effect of the eye of the basilisk, the New Mexico myth is the same as in other countries. If the basilisk sees a person first, the person dies; if the person sees the basilisk first, the basilisk dies. The story is told that in a certain place there was a basilisk in a magpie's nest on top of a tree, and the people who passed by were seen by it and died. Finally it was suspected that there was a basilisk up in the tree, and, a mirror being placed near the nest, the basilisk saw itself there and died. The belief that the basilisk dies when beholding its own image is also a prevalent one in all countries where the myth is found. Even the mirror story, with slight variations, is one that is found in Chili, France, and Spain.

In France the basilisk is also found in wells, and may be killed by placing a mirror over the well and allowing the basilisk to see its own image.

The myth of the basilisk is an old one. In Spanish literature, references to the deadly eye of the basilisk are quite common, and the same is true in French literature.

It is indeed strange that the New Mexican myth, while in many respects the same as the Spanish and general European myth, should present such a striking difference in respect to the manner of the birth of the basilisk. In Chili the myth is in all respects the European myth.

From: Aurelio M. Espinosa, "New-Mexican Spanish Folk-Lore," *Journal of American Folk-Lore* 23 (1910): 395–418.

· A Penitente Flowerpot ·

(Spanish)

It was a most curious plant to be growing there—and curious for *any* plant to grow so high on the frigid flanks of Mount San Mateo so early. Down in the valleys there was not a token of green; even the hardy chaparro had not yet dared think of budding. But up in this dark ravine, over eight thousand feet above the sea, with strips of snow still tapering northward from the pinetrunks! Someone had been at work here very lately; for the soaked earth was newly turned, and muddy fingerprints were still fresh on the neck of an enormous jar which projected a few inches above the surface. One must be crazy to pot flowers so far from home, and in an air so cold that even the rugged cedars had stopped climbing five hundred feet below, and left the heights to the shivering pines. As for the plant, that was even stranger than its garden—a great, black, shaggy ball upon a squat, brown stalk, a scant four inches tall, and more than that in thickness. It seemed to be sadly wilted, too, and was drooping very much to one side, which was small wonder considering the icy wind that drew through the ravine with dismal sighs and now and then a hollow wail. The toughest plant might well freeze in such weather.

But what a *lloron* the wind is today! One expects the March airs to screech and wail a bit; but not play crybaby the way this is doing. With almost every gust, its voice seems to turn more and more to tears, till one could almost swear it is someone crying bitterly.

Now the sun, sliding past a pinetop, falls for the first time upon the jar; and in a few moments there is a new witchcraft—for the grotesque, black blossom begins to straighten up on its stalk; not steadily, but by fits and starts. What new sort of heliotrope is this, that blooms so untimely among the New Mexican peaks, and goes nid-nodding to the sun like a boy who tries to keep awake in church?

Suddenly the howls of the wind ceased—as well they might, for they were only borrowed. A slender, brown girl, very ragged in the old black dress, and nearly barefoot, despite the cold, had been lending them; and now, rounding a big pine, she dropped her sobs in the same breath with her steps, and stood as rooted to the ground. She might be fourteen years old, and, but for the tears, very pretty; for her swollen eyes were still big and dark, and in the soft, olive cheeks was a faint bloom.

"What flower is that?" she murmured, in a voice still shaky. "And who shall plant here? Holiest Mother! It is bewitched!" and, with a scream of terror, she turned to flee down the mountainside. For, at the sound of her voice, the flower had twisted on its clumsy stalk and stared straight at her!

Her flight might have been more successful had she kept her eyes with her, instead of turning them over her shoulder to see if that horrible blossom were in pursuit. As it was, she had not gone five steps before a big pine ran against her so violently as to fling her to the ground quite breathless. Rise? Indeed, she could not. Only twenty feet away was that accursed plant glaring at her and holding her spellbound. She could neither move nor cry out, but lay watching with an awful fascination, in which her very thoughts were far off and unreal. The rude little cabin in the pass, the still form in it, the weeping woman and babes, all faded from her memory—and how she, the oldest of the young flock, had bravely tried to bring the news across the mountain to the little Mexican village, and had lost her way amid the errant cattle trails and wandered for hours crying with cold and terror. All she could think of now was this grim plant, with its wild eyes.

But *were* they so wild? Now she began to fancy that they had an imploring look, and, as she gazed, the whole weird flower took for her the guise of a prayer, a plea for mercy. Very black and tousled was it; but, oh, it looked so pitiful! and the woman in her began to swell above her fears. Perhaps the poor thing needed help.

In some conditions of the mind, one does quite absurd things in perfect good faith. Cleofes was living in a very unreal world just now; but in it she acted as seriously as if everything had been the most commonplace affair conceivable. She grew so tenderhearted for this poor vegetable which seemed to be suffering, that she found, to get up and go to its assistance, the strength she had been unable to muster to save her own life—which shows that for her years she was already very much a woman.

"*Pobrecita de flor,*" she said softly, laying her slender, brown hand on the great, black shock. "What hast thou? What can I do?" and she knelt to look at what had appeared to be its face.

A face it certainly was. The wild black hair and beard might do for the spiny wig of some strange cactus or a crazy chrysanthemum, but who ever saw eyes and mouth in chrysanthemum or cactus before? *Real* eyes, that moved and begged, bloodshot as they were, and blue lips, forced far apart by a cruel gag!

"Poor plant!" repeated Cleofes, without a thought of her own absurdity; and, tugging hard, she tore the pinecone from between the swollen jaws. The lips were dry and rough as rawhide, but now little red cracks began to show on them. The girl ran to the shadow of a tall tree and caught up a handful of snow. With that she began rubbing the frozen lips, and little by little forced bits into the mouth.

The eyes began to brighten somewhat, and, in a few minutes, a hoarse, inarticulate sound issued from the mouth—whereat Cleofes recoiled in new terror. She had not yet ceased to think of the plant as a plant; for, you must remember, she lived in a land more than half of whose people believe in witchcraft to this day. But, in another moment, her pity again conquered, and she began chafing the cold cheeks and putting more snow to the mouth.

"*Bendita—seas!*" croaked a husky voice at last.

"What art thou—plant or human?" stammered the girl, uncertain whether to stand or run.

"Juan, the—Penitente. And—they—buried me—here—to die, be-cause—I—renounced—the brotherhood!"

At this, Cleofes crossed herself and lost color. To meddle in the laws of the fanatic fraternity, whose self-tortures and crucifixions are a barbarous blot on New Mexico to this day—she knew what it meant. There are few men reckless enough to defy, even secretly, that remorseless power. And now she remembered having heard of this—that brothers who had broken their vows were buried thus in great *tinajones* (earthen jars) and left to perish.

"Thou art good, little one!" groaned the human plant; "but leave me, else will they kill thee, also." The despairing eyes seemed to push her away.

But now Cleofes was quite herself again—the *muy mujer* who had not lived fourteen years in that wilderness for nothing. The prowling Navajos that threatened their lonely hut, the bear killed in the very dooryard, meant no such danger as this. But she could not leave the poor head to perish.

"No! Though they kill me, I will get thee out!" she cried impulsively, stamping her tattered foot. "If I had only a spade!"

"That is not far. For I saw them hide it under yon scrub oak," and he thrust out his chin in that direction; "but what canst *thou?*"

"With help of God!" answered Cleofes, gravely; and she ran to the bush. There, sure enough, was the spade, burrowed under the dead leaves, and, in a moment more, she was digging around the neck of the great jar.

The eyes watched her hopelessly. But, really now, she was much woman! Good spadefuls, sisterling! With another like thee it might be done! The girl worked like one possessed; and there came a ray of light in the eyes that saw the hole slowly widening.

"But I die of cold," the voice croaked; "for these six hours I am chilled with this dead earth."

"*Tonta* that I am! When there is so much to burn!" Dropping the spade, she gathered pinecones and dead branches, and whirled one dry stick in the hollow of another till both began to smoke; and, laying dry leaves to them, blew from puffed cheeks till a wee flame leaped among them. In a few moments more a smart fire crackled to the leeward of the jar, and its life-giving heat began to thaw the frozen victim.

"Seest thou not that the saints are with us?" cried the girl, almost gayly; "all goes well, and in time we will have thee free!" Then she dug away harder than ever, while the eager eyes followed every move of her.

But they were not the only ones. Both were too much occupied with her work to think of anything else, or they might have been aware of something quite as interesting. A few rods up the hill was a narrow trail, and, over the ridge, a pair of tall ears had just risen. Very big ears they were, indeed, and cocked well forward; and, from between, a sinister face scowled down at the scene under the blasted pine. There was an ugly glitter in the eyes; and suddenly the lips drew into a hard smile that was even more unpleasant than the frown.

"See! We are at the swell of the *olla* already!" exclaimed Cleofes, panting with her work and making a wry face at a big blister on her hand. But the head did not answer; and, when she looked down at it, the face was distorted, and the eyes seemed twice their size. She whirled to follow their direction, and, in the moment, sank down with a gasp of terror. "Filomeno, the Brother of Light!"

Yes, it was Filomeno! He spurred the reluctant mule forward, grinning savagely. In good time he had come back from Cerros Cuates. What luck had sent this little she-fool to meddle in the justice of the brotherhood?

"God give you good-day!" he sneered, dismounting with rifle in hand. "It is slow digging—no? But deeper yet they shall dig who would undo the work of the Third Order. At it, little miner!—harder! Already it is late, and this must I see well done before I leave."

What? Was he going to let her finish after all—this evil Filomeno, whose crimes were known all across the county, and who was one of the most zealous of the Penitentes? The girl looked at him in wonder.

"Deeper, I tell thee! It still lacks much. *Lástima*, only, that there is not another jar for so pretty a flower!" And he gave a strange chuckle at his diabolic wit.

The spade dropped from Cleofes's hands. *Now* she understood! Not for her life could she speak a word; and, like a tattered statue, she stared at the Brother of Light.

"Here, give me the spade!" he said, after enjoying her terror for a moment. He began to throw out the earth in great wet lumps; for Filomeno had a back like the trunk of an oak. The hole grew fast, while

Cleofes, powerless and speechless, watched as in a dream. As for the head in the jar, it was luckier. It hung down limply to one side, and the horror had all faded from the half-closed eyes.

" *'State, mula!* Stop him!" For the animal, wholly suspicious of that strange object, had not ceased to snort and fling its head, and now began to sidle off, pretending to see some new terror.

"Stop him, daughter of idiots!" cried Filomeno, angrily. But Cleofes could not move; and, with a buffet as he passed her, the ruffian caught his beast and dragged it back, dealing it several blows in the face with his heavy fist.

"Now stand, thrice-accursed!" he snarled, picking up the spade again. But the mule had no notion of standing, and danced and plunged till he was like to break the bridle.

"Wilt thou not? To see, beast of infamy!" roared the enraged owner. Uncoiling the reata from the saddle horn, he knotted it about the animal's neck and brought the other end back to the hole, twisting it around his fist as he dug. Flojo seemed to grow more nervous every moment, as is the way of beasts "broken" with blows and abuse. He kept snorting and backing off and jerking on the hair-rope till it spilled the spadefuls back into the hole. Each time Filomeno stopped to give a curse and a savage yank which was soothing to neither Flojo's neck nor feelings; and, finally, bracing his heels against the edge of the hole, hauled the unwilling donkey close up to him, hand over hand.

"Now to stand, or I shoot thee the head off!" he panted, with a fearful oath; and, coiling the rope under his feet, he began to play the spade with redoubled energy.

Flojo seemed to have concluded that further protest was useless; and, with ears and head drooping and a look of utter dejection in his long face, he stood mournfully watching his master. He would be a good mule now—it cost too dear to yield to one's feelings, with Filomeno about.

These good resolutions were all very well, if only Juan's swoon had lasted a little longer. But now there was a faint sigh from the jar, and the bushy head moved feebly and the eyes began to open. Flojo cocked up one ear, and then stole a sidelong glance at the very wrong time. That black thing was alive! And without waiting for more, the terror-stricken mule reared madly backward and started off at a gallop. In an instant there came an unexpected hitch in his gait—at the same time that Filomeno's gray sombrero disappeared and his clumsy feet popped up, as if the two had incontinently changed places.

"Whoa! *Socorro!*" yelled a hoarse voice. But Flojo did not understand the last word and willfully disregarded the first; for a new panic seized him at sight of the ungainly dark form that *whopped* out of the hole and began tearing along the ground after him like a gigantic lizard. He would not have paused for all the "Whoas!" in Valencia County.

"Whoa! Stop him! Murder!" screeched Filomeno. But Cleofes could only answer with a peal of hysterical laughter. How he did bump along! No *maromero* on a saint's day could ever be half so funny when he tried his hardest. Filomeno had been just a little *too* smart. The lasso had become tangled about his feet, and now it was in a close hitch which defied his efforts to kick it off. As for doubling up and grasping the rope, Flojo's gait said a final "No" to that. Off down the hillside dashed the maddened mule, dragging his master forty feet behind.

A rocky ledge here—but it was too late to stop. The runaway leaped forward blindly and landed in the mud twenty feet below, all in a heap. A dead piñon stood almost against the rocks—so close that Flojo had cleared it safely. But the rope drew across a stiff branch and caught in a fork and stuck there—and there dangled Filomeno ten feet from the ground, head down, his torn moccasins almost touching the branch. Flojo rose painfully and tried to hobble off downhill, but the stout reata would not give, and, turning resignedly, he stood gazing with an interested air at his dangling master. For once he had Filomeno at the right end of the rope.

Three hours later, the pale March moon, resting a moment on the sturdy shoulder of San Mateo, after her climb from the east, peered down through the pines to an unaccustomed sight. A campfire burned ruddily by a deep hole, in which were jumbled the massy fragments of a huge earthen jar. Beside the grateful blaze lay a big, shaggy fellow, his tattered clothing red-caked with mud; and near him sat a girl. Filomeno had builded better than he knew. A stout hand at work was he; and when he so abruptly ceased his labors, the digging was so well advanced that, by doing a very little more, Cleofes could batter the *olla* to pieces with the spade, and presently liberate the captive. He was quite unable to move at first; but with time the glow of the fire gave back life to his chilled frame, and he was saying:

"*Pues,* little one, it is time to go—for now I am able."

"But he—but Filomeno?" cried Cleofes, as the mournful bray of a mule echoed through the woods. The shrieks and howls and imprecations had ceased long ago; only now and then there was a hollow groan from down yonder.

"Leave him, *demónio* that he is!—well hung up for the crows tomorrow!"

"No! no! We must not! Else his blood would be on us. We must let him go—and the poor mule that saved us."

"*Ea!* When he and his left me to a deeper death? And even *thee* he was to bury!"

"Even so, let us not be murderers too! Come, let him go, there's a good Juan!"

"How shall I say no to the *mujerota* who has saved me? But ask it not—for if he lives, he will have his revenge; and at his back is all the brotherhood. For me it is easy to flee, and for my son; but thy family? For I tell thee there is no corner in New Mexico where one can hide from the anger of the Penitentes."

"*Oyes,* Juan! Here thou hast his rifle, and, anyway, by now he will be past fighting. Only take him down from the tree, and bind him well by the trail, and let the mule go. When it comes home empty, they will look for Filomeno; and by Flojo's trail they will easily find him before he starves. And meantime we shall all be safe; for my mother has told me she will go to her people in Chihuahua, now that papa is dead, and this only makes it to go a little sooner. Come, good Juan, if you really thank me, do that!"

And Juan did even so. I am not at all sure that he did a service to the public; for horses continue to disappear, and travelers are sometimes waylaid in that part of Valencia County; and when one speaks of it, the people of San Mateo are wont to shrug their shoulders and say:

"*Quien sabe?* But Filomeno was not at home last night. *Ójala* they had left him up the piñon tree!"

But that is not the wish of a demure and very good-looking matron, whose home down among the hills of northern Mexico is undisturbed by anything more desperate than several round-faced youngsters. "Penitentes?" she says, with a shiver, when her husband tries to tease her.

"Boo! How I hate the very name! But none the less am I glad I made thy father turn loose that one. No, grandpa?"

And a gray and very rheumatic man, smoking in the sunshine by the door, answers:

"*Pues hija,* perhaps it is just as well—though for me, *I* would have *left* him."

From: Charles F. Lummis, "A Penitente Flower-Pot," *King of the Broncos* (New York: Charles Scribner's Sons, 1897).

CHAPTER 26

Customs and Beliefs

· Death and Funerals ·

(Various)

A Burial Place
(Native American)

A few miles below the mouth of the Klickitat there stands in mid-channel one of the most curious and interesting objects on the river: "Memaloose Island." This desolate islet of basalt was one of the most noted of the frequent "death" or burial places of the Indians. They were accustomed to build platforms and place the dead upon them. Apparently this island was used for its gruesome purpose for centuries. A large white marble monument facing the south attracts the attention of all travelers, and as we pass we see that it is sacred to the memory of Vic Trevett. He was a prominent pioneer of The Dalles, and in the course of his various experiences become a special friend of the Indians, who looked upon him with such love and reverence that when his end approached he gave directions that his permanent burial place and monument should be on the place sacred to his aboriginal friends.

From: William Dennison Lyman, *The Columbia River* (New York and London: G. P. Putnam's Sons, 1909).

The Grave of Señora Valdez
(Spanish)

Señora Concepcion Valdez was dead. For ninety long years life had lingered, and now it had vanished from the shriveled, worn little body so quietly, so imperceptibly, that the group about the bedside could not tell when the spirit passed and the woman became clay.

There was a long silence after the last faint murmur, the last soft sigh. Then old Pablo bent over the still face and listened intently. He lifted his head to motion to Anita Castro, and she went softly out of the room, to come back with a tiny white feather in her hand. With shaking fingers Pablo laid it across the stiff lips. There was no faintest flutter of the fragile thing—they all knew beyond dispute—that the end had come.

The two daughters, the last of the Valdez race, bowed their heads in the first bitter grief that loss of loved ones brings to all. Joaquina, rocking herself to and fro and calling upon the saints and the Virgin for help, wept aloud. But Concepcion knelt quietly, her little, dark face almost as drawn and wrinkled as that of the dead, and clasped the cold fingers tight in her own, while she whispered over and over again, in her own tongue:

"My mother is dead—and I cannot live without her—my mother is dead—and I cannot live without her————"

For forty years she and her mother had never been separated, had shared every feeling, every experience. It was different with Joaquina—she had been away to the convent; and had visited friends in many places—she had seen the world. But Concepcion had seldom been out of sight of this house where she was born. Here she and her mother had watched one after another of the family pass away; together they had looked on while old friends and neighbors were driven out, or pushed aside, by a strange people. Sitting quietly on their rose shaded *galeria*, or by their blazing logs, they had seen the free, happy life of Spanish California die out before the engulfing Anglo-Saxon civilization. When their own rich holdings had been decreed no longer their own—"at Washington," they were told—the two women had wept together in helpless, hopeless wonder.

And now the mother was dead and the daughter was left behind. Conception had no tears; stunned by terror of the years to come, she gazed into the face that was so peaceful now, after all its troubles, until Anita came and with gentle touch, lifted her and led her from the room.

"Mi madre must not be laid in that field up there," Joaquina was saying earnestly; "she must be laid in holy ground—is it not so, Concepcion? Did she not always say that she must be buried in consecrated ground?"

"Yes," Concepcion answered, without lifting her head from the table, "she must be laid in the churchyard and have the priest and the masses."

"Yes," Joaquina assented, "and she must have a fine, black coffin, too— she must be buried as befits a Valdez!"

Señor Don Ignacio Valdez had been dead so many years that his memory was but little more than a tradition to these last of his children; but they never forgot that they were his daughters. And Joaquina, at least, always remembered that it was the King of Spain himself who had signed the paper granting "Rancho del Potrero" to "his loyal servant, Valdez."

"Ah!" she cried, clasping her hands, "if we had now but a little part of that which is our own—but a little part—but, we have nothing, now— nothing at all! There were no more silks and laces, even, in the chests. Where shall we find the money, Concepcion? We must have money for mamácita."

Concepcion said nothing, and old Pablo sadly shook his head. Then José Garcia, who posed as the business and legal adviser of his people, spoke wisely:

"You will have to mortgage your homestead to get the money—that is the only way."

"Mortgage? What is that?" Joaquina questioned, suspiciously—Garcia was not of her class.

After many words and many questions, Joaquina spoke, still doubtful, "I see—we get money; but if we pay it not back again we lose our home. Shall it be so, Concepcion?"

"How can we lose our home?" the older woman asked. "Did not the great men at Washington say this little piece of land was ours for always?"

There were further explanations, and at last Joaquina said, confidently, "We will pay the money back. I will sew and Concha will raise many fowls and Pablo will have the fine crop of barley next year. It will be all right."

In the end, Garcia went with the sisters to the new town, with its cheap, frame houses, its brick-veneer stores, and its tiresome rows of new-set trees, that had sprung up, like some huge, ugly weed patch, on the wide sweep of the mesa there below the "Potrero." After much talk and many wearisome formalities, money was placed in their hands. They knew little of the rest; but the money would pay for the coffin and the mourning, and the priest would require money for the burial and the masses—and what else mattered, now?

Señor Valdez, and his sons, had been carried to San Luis Rey and buried in the mission graveyard beside the highborn lady who had survived but a few years of life in the new world. The second wife had been proud to bear the children of Señor Valdez and to be known by his name; but she had never dreamed of ranking with the first wife. Not even Concepcion thought of placing her there.

The forlorn little procession, dusty and spent with fatigue, after the slow drive of thirty miles over rough roads, stopped before the crumbling adobe wall of a neglected *campo santo*—the nearest consecrated ground. But the casket was satin-lined, the priest read the burial service and promised an extra mass; and among the stained and rotting, whitewashed crosses and slabs, there were a few imposing stones, bearing once proud names—the daughters turned homeward, feeling that they had done well.

Dreary days followed. The sisters were left alone with their memories, in the old *casa*. Old Pablo the faithful servitor and friend of years, had been sorely stricken with rheumatism and had gone to his daughter's home. Concepcion sobbed herself to sleep at nights, because she was "so lonesome for *mamá*," and went about her daily tasks with a settled sadness that made her sister and the few friends who were left look after her with sober faces.

At last, Joaquina borrowed a knock-kneed horse and an old cart. The two women rose before daybreak and, after gathering great bunches of Castilian roses, oleanders, and pomegranate blossoms, they drove the long, weary miles to Agua Mansa. There they laid the flowers on the unsodded grave and sat beside it for an hour. But Concepcion was consoled— "*Mamá* knew," she said. After that, once a month, they made their pilgrimage.

The moneylender drove into the yard one morning, six months later, and, after admiring the great peppers, the oleander trees, and pomegranate bushes before the house, he asked if they were ready to pay the interest.

"In'trus?" Joaquina repeated, blankly; "what is that in'trus?"

In his best mixture of English and Spanish, he tried to make it clear;

but she only shook her head and declared firmly, "In one year the paper said—then we pay the money."

He had to be content with reminding her, as he lifted his reins, that the place would become his property, if the money were not paid when the year was up. Joaquina shook her clenched hands after him as he drove away, and cried, despairingly, in answer to her sister's perplexed questions, "We shall not have that money to pay him. We shall have to lose our home!"

She had felt for some time that they should never be able to pay back the two hundred dollars they had borrowed. There had been no barley crop at all this year. She had found little sewing to do. The new settlers who had homesteaded the acres that had once belonged to their rancho knew little and cared less about the two shrinking, black-robed women they sometimes saw pass to the post office and store. And Concepcion was not so spry as she had once been—many an old hen stole her nest in the brush down by the *zanja* and never came home again, and many a fine young broiler was snatched up by prowling wild cats and coyotes, sneaking down from the mountains beyond.

Joaquina tried now to explain all this to her sister, who listened with horror-stricken eyes. "We cannot leave our home," she cried. "We have nowhere else to go—and—always I have lived here—I cannot go away———"

But Joaquina gently unfolded the plan she had not dared to mention before. She recalled friends and relations who lived in *la ciudad*. In the city there would be plenty of sewing to be done, and there would be the church—Concha might go to church every day there. On the other hand, it was impossible for them to stay on here alone. They could not find daily bread here—much less the money to pay their debt. But one thing was possible—the old home must be sold and they must move to the city.

After awhile Concepcion, with her clawlike fingers clasped tight over her breast, stole out of doors. She stood under the beautiful, wide-spreading pepper—as a happy, lighthearted girl, she had stuck the slender shoot into the ground and seen that it was watered daily. She went down into the remains of the orchard and looked up into the hoary-headed olive trees that her father had put in place with his own hands. And then she went and knelt under the Castilian rosebush that her mother had planted—and loved. Drawing her little, black shawl tighter over her

face, she moaned softly. It was all true that Joaquina had said. They—
two old women—could not live on here alone. They must sell their land—
or starve. She—Concepcion—would not mind the loneliness and the
starving; but she must think of Joaquina—had she not been the sought-
for, the beautiful one, in her youth? And she had been out into that
strange world—the old home and its associations were not all of life
for her.

"But, Holy Mother," she whispered, "*mamá* will be so lonesome, if we
go so far away! She will think we have forgotten her, if we cannot put
the flowers on her grave—" and she bent her head deeper among the
roses and shed scalding tears.

Always gentle and submissive—there was more of the blood of her
mother than of the Spanish grandee in her veins—Concepcion did not
oppose her sister's arrangements. The old home was sold for enough to
pay off the mortgage and a few hundred beside. After a last visit to the
grave, they moved to the city. Here a little house was found on a quiet
street, with a tiny yard in front for flowers and a poultry yard behind.

Joaquina was soon happy. She found work enough to supply their simple
needs. She loved the stir and bustle of the streets; she liked to see people
about. And she had friends—some of them remembered her as the gay
young daughter of Señor Ignacio Valdez.

But Concepcion again sobbed herself to sleep, now "because *mamá* was
so lonesome away off there alone." Her flowers throve as though touched
by magic; no *animales* molested her chickens; but she grew thinner and
thinner. The old, uncomplaining sadness had settled over her again, and
not even the church could bring her comfort.

Joaquina went one day to their priest, "Father," she said, "Our mother
is buried over there at Agua Mansa. Would it not be possible to bring
her here and lay her in the graveyard?"

"It could be done, daughter," the old man said, "but why? She rests as
well there as here. And it would cost more than you could afford to pay."

"But, father," and Joaquina wiped away the tears, "my sister cries and
cries because she says, 'Mamá is lonesome and thinks we forget her—for
we no longer bring flowers!' I am afraid Concepcion will die too, and
then I shall be left all alone—if she cannot put the flowers on the grave
of our mother. Here is money," and she gave him two gold pieces, the
last of their little store, "and I will pay more—if only it may be done."

In an obscure corner of a Catholic cemetery of Los Angeles, there is a grave, at the head of which stands a little, white cross. At its foot is an untrimmed rose bush—the rose of Castile. Every Sunday afternoon two women—one tall and straight, with flashing eyes and ready smile; the other tiny and frail, with a mantilla drawn close about her face—fill a broken vase with fresh flowers, gather up the scattered rose leaves, and sit in quiet content for a little while.

It is the grave of Señora Concepcion Valdez.

This is a "true" story—the sisters still live in Los Angeles. But the grave of the mother remains in the little burying ground at Agua Mansa. Agua Mansa (gentle water) was settled by a colony of New Mexicans in 1852, at a point on the banks of the Santa Ana, about two miles from the town of Colton. A chapel was built, which has now crumbled away. Its bell, made from metal collected in the vicinity and cast at Agua Mansa, now hangs in the Catholic church at Colton. Many of the early Spanish and foreign settlers of Riverside and San Bernardino were buried in the graveyard at Agua Mansa, for many years the only Catholic church and burying ground in this vicinity.

From: Rose L. Ellerbe, *Tales of California Yesterdays* (Los Angeles: Warren T. Potter, 1916).

· *Traditions of the Orient* ·
(Chinese)

Marriage

Early marriages are universal. Old bachelors are common, but elderly maiden ladies—a most useful and worthy class of people in any country—are entirely unknown in China. Marriage is the privilege, duty, and fate of Chinese girls. But the courtships leading to marriage, the betrothal, the arrangements for the marriage festivities, and life settlement are all conducted for the children by the parents and guardians, with the help of a middleman or go-between.

The Chinese maiden, before marriage, is kept in seclusion and ignorance. The principal lesson she has to learn is *obedience*. She is not sent to school. She never mingles in promiscuous society; never receives personal attention or letters of correspondence from any young gentleman whatsoever; never listens to the voice of a lover; never receives upon her waiting lips the blissful pledge of plighted troth. She is betrothed by her parents when quite young, often under ten years of age. In this important matter of marriage the girls of China have no choice, no voice. Their wishes, preferences, and affections are never consulted. Although our young people would rebel against the introduction of such a custom among us, yet it is doubtful whether the system of boy and girl courtship which prevails in this country results in any better life settlements than those arranged for the inexperienced young people of China by their parents, who can use their judgment unmoved by fancy and romance.

From: Rev. O. Gibson, *The Chinese in America* (Cincinnati: Hitchcock & Walden, 1877).

The Cue

Considerable attention is paid to the cue, or "pigtail," as it is often called in derision. This must be nicely combed and braided and left with a silk tassel at the end. Chinese dandies pay great attention to this part of their toilet. This cue is often in the way; workmen uniformly twist it around the head, but gentry, scholars, men of leisure and society, never. This shaving of the head and braiding of the cue is a very singular custom, but it is universal among the Chinese; and although thousands of these in America would be glad to adopt our custom of wearing the hair—at least while in this country—still such is the power of custom and prejudice that a Chinaman loses caste, and is tabooed by his countrymen, as soon as he makes the innovation and cuts off his cue. Even those who in their hearts would like to do such a thing openly ridicule the change. This shaving the head and wearing the cue is not, as many people suppose, a religious custom at all. It has no more to do with the religion of the Chinese, their religious rites and ceremonies, than has an American barbershop to do with the sacraments of the Christian religion.

Newspaper writers have sometimes told their readers that only Christian Chinese leave off the cue and adopt the American style of dress. That is a mistake. Some two or three Chinese Christians have adopted the American dress and have discarded the cue, but the Chinese Christians generally have not done so. The missionaries, who understand their business rather better than newspaper writers do, know that true religion requires a change of heart rather than a change in the cut of the hair.

From: Rev. O. Gibson, *The Chinese in America* (Cincinnati: Hitchcock & Walden, 1877).

Opium-Smoking

The opium-smoking curse has crossed the seas to our land, as well as to all the places where the Chinese go. Opium dens abound, both above and below ground, in San Francisco's Chinatown. To reach the subterranean dens one has to go down rickety stairs, along narrow passages where darkness reigns, and into low, wretched rooms whose horrors no words can describe. Far away from the din of outside life the silence of death reigns supreme. The air is full of the stupefying smoke of opium. No ventilation ever reaches there, and no light penetrates the gloom except from the feeble flames of a few flickering opium lamps. Men are found curled upon the bunks in different stages of stupefaction. Some are still conscious, while others are in a dreamy state of oblivion. Some are dried-up, sallow-colored sots; while others still retain much freshness and vigor, they having so far only indulged to a moderate degree.

No one can go through the Chinese quarters without seeing how prevalent the practice of opium-smoking is. Every lodging house has its opium bunks, and the air is filled with its fumes. The restaurants furnish opium couches, set in alcoves; much as our hotels do bars. Almost every store has its place in the rear where business transactions are made over the opium pipe. Every guild hall has its opium couch, and even some homes are furnished with them

The Chinaman does not get drunk with liquor. His convivial bowl is a cup of tea. The only kind of strong drink in which he indulges is samshoo, or spirit of distilled rice, which he usually drinks in small quantities, as the wine cups are not larger than thimbles. It quickly flushes the face but does not inebriate. But he loves the opium pipe, and finds solace and enjoyment in that as in nothing else.

From: Ira M. Condit and Rev. D. D., *The Chinaman As We See Him* (Chicago, New York, and Toronto: Fleming H. Revell Co., 1900).

Footbinding

First wives are always, second wives are never, small footed. This is the reason why the custom of footbinding is maintained. Parents want their girls to be first wives—not concubines, and so they bind the feet of their little ones that they may have this honorable place. Some say a queen who had club feet introduced the custom, that she might not be ashamed of her feet; but this is a doubtful explanation. Some are cruel enough to insinuate that the custom was introduced to keep wives at home, that they might not visit their neighbors to gossip. The custom has been in vogue for more than a thousand years. Few small-footed women are found here, which shows that most of the wives in this country are secondary ones; except in the case of those who are Christians. Women with bound feet seldom go out, and hence there are more of them than many have supposed.

From: Ira M. Condit and Rev. D. D., *The Chinaman As We See Him* (Chicago, New York, and Toronto: Fleming H. Revell Co., 1900).

Hatchet Men

Highbinders openly flourish in our country as they could not do in their own. There their heads would soon roll in the dust. Here they carry on high-handed crime in spite of our authorities. "Hatchet men" is the name by which the Chinese themselves commonly call them. In view of the character of the men, the name is certainly a very significant one. As to the origin of the word *highbinders*, I have heard that it was first used by an Irish policeman in New York in speaking of a Chinese tough, and the word has stuck to this kind of Chinaman ever since.

The original society in China is called Heaven and Earth League, or Triad Society. It was first formed for the purpose of overthrowing the reigning dynasty. Although it became quite powerful in South China, it was never popular with the masses, owing to the intimidation and oppression employed against those who would not join it.

The Triads, or highbinders, came to San Francisco thirty-seven years ago, and planted themselves in this soil under the high-sounding name of Chee Kung Tong, "Chamber of High Justice." While the society retains its old form, its character has changed somewhat from what it was in China. Being divested of all political color, it has come to be little more than a society of blackmailers, robbers, and assassins. Professing to be a benevolent association formed for purposes of mutual protection, it is really a closely organized band of villains and murderers.

The ordeal of initiation is said to be something terrific. Under naked swords and spears, before grim idols, with cups of mingled wine and blood, and the decapitation of a cock's head as an intimation of what will be done in case of treachery, the novice, with awful oaths, is initiated into the order. There are many secret signs, passwords, and symbols which are known only by the initiated.

If a man is to be gotten rid of, the hatchet men stand ready, for a consideration, to undertake the task. In secret conclave they deliberate over the case of one who has offended them, and select the agent who is to make way with him. He gets a round sum for the job. If arrested they agree to clear him in the courts, if he is imprisoned or killed a goodly amount is given to his family. Few Chinamen have the courage to stand against the fiat of this dark tribunal, and they all fear its power much more than they do our own courts of justice. They have different ways of dealing with those who have incurred their enmity. If it is not deemed prudent to assassinate them, charges are made out against them in our courts by means of false witnesses. A complete chain of evidence is forged by which many an innocent man is condemned. It is not only difficult to clear one against whom the highbinders have laid charges, but it is equally difficult to convict one whom they have undertaken to defend.

Many are laid under tribute to their blackmailing schemes. Their victims generally find it wiser to submit to their demands than to offer resistance, and to be ruined in their business, or lose their employment, if not their lives. The revenue of these hatchet societies is very large, hence they never lack for money to carry on their nefarious work. Money and cunning seldom fail to thwart the ends of justice, and accomplish what they undertake.

The highbinders have their regular band of paid fighters, who wear chained armor and carry revolvers, knives, and other kinds of concealed weapons. Nearly all the shooting affairs in the Chinese quarters of San Francisco and other towns may be laid to their charge. The street battles which so often occur are brought about by a contest between rival tongs. Perhaps there has been some slave girl stolen, who was under the protection of some other society, or blackmail is levied by a rival tong, or in some way the rights of others are encroached on, and a deadly contest arises, which nothing but blood can wipe out.

This class of the Chinese is confined to a comparatively small circle. The great mass of the people have no sympathy with these villains, and would be delighted to see them brought to justice. When, on several occasions, attempts have been made to put them down, the great body of the Chinese have been highly pleased with the prospect. It is hoped that the day is not far distant when these men who defy our laws, plot bloody conspiracies, and sustain vile haunts of vice, shall be suppressed. None would breathe freer, or be more delighted at this result, than the law-abiding Chinese themselves.

From: Ira M. Condit and Rev. D. D., *The Chinaman As We See Him* (Chicago, New York, and Toronto: Fleming H. Revell Co., 1900).

· Religious Beliefs ·

(Various)

A Creation Story
(Native American)

The Indians with whom I once lived in the Californian Sierras held the grizzly bear in great respect and veneration. Some writers have said that this was because they were afraid of this terrible king of beasts. But this is not true. The Indian, notwithstanding his almost useless bow and arrow in battles with this monster, was not controlled by fear. He venerated the grizzly bear as his paternal ancestor. And here I briefly set down the Modoc and Mount Shasta Indians' account of their own creation.

They, as in the biblical account of the creation of all things, claim to have found the woods, wild beasts, birds, and all things waiting for them, as did Adam and Eve.

The Indians say the Great Spirit made this mountain first of all. Can you not see how it is? they say. He first pushed down snow and ice from the skies through a hole which he made in the blue heavens by turning a stone round and round, till he made this great mountain; then he stepped out of the clouds onto the mountaintop, and descended and planted the trees all around by putting his finger on the ground. The sun melted the snow, and the water ran down and nurtured the trees and made the rivers. After that he made the fish for the rivers out of the small end of his staff. He made the birds by blowing some leaves, which he took up from the ground, among the trees. After that he made the beasts out of the remainder of his stick, but made the grizzly bear out of the big end, and made him master over all the others. He made the grizzly so strong that he feared him himself, and would have to go up on top of the mountain out of sight of the forest to sleep at night, lest the grizzly, who, as will be seen, was much more strong and cunning then than now, should assail him in his sleep. Afterwards, the Great Spirit, wishing to remain on earth and make the sea and some more land, converted Mount Shasta, by a great deal of labor, into a wigwam, and built a fire in the center of it and made it a pleasant home. After that, his family came down, and they all have lived in the mountain ever since. They say that before the white man came they could see the fire ascending from the mountain by night and the smoke by day, every time they chose to look in that direction. They say that one late and severe springtime, many thousand snows ago, there was a great storm about the summit of Mount Shasta, and that the Great Spirit sent his youngest and fairest daughter, of whom he was very fond, up to the hole in the top, bidding her to speak to the storm that came up from the sea, and tell it to be more gentle or it would blow the mountain over. He bade her do this hastily, and not put her head out, lest the wind should catch her in the hair and blow her away. He told her she should only thrust out her long red arm and make a sign, and then speak to the storm without.

The child hastened to the top and did as she was bid, and was about to return, but having never yet seen the ocean, where the wind was born and made his home, when it was white with the storm, she stopped, turned, and put her head out to look that way, when lo! the storm caught in her long red hair, and blew her out and away down and down the mountainside. Here she could not fix her feet in the hard, smooth ice and snow, and so slid on and on down to the dark belt of firs below the snow rim.

Now, the grizzly bears possessed all the wood and all the land down to the sea at that time, and were very numerous and very powerful. They were not exactly beasts then, although they were covered with hair, lived in caves, and had sharp claws; but they walked on two feet, and talked, and used clubs to fight with, instead of their teeth and claws, as they do now.

At this time, there was a family of grizzlies living close up to the snows. The mother had lately brought forth, and the father was out in quest of food for the young, when, as he returned with his club on his shoulder and a young elk in his left hand, under his arm, he saw this little child, red like fire, hid under a fir bush, with her long hair trailing in the snows, and shivering with fright and cold. Not knowing what to make of her, he took her to the old mother, who was very learned in all things, and asked her what this fair and frail thing was that he had found shivering under a fir bush in the snow. The old mother grizzly, who had things pretty much her own way, bade him leave the child with her, but never mention it to anyone, and she would share her breast with her, and bring her up with the other children, and maybe some great good would come of it.

The old mother reared her as she promised to do, and the old hairy father went out every day, with his club on his shoulder, to get food for his family, till they were all grown up and able to do for themselves.

"Now," said the old mother Grizzly to the old father Grizzly, as he stood his club by the door and sat down one day, "our oldest son is quite grown up and must have a wife. Now, who shall it be but the little red creature you found in the snow under the black fir bush." So the old father Grizzly kissed her, said she was very wise, then took up his club on his shoulder and went out and killed some meat for the marriage feast.

They married and were very happy, and many children were born to them. But, being part of the Great Spirit and part of the grizzly bear, these children did not exactly resemble either of their parents, but partook somewhat of the nature and likeness of both. Thus was the red man created; for these children were the first Indians.

All the other grizzlies throughout the black forests, even down to the sea, were very proud and very kind, and met together, and, with their united strength, built for the lovely little red princess a wigwam close to that of her father, the Great Spirit. This is what is now called "Little Mount Shasta."

After many years, the old mother Grizzly felt that she soon must die, and, fearing that she had done wrong in detaining the child of the Great Spirit, she could not rest till she had seen him and restored to him his long-lost treasure and asked his forgiveness.

With this object in view, she gathered together all the grizzlies at the new and magnificent lodge built for the princess and her children, and then sent her eldest grandson to the summit of Mount Shasta in a cloud, to speak to the Great Spirit and tell him where he could find his long-lost daughter.

When the Great Spirit heard this, he was so glad that he ran down the mountainside on the south so fast and strong that the snow was melted off in places, and the tokens of his steps remain to this day. The grizzlies went out to meet him by the thousands; and as he approached they stood apart in two great lines, with their clubs under their arms, and so opened a lane through which he passed in great state to lodge where his daughter sat with her children.

But when he saw the children, and learned how the grizzlies that he had created had betrayed him into the creation of a new race, he was very wroth, and frowned on the old mother Grizzly till she died on the spot. At this, the grizzlies all set up a dreadful howl; but he took his daughter on his shoulder and, turning to all the grizzlies, bade them hold their tongues, get down on their hands and knees and so remain till he returned. They did as they were bid, and he closed the door of the lodge after him, drove all the children out into the world, passed out and up the mountain, and never returned to the timber anymore.

So the grizzlies could not rise up anymore, or make a noise, or use their clubs, but ever since have had to go on all fours, much like other beasts, except when they have to fight for their lives; then the Great Spirit permits them to stand up and fight with their fists like men.

That is why the Indians about Mount Shasta will never kill or interfere in any way with a grizzly. Whenever one of their number is killed by one of these kings of the forest, he is burned on the spot, and all who pass that way for years cast a stone on the place till a great pile is thrown up. Fortunately, however, grizzlies are not now plentiful about the mountain.

In proof of the story that the grizzly once stood and walked erect and was much like a man, they show that he has scarcely any tail, and that his arms are a great deal shorter than his legs, and that they are more like a man than any other animal.

From: Joaquin Miller, *True Bear Stories* (Chicago and New York: Rand McNally & Co., 1900).

The Doctrine
(Mormon)

In this future state the animal creation will be in the same forms in which it now is, and all will be subservient to man. The earth and all that is upon it will be substantially as at present, and be given to the saints for their use and enjoyment.

At the resurrection the family relationships of the saints will be resumed. Orson Spencer says:

The heirs of the Abrahamic promise will retake their bodies, and resume the family relationships, just as they are here on the earth; husbands and wives, parents and children—incorruptible and immortal, however—forever.

He says again:

The promise made to Abraham, and all who are heirs of same promise through faith, extends to all generations, in this life, and to all generations to come forever and ever. That is, Abraham and Sarah will continue to multiply, not only in this world, but in all worlds to come. . . . Will the resurrection return you a mere female acquaintance that is not to be the wife of your bosom in eternity? No. God forbid. But it will restore you the wife of your bosom immortalized, who shall bear children from your own loins in all the worlds to come. . . . Companion and wife of my youth! Shall I then press you to my bereaved bosom, immortalized, beatified, glorified? Ah, yes. Sweet hope! Glorious promise! Precious wedlock! Halleluiah to the God of Abraham that has made such a covenant!

Brigham H. Roberts, congressman-elect, in a book that has been endorsed by the Mormon Church, and is therefore authoritative, says:

Instead of the God-given power of procreation being one of the chief things that is to pass away, it is one of the chief means of man's exaltation and glory in that great eternity, which, like an endless vista, stretches out before him.

The father will there, as here, be the head of the family, and will be to that family the king and priest and a god forever. The first wife will be queen in that kingdom, unless some other wife has been more obedient, or has borne more children. Those saints who have not upon the earth had a plurality of wives, or have not begotten a sufficient number of children to constitute a kingdom of their own, shall be the servants of those who have. He who has the greatest number of wives and children will have the largest dominion, and the greatest honor and glory for all eternity. The degree of the Mormon's reward and his glory in eternity, depends in no respect upon his moral qualities, or his manner of life, or his deeds, whether good or bad, or the way in which he has served God or man; but solely upon his sensuality. There is absolutely nothing whatever in the Mormon doctrines of future rewards and punishments to stir one noble impulse, or awaken one pure and holy aspiration, or prompt to a single deed of charity or benevolence. On the contrary, there is the most powerful consideration that can influence a human soul, that of a man's eternal destiny, to sink him to the lowest depths of bestiality. If he have a great many wives and a great many children, he will have very great glory, and become the peer of the eternal God.

Orson Spencer declares that a man, even in this life, cannot be in Christ in the fullest extent without being joined to a woman. The prophet Joseph goes still further. In the revelation authorizing polygamy, he dwells upon the law of polygamy as the law given to Abraham, and says:

> Go ye therefore, and do the works of Abraham; enter ye into my law, and ye shall be saved. But if ye enter not into my law, ye cannot receive the promise of my Father which he made unto Abraham.

Again, referring to plural marriage, the prophet Joseph says:

> If ye abide not that convenant, then are ye damned; for no one can reject this convenant and enter into my glory.... As pertaining to the new and everlasting covenant, it was instituted for the fullness of my glory; and he that receiveth a fullness thereof, must and shall abide the law, or he shall be damned, saith the Lord.

Those only, then, that enter into the law and practice of polygamy are assured of salvation; those that reject it are damned.

The Book of Mormon says: "I saw the finger of the Lord, and I feared lest he should smite me; for I knew not that the Lord had flesh and blood.

But still further; since God, who is thus ascertained to be of a fleshly body and of sensuous passions, is declared by scriptures to be the Father of our spirits—of all the spirits of men that now live on the earth, or ever have lived here—he must, therefore, of necessity, they affirm, be the husband of a vast number of wives, of whom these innumerable sons and daughters are the offspring. This is not an inference.

Orson Spencer says:

> The family order which God established with Abraham and the patriarchs was the order observed among celestial beings in the celestial world. And this family order is not only one at which God sits at the head, first pattern in the series of matrimonial examples, but it is of perpetual duration, both in and beyond this world. It is utterly absurd to suppose the anomaly of such an existence as a father without a mother.... But where is the scripture that ascribes the origin of all the diverse sons to one and the same mother?... This family order of Abraham (polygamy) was spread out before God, and met his entire and full approbation. And why did God approve of it? Because it is the only order practiced in the celestial heavens.

In this Spencer is simply stating in other words a revelation of Joseph the prophet, who says:

> By him, and through him, and of him, the worlds are and were created, and the inhabitants thereof are the begotten sons and daughters of God.

From: Rev. A. C. Osborn, *The Mormon Doctrine of God and Heaven* (Nashville: Southern Baptist Convention, 1899).

The Eastern Glorious Temple
(Chinese)

Now let us visit one of the Chinese Temples. The Chinese have opened their heathen temples, and set up their heathen idols and altars in this Christian land; and instead of our converting their temples into Christian churches, they have absolutely changed one of the first Protestant churches of this city into a habitation for heathen. One of these heathen temples, or an apology for one, is to be found in almost every place where any number of Chinamen have taken up their abode. Some four or five of considerable pretensions, in a Chinese way, are to be found in San Francisco, besides a number of smaller ones. Each of the famous Six Companies, with the exception of the Yan Wo Company, owns or controls a temple. In these temples are "gods many and lords many," and goddesses and attendant divinities, and tablets and inscriptions, and incense sticks and incense urns, and elaborate carvings in the most grotesque of designs, and gongs and bells with which to arouse the gods when too drowsy to hear the prayers of the people; and priests to teach the poor devotee the ceremonials of his worship. They do not have congregational worship at stated times as Christian people do. There are certain feast days and birthdays of their gods and goddesses, when large crowds throng the temples, with their offerings and prayers; but single, straggling worshippers may be found in these temples almost every hour of the day.

One of the principal Chinese "joss houses" is called the "Eastern Glorious Temple." This temple is largely owned and controlled by Dr. Lai Po Tai, a Chinese quack doctor, who is said to have accumulated a large fortune practicing medicine among a class of weak-minded, easily duped Americans, both men and women. In the central hall of this temple we find a trio of gods. The central figure is known by the high-sounding title *"The Supreme Ruler of the Somber Heavens,"* and has control of the northern regions. He is pretty good at preventing conflagrations, and so is sometimes called the "Water God." He eats vegetables only. Sitting at the left hand of the Supreme Ruler of the Somber Heavens is a black, ugly-looking fellow, the Chinese god of war, sometimes called the "Military Sage." This god is worshiped in order to become brave and courageous. At the right hand of the Supreme Ruler of the Somber Heavens is a calm-faced image, "The Great King of the Southern Ocean." This god is said to be very large-hearted, almost boundless in the sweep of his benevolence.

These are only a specimen of the many heathen deities which adorn the Chinese temples of this city and coast. No engraving or description can give any adequate idea of the debasing influence of idolatry. To the true Christian it is utterly disgusting and abhorrent. Christianity is making some weak efforts to show our Chinese brethren a better way.

From: Rev. O. Gibson, *The Chinese in America* (Cincinnati: Hitchcock & Walden, 1877).

The Order of Penitentes
(Spanish)

Strange, yet true, that none of our encyclopedias give any account of the Order of Penitentes in the United States. It is stated on good authority that the Pueblo Indians had an ancient custom of holding a penitential fast for four days in each of their pueblos. On that occasion a small number of men and women were selected to bear the sins of all. These were shut up in their sacred council chamber. Before each was placed a *tinaja* of water, of which they must not drink, while every morning a delegation came to wash their feet. This continued throughout the four fast days, and is the only form of penitence, except what is imposed by the Church, known to have existed among them.

About three hundred years ago the "Order of *Los Hermanos Penitentes*" was founded in Spain, its object being "religious study and conversation," and, so far as known, the members of this organization were "men of good morals and good sense." In course of time this order came to old Mexico, and afterward, when the Franciscan friars came to New Mexico, they introduced this system of self-torture.

It is said that the first public penance in New Mexico was celebrated in 1594 by Juan de Oñate and his men. The system degenerated more and more as the years passed, until the present "monstrosity had developed." When this order came to New Mexico they found traces of the Penitentes among the Indians previously referred to, but nothing so gross as the customs introduced by the Franciscan friars.

The number of Penitentes in New Mexico in 1903 is variously estimated from twenty-five to thirty-five hundred. They all claim allegiance to the Romish Church. Their belief is founded on the use of the whip, the cactus, and the cross as instruments of torture.

The only season in which the Penitentes practice their religious rites is Lent. During these weeks the traveler through the canyons or near their meeting places must not be surprised to witness their processions as they leave the *morada* (place of meeting), led by their priests and so-called bands of music, the latter making all kinds of noises on their musical instruments. These are followed by a number of men, each carrying on his bare shoulders one end of a huge cross, while the other end, about twenty feet distant, is dragging on the ground. After these come another band, stripped to the waist, each having a huge cactus bound over his bare shoulders, back, and breast. Then follow other men, also bare to the waist, lashing themselves with whips made from the *amole*, or soap weed, until their backs are one mass of raw flesh. Singing their weird song they pass on to an elevation about half a mile or more from the starting point, and there these deluded creatures prostrate themselves before the cross.

The whips used are about three feet long. These have braided handles, with a lash about four inches across, and braided also for about half its length, and with long, hairlike tails. This is the *"Disciplina"* of penance.

My mind goes back to one Good Friday night when, with a Mexican friend, I reached a plaza nearly one hundred miles from the railroad station. I had driven two days in order to be present and investigate for myself the tales told by Lummis in his "Land of Poco Tiempo." As we sat at supper in the home of our host, the children came running in, saying:

"The Penitentes are coming."

We at once rushed to the door to see the procession, and if possible to secure an entrance to the meeting of *tinieblas* (darkness) in that little chapel. We joined the procession, but just as we reached the door three large officers stepped in front and, beckoning with their hands, ordered us away. My guide pleaded hard, and after some discussion the men retired and talked the matter over with some of their friends. Then they returned, and I was admitted to the room, where for a couple of hours at least, with closed doors, sights were seen and noises heard that no tongue could describe.

The building is of *adobe*, with large sliding doors in one end, and with but one small, round hole in one side for light and ventilation. The floor is native earth, except at the end where the altar is located. In front of the altar is a large, curtained table, under which the choir have their seats on the floor. In front of this table, on a small stool, sit two men, each holding a stone in his hand. Directly in front of the stool, but on the earthen floor, at some distance from the front of the altar platform, is a stand on which is a wooden triangle, having one lighted candle on the apex, three on the base, and five on either side. In front of this the Penitentes stand facing the lights. These men for days have been torturing themselves in the ways previously described. Now their heads and backs and arms are bandaged. These men we would suppose to be the most religious in the community; instead, they are regarded as the most deluded and of the lower class, doing penance not only for the sins they have committed, but for those which they intend to commit during the coming year.

All things being ready, at the blast of a trumpet the meeting is in progress. The choristers under the table sing and play one verse. The men in front of the table strike three times on the seats with the stones they hold in their hands, then one of the Penitentes steps forward and extinguishes one of the lights. This continues until all the lights but one have disappeared. There is silence for a moment. Then a large, flat surface, probably nine by twelve feet, apparently of wood, covered with zinc, which in its turn is covered with leather, is placed on the floor. The doors in the front of the buildings are closed and barred. The *hermanas* arrange themselves about the room. The music is again started, and at a given signal the last light is gone. From boxes and barrels, previously ranged round the room, ropes and chains and sticks are drawn, and for about one half-hour the clashing of chains and the ranting of other instruments is maddening.

The noise, the groans, and the darkness I can never forget. If at any time I want an illustration of that "outer darkness" I only think of that awful night in the Penitentes' meetinghouse.

What does it all mean? Not "the arrival of the soul in purgatory," as someone has said. As the candles are again lighted, I see one of the Penitentes go forward and take from the wall a cross on which is an image intended to represent our Saviour, who has died during the darkness, and at once the whole mystery is clear. The darkness, with all the unearthly sounds, is intended to represent the transactions at Calvary on that Good Friday night when the "King of Glory" bowed His head and gave up the ghost.

After this service the image on the cross is borne from the little chapel to the house of a friend where entertainment has been provided, and there the music is kept up until the morning, when all return to the *morada*, from which they go to their homes in peace.

Under the flag that waves for liberty, and with the gospel in our hands that proclaims freedom for the slave of sin, we long for the day when from those lofty mountains, deep canyons, and wide-stretching plains the weird song of the poor Penitentes shall no longer be heard, but only songs of praise to Him who has cleansed us from our sins in His own precious blood.

From: Rev. Robert M. Craig, *Our Mexicans* (New York: The Board of Home Missions of the Presbyterian Church, 1904).

Bibliography

"Folk-Lore Scrapbook," *Journal of American Folk-Lore* 1 (1988): 167–68.

"Popular Superstitions," *The Pennsylvania-German Society Proceedings and Addresses*, vol. 5 (Reading, PA: 1895).

Abbott, Grace, *A Study of Greeks in Chicago* (Chicago: University of Chicago Press, 1909).

Adams, Charles F., *Some Phases of Sexual Morality and Church Discipline in Colonial New England* (Cambridge, MA: John Wilson & Son University Press, 1891).

Backus, Emma, "Weather-signs from Connecticut," *Journal of American Folk-Lore* 8 (1895): 26.

Backus, Emma, "Tales of the Rabbit from Georgia Negroes," *Journal of American Folk-Lore* 12 (1899): 108–15.

Baughman, A. J., "Historical Sketch of the Life and Work of 'Johnny Appleseed,'" *The Firelands Pioneer, New Series* 8 (December 1900): 702–11.

Beck, Louis J., *New York's Chinatown* (New York: Bohemia Publishing Co., 1898).

Bek, William G., "Survivals of Old Marriage-Customs Among the Low Germans of West Missouri," *Journal of American Folk-Lore* 23 (1910): 60–67.

Bourke, John G., "Popular Medicine, Customs, and Superstitions of the Rio Grande," *Journal of American Folk-Lore* 7 (1894): 119–46.

Brinton, D. G., "Reminiscences of Pennsylvania Folk-Lore," *Journal of American Folk-Lore* 5 (1892): 177–85.

Bronson, Edgar Beecher, *Cowboy Life on the Western Plains* (New York: Grosset & Dunlop: 1910).

Cole, Pamela McArthur, "New England Funerals," *Journal of American Folk-Lore* 7 (1894): 217–23.

Cole, Pamela McArthur, "New England Weddings," *Journal of American Folk-Lore* 6 (1893): 103–107.

Collins, Lee, "Some Negro Lore from Baltimore," *Journal of American Folk-Lore* 6 (1892): 110–12.

Condit, Ira M. and Rev. D. D., *The Chinaman As We See Him* (Chicago, New York, and Toronto: Fleming H. Revell Co., 1900).

Craig, Rev. Robert M., *Our Mexicans* (New York: The Board of Home Missions of the Presbyterian Church, 1904).

Crimmins, John D., *St. Patrick's Day: Its Celebration in New York and Other American Places, 1737–1845* (New York: 1902).

Darney, L. L., "Historic Trees," *The Bay State Monthly* 1 (February 1884): 87.

Davenport, Gertrude C., "Folk-Cures from Kansas," *Journal of American Folk-Lore* 11 (1898): 129–32.

Dawson, Charles, *Pioneer Tales of the Oregon Trail and Jefferson County* (Topeka: Crane and Co., 1912).

DeZavala, Adina, "Religious Beliefs of the Teajas or Hasanias Indians," *Publications of the Folk-Lore Society of Texas* 1 (1916): 39–43.

Drake, Samuel Adams, *A Book of New England Legends and Folk Lore* (Boston: Roberts Brothers, 1888).

Drake, Samuel Adams, *Old Boston Taverns and Tavern Clubs* (Boston: W. A. Butterfield, 1917).

Earle, Alice Morse, "Old-time Marriage Customs in New England," *Journal of American Folk-Lore* (1893): 97–107.

Earle, Alice Morse, *The Sabbath in Puritan New England* (New York: Charles Scribner's Sons, 1891).

Eddins, A. W., "How Sandy Got His Meat," *Texas Folklore Society Publications* 1 (1916): 47–49.

Edwards, G. D., "Items of Armenian Folk-Lore Collected in Boston," *Journal of American Folk-Lore* 12 (1899): 97–107.

Eglleston, Edward, *The Beginners of a Nation* (New York: D. Appleton and Co., 1896).

Espinosa, Aurelio M., "New-Mexican Spanish Folk-Lore," *Journal of American Folk-Lore* 23 (1910): 395–418.

Forbes, A. S. C., *Mission Tales in the Days of the Dons* (London: A. C. McClurg & Co., 1909).

Fortier, Alcee, *Louisiana Folk-Tales* (Boston and New York: Houghton Mifflin Co., 1895).

Fortier, Alcee, *Louisiana Studies* (New Orleans: F. F. Hansell & Brothers, 1894).

Gibson, Rev. O., *The Chinese in America* (Cincinnati: Hitchcock & Walden, 1877).

Gore, J. Howard, "The Go-Backs," *Journal of American Folk-Lore* 5 (1892): 107–109.

Harriman, Frank, "Dungeon Rock, Lynn," *The Bay State Monthly* (April 1884): 235–39.

Herrick, R. F., "The Black Dog of the Blue Ridge," *Journal of American Folk-Lore* 13 (1910): 251–52.

Herzfeld, Elsa G., *Family Monographs: The History of Twenty-four Families Living in the Middle West Side of New York City* (New York: The James Kempster Printing Co., 1905).

Hoagland, M. F., "Notes on New England Customs," *Journal of American Folk-Lore* 6 (1893): 301–303.

Hodges, N. D. C., "Survival in New England of Foundation Sacrifice," *Journal of American Folk-Lore* 12 (1899): 290–91.

Hohman, John George, "The Long Hidden Friend," *Journal of American Folk-Lore* 17 (1904): 89–152.

Hoke, N. C., "Folk-Custom and Folk-Belief in North Carolina," *Journal of American Folk-Lore* 5 (1892): 113–20.

Horford, Cornelia, "A Tradition of Shelter Island," *Journal of American Folk-Lore* 12 (1899): 43–44.

Hrbkova, Professor Sárka B., "Bohemians in Nebraska," *The Bohemian Review* 1, no. 6 (July 1917): 11.

Kirk, William F., "A Swedish Troubadour," *Cosmopolitan Magazine* 47, no. 1 (July 1909): 254–56.

Lindsay, Vachel, *A Handy Guide for Beggars* (New York: The Macmillan Company, 1916).

Lummis, Charles F., *A New Mexican David* (New York: Charles Scribner's Sons, 1905).

Lummis, Charles F., "A Penitente Flower-Pot," *King of the Broncos* (New York: Charles Scribner's Sons, 1897).

Lunt, George, ed., *Old New England Traits* (New York: Hurd & Houghton, 1893).

Lyman, William Dennison, *The Columbia River* (New York and London: G. P. Putnam's Sons, 1909).

McLennan, Marcia, "Origin of the Cat: A Negro Tale," *Journal of American Folk-Lore* 9 (1896): 71.

Miller, Joaquin, *True Bear Stories* (Chicago and New York: Rand McNally & Co., 1900).

Moore, Ruby Andrews, "Superstitions from Georgia," *Journal of American Folk-Lore* 7 (1894): 305–306.

Newel, Jane H., "Superstitions of Irish Origin in Boston," *Journal of American Folk-Lore* 5 (1892): 242–43.

Newell, William Wellis, "The Ignis Fatuus, Its Character and Legendary Origin," *Journal of American Folk-Lore* 17 (1904): 39–60.

Osborn, Rev. A. C., *The Mormon Doctrine of God and Heaven* (Nashville: Southern Baptist Convention, 1899).

Parker, Haywood, "Folk-Lore of the North Carolina Mountaineers," *Journal of American Folk-Lore* 20 (1907): 241–50.

Porter, J. Hampden, "Folk-Lore of the Mountain Whites of the Alleghanie," *Journal of American Folk-Lore* 7 (1894): 105–17.

Quigley (Dr.), *The Irish Race* (San Francisco: A Roman & Co., 1878).

Sanger, Chester F., "Sunday Travel and the Law," *The Bay State Monthly* 1 (1885): 231–33.

Siringo, Charles A., *A Lone Star Cowboy* (Santa Fe: 1919).

Skinner, Charles M., *American Myths & Legends*, vol. 2 (Philadelphia and London: J. B. Lippincott Co., 1903).

Skinner, Charles M., *Myths & Legends of Our Own Land*, vol. 1 (Philadelphia and London: J. B. Lippincott Co., 1896).

Spaulding, Arthur W., *The Men of the Mountains* (Nashville: Southern Publishing Association, 1915).

Steiner, Roland, "Observations on the Practice of Conjuring in Georgia," *Journal of American Folk-Lore* 14 (1901): 173–80.

Steiner, Roland, "Seeking Jesus," *Journal of American Folk-Lore* 14 (1901): 172.

Steiner, Roland, "Superstitions and Beliefs from Central Georgia," *Journal of American Folk-Lore* 12 (1899): 261–71.

Stetson, George R., "The Animistic Vampire in New England," *The American Anthropologist* 9 (January 1896): 1–13.

Stewart, K. Bernice and Homer A. Watt, "Legends of Paul Bunyan Lumberjack," *Wisconsin Academy of Sciences, Arts, and Letters Transactions* 18, part 2 (1916): 639–51.

Stowe, Harriet Beecher, *Oldtown Folks* (Boston: Fields, Osgood & Co., 1869).

Thanet, Octave, "Folk-Lore in Arkansas," *Journal of American Folk-Lore* 5 (1892): 121–25.

Todd, Charles Burr, "The Corpus Christi Festival at St. Mary's, Pennsylvania," *Journal of American Folk-Lore* 11 (1899) 126–32.

Voorhies, Felix, *Acadian Reminiscences* (Opelousas, LA: The Jacob News Depot Co., 1907).

Watterson, Henry, ed., *Oddities in Southern Life and Character* (New York: Houghton Mifflin Co., 1892).

Webb, W. Prescott, "Wild Horse Stories of Southwest Texas," *Publications of the Folk-Lore Society of Texas* 1 (1916): 58–61.

Whitney, Anne Weston, "Items of Maryland Belief and Custom," *Journal of American Folk-Lore* 12 (1899): 273–74.

Wilson, Howard Barrett, "Notes of Syrian Folk-lore Collected in Boston," *Journal of American Folk-Lore* 16 (1603): 133–47.

Wiltse, Henry M., "In the Southern Field of Folk-Lore," *Journal of American Folk-Lore* 13 (1900): 209–12.